THE

Christopher Knight was born in 1950 and in 1971 completed his education with a degree in advertising and graphic design. He has always had a strong interest in social behaviour and belief systems and for many years he has been a consumer psychologist involved in the planning of new products and their marketing. In 1976 he became a Freemason and is now the chairman of a marketing and advertising agency.

Dr Robert Lomas was born in 1947 and gained a first class honours degree in electrical engineering before taking up research into solid state physics. He later worked on guidance systems for Cruise missiles and was involved in the early development of personal computers and has always had a keen interest in the history of science. He currently lectures at Bradford University Management Centre. In 1986 he became a Freemason and quickly became a popular lecturer on Masonic history in lodges in West Yorkshire.

Their subsequent books are *The Second Messiah*, *Uriel's Machine* and most recently *The Book of Hiram*, all available in Arrow Books.

Dedicated to the memory of John Marco Allegro
— A man 20 years ahead of his time.

THE HIRAM KEY

Pharaohs, Freemasons and the Discovery of the Secret Scrolls of Jesus

Chris Knight and Robert Lomas

arrow books

This edition published by Arrow Books in 1997

20

Copyright © 1997 Chris Knight and Robert Lomas 1996

First published in Great Britain in 1996 by
Century
Random House, 20 Vauxhall Bridge Road,
London SW1V 2SA

www.rbooks.co.uk

Addresses for companies within The Random House Group Limited
can be found at: www.randomhouse.co.uk/offices.htm

The Random House Group Limited Reg. No. 954009

A CIP catalogue record for this book
is available from the British Library

ISBN 9780099699415

The Random House Group Limited supports The Forest Stewardship
Council (FSC), the leading international forest certification organisation.
All our titles that are printed on Greenpeace approved FSC certified paper
carry the FSC logo. Our paper procurement policy can be found at:
www.rbooks.co.uk/environment

Typeset by Deltatype Ltd, Ellesmere Port, Cheshire
Printed and bound in Great Britain by
CPI Cox & Wyman, Reading, RG1 8EX

Acknowledgements

The authors would like to express their thanks to the following people for their help and assistance during the writing of this book:

First, our families who have tolerated the long hours of absence whilst we have been researching and writing.

Reverend Hugh Lawrence, A Past Master of the Craft (who wishes to remain anonymous), Tony Thorne, Niven Sinclair, Judy Fisken, Barbara Pickard, W. Bro Alan Atkins, W. Bro Aiden Unsworth, Steve Edwards, Baron St. Clair Bonde of Charleston, Fife.

Our agent Bill Hamilton of A.M. Heath & Co. Ltd, our editor Mark Booth and also Liz Rowlinson of Century, and Roderick Brown.

'*The Hiram Key* could spark the beginning of a reformation in Christian thinking and a reconsideration of "the facts" which we have so blindly accepted and perpetuated for generations. This book is a must for freethinkers!'

David Sinclair Bouschor
Past Grand Master of Freemasonry, Grand Lodge of
Minnesota, USA

'Nothing is hidden that will not be made known, or secret that will not come to light.

What I tell you in the dark speak in the light. And what you hear in a whisper, proclaim on the house tops.'

Yehoshua ben Joseph, also known as Jesus Christ

Contents

Contents

PHOTO CREDITS – PLATE SECTION

OTHER ILLUSTRATIONS

p376 Drawing of the Westford knight taken from an original by Frank Glynn

Introduction

Henry Ford once declared that 'all history is bunk'. It may have sounded a little abrupt but when it comes to the 'facts' of the past which most Westerners are taught in school, it turns out that Mr Ford was right.

Our starting point was a private piece of research to find the origins of Freemasonry – the world's largest society that today has almost five million male members in regular lodges and has in the past included many great men amongst its number, from Mozart to Henry Ford. As Freemasons, our goal was to try to understand a little about the meaning of Masonic ritual: those strange, secret ceremonies carried out by mainly middle-class, middle-aged men from Huddersfield to Houston.

At the centre of Masonic lore is a character called Hiram Abif who, according to a story told to every Freemason, was murdered almost three thousand years ago at the building of King Solomon's Temple. This man is a total enigma. His role as the builder of King Solomon's Temple and the circumstances of his horrible death are clearly described in Masonic history, yet he is not mentioned in the Old Testament. For four of the six years we spent working on this research, we believed that Hiram Abif was a symbolic creation. But then he materialised out of the mists of time to prove himself very real indeed.

Once Hiram Abif emerged from the distant past, he provided nothing less than a new key to Western history. The intellectual contortions and laboured conclusions that have previously formed Western society's collective view of the past gave way to simple and logical order. Our researches led us first to reconstructing the ancient Egyptian king-making ritual of four thousand years ago; that in turn led us to uncover an assassination that took place around 1570 BC, gave rise to a resurrection ceremony that is the direct antecedent of modern Freemasonry. As we tracked the development of this secret ritual from Thebes to Jerusalem, we uncovered its role in the building of the Hebrew nation and in the evolution of Jewish theology.

In startling contrast to what is currently held to be fact, the Western world actually developed according to a very ancient philosophy encoded into a secret system that has come to the surface at three key moments over the last three thousand years.

The final proof of our findings may well turn out to be the archaeological find of the century. We have located the secret scrolls of Jesus and his followers.

Chapter One

The Lost Secrets of Freemasonry

'That Freemasonry dates from before the Flood; that it is a mere creation of yesterday; that it is only an excuse for conviviality; that it is a soul-destroying, atheistic organisation; that it is a charitable association, doing good under a silly pretence of secrecy; that it is a political engine of extraordinary potency; that it has no secrets; that its disciples possess in secret the grandest knowledge vouchsafed to humanity; that they celebrate their mysterious rites under the auspices and the invocations of Mephistopheles; that their proceedings are perfectly innocent, not to say supremely stupid; that they commit all the murders which are not traced to somebody else; and that they exist only for the purpose of promoting universal brotherhood and benevolence – these are some of the allegations made by babblers outside the circle of the Free and Accepted brethren. Omne ignotum pro magnifico. The less one knows the more one takes of Freemasonry.'
The Daily Telegraph London, 1871

'Masonry puts considerable stress on encouraging high standards of morality among its members. But it is hardly surprising that a society which uses secret handshakes, signs and language for the mutual recognition of its members is suspected of being an influence for bad rather than good. Why have such methods, if not to hide the truth? Why hide, if there is nothing to hide?

1

> *Those outside Masonry find the whole idea of dressing up, reciting esoteric texts and performing strange rituals so silly that they tend to believe there must be some other, and probably more sinister, attraction to it. Probably there isn't . . . but a negative is always hard to prove.'*

The Daily Telegraph London, 1995

Sheer Pointlessness

In 1871 Queen Victoria had thirty years of rule still in front of her, Ulysses S. Grant was president of the United States of America, and Freemasonry was the subject of public speculation. One hundred and twenty-five years later the first moon landing is a generation in the past, the world is switching on to the Internet, and Freemasonry is still the subject of public speculation.

We came across the first of these quotations on a neatly cut-out and folded scrap of newspaper in a dusty volume on Masonic history, where it had been placed as a book mark by some long-dead Freemason. Chris read the second mid-Atlantic between lunch and the feature film.

Almost everything, including writing styles, has changed over the last century and a quarter, but the general public's attitude to Freemasonry today is just as confused as it was in the nineteenth century. Most people do not trust what they do not understand and, if they perceive an élitism that excludes them, mistrust will quickly turn into dislike or even hatred. Whilst Freemasonry has always been open to all men over the age of twenty-one years (eighteen under the Scottish constitution) of sound mind and body, who can demonstrate good character and express a belief in God, there is no doubt that membership in the British Isles was in the past centred around the aristocracy, with the rank and file coming from the upper strata of the middle classes.

In the mid-Victorian period it was socially important,

almost essential, for a professional man to be a Freemason. The nouveaux riches of the industrial revolution sought social status through membership of an exclusive society that had a high profile amongst aristocrats of all levels, right up to the royal family itself. In theory at least, members of the working classes were equally eligible to become Masons but in practice it would hardly enter their heads to ask to join their bosses 'club', so the Lodge has long been associated with the well-to-do. Those at all levels of society who were not Freemasons could only speculate about the secrets revealed to members of this mysterious organisation. They were known to wear aprons and large collars and rumoured to roll up their trousers and exchange strange handshakes, while whispering passwords to each other.

In the second half of the twentieth century, Freemasonry is a far less élitist organisation, as men from all levels of society have sought and gained membership. However, a glance at the top of the English Masonic hierarchy quickly illustrates that being a member of the royal family or an hereditary peer is still hardly a major handicap to promotion prospects.

Most people in the Western world are at least vaguely aware of Freemasonry, and its mysteries tantalise two large groups: those who are not Masons, who wonder what the secrets of the order are; and those who are Masons, who also wonder what those secrets are! A compelling reason for silence amongst Masons is not so much a compulsion to adhere to their sacred vows, or a fear of macabre retribution from their fellows; it is more that they do not understand a word of the ceremonies they participate in, and their only fear is that people would laugh at the apparently pointless and silly rituals they perform.

Freemasonry for us, and every other 'brother' we know, is little more than a social club providing an opportunity to indulge in some amateur theatricals, followed by a meal and plenty of beer and wine. The complex and obscure ritual has to be memorised through years of chanted repetition. An emphasis is put on sincerity of delivery, but in reality only small parts of the ceremony can be understood as simple allegorical messages concerning uprightness of moral character – the rest is a strange mixture of meaningless words and re-enactments of supposed historical events surrounding the building of King Solomon's Temple in Jerusalem, some three thousand years ago.

Whilst we insiders are getting on with doing very little except learning oddball verses by rote, many on the outside are trying to destroy the organisation because they suspect it of causing corruption, seeing it as a bastion of capitalist privilege or a club for mutual back-scratching. Countless books on the subject have fed the curiosity and antagonism of the general public. Some, such as those written by American author John J. Robinson, have been superbly researched; others, such as those from the late Stephen Knight, have been little more than fiction to satisfy the worst fears of the anti-Masonic sector.

The anti-Masonic lobby is constantly at work to prove supposed misdeeds, and we have had first hand experience of this. A born-again Christian friend of Chris's recently stated that he was taking up a counselling role within his church group. Upon enquiring whom he was intending to counsel, I was horrified to hear the reply, 'Those suffering from Masonic curses.'

'What is a Masonic curse?' I asked, without telling him of my connection with the Craft (as Freemasonry is called by insiders).

'Masons have to swear allegiance to one another at the expense of all others, even their families. If they fail, they have curses brought down on them which create terrible suffering to them and those around them.'

I was momentarily lost for words. Freemasonry is many things but it is certainly not evil, although some people

4

seem determined to find it so. In direct repudiation of such ill-informed accusations, the United Grand Lodge of England publicly states that 'a Freemason's duty as a citizen must always prevail over any obligation to other Freemasons' and that 'Freemasonry should not be allowed to harm a man's family or other connections by taking too much of his time or his money or causing him to act in any other way against their interest'.

We have no wish to be apologists for Freemasonry but it does do a lot of good and, as far as we know, nothing bad. It has always donated very large sums of money to charity, usually anonymously, and it promotes levels of moral rectitude and social responsibility that are impressive and have set the standards that others follow. Colour, race, creed or politics have always been irrelevant to membership and its two driving goals are a social order based on freedom of the individual, and the pursuit of all knowledge. The only absolute requirement is a belief in God ... any god.

Our biggest criticism of Freemasonry is its sheer pointlessness. It does not know where it came from, no one seems to know what it is trying to achieve, and increasingly it seems improbable that it can have much of a future in a world that demands a clarity of purpose and benefit. Not only are the origins of Freemasonry no longer known, but the 'true secrets' of the Order are admitted to have been lost, with 'substituted secrets' being used in their place in Masonic ceremony, 'until such time as they are rediscovered'.

If the words that emerge from the ritual are taken at face value, Freemasonry would have to be at least three thousand years old. It is not only opponents of the Order who dismiss this – the United Grand Lodge of England itself does not claim such antiquity. Wary of public derision, it avoids any official view on the origins of the Craft and allows so-called 'Lodges of research' to debate the limited historical evidence that exists.

5

A Poor Candidate in a State of Darkness

When we were made Freemasons we both underwent the process experienced by every initiate to the Craft for at least two hundred and fifty years. As part of these ceremonies we were asked to swear, as men of honour, that we would not divulge any of the secrets of Freemasonry to the outside world, and we are very aware that the information we give here may be considered by some Masons a betrayal of those secrets. However, the United Grand Lodge of England considers only the means of recognition to be the protected secrets of the Order, and no one could falsely pass themselves off as a Freemason after reading this book. It is necessary to explain the rituals in considerable detail as they form the basis for all of our research. Some of the words given are secret identification devices, but we do not point out which words should be used in which circumstances, so we have done our very best to meet the spirit of our vows. In any event, we gave our agreement to maintaining these secrets on the understanding that they would not interfere with our freedom as moral, civil or religious agents; and were our vows to prevent us sharing such important discoveries as we have now made, they would have most certainly interfered with those freedoms.

* * *

Although we joined different Lodges several years apart, we recall identical experiences. This is how it felt (we have used 'I' to stand for both of us):

Having been interviewed by a panel of past masters several months before, I was now ready to be made a Freemason. What I was joining was virtually unknown to me; the only firm question that had been put to me was 'do you believe in God?' I did, and everything proceeded from there to the point where I was now standing, with a guard who was banging with the hilt of a drawn sword on the large door to the temple, seeking permission for me to enter.

I was hoodwinked (that is, blindfolded) and dressed in loose-fitting white trousers and top. One foot was in a simple slipper (the expression for this is 'slipshod'), my left leg was exposed to the knee, and the left breast of the tunic had been drawn aside so that my chest was bared on that side. Unbeknown to me a hangman's noose had been put around my neck and draped down my back. I had been relieved of all metal objects and I was now ready to be led into the Temple. (We later learnt that this mode of dress, the rough smock with the running noose about the neck, was exactly how a medieval heretic would have been treated by the Inquisition prior to making his confession.)

I recall how I sensed a large number of people present and felt very vulnerable. I felt a cold point press on the skin of my chest.

'Do you feel anything?' the voice in front asked. A whisper in my ear gave the formalised reply which I repeated out aloud.

'I do.'

'Then let this be a sting to your conscience as well as instant death should you ever betray any of the secrets now about to be imparted to you.'

Another voice from the other side of the room then spoke – I recognised it as belonging to the Worshipful Master. 'As no man can be made a Mason unless he be free and of mature age, I now demand of you – are you a free man and of the full age of twenty-one years?'

'I am.'

'Having answered that question so satisfactorily, there are others which I shall immediately proceed to put to you which I trust you will answer with equal candour. Do you seriously declare on your honour that, unbiased by the improper solicitations of friends against your own inclinations, uninfluenced by mercenary or any other unworthy motive, you freely and voluntarily offer yourself as a candidate for the mysteries and privileges of Freemasonry? Do you further seriously declare on your honour that you are prompted to solicit these privileges from a favourable opinion preconceived of our Order, a general desire for knowledge and a sincere wish to render yourself more extensively serviceable to your fellow creatures?'

'I do.'

The dagger that had been held firmly to my chest was removed (although I did not know it at the time) but the noose (called a cable tow) remained about my neck. The man to my right whispered to me to kneel and a short prayer was said, invoking the blessing of the Supreme Governor of the Universe (God – described in a neutral way so that He is equally accessible to members of any monotheistic religion).

The ceremony proceeded with my helper guiding me around the perimeter of the Temple, pausing three times to introduce me as a 'poor candidate in a state of darkness'. Although I could not see it, the centre of the Temple floor was laid out with a central rectangle of black and white squares. On the eastern edge was the Worshipful Master's pedestal, in the south sat the Junior Warden and in the west the Senior Warden, both at lesser pedestals.

After my three laps I was brought, still blindfolded, to the Worshipful Master's pedestal where he asked, 'Having been in a state of darkness, what is the predominant wish of your heart?'

Once again the answer was whispered into my ear.

'Light.'

'Then let that blessing be restored.' The blindfold was removed from behind and as my eyes adjusted I could see that I was in front of the Worshipful Master who immediately drew my attention to the emblematic 'lights' of Freemasonry, which were explained as being the Volume of the Sacred Law (for Christian candidates this

8

is the Bible), the Square and the Compasses. He then told me that I had now attained the rank of Entered Apprentice Freemason – the first of three degrees through which I would have to pass before being accepted as a full Master Mason. The secret signs, grips and password of the First Degree were then explained to me and I was told that the left-hand pillar that stood in the porchway of King Solomon's Temple has special significance to Freemasons. Both the left-hand and right-hand pillars are recreated in the Lodge and stand behind, and to either side of the Worshipful Master. The left-hand pillar, called Boaz, was named after Boaz, the great-grandfather of David, King of Israel.

After various perambulations around the Temple I was presented with a simple white calf-skin apron which symbolised the rank I had just obtained. Then I was told, 'It is more ancient than the Golden Fleece or Roman Eagle, more honourable than the Star, Garter or any other order now in existence, it being the badge of innocence and the bond of friendship ...' This section proved to be a particularly revealing part of Masonic ritual; as we show later, it contains clear evidence of being constructed at three very different periods of history, from the genuinely ancient to the relatively modern.

Throughout the course of the ceremony various moral and social virtues were recommended to me using a number of architectural analogies; amongst them, stonemason's tools were likened to methods of self improvement. Towards the end of the ceremony of initiation, I was alarmed to learn that there are test questions which must be committed to memory in order to progress to the next degree, that of Fellowcraft Freemason. Amongst these questions and answers are some pieces of information that were more intriguing than informing:

Question: 'What is Freemasonry?'

Answer: 'A peculiar system of morality, veiled in allegory and illustrated by symbols.'

9

Question: 'What are the three grand principles upon which Freemasonry is founded?'

Answer: 'Brotherly love, relief and truth.'

To any candidate the first of these principles sounds reasonable, but the next two are a little hard to fathom. Relief from what? Which truth?

Now a fully accepted brother, albeit a mere 'entered apprentice', I left the Temple feeling that something special had happened; but I did not have a clue as to what any of it might mean. The festive meal followed and as the man of the hour, I was placed at the left hand of the Worshipful Master. Toasts and speeches rolled out and a good time was had by all. The mysteries of the Craft certainly had not been revealed. Perhaps, I thought, all will become clear at the next ceremony.

It did not.

The Hidden Mysteries of Nature and Science

Some months later I passed through a Second Degree ceremony to attain the rank of a 'Fellowcraft Freemason'. This time I entered the Temple with the rest of the brethren wearing the plain white calf-skin apron that was the symbol of my genuine innocence – and my very humble status. The Lodge was then opened in the First Degree and as the candidate for elevation I was put to the test by answering the questions that were explained to me at the end of the previous ceremony. As soon as I had struggled through this examination of my ability to recite gibberish I was told to leave the Temple temporarily to be properly prepared for the 'passing ceremony'.

I was readmitted wearing the same rough clothing used at my initiation ceremony, now with left leg and right breast laid bare. As the deacons conducted me around the Temple new passwords and signs were revealed, including a hand raised posture that claims to have originated when 'Joshua fought the battles of the Lord (in the valley of

Jehoshaphat) and prayed that the sun be stayed in its course until the overthrow of His enemies had been completed'. This later proved to be highly significant.

The right-hand pillar from the porchway of King Solomon's Temple was described to complement the information given in the previous degree regarding the left-hand pillar. This pillar, identified as 'Jachin', was said to be named after the high priest who assisted at the dedication of this section of the Temple at Jerusalem. The twin pillars Boaz and Jachin were to become massively important at all points of our future research. The first is said to represent 'strength or in it is strength'; the second 'to establish' and when united 'stability'.

After the completion of the Second Degree ceremony I was 'permitted to extend my researches into the hidden mysteries of nature and science'.

Once again this ceremony was followed by eating, drinking, speeches and singing.

A Glimmer of Light

Some months later, as a Fellowcraft, wearing a white apron with two blue rosettes, I was eligible to be raised to what is often called the 'sublime' degree of a Master Mason, but first it was necessary to prove my competence once again by learning the answers to more test questions.

During the putting and answering of these questions my attention was drawn to the fact that 'our ancient brethren received their wages in the middle chamber of King Solomon's Temple without scruple or diffidence from the great reliance they placed on the integrity of their employer in those days.' Careful study of the Bible had found no mention of any middle chamber to Solomon's Temple. Such a factual mistake is unlikely, so to make sense of it, we assumed that the test questions indicated that the brethren had been able to trust their employers in the past, but might not be able to do so now.

At this stage I was also given an apparently biblical reference that does not exist in the Bible, but which points towards the mission with which I would be entrusted once I was raised to the sublime degree of a Master Mason: 'For the Lord has said in strength will I establish My Word in this Mine House that it will stand fast for ever.' This quotation proved to be extremely important, although it makes no sense to modern Freemasons and it made no sense to either of us when we first heard it.

I was then entrusted with a password which enabled me to re-enter the Temple when the proceedings had been opened as a Master Mason's Lodge. Things this time were very different and dramatic.

I re-entered the Temple to find total darkness save for the lone glimmer of a candle burning in the east in front of the Worshipful Master. In the very large windowless room the solitary candle gave precious little illumination, but once my eyes had adjusted it was possible to make out faces behind it and just pick out the form of the whole Temple in shades of black and dark grey. Dramatically, I was then informed that the subject of this degree was death itself.

The ceremony started with a brief resumé of the previous degrees:

> 'Brethren, *every degree of Masonry is progressive and cannot be attained but by time, patience and assiduity. In the First Degree, we are taught the duties we owe to God, to our neighbour, and to ourselves. In the Second Degree, we are admitted to participate in the mysteries of human science, and to trace the goodness and majesty of the Creator, by minutely analysing His works. But the Third Degree is the cement of the whole; it is calculated to bind men together by mystic points of fellowship, as in a bond of fraternal affection and brotherly love; it points to the darkness of death and to the obscurity of the grave as a forerunner of a more*

12

> *brilliant light, which shall follow at the resurrection of the just, when these mortal bodies which have been long slumbering in the dust shall be awakened, reunited to their kindred spirit, and clothed with immortality ...'*

A prayer was then said which concluded:

> *'... we beseech Thee to impart Thy grace to this Thy servant who seeks to partake with us the mysterious secrets of a Master Mason. Endue him with such fortitude that, in the hour of trial he fail not, but passing safely under Thy protection, through the dark valley of the shadow of death he may finally rise from the tomb of transgression to shine as the stars, for ever and ever.'*

The ceremony proceeded in a manner not too dissimilar to the previous occasions, up to the point where I was obliged to act out a remarkable story which explains the manner in which the true secrets of a Master Mason came to be lost. I played the role of a character who does not exist outside the rituals of masonry; his name was given as Hiram Abif:

The Worshipful Master told the story:

> *'... nature presents one grand and useful lesson more — the knowledge of yourself. She teaches you, by contemplation, to prepare for the closing hours of your existence; and when, by means of such contemplation, she has led you through the intricate windings of this, your mortal life, she finally teaches you how to die. Such, my dear brother, are the peculiar objects of this, the Third Degree in Freemasonry. They invite you to reflect upon that awful subject and teach you to feel that, to the just and upright man, death has no terror equal to that of the stain of falsehood and dishonour. Of this grand truth, the annals of Freemasonry*

afford a glorious example in the unshaken fidelity and untimely death of our Grand Master Hiram Abif who lost his life just before the completion of King Solomon's Temple, at the construction of which, as you are doubtless aware, he was the principal architect. The manner of his death was as follows:

Fifteen Fellowcrafts of that peculiar class appointed to preside over the rest, finding that the temple was nearly complete but that they were not yet in possession of the genuine secrets of a Master Mason, conspired together to obtain those secrets by any means, even having recourse to violence. On the eve of carrying their conspiracy into execution, twelve of the fifteen recanted, but three of a more determined and atrocious character than the rest persisted in their impious designs, for which purpose they placed themselves respectively at the south, west and east gates of the Temple, whither our Master Hiram Abif had retired to pay his adoration to the Most High, as was his wonton custom, it being the hour of high twelve.

His devotions being ended, he prepared to retire by the south gate, where he was accosted by the first of these ruffians, who, for want of a better weapon, had armed himself with a plumb rule, and in a threatening manner demanded of our Master, Hiram Abif, the genuine secrets of a Master Mason, warning him that death would be the consequence of his refusal; but true to his obligation he replied that those secrets were known to but three in the world and that without the consent of the other two, he neither could, nor would divulge them; but intimated that he had no doubt that patience and perseverance would, in due time, entitle the worthy mason to a participation in them. But as for himself, he would rather suffer death than betray the sacred trust reposed in him.

This answer not proving satisfactory, the ruffian aimed a violent blow at our master's forehead, but *startled by the firmness of his demeanour, it only glanced down his right temple. Yet with sufficient force to cause him to reel and sink to the ground on his left knee.'*

At this point I felt a very light blow to my temple and my two guides, known as deacons, indicated that I should go down on my knee in imitation of the story.

'Recovering himself from this situation, he rushed to the west gate where he stood opposed by the second ruffian, to whom he replied as before, yet with undiminished firmness when the ruffian, who was armed with a level struck a violent blow on the left temple which brought him to the ground on his right knee.'

Once again I felt a touch to my own temple and I was pressed down onto my right knee.

'Finding all chances of escape in both these quarters cut off, our Master staggered, faint and bleeding, to the east gate where the third ruffian was posted and who, on receiving a similar reply to his insolent demand, for our Master remained true to his obligation even in this most trying moment, struck him a violent blow full in the centre of the forehead with a heavy stone maul, which laid him lifeless at his feet ... Such was the manner of his death.'

In the light of the candle I saw the Worshipful Master reach forward over his pedestal with an instrument which touched my forehead and I felt many hands pulling me backwards to the floor. I was held straight and my feet were kept in place, so that I hinged backwards as I swung into the darkness. As I touched the ground a funeral shroud was immediately draped around me, so only my upper face was uncovered. The Worshipful Master continued:

> *'Brethren in the recent ceremony, as well as in his present situation, our Brother has been made to represent one of the brightest characters in the annals of Freemasonry, namely Hiram Abif who lost his life rather than betray the sacred trust reposed in him. And I trust that this will make a lasting impression, not only on his, but on your minds, should you ever be placed in similar circumstances of trial.*
>
> *Brother Junior Warden, you will now attempt to raise the representative of our Master with the grip of an Entered Apprentice.'*

The Junior Warden reached down, took my hand from under the shroud and pulled. My hand fell through his fingers.

> *'Worshipful Master this grip proves to slip.'*

Shadowy figures marched around my 'grave' for a few moments, before the Worshipful Master spoke again.

> *'Brother Senior Warden, you will try the Fellowcraft grip.'*

This proved as ineffectual as the first attempt.

> *'Brother Wardens, you have both failed in your endeavours. There remains yet a third and peculiar method, known as the Lion's Paw or Eagle's Claw grip, which is given by taking a firm hold on the sinews of the wrist of the right hand with the points of the fingers and raising him on the five points of fellowship, of which, with your assistance, I will now make a trial.'*

The Worshipful Master gripped my wrist tightly and pulled, hingeing me instantly upwards to my feet. Once again unseen hands took my weight. As I reached the vertical position the Worshipful Master whispered two peculiar words in my ear. I now knew both parts of the Mason's Word. At the time it was meaningless, but through our researches we have discovered its ancient and fascinating meaning, as will be shown later.

> *'Thus, my dear Brother, have all Master Masons been raised from a figurative death, to a reunion with the companions of their former toil. Let me now beg of you to observe, that the light of a Master Mason is but as darkness visible, serving only to express that gloom which hangs over the prospect of futurity. It is that mysterious veil of darkness which the eye of human reason cannot penetrate, unless assisted by that divine light which is from above. Yet even, by this glimmering ray you will perceive that you stand on the very brink of the grave into which you have just figuratively descended, and which, when this transitory life shall have passed away, will again receive you into its cold bosom.'*

As the Worshipful Master spoke these chilling words he directed my gaze downwards and to my right, where I could just pick out of the darkness the shape of an open grave, with a human skull on a pair of crossed thighbones at its head. (Fig 2) For the first time in any Masonic ceremony I felt a cold wave of goose bumps pass across my body.

> *'Let those emblems of mortality, which now lie before you, lead you to contemplate your inevitable destiny and guide your reflections into that most interesting and useful of all human studies — the knowledge of yourself.*
> *Be careful to perform your allotted task while it is*

yet day; listen to the voice of nature which bears witness that, even in this perishable frame, there resides a vital and immortal principle, which inspires a holy confidence, that the Lord of Life will enable us to trample the King of Terrors beneath our feet, and lift our eyes'

The Worshipful Master indicated upwards and to the left towards a glimmer of light in the East (the exact opposite direction to the grave) where I could see the small, illuminated shape of a star.

'... to that bright morning star whose rising brings peace and tranquillity to the faithful and obedient of the human race.'

My ceremony of 'raising' caused me to be reborn to the status of a Master Mason and concluded with the giving of more passwords and grips, and more building analogies to provide guidance on the improvement of my qualities as a Mason, and a member of society. Later, in another formal Lodge meeting, the story of events following the killing were explained:

'There was a general muster of the workmen throughout the different departments, when three of the same class of overseers were not to be found. On the same day, the twelve craftsmen who had originally joined in the conspiracy came before the King, and made a voluntary confession of all they knew, down to the time of withdrawing themselves from the number of the conspirators. His fears being naturally increased for the safety of his chief artist, he selected fifteen trusty Fellow Crafts, and ordered them to make diligent search after the person of our master, to ascertain if he were yet alive, or had suffered in the attempt to extort from him the secrets of his exalted degree.

A stated day having been appointed for their return to Jerusalem, they formed themselves into three Fellow Craft Lodges and departed from the three entrances of the Temple. Many days were spent in fruitless search; indeed one class returned without having made any discovery of importance. The second class were more fortunate, for on the evening of a certain day, after having suffered the greatest privations and personal fatigues, one of the Brethren who had rested himself in a reclining posture, to assist his rising, caught hold of a shrub that grew near, which to his surprise, came easily out of the ground; on a closer examination, he found that the earth had been recently disturbed; he therefore hailed his companions, and with their united endeavours reopened the grave and there found the body of our Master very indecently interred. They covered it again with all respect and reverence, and to distinguish the spot, stuck a sprig of acacia at the head of the grave, then hastened to Jerusalem to impart the afflicting intelligence to King Solomon.

When the King's first emotions of his grief had subsided, he ordered them to return and raise our Master to such a sepulchre as became his rank and exalted talents; at the same time informing them that by his untimely death the secrets of a Master Mason were lost. He therefore charged them to be particularly careful in observing whatever casual Signs, Tokens or Words might occur, whilst paying this last sad tribute of respect to departed merit.

They performed their task with utmost fidelity, and on reopening the grave, one of the Brethren, looking round, observed some of his companions in this position ...'

It was then explained to me how the Fellow Crafts tried to raise Hiram Abif with the words and grips used in my own figurative raising, and how since that time those elements have been adopted as the designation of all Master Masons throughout the universe, until time or circumstances should restore the genuine ones. The ceremony then continues:

> *'The third class meanwhile had pursued their researches in the direction of Joppa, and were meditating their return to Jerusalem, when, accidentally passing the mouth of a cavern, they heard sounds of deep lamentation and regret. On entering the cave to ascertain the cause, they found three men answering the description of those missing, who, on being charged with the murder, and finding all chance of escape cut off, made a full confession of their guilt. They were then bound and led to Jerusalem, when King Solomon sentenced them to that death the heinousness of their crime so amply merited.*
>
> *Our Master was then re-interred as near to the Sanctum Sanctorum as the Israelitish law would permit; there in a grave, from the centre three feet east and three feet west, three feet between north and south and five feet or more perpendicular. He could not be put in the Sanctum Sanctorum because nothing common or unclean was allowed to enter there; not even the high priest but once a year; nor then until after many washings and purifications against the great day of expiation for sins, for by the Israelitish law all flesh was deemed unclean.*
>
> *The fifteen trusty Fellow Crafts were ordered to attend the funeral, clothed in white aprons and white gloves as emblems of their innocence.'*

The ceremony continued in a manner similar to the two former degrees and I emerged a full Master Mason. Some months later, when there was no candidate to progress in the Lodge meeting, a Past Master gave an explanation of the Third Degree. The three villains who murdered

Hiram Abif were identified as Jubela, Jubelo and Jubelum, known jointly as the Juwes; pronounced Joo-ees. The 'sounds of deep lamentation and regret' that had been heard coming from the cavern were given in detail. The culprits were heard to be deeply remorseful and wishing terrible punishments upon themselves for their vile actions and in due course they get their wish; King Solomon had them executed in the manner that each had identified for themselves. These are described in the ritual, but we will not describe them as they comprise part of the means of Masonic identification.

* * *

The extracts from the three levels of Masonic ritual that we have given here will seem extremely strange to those readers who are not 'on the square', but will be very familiar to fellow Freemasons. Familiarity, however, only serves to make these inexplicable activities *seem* normal, when by any standards they are bizarre. Some Masons believe the stories to be true, just as many Christians accept the legends of the Old Testament; others take them as a bit of fun with moral overtones. Very few give any thought at all as to where such strange rituals may have originated.

Many of the principal characters are readily identifiable in Judaeo-Christian mythology – King Solomon for example, Boaz, Jachin and some others we have not identified – but the key personality is a complete mystery. Hiram Abif is not mentioned in the Old Testament at all, no builder of the Temple is named and no murder of a high priest is recorded. Some Christian critics of Freemasonry condemn the Craft because they claim that it glorifies the resurrection of a man other than Jesus Christ, and that it is essentially a pagan religion. But it is important to note that Hiram Abif, once killed, remained dead; there was no return to life nor indeed any suggestion of an after-life existence. There is no supernatural content to Masonic ritual at all and this is why members of many different religions, including Jews, Christians, Hindus and Buddhists, have found it complementary to, rather than in conflict with, their own theological beliefs.

The central story is very simple and unremarkable, having no special dramatic structure or even any obvious symbolic value. Yes, Hiram Abif did die rather than betray his beliefs; but so have countless other men and women, before and since. If some person or persons set out to invent a story that was to be pivotal to a new society, surely they would have come up with something more remarkable and self-explanatory? It was this thought that provoked us to start digging deeper in a search for the origins of the Order.

We shared the same frustrations concerning the vague conventional explanation of the origins of the Order. Our discussions became more frequent and our interest grew as we sparked off each other, and it was not long before we decided to undertake a structured investigation with the joint objectives of identifying the character we knew as Hiram Abif and finding the lost secrets of Freemasonry. At that time neither of us believed that we had any chance of succeeding in this strange quest, but we knew that the journey would be interesting. We did not know it at the time but we had just set in motion one of the biggest detective investigations of all time, and that our findings were going to be of major importance, not only to Freemasons, but to the world in general.

CONCLUSION

There is very little of the Masonic ritual that could be described as ordinary. The candidate is blindfolded, stripped of money and metal objects, dressed as an accused heretic on his journey to the gallows and finally told that the object of his last degree is 'how to die'! The journey from darkness to light is obviously important as are the two pillars called Boaz and Jachin that symbolise 'strength' and 'establishment' and when united, mean 'stability'.

Freemasonry claims to be more ancient than the Golden Fleece or Roman Eagle and has the aim of brotherly love, relief and truth – yet investigating the hidden mysteries of nature and science are presented as very important. The genuine secrets of the Order, we are told, have been lost and substituted secrets are in their place until such time as the true ones will be found.

The central character of Freemasonry is the builder of King Solomon's Temple who is named as Hiram Abif, who was murdered by three of his own men. The stylised death and resurrection of the candidate is the act that makes one a Master Mason and when raised from his tomb, the bright morning star is on the horizon.

Where could such strange ideas have developed, and why? We could only start our investigation by considering the known theories.

Chapter Two

The Search Begins

Where Did the Order Originate?

A great number of well-informed men have set out before us to try and find the origins of Freemasonry, and they overlooked none of the obvious possibilities; nor did the ranks of the romancers and charlatans who have joined in the hunt. For some the line is simple: Freemasonry is only as old as its publicly recorded history (the seventeenth century) and everything purporting to predate those records is whimsical nonsense. This pragmatic attitude is uncomplicated, but it is the easiest of hypotheses to reject for many reasons, as we will show, not least the fact that there is widespread evidence to show that the Order materialised slowly over more than three hundred years before the establishment of the United Grand Lodge of England.

From the establishment of the Grand Lodge of England in 1717 onwards the Order has been open about its existence; only its methods of recognition have been kept from public gaze. But the organisation that we now call Freemasonry was a secret society before the mid-seventeenth century and secret societies, by definition, do not publish official histories. We therefore decided to look into the possible history of the Craft before it 'went public' and felt that there were three serious theories that had received consideration from Masonic historians:

1. That Freemasonry is as ancient as the Masonic ritual claims – it was indeed created as a result of happenings at the building of King Solomon's Temple and has been passed down to us though mechanisms unknown.

2. That it is a development of medieval stonemasons' guilds, whereby 'operative' Masonic skills with stone were translated into what Masons call 'speculative' Masonic skills of moral improvement.

3. That Masonic ritual originates directly from the Order of the Poor Fellow-Soldiers of Christ and the Temple of Solomon, now better known as the Knights Templar.

The first theory, that Freemasonry was the creation of King Solomon, struck us as impossible to research because the Old Testament is the only source, so we pursued it no further at that time.

The second one, that medieval stonemasons developed the Craft for their own moral improvement, is a theory that has found acceptance in virtually every quarter, Masonic and non-Masonic. Nevertheless, despite the apparent logic of this idea and the large number of books that have promoted this idea over many generations, we found it difficult to substantiate once we considered it in depth. For a start, despite rigorous searching, we were completely unable to find any records to show that medieval stonemasons' guilds existed at all in England. Had they existed we felt certain that some trace would still remain; in many European countries they certainly did exist and there is plenty of evidence of their activities. Gould's *History of Freemasonry* carries page after page of crests of the guilds of stonemasons across Europe, but none are British!

Such workers were skilled artisans in the employ of the church or rich landowners, and it seems unlikely that their masters would have been enlightened enough to permit some form of proto-trade union, even if the workers had developed a desire for such a unifying body. Many of them would have spent their entire lives working on a single building such as a cathedral, and the need for secret signs of recognition and passwords struck us as non-existent when these masons were trundling around the same building site for fifty years.

Most stonemasons in the Middle Ages were illiterate and would have had little or no education outside of their apprenticeship which provided only craft skills. To imagine that they could have understood, let alone have originated, as complex a ritual as that now used by Freemasons strains credibility. Their vocabulary and most likely their ability for abstract thought must have been very limited indeed. Travel for all but the most highly skilled master masons was a rare event so secret signs, grips and passwords would not be of much value; and even if they did travel from one building construction to another why would they need secret means of recognition? If someone falsely claimed to be a stonemason it would not take long to spot their inability to work stone.

As many kings and their mightiest lords have been Freemasons from the Order's known beginnings to the present (see Appendices), we could not imagine the circumstances in which a band of noblemen turned up at a stonemasons' gathering asking if they could copy their proceedings to use them, in a symbolic manner, for their own moral betterment.

We found the definitive evidence to dispose of the 'stonemason theory' when we studied what are known in Freemasonry as 'The Old Charges', the oldest of which is believed to date back to the late fifteenth century. It sets out rules of conduct and responsibility for Freemasons and it has always been assumed that these were taken from the codes of conduct belonging to medieval stonemasons' guilds. One of these Charges states that 'no brother is to reveal any legitimate secret of another brother if it might cost him his life and property'. The only legitimate Masonic secret at that time that would automatically carry such a penalty if discovered by the state, would have been heresy; a crime that surely would not have been committed or condoned by simple, Christian stonemasons. The question we asked ourselves was, 'Why on earth would heresy be anticipated as a possible guilty secret of these castle and cathedral builders?' It did not make sense. Organisations do not evolve important rules in case one of their members might one day be secretly guilty of a crime against the Church; clearly whoever originated this Old Charge was aware that every brother lived with the danger of being branded a heretic. We were certain that these rules were not created by simple stonemasons, but for a group that lived on the fringes of the law of the land.

Having satisfied ourselves that there was no evidence to support the stonemason theory and plenty to damn it, we became increasingly puzzled as to what kind of people the 'Ancient Charges' could have referred to. Another Charge from the same period, much discussed by historians, indicates a very clandestine ancient purpose. This refers to the provision of 'employment' for a visiting brother for the period of two weeks after which time 'he should then be given some money and put on the road to the next Lodge'. This is the kind of treatment that one would expect to be extended to a man on the run, seeking safe-houses as he goes. Yet another Charge prohibits Masons from having sexual relationships with the wife, daughter, mother or sister of a brother Mason, which would be an absolute necessity to maintain the 'safe-house' system – to come home and find a Masonic guest in bed with one's wife or daughter would rather strain the oath of brotherly charity.[1] We could not imagine what possible heresy this early Masonic group could have been guilty of, to create

[1] John J. Robinson: *Born in Blood*

such a highly structured system of recognition and survival outside of the Church and State. In addition to these factors which discredit the stonemasons theory, it is essential to remember that the central imagery that runs right through Freemasonry is the building of King Solomon's Temple. There is no link connecting medieval stonemasons to this event, but there most certainly is where the third theory is concerned – the Knights Templar theory.

The Knights Templar, or to give them their full title, the Poor Fellow-Soldiers of Christ and the Temple of Solomon, were formed almost six hundred years before the establishment of the Grand Lodge of England. If there is a connection between these crusading warrior-monks and Freemasonry, we will have to explain the gap of four hundred and ten years between the sudden demise of the Order in October 1307 and the formal appearance of the Craft. This break has prompted many observers, Masonic and otherwise, to dismiss suggestions of a link as wishful thinking; some have published books to show that the supporters of this theory are mere romantics predisposed to believe esoteric nonsense. More recently available evidence has, however, strongly shifted the weight of argument in favour of the Templar/Freemasonry connection, and our own researches have put it beyond any doubt at all.

Before we look at the formation of this fascinating Order, we examined the circumstances of the building that gave the Templars their name and Freemasonry its theme.

The Temple of King Solomon

We found that there were, in the wider sense, four Temples associated with Mount Moriah in the city of Jerusalem. The first was that built by King Solomon three thousand years ago. The next never existed in stone; it was that seen in a vision by the prophet Ezekiel during the captivity of the Jews in Babylon in about 570 BC. Imaginary though this Temple was, it cannot be ignored as it has had a significant effect on later Jewish writings and beliefs that passed down to Christian belief. The third was built by King Zerubbabel in the early part of the sixth century BC after the Jews returned from their Babylonian captivity, and the final Temple was being erected by Herod at the time of Jesus Christ and was destroyed by the Romans in AD 70, just four years after its completion.

As we were later to discover, Solomon set about creating many great buildings including a temple to house the god we now call Yahweh or Jehovah. Both names are attempts at translating from Hebrew, a form of writing with no vowels. Solomon is often referred to as a wise king, but as we progressed in our researches we discovered that the designation 'wise' had been bestowed on all the builders and kings who sponsored buildings for thousands of years before Solomon, as will be demonstrated later.

The Jews themselves had no architectural heritage, and none of them had the building skills required to erect anything more than a simple wall; consequently, the Temple at Jerusalem was built by craftsmen hired from Hiram, the Phoenician King of Tyre. Despite the name it was clear to us, and every previous observer, that King Hiram has nothing to do with Hiram Abif. The ritual of the Holy Royal Arch Degree, which we will discuss further in Chapter Thirteen, makes it very clear that Hiram, King of Tyre supplied the materials whilst another individual, Hiram Abif, was the actual architect of the Temple. It even mentions that these three individuals (Solomon and the two Hirams) held an important Lodge and were the sole joint holders of the true secrets of a Master Mason.

Despite a commonly held Masonic view that this

Temple was a landmark in the history of building, Clarke and other experts consider its style, size and layout to be almost a carbon copy of a Sumerian temple erected for the god Ninurta a thousand years earlier. It was a small building, similar in size to an ordinary English village church and believed to be less than half as big as Solomon's palace. We can guess at where the great king's priorities lay when we discovered that the building to house his harem was at least as big as Yahweh's Temple.[2]

From a knowledge of the purpose of churches, synagogues and mosques, it would be easy to assume that Solomon's Temple was a place where the Jews worshipped their God. This, however, would be a mistake as this Temple was not constructed to be visited by men – it was, quite literally, the House of God; a home for Yahweh Himself.

There are no physical remains of the Temple of Solomon and there are no independent records of it, so no one can be sure whether or not it really existed; it might be an invention of the later Jewish scribes who wrote down their verbal traditions long after the alleged building took place.[3] They tell us that this, the most famous of all temples, was built of stone and completely lined inside with cedar brought from Tyre. The walls are said to have been nine cubits (about 13 foot 6 inches) thick at their base and rose to support a flat timber roof of cedar topped with fir. The distinguishing characteristic of the Temple was the amount of gold which covered the floor, walls and ceiling, set amongst carvings of cherubim and open flowers. The interior was 90 feet long and 30 feet wide and the whole building was aligned from west to east with a single entrance at the eastern end. A partition with a pair of folding doors set into it divided the interior into a two

[2] 'A New Look at King Solomon's Temple and its Connection with Masonic Ritual', J. R. Clarke. Published in *ARS Quatuor Coronatorum*, November 1976
[3] *Peake's Commentary on the Bible*

thirds to one third split, creating a cube 30 feet in height, width and length. This was the Oracle of the Old Testament, also called the Holy of Holies and known in Masonic ritual as the Sanctum Sanctorum, which was completely empty except for a rectangular box of shittim wood (acacia) 4 feet long by 2 feet wide and 2 feet high, placed in the exact centre of the floor. This was the Ark of the Covenant which contained just three things: two tablets of stone bearing the Ten Commandments and the god Yahweh himself. On top of it was a thick sheet of solid gold and two wooden cherubim, themselves heavily covered with gold, with outstretched wings guarding the precious contents.

These cherubim were not the chubby, haloed, flying infants popular with Renaissance painters. They would have been Egyptian in style, looking exactly like the figures depicted on the walls and sarcophagi of the pyramids.[4] The Holy of Holies was in permanent darkness except for once each year on the Day of Atonement, when the High Priest entered with the blood of the national sin-offering, the scapegoat. After the High Priest left, a large chain of gold was placed across the doors sealing off the smaller chamber from the larger. According to later Jewish tradition this room was used by the Priests and Levites (hereditary priests) alone and it contained a gold-covered cedar altar placed square on just in front of the doors and, of course, outside of the eastern doorway stood the two pillars, Boaz and Jachin.

This then was the building that the Templars venerated as the central icon of their Order. But it was the ruins of another Temple that they excavated, built almost exactly a thousand years later on the same site by the infamous King Herod. Why then, we wondered, did they choose to name themselves after Solomon's Temple?

[4] W. F. Albright: *The Archaeology of Palestine*

CONCLUSION

We had easily decided that the stonemason theory of the origin of Freemasonry does not hold up under close examination for the simple reason that guilds of stonemasons did not exist in Britain. The fact that they existed on the Continent is not relevant because Freemasonry did not develop in the areas where these European Guilds were formed.

The protocol found in the Ancient Charges of the Order, with their obligation to provide work and a concern about ensuring the protection of the female relatives of brothers, seemed to us to be much more fitted to a secret society rather than a group of itinerant builders.

We had searched long and hard, spending hundreds of hours in various libraries immersed in reference books but try as we might we could not find any connection between King Solomon's Temple and medieval stonemasons.

History had told us that there had been three temples of stone on the site and one imaginary one that could not be ignored as it had inspired many people down the ages. The original Temple built for Solomon was a small Sumerian-type building, smaller than his harem, erected to house the troublesome storm god Yahweh rather than as a place of worship. Yahweh himself lived inside the Ark of the Covenant which was housed in the Holy of Holies of the Temple, an area known to Freemasons as the Sanctum Sanctorum. This Ark was constructed and decorated in an Egyptian style and at the eastern doorway of this first temple stood the two pillars known to Freemasons as Boaz and Jachin.

The idea that the Order might have come down from Solomon himself as a continuous secret society hidden from the world seemed completely impossible, and we were left, through a process of simple elimination, with just one plausible origin to investigate. We knew that the first Knights Templar had excavated the site of the last Temple, and many writers had suggested connections between these knights and Masonry.

Chapter Three

The Knights Templar

The Beginnings of the Order

The image of a brave crusader wearing a white mantle decorated with a red cross and sporting a full beard, slaying the wicked and protecting the good, is one that most of us have been familiar with since childhood. The reality was quite different. The red cross on the white robe was the garb, not of all crusaders but of a group of warrior monks: the Knights Templar. Their mysterious rise from nowhere, their subsequent massive wealth and influence and their sudden and total fall from grace on Friday 13 October 1307 has made them the subject of debate and imaginative speculation from that day to this.

For almost two hundred years the Templars were powerful beyond the scope of most kings, with legendary fighting abilities and fabulous treasures. Could there really be a connection between this long-gone medieval Order and the middle-class men who mumble Masonic ritual behind closed doors in just about every sizeable town in the Westernised world? At face value they seem so far apart that it would take a massive amount of evidence to claim a direct relationship, but as we looked at the details of both side by side, the disparity between the two began to shrink surprisingly rapidly.

The Muslims had ruled Jerusalem since the seventh century and had allowed Jews and Christians access to the city which was important to all three religions for different reasons. Towards the end of the eleventh century Seljuk Turks took control of Jerusalem and banned Christians from making pilgrimages. The powers of Christendom were unhappy at this state of affairs and mobilised their forces to recapture the land of Jesus. Despite the purity of the apparent motive behind them, the so-called 'Crusades', the battles for control of the Holy Land, were hard-fought, merciless conflicts.

The crude and self-seeking Christian invaders from the north believed that the Muslims were in the habit of swallowing their gold and jewellery to hide them in times of crisis and consequently many Muslims died in agony with their bellies torn open as white, infidel fingers probed their entrails for nonexistent valuables. The Jews of Jerusalem fared little better. They had lived happily side by side with the Muslims for hundreds of years and on 14 June 1099 they died beside them; the bloodlust of the crusaders knew no bounds. One crusader, Raymond of Aguilers, was moved by the sight of the devastated city and the mutilated corpses of its residents to quote Psalm 118: 'This is the day the Lord has made. Let us rejoice and be glad of it.'

In the years that followed the capture of Jerusalem, Christians from all over Europe began to make the pilgrimage to the Holy City, a journey so long and arduous that a fit body and a strong constitution were needed to survive it. The growing number of pilgrims travelling from the ports of Acre, Tyre and Jaffa to the city of Jerusalem created problems and an infrastructure had to be created to provide for them. An important part of these arrangements was the Amalfi Hostelry in Jerusalem, which was established by the Knights Hospitaller to provide food and lodgings for the constant flow of travellers. The importance and wealth of the small and obscure order of monks who ran it grew in proportion to the increasing number of visitors, and the new Christian rulers of the City rewarded their efforts with generous gifts. The Order developed quickly and its prior must have been an ambitious and politically astute individual as he took the unusual step of creating a military arm by accepting knights to join, after which he changed the title of the Order to 'the Hospital of St John of Jerusalem'. It obtained papal blessing in 1118 when it was provided with a formal constitution, known as a 'Rule'.

This was an organisation which probably influenced a French nobleman from Champagne by the name of Hugues de Payen, because in the same year he and eight other knights established the unofficial Order of the Poor Soldiers of Christ and the Temple of Solomon. According to tradition King Baldwin II, the Patriarch of Jerusalem, readily gave his support to the new Order and provided quarters for them in the eastern part of his palace which adjoined the former Al-Aqsa Mosque and stood on the site of King Solomon's Temple. The Templars, as they are now usually called, were said to have come into existence for the purpose of providing protection for the increasing flow of pilgrims as they made their hazardous journeys between the coastal port of Jaffa and Jerusalem.

All of these original knights were laymen who took an oath to live as though they were monks, in poverty, chastity and with obedience. Initially they wore no special clothing, but they said prayers at regular intervals and in every way they behaved as though they were members of a religious order.

Some time in 1118 these nine knights apparently arrived from France and appointed themselves guardians of the Judaean desert roads leading to Jerusalem. This standard account struck us as odd. Why had these Frenchmen set themselves a task which was extremely optimistic at best and foolhardy at worst? Even a small band of Saracen insurgents would surely have over-whelmed them no matter how well trained and armed they were. Surprisingly we found that Fulcher of Chartres, Baldwin II's chaplain, did not make a single mention of them in his extensive chronicles that cover the first nine years of the unofficial Order's existence. The earliest certain evidence of the Templars dates from 1121, when a certain Count Fulk V of Anjou lodged with the Templars and thereafter left them an annuity of thirty Angevin livres.

From the evidence available it seems clear that the band of nine knights did not expand for a long time after its establishment. It was not until after they had spent no less than nine years in their lodgings on the site of Herod's Temple that Hugues de Payen left for the west in search of worthy recruits who would swell the Order to a size more appropriate to the fulfilment of its self-proclaimed mission.

What Were They Searching For?

We instinctively felt that there was something wrong here. There is no evidence that these founding Templars ever gave protection to pilgrims, but on the other hand we were soon to find that there is conclusive proof that they did conduct extensive excavations under the ruins of Herod's Temple. We soon realised that many other writers had had reservations about the accepted version of the Templars' aims; the more we looked, the more we came across theories about the real motives of the Templars. In one, the French historian Gaetan Delaforge commented:

> '*The real task of the nine knights was to carry out research in the area in order to obtain certain relics and manuscripts which contain the essence of the secret traditions of Judaism and ancient Egypt, some of which probably went back to the days of Moses.*'[1]

[1] G. Delaforge: *The Templar Tradition in the Age of Aquarius*

This comment was used by the researcher and author Graham Hancock in arguing that these knights were not what they seemed.[2] He concluded that the Temple site itself was the focus of their interest and that there is evidence of their major excavations. He quotes from an Israeli archaeologist's official report which established that these nine knights were searching the Temple ruins for something unknown:

> *'The tunnel leads inwards for a distance of about thirty metres from the southern wall before being blocked by pieces of stone debris. We know that it continues further, but we had made it a hard-and-fast rule not to excavate within the bounds of the Temple Mount, which is currently under Moslem jurisdiction, without first acquiring the permission of the appropriate Moslem authorities. In this case they permitted us only to measure and photograph the exposed section of the tunnel, not to conduct excavation of any kind. Upon concluding this work ... we sealed up the tunnel's exit with stones.'*

We found further evidence that the Templars had been involved in digging for something under the ruins of Herod's Temple in the writings of Lieutenant Charles Wilson of the Royal Engineers who led an archaeological expedition to Jerusalem at the turn of the century.[3] He recovered many old items that can be positively identified as Templar artefacts, from diggings deep below the Temple. As our researches for this book were nearing completion, we had the good fortune to meet Robert Brydon, a scholarly Templar archivist based in Scotland, who now has many of these items in his care.

Our motive for looking at the origins of the Templars

[2] G. Hancock: *The Sign and the Seal*
[3] C. Wilson: *The Excavation of Jerusalem*

was to try and confirm any direct connection between their Order and modern Freemasonry. As we absorbed the known facts and read official and unofficial perspectives on the first Templars, we concluded that it was clear they were indeed excavating the Temple. The questions we needed answers to were: what were they looking for, and much more importantly, what did they actually find?

Other writers have speculated that they may have been looking for the lost treasures of the Temple, searching for the Holy Grail or even trying to find the Ark of the Covenant itself.[4] These speculations may well be correct but, of course, we were more interested in what they actually found rather than what they originally set out to locate.

For nine years then, these nine devoted 'treasure' hunters had excavated the site of the great Temples of the Jews and during that time they had not sought or allowed any further knight entrants to their Order, living solely on the charity of Baldwin.

All must have gone reasonably well year after year as they tunnelled through solid rock, inching closer and closer to the base of the 'Holy of Holies'; but then something happened to change the basic plan. It occurred to us that it was probably something less than a coincidence, that Hugues de Payen's journey west to find recruits for the first time happened just months after the death of their benefactor Baldwin in October 1126. Had they run out of funds and food before their unknown task was completed, or did they wait for Baldwin to die in order to cut him out of any share of treasure?

The Rule of the Order

It appears that Payen's journey had been prompted by a real fear for the continuance of their group. A letter he

---

[4] G. Hancock: *The Sign and the Seal*

wrote as he travelled through Europe clearly illustrated his concern that his fellow knights back in Jerusalem needed their convictions bolstering. It referred to the knights' original vocation being weakened by the devil and went on to quote biblical passages to reassure his remaining seven knights. There were only seven left back on the Temple Mount as Payen was accompanied on his journey by André de Montbard, the uncle of the very young but highly influential Abbot of Clairvaux (destined to become St Bernard). It must have been this family connection that took them first to Bernard, who was clearly impressed by the story he heard from his uncle. Bernard's words promoting their campaign for assistance left little doubt about his opinion of these knights from Jerusalem: 'They go not headlong into battle, but with care and foresight, peacefully, as true children of Israel. But as soon as the fight has begun, they rush without delay upon the foe ... and know no fear ... one has often put to flight a thousand; two, ten thousand ... gentler than lambs and grimmer than lions; theirs is the mildness of monks and the valour of the knight.'

The future St Bernard quickly brought the fledgling Order to the attention of Pope Honarius II, asking that his adopted little band of knights from Jerusalem should be provided with a 'Rule'; a constitution of their own that laid out requirements for conduct and practice which would give them legitimacy and defined status within the Church. This was finally granted on 31 January 1128 when Hugues de Payen appeared before the specially convened Council of Troyes. This impressive body was presided over by the Cardinal of Albano, the Papal legate and comprised the Archbishops of Rheims and Sens, no fewer than ten bishops and a number of abbots, including Bernard himself. The proposition was carried and the Templars were given the right to wear their own mantles, which at that time were pure white, as well as receiving their Rule.

To the whole world, they were now truly monks as well as knights.

What fascinated us about the Rule given to the Templars was not so much what it said but much what it did *not* say. Nowhere was there any mention of pilgrims or their protection. Strange, we thought, how the apparent sole reason for creating the Order could be so totally overlooked! By this point we were convinced that something very mysterious was at the centre of the founding of the Templar Order.

The original nine knights had long been extremely reluctant to take in new recruits, but now they were forced by the need for funds, extra workers and perhaps even clerics to change their attitude. Their new Rule made joining members probationers for the first year and required from them an immediate vow of poverty, so a new 'brother' had to hand over his personal wealth to the Order. All candidates were required to have been born in wedlock, be of noble birth, be free from any vow or tie and be of sound body. Upon admission the accepted brother owned only his sword and nothing else; he had no identity apart from his sword, which he dedicated to the service of the Order. When he died his grave carried no inscription, being marked only with a rectangular stone into which the shape of his sword was carved.

Immediately after the granting of their Rule the Templars' circumstances went from strength to strength. They gained the support of scores of influential landowners and donations started to arrive from all corners of the Christian world. Bernard had convinced the Pope of their worth and suddenly they became the fashionable cause with wealth being thrust upon them. When Hugues de Payen and André de Montbard returned to Jerusalem a mere two years after setting out, the level of their success was outstanding. They had gone west with nothing and came back with a Papal Rule, money, precious objects, landed wealth and no less than three hundred recruited noblemen to follow Hugues de Payen's lead as Grand Master of a major order.

Hugues de Payen must have been producing something very tangible to generate such interest and support. With our curiosity mounting, we looked further into what is still known of these warrior monks.

The new members of the Order were sworn to poverty, chastity and obedience but whether or not this Rule was applied retrospectively to the founders is never mentioned. Certainly Hugues de Payen remained married to Catherine de St Clair (a Scottish woman of Norman descent) and set up the first Templar Preceptory outside the Holy Land on her family's land in Scotland, a fact that would later turn out to be of major relevance. Entrants were obliged to cut their hair but forbidden to cut their beards. This is where the image of the Templar Crusader with the long flowing beard arose. Diet, dress and all other aspects of their daily lives were controlled by the Rule. In particular, their behaviour on the battlefield was strictly ordered. Templars were not allowed to ask for mercy or to ransom themselves but were compelled to fight to the death. They were never allowed to retreat unless the odds against them exceeded three to one and whilst history shows that they ultimately lost, it is also clear from Muslim as well as Christian records that the Order was both feared and respected for its fighting skills.

We were amazed to find that about ten years after the granting of their original 'Latin Rule' the Templars began to think so highly of themselves that they unilaterally developed a 'French Rule' to replace the former with one in the working language of the members of the Order. The fact that they had the confidence to do this illustrates the power and independence that the Templars enjoyed. This new Rule contained several significant changes but intriguingly, it still made no mention of the protection of pilgrims. It did away with the requirement for a probationary year for novices and turned one highly important rule on its head, instantly changing the legal basis of the Order.

In the Latin Rule an instruction read '... moreover where non-excommunicated knights are gathered you must go'. However, in the translated and amended French Rule the same sentence became '... we command you to go where excommunicated knights are gathered'. This can only imply that they were outside Vatican law. There can be no possibility that this was simply an error of translation as the clerics were working in their own language, not some unfamiliar script, and such a total reversal of meaning would have been spotted by the rest of the Order even if the original scribe made a mistake. Taken with what we now know of the Templars, both their arrogance and their suspected deviation from the Church of Rome, it is entirely understandable that they dared to write such a thing but we could not find anything to indicate what their reason might have been.

Eventually the Templars' luck was to run out. The Pope and Philip, King of France moved in on the errant Order, bringing it to its knees in just one terrible day ... Friday 13 October 1307. Ever since that day the number thirteen has been considered unlucky and a Friday the 13th of any month has become a date to keep any overly superstitious person indoors clinging to their lucky rabbit's foot.

The Seal of the Order

The first seal of the Templars depicted two knights riding on a single horse and it is usually claimed that this is a device to signify the poverty to which the members were sworn, in that they could not afford a mount for every knight. This would have made them a very inefficient fighting force had it been based on truth. The French Rule, however, states that the Master 'must have four horses, and one chaplain-brother and one clerk with three horses, and one sergeant brother with two horses, and one gentleman valet to carry his shield and lance, with one horse …'. Clearly there was no shortage of available mounts.

It occurred to us that this seal might represent the two grades of knights within the one Order; those who were more advanced who were allowed to share in the Templar secret, and those in the 'back seat' who did not. This interpretation of the seal is, of course, pure speculation, but it seems certain that they did have a secret and once the Templars had done away with the twelve-month probationary period, they would have needed some method to protect themselves from unproven and potentially untrustworthy newcomers.

Organisation of the Order

The Order did not consist only of knights. There were two lesser classes besides the full brothers. The first were known as sergeants who were recruited from what we would now describe as the working class, rather than the nobility that was the source for the knights. They undertook such positions as grooms, stewards, sentries and general support troops. Like their betters they wore a red cross, but the mantle itself was a dark brown rather than white, reflecting their lack of purity in relation to knights of the Order. The other group comprised the clerics who looked after the spiritual needs of the knights. They were the only literate members of the Order and were themselves priests, taking care of record keeping and communications, sometimes writing in very complex codes. French was the spoken and administrative language of the Templars but these versatile priests could say the Mass in Latin, haggle with local traders in Arabic and be quite capable of reading the Old Testament in Hebrew and the New Testament in Greek. They served the spiritual needs of the fighting men and were distinguished by the wearing of the Templar Cross on a green mantle.

These clerics would consecrate the bread and wine at the Eucharist like a modern-day priest but they took this duty so seriously that they were said to wear white gloves at all times except when actually handling the Host during the service. As the bread was the body of Christ it was important not to soil it with the dirt of profane day-to-day activities and white gloves were worn to keep their hands clean enough to handle the body of God. This wearing of white gloves was to us an obvious parallel with the modern Freemason, who always wears white gloves to his Lodge meetings. No reason has ever been given for this practice. Could this, we wondered, be a Templar connection?

Another distant echo of current Masonic practice lies in the Templars' use of sheepskin as their only permitted form of decoration, as well as the requirement of their Rule that they were to wear tight sheepskin breeches beneath their outer clothing at all times as a symbol of innocence and chastity. It is an alarming thought in this age of personal hygiene, but these conscientious knights did not remove their breeches even to wash themselves. After a few days, let alone the many decades that many of them spent under the desert sun, their chastity must have been totally guaranteed! Whilst Freemasons today do not wear breeches, they do wear white lambskin aprons in Lodge meetings, which we were told is the badge of innocence and the emblem of friendship.

One more similarity struck us as pointing to a possible Templar connection. We found that the Beausant, the Templar battle flag, consisted of two vertical blocks, one white and one black – the black symbolising the world of sin the knight had left behind to enter the Order, and the white reflecting the move from darkness to light. The modern Freemasons' Lodge always displays at its centre a pattern of black and white squares and at Lodge meetings every brother wears a white shirt with a black tie and suit; if he does not he will not be admitted as he is not properly clothed. No one has ever explained why Freemasons wear lambskin and black and white in order to be considered properly clothed. The only reason offered is that 'our ancient brethren always dressed this way'.

Whilst there are a number of parallels here we did not seek to make too great a play on these similarities, as we wanted to be sure that we were not starting to see what we wanted to see. These powerful coincidences were circumstantial pieces of evidence, but they did fuel our enthusiasm for exploring the connection between the two Orders more closely. We now had a burning question:

What had the Knights Templar found which had so influenced their development?

CONCLUSION

We now knew that the Templars had painstakingly excavated the ruins of Herod's Temple and that the downfall of the Order came as the result of accusations of heresy. If the Templars did hold heretical beliefs and conduct strange rituals, it seemed to be a real possibility that these could have orginated with a document or documents found by them. Had these twelfth-century knights uncovered any ancient texts, they would have been in an almost unique position at that time to interpret and appreciate them. Whilst the knights themselves are believed to have been illiterate, their clerics were able to read and write in many languages and were famous for their abilities to create and break ciphers. We pursued this avenue as our best guess, unaware that evidence of a Templar find was almost under our noses in the ritual of a Masonic degree that neither of us had joined.

Chapter Four

The Gnostic Connection

The Early Christian Censors

The twentieth century has been very fruitful in the unearthing of lost manuscripts, the most important discoveries being the so-called 'Dead Sea Scrolls' found at Qumran in a series of caves in the desert twenty miles to the east of Jerusalem and the extensive collection of so-called 'Gnostic Gospels' discovered at Nag Hammadi in Upper Egypt in 1945.

It seems reasonable to suppose that there are yet more discoveries to be made in the future and that many unrecorded discoveries have been made in the past. The finds that are behind us in time can be categorised under three headings: those that are known and logged; those destroyed or subsequently lost; and those that have been found but have been kept secret. Perhaps, we speculated, the Templars had unearthed a collection of writings similar to these recent finds but they hid them from the gaze of the general world.

Modern Freemasonry has often been described as being 'Gnostic' in many respects, so we decided that our best starting point would be a study of the Nag Hammadi library to see if we could find any clues as to what the Templars may have found.

The Gnostic Gospels

The term 'Gnostic' is used today as a collective name for a

range of heretical works which infected the true Church for a while in the distant past but which were outlawed as nonsense imported from other religions. It is a very inexact label and it does not identify a single school of thought. Writings described as Christian Gnosticism range from those with Indian, Persian and other influences to those with more traditionally Jewish concepts at their heart. Some of these works are bizarre in the extreme with such stories as the boy Jesus murdering other children in a rage then returning some of his victims to life. Others are clear and simple philosophical messages attributed to Jesus.

The word itself is from the Greek *gnosis* meaning knowledge or understanding, not meant in the scientific sense but in a more spiritual interpretation, in the manner that Buddhists may find enlightenment through self contemplation and an empathy with the world around them. An awareness of one's self, an appreciation of nature and the natural sciences are pathways to God for the Gnostic. Most Christian Gnostics saw Jesus Christ, not as a god, but as the man who illuminated that pathway, in the same way that Gautama Buddha and Muhammad are understood by their followers.

Gnostic Gospels have been around at least as long as the New Testament Gospels but these non-canonical works became known to a broader, non-academic audience following the publication of the translation of fifty-two papyrus scrolls written in Coptic script unearthed in December 1945 near the town of Nag Hammadi in Upper Egypt. Whilst these particular documents date from AD 350–400, many are known to be copies of works that are some three hundred years older. They were found by an Arab boy called Muhammad Ali al-Samman and his brothers in a sealed red earthenware jar, about three feet tall, which was buried in soft soil near to a massive boulder. The brothers had smashed the jar open hoping to find treasure but were disappointed to find inside only thirteen papyrus books bound in leather. They took the books home and as they were nice and dry they were thought to be an excellent material for lighting the family oven. Thankfully young Muhammad Ali was due to be investigated by the police so, fearful of being accused of stealing the texts, he asked a local priest, al-Qummus Basiliyus Abd al-Masih, to hide the books for him. Naturally, the priest saw the possible worth of the documents and sent some to Cairo to be valued; there they passed through the hands of a number of dealers and scholars until a section of the Gospel of Thomas, far older than any he had seen before, finally ended up in the hands of Professor Quispel of the Jung Foundation in Zurich. He was astounded at what he saw and quickly traced the rest of the hoard, which had understandably by then found its way to the Coptic Museum in Cairo.

Once he had the opportunity to study the full documentation Professor Quispel found that he was looking at many previously unknown texts that had been buried nearly 1,600 years ago in a period which was critical in the formation of the Roman Catholic Church. The rediscovered works had been suppressed by the Ecclesiastical Christians as heretical. Had they not been, Christianity would have developed in a very different direction and the orthodox form of the religion that we know today might not have existed at all. The survival of the organisational and theological structure of the Roman Catholic Church has always been dependent on the suppression of the ideas contained within these books.

The Gnostic Resurrection

There were major differences between two early Christian traditions concerning the truth behind the resurrection of

Jesus.[1] In the Gnostic work *Treatise on Resurrection*, ordinary human existence is described as spiritual death whereas the resurrection as the moment of enlightenment, revealing what truly exists. Whoever grasps this idea becomes spiritually alive and can be resurrected from the dead immediately. The same idea can be found in the *Gospel of Philip* which ridicules 'ignorant Christians who take the resurrection literally':

> *'Those who say they will die first and then rise are in error, they must receive the resurrection while they live.'*

This description of a living resurrection reminded us of the subject matter of the Masonic Third Degree ceremony and encouraged us to investigate further the cause of the row over the literal truth of the resurrection of Jesus's body.

There are major consequences of a literal belief in the resurrection of Jesus's body which later ascended into heaven. All the authority of the Roman Catholic Church stems from the experiences of Jesus's resurrection by the twelve favoured apostles, an experience which was closed to all newcomers following his ascent into Heaven. This closed, unchallengeable experience had enormous implications for the political structure of the early Church.

It restricted the leadership to a small circle of persons who held a position of incontestable authority and conferred on this group the right to ordain future leaders as their successors. This resulted in the view of religious authority which has survived to this day: that the apostles alone held definitive religious authority and that their only legitimate heirs are priests and bishops, tracing their ordination back to that same apostolic succession. Even today the Pope derives his authority from Peter, first of

[1] Elaine Pagels: *The Gnostic Gospels*

the apostles, since he was first witness of the resurrection. It was very much in the interests of the rulers of the early Church to accept the resurrection as a literal truth because of the benefits it conferred on them in the form of an uncontested source of authority. Since no one of a later generation could have access to Christ in the way that the apostles did during his lifetime and at his resurrection, every believer must look to the Church at Rome, which the apostles are said to have founded, and its bishops for authority.

The Gnostic Church called this literal view of the resurrection 'the faith of fools', claiming those who announced that their dead master had come physically back to life confused a spiritual truth with an actual event. The Gnostics quoted the secret tradition of Jesus's teaching as recorded in his speech to his disciples in Matthew:

> *'To you it has been given to know the mysteries of the kingdom of heaven, but to them it has not been given.'*

The Gnostics recognised that their theory of secret knowledge, to be gained by their own efforts, also had political implications. It suggests that whoever 'sees the Lord' through inner vision can claim that his or her own authority equals or surpasses that of the apostles and their successors.

We found that Irenaenus, known as the father of Catholic theology and the most important theologian of the second century AD, saw the dangers to the authority of the Church that this view presented:

> *'They consider themselves mature so that no one can be compared with them in the greatness of their gnosis, not even if you mention Peter or Paul or any of the other apostles... They imagine that they themselves have discovered more than the apostles and that the apostles*

preached the gospel still under the influence of Jewish opinions, but that they themselves are wiser and more intelligent than the apostles.'

Those who consider themselves wiser than the apostles also consider themselves wiser than priests, for what the Gnostics say about the apostles and in particular about the Twelve expresses their attitude towards the priests and bishops who claim to stand in the orthodox apostolic succession. In addition, many Gnostic teachers also claimed access to their own secret sources of apostolic tradition, in direct rivalry to that commonly accepted in the churches. In the Gnostic *Apocalypse of Peter* the orthodox Church's claim to religious authority is undermined by an account of the risen Christ explaining to Peter that:

'those who name themselves bishop and deacon and act as if they had received their authority from God are in reality waterless canals. Although they do not understand mystery they boast that the mystery of truth belongs to them alone. They have misinterpreted that apostle's teaching and have set up an imitation church in place of the true Christian brotherhood.'

This point had been picked up and expounded by the scholars who had translated the Gnostic Gospels. We were both struck by the political importance of this idea of a living resurrection when one afternoon in Sheffield University Library we found this comment by the respected Gnostic scholar Elaine Pagels:

'Recognising the political implications of the doctrine of the resurrection does not account for its extraordinary impact on religious experiences of Christians ... but in terms of the social order ... the orthodox teaching on the resurrection had a different effect. It legitimised a

hierarchy of persons through whose authority all others must approach God. Gnostic teaching was subversive of this order, it claimed to offer to every initiate a means of direct access to God of which the priests and bishops themselves might be ignorant.[2]

We now knew that the interpretation of the resurrection had been a tremendous source of controversy in the early Christian Church and that there had been a secret tradition concerning living spiritual resurrections connected with a group of Christians labelled Gnostics and denounced for political reasons as heretics, because their interest in gaining knowledge undermined the authority of the bishops of the orthodox Church.

The resurrection also figured very prominently in the ritual of the Masonic Third Degree, but there it was very much a story of a living resurrection mixed in with the story of an unlawful killing and the recovery and reburial of a dead body. We had found references to the living resurrection element in the Gnostic Gospels but we now needed more information to try to work out what the Templars might have found, so in order to pursue this further we read the discoveries from Nag Hammadi in translation.

The books relating to Thomas in particular gave us additional clues. In the *Gospel of Thomas* we found a sentence which corresponds directly with the basis of the Mark Mason's Ritual:

'*Jesus said, "Show me the stone which the builders have rejected. That one is the cornerstone."*'

We were aware that similar passages occur in the New Testament:

[2] Elaine Pagels: *The Gnostic Gospels*

'*Jesus saith unto them, "Did ye never read in the scriptures, The stone which the builders rejected, the same is become the head of the corner: this is the Lord's doing, and it is marvellous in our eyes?"'*

Matthew 21:4

'*And have ye not read this scripture; The stone which the builders rejected is become the head of the corner.*'

Mark 12:10

'*And he beheld them, and said, "What is this then that is written, The stone which the builders rejected, the same is become the head of the corner?"'*

Luke 20:17

These quotations from the Synoptic Gospels (Matthew, Mark and Luke) all speak of Jesus teaching from the scriptures about the importance of a rejected cornerstone; but only in the *Gospel of Thomas* does he demand to be shown the stone which the builders have rejected – in an exact parallel of the ritual of the Masonic Mark Masonry degree. This seemed to indicate a connection between Freemasonry and Gnosticism.

Furthermore, in another work, the *Acts of Thomas*, we found the story of that apostle building a fine palace in Heaven by means of good works on Earth. This story is the epitome of the address in the north-east corner which figures in the Masonic First Degree ritual.

Whilst these points were interesting, they did not seem enough to explain the behaviour of the Knights Templar, which was the initial reason for our perusal of these texts. So at this stage, though we had come across tentative connections between Gnostic Christianity and modern Freemasonry, nothing really concrete had emerged. We had found some core concepts that had parallels with the tenets of Freemasonry, particularly the idea that people should undergo a 'resurrection' when still alive, but at this point we decided we needed to look far more closely at the formation of the Early Christian Church if we were ever to deduce what it was that the Templars found.

CONCLUSION

We had speculated that the Templars may have found a cache of writings which changed their world-view and in an attempt to find out what they had found we had looked into a collection of early Christian writings collectively known as the Gnostic gospels. We concluded that the concept of '*gnosis*' (knowledge) is the opposite of the Church's concept of 'faith' and that it is a type of thought process that fits well with Freemasonry.

We had come to the conclusion that much of the selective doctrine of the early Church was based on political expediency as much as religious opinion. In the Nag Hammadi discoveries, hidden between AD 350–400 and rediscovered in Egypt, we found a quite different interpretation of the truth behind the resurrection of Jesus. Here was a Gnostic Christian tradition of a living resurrection which reminded us strongly of the Masonic Third Degree ceremony.

The literal belief in the resurrection of Jesus's body, which later ascended into Heaven, was a vital factor in the authority of the Roman Catholic Church. This authority stems from the claimed experiences of Jesus's resurrection by the twelve favoured apostles, an experience which was then closed to all newcomers following his ascent into Heaven. This closed and unchallengeable experience was the source of the power of the Bishop of Rome in the political structure of the early Church, and conferred incontestable authority over those who had faith.

We had read Gnostic writings which called this literal view of the resurrection 'the faith of fools', claiming that anyone who announced that their dead master had come physically back to life mistook a spiritual truth for an actual event and were as 'waterless canals'. This view was supported by appealing to a secret tradition of Jesus's teaching in Matthew's Gospel. Irenaenus, a second-century theologian, had written about the dangers of this idea of a living resurrection to the power of the established priests. From our study of the Nag Hammadi texts we had discovered that the interpretation of the resurrection had caused tremendous controversy in the early Christian Church and that a group of Christians labelled 'Gnostics' had a secret tradition concerning living spiritual resurrections connected with Jesus. We concluded that the Gnostics had been denounced for political reasons as heretics; furthermore, their interest in gaining knowledge undermined the authority of the bishops of the orthodox Church.

Further reading of the Gnostic Gospels gave us strong ancient echoes of Masonic ritual that we knew well and, encouraged by these finds, we decided to look more closely at the Early Christian Church with an open mind. We started by considering the uniqueness of the claims made for Jesus himself.

Chapter Five

Jesus Christ: Man, God, Myth or Freemason?

Another Virgin Birth

If the Church's version of events surrounding the man we call Jesus Christ were not historically accurate, we would expect a majority of contemporary writings to conflict with that 'official' history. We quickly found this to be the case, as the Nag Hammadi scripts and the Dead Sea Scrolls both shed a very different light on the interpretation given in the New Testament.

A fundamental difficulty for the Church lies in the fact that the central Christian myth predates Jesus Christ. The outline of Christ's story is as ancient as man, from the virgin birth in humble surroundings to the sacrificial death that saved his people – it has all been written down, time after time, for religious figureheads in many cultures. This is not a case of similarities; we're talking about total interchangeability. So close was the story of Mithra (or Mithras), another cult popular in the Roman Empire, that the Church Fathers identified it as the work of the devil intended deliberately to parody the story of Christ. The fact that the cult of Mithra existed long before the Christian Messiah was born did not faze these resourceful individuals; they simply claimed that the devil was a sly old fox who had gone backwards in time to plant a man who would discredit the 'obvious' originality of the story of Christ. Here are just some of the ancient figures who were considered gods, who all predate Christ:

Gautama Buddha: born of the virgin Maya around 600 BC.

Dionysus: Greek god, born of a virgin in a stable, turned water into wine.

Quirrnus: An early Roman saviour, born of a virgin.

Attis: born of the virgin Nama in Phrygia around 200 BC.

Indra: born of a virgin in Tibet around 700 BC.

Adonis: Babylonian god – born of the virgin Ishtar.

Krishna: Hindu deity – born of the virgin Devaki in around 1200 BC.

Zoroaster: born of a virgin 1500–1200 BC.

Mithra: born of a virgin in a stable on 25 December around 600 BC. His resurrection was celebrated at Easter.

It seems that over the centuries quite a lot of innocent young ladies were giving birth to the children of gods!

The cult of Mithra is particularly awkward for Christians who do not subscribe to the satanic time-traveller theory. Mithraism is a Syrian offshoot of the more ancient Persian cult of Zoroaster, which was introduced into the Roman Empire about 67 BC. Its doctrines included baptism, a sacramental meal, belief in immortality, a saviour god who died and rose again to act as a mediator between man and god, a resurrection, a last judgement and heaven and hell. Interestingly candles, incense and bells are used in its ceremonies. Its devotees recognised the divinity of the Emperor and were relaxed about coexisting alongside other cults, but it was finally absorbed by the much less tolerant Christians. As we will show later, the true Jesus sect, the Jerusalem Church, had lacked most of these pagan trappings; these were much later Roman additions to create a hybrid theology that would meet the needs of the widest possible number of citizens. If the plebeians had to have their superstitions, the Romans eventually reasoned, why not have one that was state controlled?

But for a tiny twist of fate in the later years of the Roman empire, nice families would today be driving off to Sunday worship with 'Mithra loves you' stickers in their car windows. Another essential problem is the true name of Christ. Most people are aware that the name 'Jesus Christ' is a later Greek title, but they do not often bother to wonder what this man-god's real name was. The name that he was born with is not known for sure, but it is possible that he was known in his lifetime as Yehoshua, meaning 'Yahweh delivers' and equating in modern terms to something like 'the one that will bring victory'. In the form that we would recognise it today, it would translate to Joshua; the same name given to the man in the Old Testament who delivered victory to his people at the battle of Jericho, when the walls of that city were supposedly brought down by trumpet blasts. The name Jesus is simply a Greek interpretation of the Hebrew name Yehoshua, but the addition of the title 'Christ' is far more worrying. It is a Greek rendering of the Jewish title 'Messiah' which has been given the meaning 'the bringer of salvation through the redemption of sin,' despite the fact that the Hebrew/Aramaic term simply meant 'a person that will become rightful king of the Jews'. Jewish tradition says that Israel's kings were also associated with messiahs. To them the word meant a king-to-be or a king in waiting. These were straightforward, practical meanings: we can be certain that the Jewish concept of a messiah and his coming kingdom had no supernatural overtones at all.[1]

Amazingly the word 'messiah' appears only twice in the Authorised Version of the Old Testament, and is totally absent from the New Testament. Nonetheless, by the time of Jesus it had became a popular concept amongst the Jews as they looked forward to a time when they would govern themselves again, instead of being under the control of occupiers ('Kittim', as they called them) such as the Syrians, Babylonians or, more particularly for them, the Romans. For these Jewish nationalists of the first centuries BC and AD, once a rightful person took the throne of Israel he would become king and the future-tense title of 'messiah' would no longer apply.

The fact that the word 'messiah' is not used at all in the New Testament can only be explained if the translators have used the Greek word 'Christos' wherever the Hebrew word 'messiah' appeared in early texts. Over time, the designation 'Christ' has come to be synonymous with Jesus Christ rather than any other messiah, or Christ, although the term was far from unique, and was not restricted to one individual.

For the later Gentile hijackers of Jewish tribal beliefs, the Hebrew usage of the word 'messiah' was far too passive, alien and based in the real world of Jewish political aspirations; consequently in the Greek translation the word took on overtones of a Hellenistic mystery cult with the supernatural power to save souls and redeem the whole world. Norman Cohen succinctly described the situation when he said of the Jewish Messiah:

'He will be, at most, a great military leader and a wise and just ruler, guided by Yahweh and appointed by him

[1] S. Mowinckel: *He That Cometh*

to rule over his people in Judah. The notion of a transcendental saviour in human form, so important in Zoroastrianism and so central to Christianity, is totally unknown to the Hebrew Bible.'[2]

That Christians claim an authority for their beliefs from the Old Testament must be very galling for modern Jewish scholars when they can see that their heritage has been used to lend credence to a Roman mystery cult, largely of ancient Persian origin. This plundering of the twenty-two Jewish texts which constituted the core of the Old Testament became widespread as early as the beginning of the second century, when Christians searched for references which supported the beliefs of their fledgling cult.

Members of the early Church considered themselves to be Jews, and until the end of the first century everyone else saw Christians as a Jewish sect. By the beginning of the second century, however, the vast majority of Christians were Gentile converts from around the Roman Empire who no longer considered themselves to be Jews at all. These cultural looters had little or no regard for context or accepted interpretation and felt themselves free to quote at will from Jewish texts that were not recognised as scripture by their owners.

The Old Testament Bible had been translated into Greek in the third century BC, and became known as the Septuagint (usually shown as the '*LXX*'). Christians inserted new passages and whole books and then had the audacity to accuse the Jews of having deleted these sections from their own scriptures! This belief became enshrined in Christian thinking and resulted in many future acts of vandalism, such as an occasion in Paris in 1242 when twenty-four cartloads of Jewish scriptures were looted from synagogues before being burned, and

---

[2] Norman Cohen: *Cosmos, Chaos and the World to Come*

another twenty years later when King Jayme I of Aragon ordered that all Jewish books be destroyed.

Some early Christian scholars believed that the Old Testament was alien to their new religion but the majority read imaginatively between the lines to see 'obvious' references to their Saviour. The twenty-two books of holy scripture were suitably enlarged to create a 'bumper' Old Testament.

These additions by early Christian writers included Esdras, Judith, Tobit, Maccabees, Wisdom, Ecclesiasticus, Baruch, the Prayer of Manasseh and, within the Book of Daniel, the Song of the Three Holy Children, the History of Susannah, and Bel and the Dragon.

For a time the Christians were happy with their 'new' Old Testament but as more serious scholars such as the third-century Alexandrian Origen began to study texts afresh, real doubts were raised which led to a realisation that the original Jewish version was the only correct one. The suggestion was made that all of the new scriptures in Christian churches should be destroyed, but these arguments were soon buried in the general Christian desire to be a stand-alone religion with a differentiated scripture.

But whilst the main Church took the easy option, the debate did not end, and many Christian thinkers remained unconvinced. In the fourth century Cyril of Jerusalem forbade the reading of these extraneous books, even in private, and as late as the eighteenth century some leading Christian thinkers, such as John Damascene, maintained that the Jewish twenty-two were the only components of the true scripture.

The same cavalier people who had doctored the Old Testament assembled the New Testament. To take a considered view of the events that led to the creation of this relatively instant block of brand new scripture, it is essential to understand something of the Jewish world-view at this crucial point.

Today, virtually all Western people appreciate the line

between politics and religion, but it is a mistake to assume that other countries or other periods of history view things in the same way. Modern Iran, for instance, does not recognise any difference whatsoever between the two subjects, and the people of Judaea and Galilee, two thousand years ago, would have thought you mad if you tried to imply that their relationship with their god was in any way different to their national struggle. Politics at the time of Jesus the Christ was a serious theological matter; the stability of the nation rested upon God's view of its worth. If they proved worthy, the Jews would have their own king and would destroy their enemies in battle. For hundreds of years they had been unworthy, so God had deserted them to the whims of their enemies, but as the devout Jews started to live a more austere life, they started to expect the arrival of a Messiah to begin the process of a return to self rule.

There is a very fundamental point here which cannot be ignored: nowhere in the Old Testament does it prophesy the coming of a world saviour. The Jews expected a leader to emerge who was an earthly king in the mould of David and, however much Christians would like it to be so, Jesus was *not* the Messiah of the line of David (the Christ), because he did not succeed in becoming the undisputed king of Israel. For the Jewish people of the time, including Jesus himself, there was no other meaning for the word; it is not a question of faith, it is a fact of history beyond theological debate. The Church is now fully aware of this early misunderstanding and may claim that its 'spiritual' interpretation of the word is true and valid, despite the fact that the Jews used the word quite differently. However, once the Church acknowledges that the Christian and Jewish use of the term 'messiah' have nothing in common, it follows that the Church has no right to use the Old Testament as a source of evidence regarding the coming of its Christ. To do so is bare-faced fraud. We stress the point that the Jews were not expecting a god or a world saviour; they were simply expecting a political leader with credentials stretching back to their first king – David.[3]

A further problem for mainline Christianity is the belief that Jesus was the offspring of a magical mating of Yahweh and Mary. As we have seen, this god-and-woman union is an ancient necessity for the parentage of all would-be man-gods in Middle Eastern cultures. The justification for this claim amongst Christians is taken from the title that Jesus used for himself – 'Son of God' – which was an ancient title for everyone who was claiming kingship. All kings from the times before the pharaohs onwards have established their right to rule through their descent from the gods.

As we were researching the whole complex area of the expected role of the messiah we came across a very strange and startling point that no one seems, to the best of our knowledge, to have considered before. It concerns the name of the murderer who was released instead of Christ at his trial. His name, you may recall, was Barabbas. Just another biblical name, you may think, and one that feels to have an evil ring to it: 'Barabbas the wicked murderer whom the equally wicked Jews chose to release in preference to our Saviour.' The baying of the crowd to crucify the Christ in preference to a common criminal is one of the New Testament's pieces of evidence regarding the allegedly despicable nature of the Jews that has led to two thousand years of anti-Semitism.

However, one only needs a rudimentary knowledge of the language of the time to understand that 'Barabbas' is

[3] If there ever was a true Jewish messiah it can only have been David Ben Gurion, the Zionist activist who became the first 'king' of a self-governing Jewish state in 1948. His modern title was 'prime minister' rather than 'king', but the effect was the same. Whether or not he could claim descent from the line of David we do not know.

not a name at all but a title, meaning precisely 'Son of God'! 'Bar' means 'son of' and 'Abba' literally means 'father', but its usage was, and generally still is, a reference to The Father; that is, God. This intrigued and puzzled us but we were staggered when we went on to discover that early manuscripts of Matthew, in verse 27:16, this man's designation is used in its full form: 'Jesus Barabbas'.

So the individual who was released and not crucified at the request of the crowd was, as an indisputable matter of Gospel record, known as 'Jesus, the son of God'. The first part of the name was deleted from the Gospel of Matthew at a much later date, by those that sought to establish facts to fit their Gentile beliefs. Such selectivity is what we would now euphemistically call 'being economical with the truth', but it is little more than a deceit to avoid difficult questions that the Church would not, or more likely could not, answer.

The plot was certainly thickening.

The Gospels state that this other 'Jesus, son of God' was accused of being a Jewish rebel who had killed people during an outbreak of insurrection. Thus Barabbas was not a criminal but a Jewish fanatic, one facing a similar accusation to the one brought against Jesus.[4]

When these fuller facts are taken into account, the whole circumstances of the trial of Jesus become much more complicated. Two men of the same name with the same claim and much the same crime; how can we know which one was released? Certainly many of the oldest Christian sects believe that Jesus did not die on the cross because another died for him. Muslims today hold Jesus Christ in very high regard as a prophet who was ordered to be crucified but whose place was taken by another. The symbolism of the crucified Christ is absolutely central to

---

[4] *Peake's Commentary on the Bible*

mainline Christianity, yet so many groups, both contemporary with the event and modern, hold that he did not die in this manner. Could they be right?

The evidence that we had just come across was not from some disputed Gnostic Gospel but from the New Testament itself, so our inevitable Church critics should have a hard time pushing this truth under the carpet. There is little doubt that some will pretend they did not read it or that it is some sort of mistake that can be rationalised away by the traditional process of talking in circles.

Being free from the requirements of the dogma of blind faith, we had accepted that the legend of Jesus the Christ was an amalgam of supernatural yarns brought in from other mystery religions. Given what we had now learnt we started to wonder whether even the more general details of Jesus's life could be a composite of the story of two men – much in the same way that it is believed that the story of Robin Hood grew out of the telling of tales about a number of Anglo-Saxon noblemen who operated outside the laws of the Norman rulers.

Had the Roman authorities, threatened by the rise in nationalism in Judaea, moved against all known trouble-makers at one moment? The Jews were a small but permanent thorn in the side of the Emperor and the widespread expectation of the arrival of a new messiah to kick out the Romans was getting the local population far too excited. The Sicari, armed Zealot fanatics, were assassinating Jews who were friends of Rome and the general population was getting over-confident about the possibility of seizing independence. It would have been quite normal for the Roman authorities to wipe out trouble before it got out of hand. We could only speculate as to what might have happened to create the strange situation that is recorded in the New Testament.

Our first scenario was that two competing messiahs had sprung up amongst two different groups in Judaea, since it is well documented that there were many claimants for the title of messiah during the first and second centuries. What if two of these messiahs were at their peak of popularity at the same time? They would have both been called Jesus by their followers, because it is a description given to the saviour of the Jewish people – their provider of victory and future prosperity. At the point of this general pre-emptive arrest, one of these messianic figures may have been known best as 'Jesus, king of the Jews' and the other 'Jesus, son of God'. As these criminals were paraded in public, Pontius Pilatus became aware that the situation was becoming explosive, and fearing a bloodbath in which he might be a victim, offered to let one of these two captive messiahs go. The crowd had to choose between their kingly messiah or their priestly messiah, and they chose the latter.

We call this scenario the Schrödinger's Cat theory of the Messiah (after the famous logic experiment which showed that two mutually exclusive outcomes can co-exist in the strange world of quantum mechanics) because it is impossible to say whether the 'real' Jesus of the Christian faith was crucified or released. The stories of both men are now so totally merged that the Christian sects that claim he was never crucified are quite correct, yet so is the mainstream Church which says that he was crucified.

Our second scenario was based on the knowledge that there was a traditional requirement for there to be two messiahs, who would work hand-in-hand to achieve the final victory of Yahweh and His chosen people. A kingly messiah from the tribe of Judah, the royal line of David, would be joined by a priestly messiah from the tribe of Levi. This was expected because according to tradition, Jewish priests had to be Levites. This theory assumes that at the point of the trial both messiahs had been arrested and charged with causing civil insurrection. The Jesus from the royal line of Judah was held and died on the cross whilst the Jesus from the priestly line of Levi went free.

Which was which? The Jesus who was born to Mary claimed to be a messiah because he came from the royal line of David, and was supposedly born in David's city of Bethlehem. However, as can be read in the opening verses of the New Testament, this descent, through a string of 'begets', is based upon the genealogy of Mary's husband Joseph who was not, according to Christian belief, the father of Jesus. A cruel twist of cold logic – if he was the son of God, he could not be the royal messiah!

The Jesus born to Mary could not technically be a kingly messiah, but he *could* possibly be the priestly version: his mother is known to be a relation of John the Baptist, who was a Levite; so Jesus must have had some Levite blood himself. If this Jesus had followed this argument it would be clear that it was not he who died on the cross.

In this 'double Jesus' situation we had come across an obvious flaw in the Christian story of the messiah, but apart from discussing these two scenarios as possible solutions we could get no further at this point. It was not until we had unlocked a deeper Masonic riddle that the real solution became clear; this we will cover later in the book.

The Principal Groups of Jerusalem

The three principal groups amongst the population of Judaea in the first century were Sadducees, Pharisees and the Essenes. The first two are defined in the footnotes of the Douai Bible as follows:

> '*Pharisees and Sadducees. These were the two sects among the Jews: of which the former were for the most part notorious hypocrites; the latter, a kind of free-thinkers in matters of religion.*'

For such a little piece of information the degree of inaccuracy is remarkable.

The Sadducees were, by established right, the priestly and aristocratic bureaucracy of Jerusalem. They were very conservative in their religious views, not believing in any existence beyond the grave and they no doubt considered the complex views and actions of the Pharisees to be the work of superstitious fools. In most respects they ran the country according to Roman requirements rather than Jewish ones; they were what we now call Quislings. They maintained the freedom of the individual to shape his own destiny and unlike the Pharisees they believed that history took its own course rather than being a part of some divine plan. Whilst they were wealthy and of high social standing they were boorish, rude and extremely hard on anyone who broke the law or interfered with their administration. They were not men of ideas or ideals but they kept the country running whilst looking after the status quo which was to their advantage. To be fair, they were probably not much different to the ruling classes in most countries before and since, but to call them 'free thinkers in matters of religion' is about as far from the truth as one can get.

The Pharisees, on the other hand, were not, strictly speaking priests at all, but were devoted to the Law and constantly tried to apply it in every avenue of life. To assist them in this search for fulfilment of the Law they had developed a tradition of interpretation by which all actions were minutely regulated. They set high standards which became the landmarks of modern orthodox Judaism, and whether one shares their beliefs or not they were impressively single-minded. Traditionally, all worship of Yahweh had been restricted to occurring in His Divine Presence in the Temple at Jerusalem under the control of the high priest, but the Pharisees created the opportunity for the eventual evolution of the structure of the rabbi and the synagogue, as a basis for Jews everywhere to have access to God.

Today the fears and the hopes of the Pharisees live on in the form of Orthodox Judaism. Throughout the entire world Orthodox Jews will not conduct business on the Sabbath, neither will they drive a motorcar, use public transport, push a baby buggy, sew or mend, watch television, cook or squeeze out a sponge, press a doorbell or use a lift. Recently a Jewish manager of a kosher hotel in the southern English holiday resort of Bournemouth was sacked for operating the electrical switch to activate a central heating system on a Saturday morning. The fact that his guests were possibly about to die from hypothermia was no excuse for this blatant abuse of the Law, which stems from the fact that the Torah, the book of Jewish law, forbids the 'kindling of fires' on the Sabbath.

The Essenes remained a less understood group until 1947, when the Dead Sea Scrolls were discovered at Qumran twenty miles east of Jerusalem. The scrolls tell us a great deal about these strange men who lived in this dry rocky valley from around the middle of the second century BC to AD 68. There is evidence that the caves were subsequently occupied by a smaller number of people up to AD 136 (the time of the final Jewish uprising under another Jesus), but it is uncertain whether or not these later dwellers were Essenes.

It is a measure of the all-embracing strictness of the Essene mind that their religious observances made the Pharisees look like carefree hedonists. Although it is now accepted by many scholars that the Essenes and the early Church had numerous features in common, the Church of Rome has always denied any connection between the two. One of the most obvious common links was the uniquely shared apocalyptic expectation. Both expected their existing world to end abruptly and imminently.

The main factor differentiating the Essenes from the Sadducees and the Pharisees was that membership of the

Essenes was attained only through individual, adult choice, not by virtue of birth. The Qumran Essenes thought of themselves as the sole custodians of the true religious teachings of Israel and believed that through their priestly founder, known in the Scrolls as 'the Teacher of Righteousness', they had established a 'new covenant', the ultimate and final form of the perfect alliance between the people of Israel and their God. This arrangement was reserved solely for the members of the Essene community, due to their unerring respect for every one of the 613 commandments of the Law and their total belief in the depth of their own unworthiness. Like the Pharisees they had adopted the idea of lesser gods known as angels.

That the authors of the Dead Sea Scrolls, who we now call the Qumran Community, were Essenes is now beyond doubt; and that these people were the Nasoreans or the original Jerusalem Church was to become very clear to us. The evidence that these groups were essentially all one and the same is huge, and the Church's argument that they are separate appears to be an attempt to protect the 'specialness' of Jesus, when the Dead Sea Scrolls tell such a similar story without reference to him. If the Church today was to accept that the Qumranians were the Jerusalem Church, it would have to explain why its godhead was not the leader of his community.

The Dead Sea Scrolls describe a group with an identical world-view, the same peculiar terminology and precisely the same eschatological beliefs as the Jerusalem Church. It has been shown by experts, such as Professor Robert Eisenman, that the leader of the Qumran Community around the fourth and fifth decades of the first century AD was James the Just, the brother of Jesus, who the Church accepts was the first Bishop of Jerusalem. (Also subsequently confirmed in a private conversation with Professor Phillip Davies.)

How did James divide his time between the two groups? Alternate days or mornings and afternoons perhaps? Hardly. The inescapable answer is they were both the same thing. For the last three decades of its existence the Qumran Community *was* the Jerusalem Church.

In spirit the Essenes were ultra-conservative Jews, but in some ways they were progressive and creative beyond measure. Qumranian vocabulary is present in Christian literature and misunderstandings of its original meaning has given succour to those who would sustain Gentile gods through the valued currency of Judaism. The new vocabulary of the Qumranians began to enter Jewish theological culture in the first century BC and developed in the first century AD, when Targmic literature was commonplace. This was the translation of the Hebrew Bible into Aramaic, the language of Jews at the time of Jesus the Christ. As services were conducted in little-understood Hebrew, they were simultaneously freely translated into Aramaic for the benefit of the general worshipper. The translators would use terms and phrases that would be understood in the light of their current circumstances, thus Qumranic lines in Christian ritual such as 'Thy kingdom come', 'the kingdom of the Lord', 'the kingdom of God' and 'The kingdom of the House of David' all referred to the same political objective. George Wesley Buchanan observes:

> 'When Jesus was reported to have said, "My Kingdom is not of this world" (Jn 18:36), he did not mean that it was in heaven. In the Gospel of John all people are divided into two groups: (1) those of the world and (2) those not of the world. Those not of the world included Jesus and his followers who believed in him. They lived on the earth. They were not in heaven, but they were not the heathen. They belonged to "the church" in

contrast to "the world". "The world" included all the pagans and those who refused to believe in him.'[5]

We can see that the terms used at the time were simple political statements. If you followed the independence movement you were in the 'Kingdom of God' and if you were not you were in the ordinary 'world'. In Luke 17:20–21 a Pharisee asked Jesus when the Kingdom of God will come and received the reply:

'The Kingdom of God will not come with observation, and they will not say, "Look here! or there!" Look, the Kingdom of God is in your midst.'

The terms 'the kingdom of heaven' and 'the Kingdom of God' had a very clear and simple meaning to the original users, but when they were adopted by Gentile Christians, their new owners fondly thought of a paradise where good people go after their lives are over, possibly being reunited with their lost loved ones in a timeless ecstasy. This is a very long way from anything that any Jesus (that is, any 'bringer of victory') taught in the first century. The Aramaic word which was translated into Greek to mean 'kingdom' has been misunderstood in this context, as it also means 'government' or 'rule' and, when one looks at the full usage of the term it means 'the land of Israel being ruled according to the Mosaic law'. In effect, when Jesus and his contemporaries referred to 'the coming of the kingdom of heaven', they quite simply meant 'the time soon when we kick the foreign occupiers and their puppets out of Judaea, and get down to some strict observance of hard-line Jewish rules'. The most religious amongst them saw their problems resulting from Yahweh's desertion of them due to their sinfulness in not upholding the law of Moses strongly enough. The only

---

[5] George Wesley Buchanan: *Jesus – The King and His Kingdom*

remedy for all of the problems which plagued them was purity and righteousness; they had to observe every letter of God's law.

The Hard Evidence of the Dead Sea Scrolls

As we have shown, the connections between the terms used in the New Testament and the Dead Sea Scrolls are obvious, but from the start the Catholic Church has tried to play them down. The interpretation of the scrolls was led by a Catholic group including Father de Vaux, Father Milik, Father Skehan, Father Puech and Father Benoit. Other independent figures involved complained at the time that they were not being given open access to many of the scrolls, and John Allegro and Edmund Wilson both stated that they felt that there was a deliberate policy to distance the Qumran Community from early Christianity despite growing evidence of a commonality.[6]

Father de Vaux strongly maintained that the Qumran Community was entirely different from the early Christians; he also observed that because John the Baptist was so close to the teachings of the Qumran Community he could not be considered to be a Christian, but merely a precursor of Christianity. As it is clear from the New Testament that John the Baptist was central to the establishment of Jesus's ministry, such a connection is hard to play down. De Vaux also ignored the fact that both groups used baptism, both shared their possessions as a community, both had a council of twelve leading personalities and both were concerned with Messianic figures and the imminent coming of the 'kingdom of God'. On 16 September 1956 John Allegro wrote to Father de Vaux saying:

'... *you are unable to treat Christianity any more in an*

[6] M. Baigent and R. Leigh: *The Dead Sea Scrolls Deception*

objective light ... You go on to talk blithely about what the first Jewish-Christians thought in Jerusalem, and no one would guess that your only real evidence – if you can call it such – is the New Testament.'[7]

Father de Vaux and his team could not help but view these new scrolls in the light of their existing belief, and consciously or unconsciously they twisted the facts to try and show that the Qumran Community and Nasoreans/Jerusalem Church were unrelated.

That pretence is now over.

To us it seems inescapable that the man who was Jesus the Christ must have been a leading Qumranian figure during the crucial years of the third and fourth decades of the first century. The Community's numbers were tiny at that time, possibly no more than two hundred people, and perhaps there were little more than around four thousand Essenes in total. They were a gathering of like-minded people who saw imminent salvation from their problems through holiness and, although they were not hereditary priests, through living a monastic existence. This involved a society that was extremely hierarchical, from the Guardian or the Grand Master downwards to such inferior beings as married men or, worse still, women, especially menstruating women. Females at that point in their bodily cycle had to withdraw from any contact with men, including visible contact. Reproduction was an unfortunate necessity of life, but those that chose to indulge in matters of the flesh had a considerable cleansing process to go through before returning to the main community.

There were various levels of membership, from a broad outer group to an inner sanctum. Initiation to the higher echelons required vows of secrecy that carried threat of

[7] Letter from Allegro to de Vaux, dated 16 September 1956

horrible punishments should the secrets of their brotherhood be revealed to the outside world. This sounds like highly Masonic practice but one difference is that the Qumranians did not consider such threats as token; they meant them literally.

These people of Qumran were of great interest to us. They wore white robes, took vows of poverty, swore to secrecy under threat of terrible punishment and claimed to possess secret knowledge. We were building up a picture of a revolutionary Jewish group which seemed likely to have included Jesus, and which was central to the Jewish revolt that eventually led to the destruction of Jerusalem and its Temple once again.

* * *

We had established beyond all reasonable doubt that the Templars had excavated the ruins of Herod's Temple, and whatever they had found must have been hidden around the early years of the first century, when it was in the early stages of construction, and AD 70, when it was destroyed. This left a period of no more than seventy years during which the material could have been hidden. The Copper Scroll – so called because it was actually engraved on sheets of copper – found at Qumran tells how the Community hid its treasures and writings under the Temple shortly before AD 70, so we have no need to speculate whose scrolls the Templars found. And, if we were right, and the Qumran Community and the Jerusalem Church were one and the same thing, the Templars clearly had possession of the purest 'Christian' documents possible – far more important than the Synoptic Gospels!

By far the most important connection between the Qumran Essenes, the Knights Templar and Freemasonry is the fact that all three focus on the mystical and physical rebuilding of King Solomon's Temple. This is extremely unlikely to be a coincidence and it could not be a case of fraudulent association as far as Freemasonry is concerned, because the Grand Lodge of England and its teachings about the building of a spiritual Temple predates the discovery of the Dead Sea Scrolls by well over two hundred years.

When looking at Gnostic Christianity we had found that there was a link between it, the New Testament and Freemasonry in that all three had references to 'cornerstones'. We found the same references in the Qumranian texts. Eisenman and Wise make this point amongst other observations regarding linkages between the scrolls and Christianity:

> '*Readers familiar with the New Testament will recognise "Community" and "Temple" here as basically parallel allusions, because just as Jesus is represented as "the Temple" in the Gospels and in Paul, the Community Rule, using parallel spiritualised "Temple" imagery in viii 5–6 and ix 6, pictures the Qumran Community Council as a "Holy of Holies for Aaron and a Temple for Israel". This imagery, as we shall see, is widespread at Qumran, including parallel allusions to "atonement", "pleasing fragrance", "Cornerstone", and "Foundation" which go with it.*'[8]

The use of the idea of 'foundation' also rang bells for us.

The Family of Jesus

A significant element, which the Church is reluctant to discuss, is the evidence that Jesus had brothers, and probably sisters as well. References to the brothers of Jesus are found in a wide range of first- and second-century documents, including the New Testament itself.

[8] Robert Eisenman and Michael Wise: *The Dead Sea Scrolls Uncovered*

Having siblings is quite normal, but when you are supposed to be the son of God a question arises – who fathered the others? Fortunately, there is evidence indicating that Jesus was the eldest, so that *his* virgin birth is not instantly ruled out. This issue of siblings has long been recognised, and three principal theories have been put forward to explain this situation:

Early debates on Christianity carried the name of their leading theologian. The 'Helvidius' view accepts that there were indeed brothers of Christ; the 'Epiphanius' argument puts forward the notion that they were Joseph's sons by a previous marriage; and the desperate explanation put forward by Jerome was that the term 'brother' really meant 'cousin'. Despite the fact that the Bible clearly refers to Christ's brothers on many occasions, the Roman Catholic Douai Bible clearly indicates its preferred option in explanatory notes:

'... *Helvidius and other heretics most impiously inferred that the blessed Virgin Mary had other children besides Christ:*'

This contradicts Matthew 13:55–56, which states:

'*Is not this the carpenter's son? Is not his mother called Mary, and his brothers James, Joseph, Simon and Jude? And his sisters, are they not all with us?*'

The response of the editors of the Douai Bible is creative, if somewhat less than convincing to the critical reader, when it claims:

'*These were the children of Mary ... the sister to our Blessed Lady and therefore, according to the usual style of the scripture, they were called brethren, that is, near relations to our Saviour.*'

If there were a shred of truth in this strange explanation, one would have to observe that it was not very imaginative of Jesus's maternal grandparents to have two daughters and call them both Mary. However, it is now just about universally accepted that Jesus had brothers and sisters. His younger brother Ya'acov (in English, Jacob, and in the Greek versions of the Bible, James) outlived Jesus by approximately thirty years and, as we will show later, was responsible for preserving his true teachings so that they could eventually triumph in the face of unbelievable odds.

The Birth of a New Religion

We now knew that there was a big difference between the original Jerusalem Church and the later organisation which stole their clothes after they had been wiped out in the war with the Romans. Looking into the writings of the people that the Roman Church calls 'the early Church fathers' and later Church leaders, we were staggered at the confusion, misunderstanding and muddled thought that has existed through the ages. We also came across some surprising honesty; Pope Leo X (the Pope who dubbed King Henry VIII the 'defender of the faith'), is on record as saying:

'It has served us well, this myth of Christ.'

From the fall of Jerusalem in AD 70, the faith called Christianity had started to part company with its Jewish origins and soon all sight of the hero called Yehoshua was lost in foreign myths and legends. Old pagan stories were piled into a story of the man who tried to be the saviour king of his people. In Rome the legend of Romulus and Remus was retold with two new lesser gods, the great saints Peter and Paul. The sun god Sol had his birthday on 25 December and this date was thought to be suitable for Jesus's birthday too, so that the great gods could be celebrated on the same feastday. The Sabbath was moved from Saturday to the sun god's day, Sunday, and the symbol of the sun found its way behind the heads of the divine and the saintly in the form of the halo.

The citizens of the Roman Empire found the new religion both familiar and reassuring; they might not be doing so well in this life but they would get a better deal in the next. Like most people throughout history they had little use for logic, preferring to take enjoyment from the emotion of it all, asking their (now one) God for help in times of need and praising him when things went well. Christianity became a cult of ritual rather than ideas, and theology took a backseat to political control.

The Roman Empire had been a hugely successful political force, but despite its ruthless approach to holding power its might could not last for ever. It began to crumble as a cultural force but it found that the control of the minds of people was far more effective than just controlling their bodies. Christianity gave Rome the mechanism to establish unparalleled political might based on unsophisticated masses who would be offered a better life after death if they did the Church's bidding. Thomas Hobbes, the seventeenth-century philosopher and political thinker, expressed the situation clearly when he said:

> '*The Papacy is not other than the Ghost of the deceased Roman Empire, sitting crowned upon the grave thereof.*'[9]

Probably the most significant event in the creation of what we now call 'The Church' took place in Turkey on 20 May AD 325. This was the Council of Nicaea, the result of the Emperor Constantine's decision to take control of his fragmenting Empire once and for all. At the

---

[9] Thomas Hobbes: *Leviathan*

time Constantine was extremely unpopular and discontent was rife; the idea he came up with to solve his problems was a stroke of true genius. He was realistic enough to accept that Rome was no longer the power that it had been, and whilst he could not hold his position secure through force or financial reward, he could hold sway over his people if he could insert himself into the spiritual beliefs which seemed to be dividing his subjects' loyalties. The whole Empire had become a pot-pourri of cults with some of them, such as Christianity, present in many very different forms. Over several generations just about every eastern religion had found its way to Rome and had been absorbed and metamorphosed to fit local tastes. So thorough had the Romanisation process become that few of the original cult founders would have recognised their own faiths as they merged one into the other to become highly interchangeable; a theological mix-and-match. In this period of change, those who called themselves Christians squabbled amongst themselves with quite fundamental differences in belief.

Despite his role as the legitimiser of Christianity, Constantine was a follower of the Sol Invictus sun-god cult right up until the time he was on his death bed, when he finally accepted baptism on the off-chance that the Christians might have got it right all along. A sensible and inexpensive piece of after-life insurance.

When the Emperor first became involved with the Christians, their population was quite significant; one in ten citizens claimed to be a follower of this Jewish splinter group. He settled disputes for different Christian factions who accused each other of falsehoods, and must have felt that this religion was emerging as the dominant force.

Constantine earned the title that history was to confer upon him – 'Constantine the Great'. He hatched his plan and executed it immaculately. At the time there were two emperors, with Constantine ruling the west and Licinius the east and when Constantine put it to his counterpart that all monotheists should no longer be persecuted, Licinius readily agreed. As these persecutions had all but stopped anyway, Licinius must have been puzzled as to why Constantine should suddenly be so interested in the well-being of accepted cults such as Christianity. He found out shortly afterwards when Constantine accused him of reneging on the agreement and had him murdered on the basis of protecting the religious freedoms of his citizens. Constantine immediately became the one and only Emperor with the full backing of the increasingly vocal and influential cult of Christ. This was clearly an excellent route to maintaining order and engendering cohesion and Constantine must have felt that it deserved further development. There were two obstacles to this strategy: firstly, there were still too many religions active generally and, in particular, within the army; secondly, Christians themselves were in such disagreement that they seemed in danger of splitting up into different faiths. Constantine's solution was dazzlingly brilliant.

Although he was still a devotee of the Sol Invictus religion, Constantine convened the first international council of Christians to establish, once and for all, a single, official view concerning the Christian cult and their Jewish prophet Jesus the Christ. He brought church leaders from every part of the ancient world including Spain, France, Egypt, Persia, Syria, Armenia and the Holy Land itself. Because the Christians were by far the most vocal sect of the Empire, this council held at Nicaea (now Iznik) in Turkey, amounted to a de facto parliament of the new, united Empire. The event was superbly stage-managed: Constantine sat at the centre with the bishops sitting around him so that his authority was stamped on all discussions. The Emperor thus positioned himself as the 'current' Christ with his disciples in attendance and, as later legend held, the power of the Holy Ghost was also present, acting through the man who was to be the founder of the Church. Constantine was principally interested in two things: the God of the Christians, whom he saw as a manifestation of his existing sun god; and the figure of Jesus the Christ, whom he saw as a Jewish messiah, just as he was, he felt, the messiah of the Empire. He considered Jesus to be a warlike and sacred figure like himself who fought to establish God's rule; but whereas the Jewish king had failed, he had not.

Ever since the time of Constantine, Christians have viewed him as a great leader of the faith who defeated the heretics. A story was soon told of his conversion to Christianity when at the Battle of Milvian Bridge: the Emperor followed an instruction received in a prophetic dream and painted the symbol of the true God on the shields of his army. Following Constantine's later involvement with the Christians it was assumed that this image must have been the sacred Greek letters 'chi' and 'rho', the first two letters of the word 'Christos'. However, as Constantine never became a Christian, the image on those shields was almost certainly the blazing sun of his 'true god', Sol Invictus. There are no recorded accounts from the time that describe this symbol but as the Emperor had just been admitted a member of the Sol Invictus cult and spent the rest of his life as its high priest, it seems highly improbable that he would have used any other imagery.

The result of the Council was the 'Nicene Creed', which sought to reconcile the differences between various Christian factions and to avoid doctrinal gulfs that had looked as though they might split the Eastern Church away completely. The rulings that emerged still provide the basis for most Church establishments today, covering many points of detail such as when congregations should stand and when they should sit during services. The central issue, however, was the problem of whether Jesus the Christ was a man or a god, and if he were indeed a god, what was the precise nature of his divinity?

The members of the Council had a major task in front of them which must have tied their theological brains in knots. To find a logical solution was painfully difficult: if there was only one God, how could Jesus be a god without being that God? And if he had been conceived in Mary, then it followed that there must have been a time when God was not born, so there must be a senior deity who is not totally separate. This was rationalised in Constantine's Gentile mind by explaining the relationship as 'God the father' and a 'God the son'. This seems to us a pretty poor conclusion because nobody believes that they and their own father are different manifestations of the same entity; if it were so there would only be one human, as we are all from an almost infinitely long parent/child lineage. The inescapable conclusion is that Christianity is not a monotheistic religion at all; it just deludes itself by keeping its thinking supremely muddled.

The Nicaean Council members also posed themselves the awkward question, 'There must have been a God the Father before he built the world, but what could he have been doing when he was all alone?' No answer emerged but a century later St Augustine of Hippo neatly suggested that 'God had spent that time building a special hell for those that ask such questions!'

Arius, a priest from Alexandria, was the champion of the non-god lobby. He had argued that Jesus the Christ could not be God because he was a man. God was God and it had to be blasphemous to think that Jesus was divine by nature; he could only have become divine through his actions. Arius was an extremely clever theologian and he produced a staggering array of scriptural argument to support his thesis that Christ was a man, just as the members of the Council were. He was opposed by another Alexandrian called Athanasius, who claimed that the Father and the Son were (paradoxically) of one substance. Opinion on the divinity of Jesus the Christ was split and it had to be put to the vote. Arius lost, and the penalty he paid for losing the ballot was that his name became despised as synonymous with evil under the designation 'the Arius Heresy'.

Heresy had been an accusation readily but imprecisely thrown by one Christian group at another, but after Constantine took control its meaning became crystal clear. In essence, the truth became what the Emperor said it was; the rest was heresy, the work of the devil. Many scriptures were outlawed, and application of the label 'Gnostic' to them effectively removed them from the now narrowly defined creed of Christianity.

Interestingly, one of the most important documents *not* to come out of the Council of Nicaea was the 'Donation of Constantine'. This was an eighth-century discovery which purported to be Constantine's instruction that the Church of Rome should have absolute authority in secular affairs because St Peter, the successor to Jesus as leader of the Church, had passed such authority to the bishop of Rome. This is now universally accepted to be a poor forgery but despite this the Roman Catholic Church still clings to the rights that this bogus document conferred upon it. We should also mention at this point that the claim that Peter gave the keys of Heaven to the Pope is another deliberate falsehood, intended to sustain the claims of the Roman Church. It is clear from the Acts of the Apostles and the Letters of Paul that James, the younger brother of Jesus the Christ, took the leadership role of the Jerusalem Church. It is also interesting to note that the first ten bishops of the Jerusalem Church were, according to the 'Church Father' Eusebius, all circumcised Jews who kept Jewish dietary laws, used Jewish liturgy for their daily prayers and recognised only the Jewish Sabbaths and festivals, including the day of atonement. This last observance clearly demonstrates that they did not regard the death of Jesus as atoning for their sins!

Constantine above all others did a splendid job of hijacking Jewish theology. Although he was effectively the architect of the Church, he never became a Christian himself – but his mother, the Empress Helena certainly did. Helena wanted all of the holy sites to be identified and suitably marked with a church or other shrine, so she sent out teams of investigators who had instructions not to return until they had discovered every holy location and artefact from the burning bush of Moses to the True Cross itself.

Christ's tomb was duly found in Jerusalem beneath Jupiter's temple and the site of the crucifixion identified a short distance away. The very spot where Mary Magdalene stood when she heard the good news of the resurrection was located and marked out with a star – all this three hundred years after the events had taken place and two hundred and fifty years after the Romans had destroyed the city. By a miraculous coincidence it was Helena herself who stumbled across the True Cross, complete with Pontius Pilatus's 'King of the Jews' plaque. Perhaps her servants were just a little too eager to please.

The Empress founded churches on the Mount of Olives marking the place where Christ ascended up to Heaven, and at the supposed site of his birth in Bethlehem. We cannot help thinking that Helena found what she wanted to find. One of the sites identified was the exact place where God spoke to Moses from the burning bush on top of Mount Horeb in the Sinai Desert which is now the location of St Catherine's Monastery.

Once the Imperial family saw the practical value of Christianity, it certainly threw itself into public celebration of the legends of the new cult.

Truth Within the Heresies

The early Roman Church set about the task of destroying everything that did not meet its required dogma. Truth was unimportant; what the Church wanted to be was so, and everything contradictory to that was removed. Until recently almost nothing at all was known about Jesus the

Christ outside of the meagre information given in the New Testament. It is strange how a man who is the basis of the principal religion of the Western world can leave so little trace. It is often possible to prove the existence of an historical figure by the negative things said about them by their enemies, yet Jesus is apparently not mentioned in such sources as the writings of Josephus, the first-century historian of the Jews – apart, that is, from a recently discovered text known as the Slavonic Josephus, to which we will return later in the book. The almost total absence of references to Jesus is due to the knives of the censors, but fortunately they were not completely successful, as the long-hidden Slavonic Josephus will demonstrate.

The Romanised Church destroyed any evidence that portrayed its saviour as a mortal rather than a god. In one of the greatest acts of vandalism Christians burnt the library at Alexandria in Egypt to the ground because it contained so much information about the real Jerusalem Church. In doing so they destroyed the greatest collection of ancient texts the world has ever seen. Fortunately their task proved, ultimately, impossible as they could not remove every trace of evidence. Hence, as we have been, the revelations of the Gnostic Gospels and the remarkable Dead Sea Scrolls. Furthermore, the writings of the founding fathers of the official Church unintentionally shed a lot of light on the people and the thoughts they sought to destroy. In addition, the works of early Christian thinkers sometimes escaped the censor because they were felt to be harmless, yet their words can actually tell us a great deal.

One such informative piece came from the pen of Clement of Alexandria, a leading Christian thinker of the second century. He was considered to be rather Gnostic in his outlook but his work was not generally destroyed since it was deemed acceptable. A letter that he wrote to an unknown man by the name of Theodore survived: it reads as follows:

'You did well in silencing the unspeakable teachings of the Carpocratians. For these are the "wandering stars" referred to in the prophecy, who wander from the narrow road of the commandments into a boundless abyss of the carnal and bodily sins. For, priding themselves in knowledge, as they say, "of the deep of Satan", they do not know that they are casting themselves away into "the nether world of the darkness" of falsity, and, boasting that they are free, they have become slaves of servile desires. Such [people] are to be opposed in all ways and altogether. For, even if they should say something true, one who loves the truth should not, even so, agree with them. For not all true [things] are the truth, nor should that truth which [merely] seems true according to human opinions be preferred to the true truth, that according to faith.

Now of the [things] they keep saying about the divinely inspired Gospel according to Mark, some are altogether falsifications, and others, even if they do contain some true [parts], nevertheless are not reported truly. For the true [things], being mixed with inventions, are falsified, so that, as the saying [goes], even the salt loses its flavour. [As for] Mark, then, during Peter's stay in Rome he wrote [an account of] the Lord's doings, not, however, declaring all, nor yet hinting at the secret [ones], but selecting those he thought most useful for increasing the faith of those who were being instructed.

But when Peter died a martyr, Mark came over to Alexandria, bringing both his own notes and those of Peter, from which he transferred to his former book the things suitable to whatever makes for progress toward knowledge [gnosis]. [Thus] he composed a more spiritual Gospel for the use of those who were being perfected. Nevertheless, he yet did not divulge the things not to be uttered, nor did he write down the hierophantic teachings of the Lord, but to stories already written he added yet others and, moreover, brought in certain sayings of which he knew the interpretation would, as a mystagogue, lead the hearers into the innermost sanctuary of that truth hidden by seven. Thus, in sum, he prearranged matters, neither grudgingly nor incautiously, in my opinion, and, dying, he left his composition to the church in Alexandria, where it even yet is most carefully guarded, being read only to those who are initiated into the great mysteries.

But since the foul demons are always devising destruction for the race of men, Carpocrates, instructed by them and using deceitful arts, so enslaved a certain presbyter of the church in Alexandria that he got from him a copy of the secret Gospel, which he both interpreted according to his blasphemous and carnal doctrine and, moreover, polluted, mixing with the spotless and holy words utterly shameless lies. From this mixture is drawn off the teaching of the Carpocratians.

To them, therefore, as I said above, one must never give way, nor, when they put forward their falsifications, should one concede that the secret Gospel is by Mark, but should even deny it on oath. For, "Not all true [things] are to be said to all men". For this [reason] the Wisdom of God, through Solomon, advises, "Answer the fool from his folly," teaching that the light of the truth should be hidden from those who are mentally blind. Again it says, "From him who has not shall be taken away," and, "Let the fool walk in darkness." But we are "children of light", having been illuminated by "the dayspring" of the Spirit of the Lord "from on high," and "Where the spirit of the Lord is," it says, "there is liberty," for "all things are pure to the pure".

To you, therefore, I shall not hesitate to answer the questions you have asked, refuting the falsifications by the very words of the Gospel. For example, after "*And they were in the road going up to Jerusalem,*" and what follows, until "*After three days he shall arise,*" [the secret Gospel] brings the following [material] word for word: "*And they come to Bethany, and a certain woman, whose brother had died, was there. And, coming, she prostrated herself before Jesus and says to him, 'Son of David, have mercy on me.' But the disciples rebuked her. And Jesus, being angered, went off with her into the garden where the tomb was, and straightway a great cry was heard from the tomb. And going near, Jesus rolled away the stone from the door of the tomb. And straightway, going in where the youth was, he stretched forth his hand and raised him, seizing his hand. But the youth, looking upon him, loved him and began to beseech him that he might be with him. And going out of the tomb they came into the house of the youth, for he was rich. And after six days Jesus told him what to do and in the evening the youth comes to him, wearing a linen cloth over [his] naked [body]. And he remained with him that night, for Jesus taught him the mystery of the kingdom of God. And thence, arising, he returned to the other side of the Jordan.*"

After these [words] follows the text, "*And James and John come to him,*" and all that section But "*naked [man] with naked [man]*" and the other things about which you wrote are not found.

And after the [words], "*And he comes into Jericho,*" [the secret Gospel] adds only, "*And the sister of the youth whom Jesus loved and his mother and Salome were there, and Jesus did not receive them.*" But the many other [things about] which you wrote both seem to be and are falsifications.

> *Now the true explanation and that which accords with the true philosophy ...'*[10]

At this point the letter stops mid-page.

This reference to a secret Gospel, and more importantly, to a secret inner ceremony conducted by Jesus himself, was a great find. Could it be true, we wondered? Clement might have been wrong – but that did not seem likely. Then the letter could be a forgery; but if so, why? We could not imagine what motive anyone would have had in forging it so long ago. Returning to the gist of the letter, we think there is a strong similarity between the references to 'the young man naked except for a linen cloth' and the unexplained incident at the time of the arrest of Jesus at Gethsemane, as described in Mark 14:51–52:

> *'And a certain young man followed him, having a linen cloth cast about his naked body. And they laid hold on him. But he, casting off the linen cloth, fled from them naked.'*

The Carpocratians were a particularly unpleasant early Christian sect who believed that sin was a means of salvation and the implication about two naked men may be a deliberate misreading of events to justify their own bizarre behaviour. The content of the letter does ring true, given the event in Mark's Gospel. Again, there are Masonic parallels: it reminded us of Masonic ceremonies when the candidate is clothed only in white linen – and, of course, the mantle of the Templars was originally plain white linen.

If a second-century Christian did have some knowledge

[10] Morton Smith: *The Secret Gospel*

of secret ceremonies conducted by Jesus the Christ and his followers, we would almost expect such a person to be from Alexandria, which had strong connections with the early Jerusalem Church. Given the dramatic contents of that letter, we were impelled to look at Clement's surviving treatises, although they may have been tampered with by later Christian censors. In a short work entitled *The Mysteries of the Faith not to be Divulged to All* he indicates that knowledge is not made available to everyone:

> '... the wise do not utter with their mouth what they reason in council. "But what ye hear in the ear," says the Lord, "proclaim upon the houses," bidding them receive the secret traditions of the true knowledge, and expound them aloft and conspicuously; and as we have heard in the ear, so to deliver them to whom it is requisite; but not enjoining us to communicate to all without distinction, what is said to them in parables.'

This suggests that there was a secret tradition and that it is, at least in part, present within the Bible, written in such a manner that the uninitiated would accept the parable on a literal level while the informed would discern something far more important and meaningful. Clement could only be referring to parts of the New Testament that are not normally considered to be parables, because such obvious parables as 'the Good Samaritan' are potted lessons in morality and nothing more. In which case, could there be a hidden meaning in the stranger parts of the story of Jesus the Christ, which are taken by modern Christians as literal truths? Do such episodes as Jesus turning water into wine or raising the dead conceal a cryptic message behind the impossible acts they seem to refer to? We were starting to be just as interested in the detail of biblical scriptures as in Masonic texts.

Reading through a work attributed to another second-century Christian, Hippolytus, entitled *The Refutation of All Heresies* we found fascinating reports of a heretical sect that he identifies as the Naassenes, who claimed to have beliefs handed down from James, the brother of the Lord by Mariamne. They are supposed to consider the intercourse of women with men to be a wicked and filthy practice, while washing in life-giving water was a splendid thing. Hippolytus goes on to say:

> *'They assert, then, that the Egyptians, who after the Phrygians, it is established, are of greater antiquity than all mankind, and who confessedly were the first to proclaim to all the rest of men the rites and orgies of, at the same time, all the Gods, as well as the species [of things], have the sacred and august, and for those who are not initiated, unspeakable mysteries of Isis. These, however, are not anything else than what by her of the seven dresses and sable robe was sought and snatched away, namely, the pudendum of Osiris. And they say that Osiris is water. But the seven-robed nature, encircled and arrayed with seven mantles of ethereal texture (for so they call the planetary stars, allegorising and denominating them ethereal [robes], is as it were the changeable generation, and is exhibited as the creature transformed by the ineffable and unportrayable, and inconceivable and figureless one. And this, [the Naassene] says, is what is declared in scripture, "The just will fall seven times, and rise again." For these falls, he says, are the changes of the stars, moved by Him who puts the stars in motion.'*

There were a lot of bells ringing as we read this passage. The term Naassene is another form of 'Nasorean', the name adopted by the original followers of Jesus who formed the Jerusalem Church. The description of the distaste for sexual contact with women and the major role of cleansing also fits in perfectly with what we now know

about the Essene Community at Qumran which produced
the Dead Sea Scrolls. The fixation with the number seven
dovetails interestingly into the reference in Clement's
letter to 'the innermost sanctuary of that truth hidden by
seven'. The whole thing also struck us as having a very
Masonic feel to it; though we couldn't identify the
connection then, subsequently it became clear when we
came across the ritual of the Royal Arch Degree of
Freemasonry – but more of that a little later.

A Positive Link between Jesus and the Templars

From the evidence available we were now convinced that
Jesus and his followers were originally called Nasoreans
(or Nazarenes) but it was important to understand what
was meant by this designation and to consider why it went
out of use. Jesus himself had been given the title in
Matthew 2:23:

> *'And coming he dwelt in a city called Nazareth; that it
> might be fulfilled which was said by the prophets: That
> he shall be called a Nazarene.'*

This seemed to be an indicator that the Gospel of
Matthew was written by someone well removed from the
true Church, or, more likely, that it was added at a later
date by someone who wanted to tidy up some unattractive
loose ends. It struck us as a painful contortion of logic to
say that Jesus was duty-bound to go and live in a
particular place because some long-gone soothsayer had
said that he would. What's more, a major flaw in the New
Testament claim that people called their saviour 'Jesus of
Nazareth' is the evidence that the town of Nazareth
simply did not exist at the time of Jesus! There are no
historical records referring to the town that predate the
mentions in the Gospels, which is a unique situation as
the Romans kept excellent records throughout their

empire. The term actually used was 'Jesus the Nasorean' because he was a senior member of a movement that bore that name. The New Testament places Jesus's early activities around the Sea of Galilee and his supposed move to Capharnaum, described in Matthew 4:13, was merely a necessary correction to bring history back into line.[11]

We were struck by the phrasing here: it implies that Jesus was a *member* of the Nasorean sect, which strongly suggests that he was not necessarily its original *leader*. It seems that Jesus might not have been the founder of the Church at all.

The Nasoreans were clearly going to be very significant in the story that was starting to unfold in front of us. And then an important clue came from a totally unexpected source. Whilst visiting the Sinai, Chris, a keen scuba diver, took the opportunity to dive on the coral reefs of the Red Sea, which he knew from previous experience were the finest in the world.

The underwater visibility around Sharm el Sheik in Egypt is normally excellent but on one particular day it dropped dramatically due to the annual spore bloom from the coral. This turned the water hazy and in places the visibility dropped to a couple of yards. Chris takes up the story:

'I was aware that was not all bad news as the plankton brought in such wonderful creatures as manta rays, seeking to feast on the suddenly plentiful food. It was about ten in the morning when I jumped off the extremely hot deck of the all-steel *Apuhara* (an Egyptian vessel that had started life as a Swedish icebreaker) and dropped a hundred feet to the multicoloured sea bed.

'I headed towards the headland, rising slowly as the water became increasingly shallow to give me a safe dive profile for nitrogen decompression. At about thirty feet I

---

[11] *Peake's Commentary on the Bible*

entered a large cloud of zoo-plankton and completely lost sight of my dive buddy, so I backed out towards the clearer area. No sooner had I got my vision restored than I realised that a giant manta ray was heading straight at me, mouth wide open as it scooped in tons of water to filter out its morning meal. It stopped just a dozen or so feet in front of me and hovered motionless like an alien flying saucer. This fish was over twenty feet wide, and as my head twisted from left to right to take in the splendour of this magnificent creature I was filled with awe and excitement. Suddenly, without any discernible movement of its wings, it broke away to my left and then I saw two smaller mantas sweeping in behind it to take advantage of the food-carrying current off the headland.

'This rated as one of my best dives ever and as soon as I was back on board I asked Ehab, the friendly and usually knowledgeable Arab guide, for the name of the location and he told me it was called Ras Nasrani. Conversationally I asked him what the word meant, and was told that Ras translated simply to "head" or "point" and "Nasrani" was a word for lots of little fish. I pressed further and asked what type of fish and he replied, "Just ordinary little fish, when there is lots of them together".

'A few days later, at the monastery of St Catherine, I heard an Arab describe Christians with precisely the same word, "nasrani", and when I checked, it was confirmed that this is the normal Arabic word for the followers of the major prophet called Jesus.'

The literal meaning immediately sprang back into mind and suddenly made a lot of sense. Could this be the very simple meaning of the term – that is, in the earliest times, Christians were 'the little fishes'?

This could be based on the 'fisher of men' imagery that the Church attributes to Christ; more likely it is based on the ancient association of the priest and the fish. The members of the Essene sect were all priest-like in their devotions and obedience of the law and they bathed in water at every opportunity, which also would have given good reason to use the term. This theory fits the fact that members of the Nasorean sect went around the holy places of the early Christian era and marked their sacred places with two arcs that formed the famous sign of the fish. It is interesting to note that the symbol of the organisation was originally a fish and not a cross, indicating that the execution of Jesus was not so important at that time.

It could also be that Peter and John were high-ranking members of the Nasorean sect who recruited others and therefore became known as 'fishermen' in recognition of their recruitment activities rather than as a literal reference to a trade. This would make a lot of sense because the Dead Sea area has no real fish; so to give a literal reading any validity, the later authors of the New Testament had to shift the origins of these 'fishermen' to the Sea of Galilee – which was well stocked with fish – to overcome this contradiction.

Further research showed that the adjective 'nazôraios' has been identified as a very early term used by outsiders for the sect that later became known as Christians. Epiphanius speaks of a pre-Christian group called the Nasaraioi who, it has been suggested by a number of leading scholars such as Lidzbarski, originally designated the sect out of which the figure of Jesus (and therefore the Church) had emerged. Again this suggests that Jesus may well have been a mere member rather than a founder.

There was no doubt in our minds about two things:

Jesus did not come from the town of Nazareth; instead, he was a member of the Nasorean sect whose members almost certainly considered themselves to be 'fishes'.

This discovery made so much sense that we combed through as much information as we could, looking for any small titbits of information that might shed more light on a very promising hypothesis. Various pieces of data were intriguing, but we were staggered to discover that the Nasorean sect never quite died out; it still survives in southern Iraq as part of the larger Mandaean sect whose members trace their religious heritage back, not to Jesus but to Yahia Yuhana, better known to Christians as John the Baptist! Their literature uses the similar word 'natzor-aje' to describe themselves. They believe that Yshu Mshiha (Jesus) was a Nasorean but one who was a rebel and heretic who betrayed secret doctrines that had been entrusted to him. We wondered what secrets he might have possessed and to whom he had passed these secrets. The possible answers were not far away.

We did not know very much about the Mandaeans and researching them, were riveted by the following statement:

> '*The Mandaeans, a small but tenacious community which dwells in Iraq, follows an ancient form of Gnosticism, which practices initiation, ecstasy and some rituals which have been said to resemble those of the Freemasons.*'[12]

There it was. A group that has direct descent from the original Church of Jerusalem, and one of the first descriptions of them that we come across identified their rituals with Freemasonry. Could the secret that Jesus had supposedly betrayed been some sort of Masonic-style secret? It seemed an amazing thought. This had to be the

---

[12] Arkon Daraul: *Secret Societies*

beginning of something very important, a view confirmed when we discovered that the Mandaeans of today call their priests 'Nasoreans'! We were fascinated to find that these people take their name from the word 'Manda' which means 'secret knowledge' and we quickly found some evidence of possible connections with Freemasonry. The Mandaeans use a ritual handshake called 'Kushta' which is a grip given to ceremonial candidates, signifying 'Righteousness' or the doing of right things. This we considered to be a very Masonic idea.

Another aspect of their ritual that appeared to have Masonic overtones was the fact that the Mandaeans say a silent prayer when their initiates are considered to be ritually dead, just as the most secret words of Freemasonry are always whispered into the ear of the Master Mason candidate when he is raised from his ritual grave. This was later to provide a very important link between the ancient past and modern Freemasonry.

The Star of the Mandaeans

Chris started to look more closely at the beliefs and rituals of this remarkable theological fossil of a culture dating from the time of Jesus, and he came across a few words that were to lead to a remarkable unravelling of history.

Josephus, the historian of the Jews in the first century, observed that the Essenes believed that good souls have their inhabitation beyond the ocean, in a region that is neither oppressed with storms of rain or snow nor with intense heat, but refreshed by the gentle breathing of the west wind which perpetually blows from the ocean. This idyllic land across the sea to the west (or sometimes the north), is a belief common to many cultures, from the Jews to the Greeks to the Celts. The Mandaeans, however, believe that the inhabitants of this far land are so pure that mortal eyes will not see them and that this place is marked by a star, the name of which is 'Merica'.

A land across the ocean; a perfect place marked by a star known as Merica ... or perhaps A-merica? We knew that the morning star had been important to the Nasoreans and the evening star, the star of the west, is the same celestial body – the planet Venus.

As we were to find out in great detail later in our researches, the United States of America was created by Freemasons and its constitution is based on Masonic principles and, as we already knew, the morning star is the one that every newly raised Master Mason is required to look towards. The star as a symbol has always been important to the United States. Our minds immediately turned back to Masonic ritual and the closing of the Lodge meeting when the following questions are asked of the Senior and Junior Wardens by the Worshipful Master:

> *'Brother Senior Warden. Whither are you directing your steps?'*
> *'Towards the West, Worshipful Master.'*
> *'Brother Junior Warden. Why leave the East to go to the West?'*
> *'In search of that which was lost, Worshipful Master.'*
> *'Brother Senior Warden. What was that which was lost?'*
> *'The genuine secrets of a Master Mason, Worshipful Master.'*

These connections could be coincidental but it seemed to us that too many coincidences were happening all at once.

The Star of America

It may seem a strange diversion when researching Jerusalem at the time of Jesus, but the origin of the name of America is an important by-product of our researches. We believe that one of the problems of traditional historical research is that experts have looked at individual 'packets' of history as though certain significant sets of circumstances just arrived at a given date for us to label and observe. Increasingly, serious investigators are appreciating that there are unexpected and powerful connections between all kinds of events previously seen as unrelated.

We knew the Mandaeans were the direct descendants of the Nasoreans, who we had also established were the same group as the Qumranians, the people who buried their secret scrolls under Herod's Temple. It follows that if the forefathers of the Mandaeans were the authors of the scrolls which the Templars unearthed, the mystical land beneath a star called 'Merica' might have been recorded in their secret writings. In short, it seemed possible that the Templars learnt about a wonderful land beneath the bright lone star 'Merica' from the scrolls, and if so, there is a strong possibility they sailed west to find it.

The continent of America is popularly believed to have taken its name from the Christian name of Amerigo Vespucci, a wealthy ship-chandler in Seville who did not sail to the New World until 1499, seven years after Columbus. It is now also accepted that many Europeans and Asiatics had arrived on the continent a long time before these famous, high-profile expeditions backed by the Spanish. Maybe Templar descendants had been involved in naming the new continent; maybe the Templars themselves actually went in search of a land under the evening star they knew from their discoveries to be called 'Merica'.

Templar ships were built to withstand a variety of conditions including the storms of the Bay of Biscay and their navigation, by lodestone compass and astrological maps, was far from crude. A transatlantic voyage was not only possible; if they had knowledge of the land of the morning star, the land of Merica, they also had the perfect motive both to find the New World and to leave the Old – survival, once their Order was denounced as heretical in 1307.

In the light of all this new evidence, Chris felt that it was reasonable to speculate that some of the Templars had set sail westward into the unknown, flying their maritime battle flag, the skull and cross-bones. They then found the land of the western star, a hundred and eighty-five years before Columbus. The idea seemed to make a lot of sense, but the evidence still remained very circumstantial.

Chris had been working on interpreting the complexities of the cults of the first century AD and when he first came across the thought that there could be a connection between 'Merica' and 'America' he felt that it could be very significant, but he knew it was well short of anything approaching proof. Chris recalls:

'I remember feeling sure that at our next meeting Robert would be very excited at the possibility that there was a Nasorean origin to the name of the American continent. I did not mention it at all and waited for him to read my draft chapter. He inserted my floppy disc into his computer and scanned the screen. As he reached the important section, his response was stony silence. I was sorely disappointed; if Robert did not find this hypothesis interesting, nobody would.

'Robert stood up and muttered to himself as he rummaged through the piles of books that filled every square foot of his study floor. He tutted as several volumes of Gould's *History of Freemasonry* collapsed into an untidy heap, then smiled as he withdrew a very new and shiny book from their midst.

'He flicked through the pages of the AA road map of the British Isles and pointed his index finger in the general region of southern Scotland.

"How do you fancy a day out?" he enquired.

"Where are you pointing?" I asked, trying not to look too deflated. "Edinburgh?"

"No. Just a few miles south, the village of Roslin ... the site of Rosslyn Chapel."

'It was two days later when we set off for Edinburgh and Robert still had not explained where or why we were going. From the beginning of our work we had split responsibility roughly at the Templar period, with Robert concentrating on events since the thirteenth century and myself everything before it. Just at the point that I was investigating the first century AD in Jerusalem, Robert was focused on fourteenth-century Scotland. Previous visits across the border had already revealed a large number of Templar and Masonic graves, which had demonstrated to us just how important this country was in the development of Freemasonry. So what else had Robert come across?

'We used the time on the journey to discuss various areas of our general work but as we approached the Scottish border at Gretna, I became impatient and insisted that Robert explained our mission for the day.

"Okay," he said with a smile. "You know I've been looking at the history of the Sinclair family and the chapel that William St Clair built in what is now the village of Roslin."

"Yes," I replied sharply as an indication to get to the point without a rambling intro.

"Well, it hadn't registered when I first read about it, but there is something very strange about Rosslyn Chapel that fits with your 'Merica' idea." Robert had my complete attention as he continued. "The whole building is decorated inside with carvings of Masonic significance ... and botanical significance. Arches, lintels, pillar bases and suchlike are mostly covered in decorative but highly detailed plant motifs, with many different species represented."

'This was certainly fascinating but the connection to my Mandaean discovery was still not clear.

"The point is ..." Robert hesitated to build the

suspense. "Those plants include the aloe cactus and maize cobs."

'The importance of this churned around in my mind for a couple of seconds. "What date did you say the chapel was built?"

"Exactly the point," Robert said as he slapped his knee. "The first turf was cut in 1441 and all work was completed forty-five years later in 1486. I reckon those carvings must have been in place ... oh, no later than 1470."

"Remind me, when exactly did Columbus discover America?" I needed confirmation of what my memory was telling me.

"He landed in the Bahamas in 1492, Puerto Rico in 1493, Cuba in 1494 but never did actually set foot on the mainland." Robert continued before I could ask the next question. "And yes, the aloe cactus and Indian maize, or corn as Americans call it, were both New World plants that were supposedly unknown outside that continent until well into the sixteenth century."

'I stared across at Robert as the inescapable conclusion hit me. Even if Columbus had found these plants on his first brief voyage, Rosslyn Chapel had been completed six years previously, and therefore the carvings of the maize and the aloe cactus were created when Christopher Columbus was still a schoolboy. Someone else had travelled to America and brought back plants long before Columbus is supposed to have discovered the New World. And the proof is present in a Templar/Masonic building!

We arrived at the chapel around midday, both feeling excited and honoured to be in such a special place. Gazing around the interior we looked up at the solid stone, three-foot thick vaulted roof that runs the length of the interior and marvelled at the heavy decoration. Wandering around the chapel we soon found the plants that we were looking for, maize cobs arched over a window in the south wall and the aloe cactus appeared across a lintel connected to the same wall (Figs 7 and 8). Elsewhere we could see many other recognisable plants and everywhere there were manifestations of the 'green man', the Celtic figure that represented fertility. Over a hundred 'green men' have been counted but it is believed that there are even more subtly peeping out of the vegetation.

Rosslyn Chapel is a remarkable and magical place. It links Christianity with ancient Celtic folklore and Templarism Freemasonry. We knew with certainty that this would not be our last visit to this unique building.

* * *

Everything we had discovered about the Essenes/Nasoreans seemed to exhibit striking links with Freemasonry; the unexpected revelation that a sect descended from the Mandaeans still exists in Iraq threw out more parallels. One line of research had unexpectedly taken us to a building in Scotland which displayed tantalising Freemason/Templar imagery. But to understand the Nasoreans fully, we knew that we had to go back as far in time as possible to unravel the initial threads of our mystery: we needed to find out where the key elements of the Jewish religion first appeared.

CONCLUSION

Having found that the Qumranians and Jesus himself had some strong connections with the Templars and Freemasonry, we now wanted to know the origin of their beliefs and rituals. The people of Qumran were a distillation of everything that can be described as Jewish, yet there was obviously far more to their structure and belief system than can be attributed to the Old Testament.

Once again we were lost for a next step in our research.

Just as we had had to leap back to the period of Jesus in the hope of finding an explanation for Templar beliefs, we now had to go back in time once again to reconstruct the theology of the Jews. The rituals of Freemasonry might have been invented by the Qumranians, but we somehow felt sure that they must be much, much older.

We decided to go back as far as it is possible to go, then work forward, so that we could better understand the driving passions of the Qumranian mind.

Chapter Six

In The Beginning Man Made God

The Garden of Eden

Having decided that we needed to understand the history and evolution of Jewish religious beliefs, we turned our attention to something vital to all civilisations – language. The evidence is that most languages of the Indian subcontinent, western Asia, Europe and parts of North Africa stem from a common, ancient source. The commonalities of hundreds of tongues have proven the point. It seemed to us that the same might apply to religion, because as people spread out, taking their languages with them, they are bound to have taken their legends and their gods as well. The connections between apparently different religions can, we believe, reveal linkages just as clear as those found by philologists (those who study the development of language).

The origins of language have been sought for thousands of years. Many early peoples supposed that language was of divine origin, and that if one could discover the first or purest form of speech, one would have found the lexicon of the gods. Many 'experiments' have been conducted to find this primeval tongue, including one by Psamtik I, Pharaoh of Egypt in the seventh century BC, who had two children brought up to hear no spoken word in the hope that they would instinctively develop the pure and godlike language. They are said to have spontaneously spoken Phrygian, an ancient language from Asia Minor. The same experiment was carried out more than two thousand years later by King James IV of Scotland with the resulting language being, equally unconvincingly, Hebrew.

The first language from which virtually all subsequent tongues of the Old World sprang has been labelled, rather unpoetically, Proto-Indo-European. This has been shown to be the common source of Urdu, French, Punjabi, Persian, Polish, Czech, Gaelic, Greek, Lithuanian, Portuguese, Italian, Afrikaans, Old Norse, German and English, amongst many others. How long ago Proto-Indo-European was a living single language we will never know, because our detailed knowledge of the past relies on the next great evolutionary step that grew out of language, and that is the written word.

The Book of Genesis was first written down around 2,700 years ago, well after the time of King Solomon. Ancient though this is, we now know that writing began more than twice as far back in history in a land called, rather beautifully, Sumer.

Sumer is the accepted birthplace of civilisation. Its writing, theology and building technology formed the foundation of all later Middle Eastern and European cultures. Although no one is sure where the Sumerians came from, they believed that they had come from a land called Dilmun, which is generally held to be modern day Bahrain, on the west coast of the Persian Gulf. By 4000 BC they had a thriving existence in what is now southern Iraq between the two rivers, the Tigris and the Euphrates. The broad alluvial plains there provided rich agricultural land on which to grow crops, raise cattle, and the rivers abounded with fish to catch. By the fourth millennium BC, Sumer had a well-established culture that had cities, specialised craftsmen, co-operative irrigation works, ceremonial centres and written records.

City cultures are very different to those found in villages as concentrations of large numbers of people demand a sophisticated social structure, with the majority of the workforce removed from agricultural production without loss of productivity. The Sumerians developed excellent farming techniques and it has been calculated from texts in cuneiform scripts that their yield of wheat 4,400 years ago would compare favourably with the best of modern wheat fields of Canada!

Besides establishing a highly efficient agriculture and such basic industries as the making of textiles and ceramics, the Sumerians invented new materials including glass and became outstanding glaziers as well as metal-workers, using gold, silver, copper and bronze. They became accomplished stone carvers and creators of delicate filigree work and carpentry, but without doubt the most important invention of these amazingly competent people was the wheel.

Their achievements as builders were impressive; their many important innovations included the pillar, which was directly inspired by the trunk of the date palm. Their earliest cities were made up of mud brick buildings; these crumbled in the course of a few generations so another building would be erected on top of the old. Over the thousands of years of Sumerian civilisation, this process of decay, collapse and rebuild created large mounds that we call 'tells', many of which, as much as sixty feet in height, still exist.

The wealth of the Sumerians attracted travellers from distant lands who sought to trade their simple goods for the wonderful produce of this advanced civilisation. In response, the Sumerians developed a whole class of international merchants with large warehouses for imports and exports. The Sumerians were in a good position to demand advantageous terms for their trading and it is likely that the populace would have had access to the most exotic and splendid goods from the corners of the known world. Many of their raw materials were brought down the rivers in boats, which were then either sold or dismantled for their valuable wood. The only tree that grew locally was the date palm and its wood was too flexible to use in general building. Sumer had no stone quarries so when the Sumerians wished to construct in stone, cut blocks were shipped down the rivers and carried through their elaborate canal system to the required site. Boats could not travel upstream so manufactured goods to pay for the purchase of raw materials had to be carried north by donkey; the horse was unknown in Sumer.

The Cities of Sumer
(*See* Appendix 6)

There were as many as twenty cities in the land of Sumer, the most important of which were Ur, Kish, Eridu, Lagash and Nippur. Each was politically autonomous, with a king and a priesthood. For the Sumerians the land was God's, without whose procreative power life would end; the king was a lesser, earthbound god whose responsibility it was to ensure the productivity of the community. At the centre of each city was their god's house – the temple, from which the priests controlled every aspect of life in the community, including the dispensing of justice, land administration, scientific and theological learning and religious ritual.

The schools, known as 'edubba', produced the professional classes who would start their education from a young age. They were expected to become proficient in writing and then to study a range of subjects including mathematics, literature, music, law, accountancy, surveying and quantity surveying. Their development was oriented to produce well-read leaders of men. Whilst elements of the Sumerian language remain in use today, it was not the origin of Proto-Indo-European; in fact it was only of the few tongues completely unconnected with this root language.

Our interest in the Sumerians was to see if elements of their theology had been the common source of religious beliefs that had spread in the same way that language had done; developing to suit local preferences as it travelled but retaining an identifiable core.

From the ruins of Nippur archaeologists have recovered many thousands of tablets that record the history of its people. Their early writing started out, as far as we know, around 3500 BC and in much the same way as language must have developed, fundamental objects such as head, hand and leg were the first items to be identified. These were easily recognised pictograms with a profile of the object, but quickly more symbolic words were created. The symbol for a man was an ejaculating penis, looking very much like a candle. From that came the word for a male slave, which was the candle-shape with three triangles superimposed to represent hills. This denoted a stranger; Sumer had no hills and the only resident non-Sumerian males were slaves. The marks they made were created by pushing a stick into wet clay and this tended to give a broader indentation and deposit where the writing instrument started and finished a line. This triangular effect at each end of the line was later translated as a serif; the small marks that you can see on the extremities of the letters on this page.

It is not just the stylistic treatment of our letters that stems from the land of Sumer; our very alphabet owes it much. The letter 'A', for example, derives from the image of a bull's head, which was a near triangle with two of the sides being overlong giving the impression of horns. This was first evolved by the Phoenicians, then entered early Greek where it looked like the bull's head on its side, for as the Greeks developed capitals in their alphabet the letter 'A' was rotated another ninety degrees and became 'alpha', a character very similar to our modern capital 'A', which is essentially a bull's head upside down. Today the

English language still contains a few almost pure Sumerian words, such as alcohol, cane, gypsum, myrrh and
saffron.

As well as passing down to us, amongst other things,
the wheel, glass, our alphabet, our divisions of the time of
day, mathematics, the art of building, the Sumerians gave
us something else: God. They also have provided us with
the earliest written histories, and as Freemasons we were
particularly interested in Sumerian references to Enoch,
who is important in Masonic lore, and the Sumerian story
of the great flood which figures so largely in the ritual of
the Masonic Ark Mariners Degree.

Etymologists have shown that the story of the Garden
of Eden in the Book of Genesis is the story of Sumer;
moreover, cities such as Ur, Larsa and Haram, mentioned
in the Book of Genesis, were actually in the land of
Sumer. Genesis gives us the creation story:

> '*In the beginning God created the heaven and the earth.
> And the earth was without form, and void; and
> darkness was upon the face of the deep. And the Spirit
> of God moved upon the face of the waters. And God
> said, Let there be light: and there was light ... And
> God said, Let there be a firmament in the midst of the
> waters, and let it divide the waters from the waters.
> And God made the firmament, and divided the waters
> which were under the firmament from the waters which
> were above the firmament: and it was so ... And God
> said, Let the waters under the heaven be gathered
> together unto one place, and let the dry land appear:
> and it was so. And God called the dry land Earth; and
> the gathering together of the waters called he seas ...
> And God said, Let the earth bring forth grass, the herb
> yielding seed, and the fruit tree yielding fruit after his
> kind ...*'

Compare this to an abstract from a Babylonian account

of the creation known as 'Enuma Elish' from its first two words, meaning 'when on high'. It was written down in both Babylonian and Sumerian nearly a thousand years before Genesis and survives almost complete on seven cuneiform tablets:

> *'All lands were sea. Then there was a movement on the midst of the sea; At that time Eridu was made ... Marduk laid a reed on the face of the waters, He formed dust and poured it out beside the reed. That he might cause the Gods to dwell in the dwelling of their heart's desire, He formed mankind. With him the goddess Aruru created the seed of mankind. The beasts of the field and living things in the field he formed. The Tigris and the Euphrates he created and established in their place: Their name he proclaimed in goodly manner. The grass, the rush and the marsh, the reed and the forest he created, The lands, the marshes and the swamps; The wild cow and her young, the lamb of the fold, Orchards and forests; The he-goat and the mountain-goat ... The Lord Marduk built a dam beside the sea ... Reeds he formed, trees he created; Bricks he laid, buildings he erected; Houses he made, cities he built ... Erech he made ...'*

This Mesopotamian epic of creation is without doubt the source of the Genesis creation legend, and it attributes to God all of the good things brought into existence by the remarkable Sumerians. The references to buildings being created by God did not carry through into the Israelite story because the nomadic nature of the Jews meant that the only cities they had lived in by the time the Book of Genesis came to be written down had been built by others; often taken after the original inhabitants had been put to the sword. The God of Genesis, Yahweh, did not come into existence for several hundred years after the writing of these cuneiform tablets.

According to many experts, the gods of later civilisations are developments of the Sumerian fertility and storm gods. Could this be true? Certainly the storm god had a large part to play in the land of Sumer and the legend of Noah. The Sumerians saw nature as a living entity and the gods and goddesses were embodiments of the forces of that living land; each had a part to play in the forces of nature. Some deities were responsible for the fertility of the land and its people; others took responsibility for organising the storms which occurred. It was obviously important for the continuance of the people that the favour for the fertility gods should be actively sought; equally, given the devastating effects of their labours, the storm gods had to be placated to preserve the Sumerian way of life.

It would have been a storm god with power over the weather who caused the Great Flood which gave rise to the story of Noah, and as Freemasons we were naturally interested in storm gods and floods, since the Order devotes a whole side degree – the Ark Mariner's Degree – with a complete and detailed ritual to preserve the story of Captain Noah and the legend of the Flood.

The one major problem that the people of Sumer had to contend with was the flooding of the low plains through which the Tigris and the Euphrates flowed south to the sea. Periodically the flooding would be disastrous, but on one particular occasion it must have been unusually cataclysmic, and so entered folklore for all time. Whether or not a boat builder called Noah actually existed we cannot know, but we can be sure that the Great Flood did happen.

Further analysis of Genesis, especially the genealogy of Seth and Cain, clearly traces the creation story back to Sumer. There are lists of Sumerian kings from Larsa which name ten kings who reigned before the Flood, and give the length of their reigns, ranging from 10,000 to

60,000 years. The Larsa list ends with the words, 'After the Flood kingship was sent down from on high'. This suggests that a new beginning was made after the Flood. The last name in the second Larsa list is Ziusundra, which is another name for Utanapishtim, the hero of the Babylonian story of the Flood written on the eleventh tablet of the Gilgamesh Epic. The seventh king in the Sumerian list was regarded as possessing special wisdom in matters pertaining to the gods and as being the first man to practice prophecy; that seventh name is Enoch, of whom scripture says 'he walked with God', and who in later Jewish tradition was held to have been taken to Heaven without dying. It seemed to us that there could be little doubt that the writer of Genesis was using Sumerian material which had passed into early Jewish tradition. The links between the religion of the Jews and the ancient land of Sumer are clear but the situation becomes even more intriguing when we look at the reason why the original writer, or the Yahwist using his material, assigned such longevity to Seth's descendants before the Flood. We suspect it was to emphasise the contrast between the conditions of life before and after the divine judgement of the Flood. There is, however, another possible reason. It has been suggested by some writers that the astronomical numbers in the Sumerian king-lists may be the product of astrological speculations which applied measurements derived from the observation of the stars to the calculation of mythical regnal periods. In the same way, the early Jewish writers may have arranged the numbers of the list to correspond with a chronology which assigned a fixed number of years from the Creation to the foundation of Solomon's Temple, and divided this period into epochs, the first of which, from the Creation to the Flood, contained 1,656 years.[1]

[1] *Peake's Commentary on the Bible*

Ur, the City of Abraham

Ur, famous today for its great ziggurat, was looked upon in the third millennium BC as one of the great city-states of the world. The northern and western sides of the city had major canals that brought ships in from the Euphrates and the sea, which was much closer to the city 4,400 years ago than it is now. One surviving bill of loading lists gold, copper ore, hardwoods, ivory, pearls and other precious stones in a single cargo.

Ur was at its finest under Ur-Namma in around 2100 BC, when large parts of the city were rebuilt and developed, and supported a population of as many as 50,000 people. The great ziggurat was enlarged and inset with mosaics and planted with shrubs and trees. At the summit was the temple of the city's own deity – Nanna, god of the moon. In 2000 BC the inhabitants incurred the wrath of their god because, along with sixteen other Sumerian cities, Ur was sacked by Elamites. This defeat, like all others, was put down to the people failing their god in some way and he in turn leaving them unprotected from their enemies. This destruction was described by a scribe who witnessed the terrifying occasion:

> *'In all its streets, where they were wont to promenade, dead bodies were lying about; In its places, where the festivities of the land took place, the people lay in heaps.'*

Temples and houses were pulled to the ground, valuables looted and many of those not killed were taken into slavery. The city survived but never truly regained its former glory and by the eighteenth century BC Ur was a relatively minor city. During this period of decline the relationship between the Sumerians and the pantheon of gods became strained and the concept of personal gods grew in importance.

These personal gods, who were usually nameless, related directly to the individual – what we might call a guardian angel. A person would inherit their god from his father so when someone said that he 'worshipped the god of his fathers' he was not making a general statement about the status of the god, he was expressing his individual family identity – his birthright. This personal god would look after him and take his cause to the greater gods when necessary, but he demanded obedience and close attention in return. Should the man behave badly his god might desert him. The man was, of course, the arbiter of what was right and wrong; if he felt he had done wrong he would be in fear of his god's reaction, but if he did something that all the world except himself thought was wicked, he was safe. This seems like a very good means of controlling most bad behaviour, along the lines of Jimminy Cricket's catchphrase in the film *Pinocchio*: 'Always let your conscience be your guide.'

At some point in the period of decline between 2000 and 1800 BC a man called Abram decided to leave his city of Ur and head northwards in search of a better life. The direction he chose was almost the opposite direction to that of Dilmun, the sacred land his people aspired to, and the land of their ancestors. At some point in Jewish history Abram became Abraham, the father of the Jewish people. It was clear to us that the ideas that he took with him from Ur must be an important part of what we needed to learn.

We had been prompted to look so far back in time in the hope of gaining a better understanding of both Abraham and his god, as together they represent the earliest encounter in the Bible between a real man (as opposed to a mythical character) and the deity that became the god of the Jews. Neither of us knew very much about the land of Sumer beforehand; indeed this whole period of history was totally unknown to anyone until the middle of the nineteenth century when P. E.

Botta, a French archaeologist, started to uncover major finds in the area now known as Mesopotamia.

The spread of Sumerian culture must have occurred more than 5,000 years ago. One of the best known examples of this cultural development from a North African/south-west Asian origin is the Celts who moved throughout central Europe and finally settled in coastal areas of western Spain, Brittany, Cornwall, Wales, Ireland and Scotland where some social groups remain genetically undiluted by the virtual absence of intermarriage with other peoples. Their knotted, intertwining designs show a strong relationship to art of the Middle East and if there was any doubt remaining, DNA analysis of some modern-day Celts from remote communities has been shown to be a match with North African tribal groups.

No one knows for sure how long Sumer had existed, but from the records that we have consulted it seems reasonable to believe that everything we know of Sumer postdates the Flood; many of the towns and cities were probably even greater before the deluge struck them off the face of the earth.

God, the King, the Priest and the Builders

The Flood is recorded as an ancient happening, even to those that are themselves ancients to us. The Bible tells the story of Noah surviving with his family and assorted animals. In a Mesopotamian flood myth, King Utanapishtim saves seeds as well as animals from the destructive flood, sent by Enlil to terrorise other gods. In Greek mythology, Deucalion and his wife Pyrrha build the Ark to escape the devastating wrath of Zeus.

Guessing is no longer the only way forward; evidence of a major flood just over 6,000 years ago has been found around Ur, where a layer of water-laid clay two and a half metres deep covers an area of more than 100,000 square kilometres. This amounts to a spread across the entire width of the Tigris-Euphrates valley from north of modern Baghdad to the coast of the Persian Gulf in what now includes parts of Iraq, Iran and Kuwait. To leave such a deposit the flood must have been of gigantic proportions and would certainly have swept away human culture throughout what would later be the land of Sumer. This dating for the Flood explains why the Sumerians seemed to have appeared from nowhere in around 4000 BC – virtually overnight in archaeological terms. A full-blown and sophisticated culture without any history or evidence of origins elsewhere is indeed mysterious.

But it is a mystery with a simple solution.

The answer is that the earlier and perhaps even greater period in the history of Sumer was all but lost in the cataclysm and the surviving Sumerians had to rebuild everything from the foundations upwards. The main problem that confronted the remaining people was to find survivors who had been 'keepers of royal secrets'; those who had been high priests of the vanished temples and therefore may have the power of science, especially the science of building. Some must have survived; perhaps their knowledge of the hidden mysteries of nature and science afforded them sufficient warning of the coming Flood, giving them time to head for high ground or indeed build an ark. Whilst the secrets and symbolism of building predated the Flood, we believe that the sudden and urgent need to reconstruct the 'whole world' created a new outlook based on building the square, level and upright foundations of a new order. We are not claiming that this was Freemasonry in any form, but it did give rise to the connection between the science of masonry and the concept of resurrection, as the world itself had undergone 'death' and once again had been raised out of the waters of creation.

Many people may have found the rebuilding of Sumer

too challenging and left the region in search of a new home away from the soft wet clay that covered their land. They carried with them their language which was as sophisticated in grammatical structure as many today. In addition they took the knowledge of farming, the story of their buildings and their gods and their myths. To less advanced peoples of Europe and Asia they must have seemed like gods themselves.

Our problem in writing the story of our investigation is the breadth of topics that we had to dig into, all apparently unrelated but in fact heavily interlinked. At times our studies were buried in source material that ranged from the beginning of time to the modern day. Putting everything we found into some sort of intelligible sequence has proved a challenge, but the more information we collated the clearer the picture became. This was especially true for matters relating to Sumer. The more we looked for the influences upon other cultures the more we found. This book cannot deal with them all, but we give you just one example to show how extraordinary the role of this culture has been.

The concept of a pillar or holy mountain connecting the centre of the Earth with the sky (Heaven) is a Sumerian concept that has found its way into many belief systems including those of northern Asia. The Tartars, Mongols, Buryat and the Kalmyk peoples of northern Asia possess a legend that claims their holy mountain was a stepped building consisting of seven blocks, each one smaller than the last as it rises up towards the sky. Its summit is the pole star, 'the navel of the sky', that corresponds to the base below, 'the navel of the Earth'. This structure describes no building known to these tribesmen but it does fit the description of a Sumerian ziggurat, which was created as an artificial mountain. We can be certain that this connection is no coincidence because the name that these northern nomads give to this sacred, mythical tower is simply ... 'Sumer'². Whilst all Sumerian temples are believed to have followed this format, the most famous of them all is known to us as the Tower of Babel, the great building closely associated with the descendants of Noah. This tower was built in Babylon by Nabopolassar and was a seven-storey ziggurat some three hundred feet in height with a shrine to the god Marduk on its summit. Like the story of the Flood, the story of the Tower of Babel was written down in the Book of Genesis by combining different versions of ancient legends and allowing the authors to make sense of the way they found the world. Chapter Ten of Genesis deals with peopling of the countries of the Earth after the Flood, explaining how the sons of Noah gave rise to new tribes in each part of the world. For the Hebrews the most important of these sons was Sem, who gave rise to the peoples known as Semites (in the course of his impressive six-hundred-year life), which of course include the Jewish people. The next chapter of Genesis tells the story of the Tower of Babel, starting by acknowledging that there was once only one language. It begins:

> '*And the earth was of one tongue, and of the same speech. And when they removed from the east, they found a plain in the land of Sennaar [Hebrew for Sumer], and dwelt in it.*
>
> *And each one said to his neighbour: Come, let us make brick, and bake them with fire. And they had brick instead of stones, and slime instead of mortar. And they said: Come, let us make a city and a tower, the top whereof may reach to heaven: and let us make our name famous, before we may be scattered abroad into all lands and the Lord came down to see the city and the tower, which the children of Adam were building.*
>
> *And He said: Behold, it is one people, and all have*

² Mircea Eliade: *Shamanism, Archaic Techniques of Ecstasy*

*one tongue; and they have begun to do this, neither will
they leave off from their designs, till they have
accomplished them in deed.*

*Come ye, therefore, let us go down, and there
confound their tongue, that they may not understand
one another's speech.*

*And so the Lord scattered them from that place into
all lands, and they ceased to build the city.'*

This neat bit of rationalisation made clear to the Jews
why it was that people spoke different languages, and
because the world had been an empty wilderness before
God decided to repopulate it through the line of Noah, it
was entirely reasonable that He could promise the land of
Canaan to the sons of Sem without a thought for the
people there before them. From His beginnings in Sumer,
'God' took different pathways, to the valleys of the Nile,
the Indus and possibly even the Yellow River, giving rise
to the great religions of the world. All this happened in
very ancient times and one of the very latest variations of
Sumerian theology was the god of the Jews.

The Figure of Abraham, the First Jew

Once Abraham had made the decision to leave Ur the
natural direction was northwards up the route of the two
rivers in search of a new home in which he would be at
peace with his God. The Old Testament tells us that until
Abraham arrived on the scene the ancestors of Israel
'served other gods' (Joshua 24:2), which is hardly surprising as Yahweh, the god of the Jews (and eventually
Christians) was as far in the future for them as the
personal computer was for William Caxton! Even after
Yahweh had made Himself known to His 'chosen people',
allegiance to Him was at best patchy for almost a thousand
years – other gods of all descriptions were just as popular.
When the time came for the Israelites to write down the

history and heritage of their people they looked back through immense periods of time and confirmed ancient oral traditions by fitting in the details that 'should' have been.

Abraham was probably prompted to leave his native city of Ur because the 'godless' nomads from the North that were taking over daily life were no longer acceptable to him; at that time, political discontent would always be expressed as theological discontent. The Bible states that Abraham came out from man-made order, where the rule of God had been rejected. This refers to the unseating of God's representatives upon Earth – the king of Ur and his priests.

Abraham is generally considered to be the first historical figure in the Bible; by contrast, Adam, Eve, Cain, Abel and Noah are representatives of peoples and times that embody early Hebrew ideas and traditions concerning the beginnings of life on Earth. It is probably true that he went on to travel to the land of Canaan, passing himself off as a tent-dweller and en route having heavy discussions with his personal god who naturally travelled with him from Sumer.

The description of Abraham as a nomad like themselves makes a lot of sense, as he and the people who travelled with him were without a land to call their own. The name Hebrew, we discovered, derives from the term 'Habiru' which was apparently a derogatory term (sometimes also shown as 'Apiru') used by the Egyptians to describe the Semitic tribes that wandered like the Bedouin.

As we saw above, the history of the Jews claims descent from Sem, the son of Noah, who was himself a character from Sumerian legend, and later from Abraham who left Sumer to find 'the promised land'. Given that there is no trace of these dwellers of the land of Sumer, we feel that many Sumerians must have trekked north and west to become a significant part of the wandering peoples that became the Jewish nation. However, all the evidence shows that the Jews are not a race or even a historical nation as they have come to believe; they are an amalgam of Semite groups who found commonality in their statelessness and adopted a theological history based on a Sumerian sub-group. Perhaps one in ten of the Israelites at the time of David and Solomon was of Sumerian stock and a tiny fraction of this number were descendants of Abraham, who logically was not the only Sumerian to travel into Canaan and Egypt during the second half of the second millennium BC. The Habiru were identifiable from the nomads who had existed in Egypt, because they were Asiatics who wore strange clothes, were bearded and spoke in an alien tongue.

Abraham is considered to be the key to the founding of Israel, with his God promising him a new home for his people in the land, later identified as part of the northern 'Fertile Crescent' called Canaan. Given the nature of Sumerian deities outlined above, it is likely that Abraham was a priest with a particular god who was his companion and guardian.

The average Jew or Christian reading the Old Testament can be forgiven for thinking that the land of Canaan was a rightful gift of God to His chosen people, but the eventual taking of this 'promised' land was nothing less than theft. If the words of the Old Testament are to be taken at face value, then the Jews and their god were nothing less than wicked. No supernatural justification can excuse the slaughter of so many of the original inhabitants, which is what the Old Testament claims happened.

Most Christians today have a blurred and vague impression of the history of their God who was first the God of the Hebrews. They imagine their all-powerful and loving God as promising His 'chosen people' a beautiful land, flowing with milk and honey (a kind of Sumer or Garden of Eden rediscovered), a land called Canaan. But

Canaan was no uninhabited wilderness where noble wanderers could carve out a new homeland, and Yahweh was no sweet benefactor. He was a storm god, a god of war.

Recent archaeological studies have revealed that the Canaanites whose lands the Israelites seized had an advanced civilisation with walled cities and countless lesser towns and villages and sophisticated systems of food production, manufacture and world trade. If the stories contained in the Bible are accepted, then the original God of the Hebrews was in reality a figurehead who justified invasion, theft and slaughter, with much in common with Genghis Khan!

It amazes us that many Christians believe that the Old Testament is a real historical record of events, despite the fact that it portrays God as a vain, vengeful maniac without a drop of compassion. Besides ordering the slaughter of hundreds of thousands of men, women and children in the cities he ordained should be stolen from the indigenous population, he also was known to attack his friends for no apparent reason. In Exodus 4:24–25 we read that Yahweh decided to kill Moses shortly after commanding him to make his way to Egypt to rescue the 'enslaved' Israelites. He was talked out of this particular piece of bad behaviour by a woman that claimed Moses as her bridegroom. This was later rewritten in the apocryphal work *Jubilees* to move the blame from Yahweh to a spirit called Mastema, which is only a word meaning the 'hostile' side of Yahweh's nature. However, it is clear from the Book of Exodus that God did murder Moses's son when the mood took him.

Whilst nobody has so far managed to date Abraham's travels with any certainty, it is widely accepted that he existed no earlier than 1900 BC and no later than 1600 BC. If he were at the later end of this period he would have been right in the midst of the occupation of Egypt by the so-called 'Hyksos' or 'Shepherd Kings', who invaded and oppressed the Egyptians for over 200 years, from around 1786 to 1567 BC. By now we had come to the view that if there was a connection between Abraham and the Semites who occupied Egypt from the area of Jerusalem, history could start to make a lot of sense. Abraham had set out with his followers for Haran, a major city in modern Syria on the banks of the Balikh river which was on the trading route from Sumer up the Euphrates. From there he took his group into the land of Canaan, which is of course Israel.

Somewhere en route Abraham became concerned that he had done some wrong, because he felt that his personal god was unhappy with him. This was probably the way he rationalised a bad problem or incident that befell his group, translating the calamity as being the result of his god removing protection because he was vexed. So upset was Abraham's God (which equates to how big a problem faced them) that he felt that the only way out was to offer his son Isaac as a sacrifice. A passage in Micah 6:7 shows the seriousness of the situation:

> *'Shall I give my firstborn for my transgression, the fruit of my body for the sin of my soul?'*

Twice in the story of Abraham the words 'after these things' appear; it has long been observed that these were the moments of major crisis where the god of Abraham was to be appeased. This was one of them. Fortunately for the young Isaac, the problem must have eased and his deeply superstitious father changed his mind about the need to kill him. There is, however, a far later story that Isaac was sacrificed by Abraham but subsequently resurrected and Isaac, like Jesus the Christ, is portrayed as a 'suffering servant' who brings salvation and redemption to others.

Somewhere between thirteen hundred and a thousand years passed before the story of Abraham was first written down, having been a tribal legend handed down by word of mouth for that immense period of time. When it came to be written it seemed natural that Abraham's god must have been Yahweh despite the fact that Yahweh was not introduced until the time of Moses. The terminology of Moses when he led the Israelites out of Egypt, telling them that his message came from 'the god of their fathers', is a uniquely Sumerian way of referring to a personal god that belongs to the offspring of Abraham.[3] Whilst only a tiny fraction of these displaced Asiatics (proto-Jews) can have been descendants of Abraham, all of them by this time had bought into the legend and had adopted it as an acceptable and noble reason for their current circumstances.

If Moses had stood in front of these slaves in Egypt and told them his message had come from Yahweh or a god of the whole world who cancels out all other gods, he would have been thought mad.

Unlike previous characters, Abraham did not become the source of a whole tribe that took his name; instead his personal god, 'the god of Abraham' became the distinguishing characteristic of his future people. We find it truly amazing that one Sumerian man's psyche has formed the basis for the three great monotheistic religions of the world.

By now our quest had led us to an understanding of the concept of a personal god and of the people who drew their cultural heritage from a man who had left the Sumerian city of Ur taking his personal god with him. Although we had found comment on a possible resurrection ceremony connected with Isaac, the son of the father of the Jews, this story seemed to be of much later origin. There were no links with Freemasonry to be found here, so we felt that before again picking up the development of the Jewish people we had to look at the greatest ancient

[3] John Sassoon: *From Sumer to Jerusalem*

civilisation of them all, which sprang up around the River Nile. Abraham had spent time in Egypt during the formative period of the Jewish nation and we were aware that later Jews had risen to prominence in the land of Egypt. Ancient Egypt had to be the next object of our enquiries.

CONCLUSION

It was only when we looked at the early development of God that we realised just how little we had ever been taught of early history. We had known nothing of the land of Sumer, the birthplace of civilisation and the place where writing and education first originated. The Sumerians, we had discovered, were the inventors of the pillar and the pyramid which had spread far beyond their own land. The story of the Genesis account of the Flood turns out to be predated by nearly a thousand years by the Sumerian account of creation known as the Enuma Elish.

It was from the Sumerian city of Ur that Abraham came bringing with him his personal god known as the 'God of his fathers' sometime between 2000 and 1600 BC. We had wondered whether Abraham could have had any connections or overlap with the Hyksos kings of Egypt who ruled from 1786 to 1567 BC, but we did not have enough knowledge of the Egyptians to answer the question. And despite a few tantalising hints of characters who figured in Freemasonry, we had found no other links at all with the modern Craft. If we were ever to crack the puzzle, then we would have to come forward again in time and study the civilisation of Egypt.

Chapter Seven

The Legacy of The Egyptians

The Beginnings of Egypt

The Egyptians are most famous for pyramids. As we were to find out, the legacy of this very special people goes far beyond ancient artefacts as they were responsible for some major contributions to our modern way of life. Egyptians today are a mixture of Arab, Negro and European racial types creating a variety of skin tones and features. Many of these are strikingly beautiful, and some are identical to the images found in the ancient tombs within the pyramids. This beauty is not merely skin deep; they have also always been a friendly and, by all normal standards, a tolerant nation. The widespread idea that the 'wicked' Egyptians used Hebrew slaves to build the pyramids is nonsense, not least because there were no Hebrews in existence at that early time.

The earliest Egyptians must have been strongly influenced if not entirely guided by the city builders of Sumer. Perhaps after the Great Flood, some holders of the secrets and mysteries of building made their way northwards and westwards until they discovered another river-based people who sustained their life through a rhythmic and controlled flooding of the river's waters to bring goodness and moisture to the arid desert soil. As Egypt has a level of rainfall that cannot support crops, the Nile has always been central to the continuation of life there and it is little wonder that this river has become virtually synonymous with Egypt.

From the end of August to September an annual inundation flows from the south to the Mediterranean in the north, depositing black mud from which the food of the nation will grow. Too much inundation in a year led to serious flooding, destroying homes and killing livestock and people; too little meant no irrigation and therefore famine. The balance of life was dependent upon the generosity of the Nile.

Ancient records show that when Egyptian soldiers had cause to chase their enemies into Asia they were horrified at the conditions they found in places such as the Lebanon. Vegetation was reported to 'grow at will and to hamper the progress of the troops' and the 'Nile confusingly fell from the sky instead of flowing from the hills'. This reference shows that they had no word for rain and that even this usually vital phenomenon can be unwelcome once you have learned to live without it. They were also disgusted at the temperature of the water they drank from the cool rivers, choosing to lay it out in bowls to warm in the sun before putting it to their lips.

The Nile had supported small, isolated groups of nomadic hunters for tens of thousands of years but during the course of the fourth millennium BC farming settlements began to appear. These developed into proto-kingdoms with territorial boundaries to debate and protect. Fighting became common before there was a general realisation that co-operation was more effective than aggression and harmonious communities emerged. Sometime before 3100 BC a single kingdom was finally established with the unification of the two lands of Upper and Lower Egypt (*See* Appendix 6).

The theology of the earliest periods of the united kingdom was still fragmented, with each city retaining its original gods. Most people believed that in a time before memory gods had lived in the same way that men do, with fears, hopes, weaknesses and ultimately death. Gods were not immortal let alone omnipotent; they aged and died with cemeteries set aside for them. This total mortality is clearly at odds with any definition of a god and raises the question as to why these earlier inhabitants were described as such. Our only guess is that the people who controlled the Nile region over five and a half thousand years ago were foreigners who possessed knowledge or technology which was so advanced compared to the indigenous population that they seemed to be capable of magic. In ancient times magic and religion were inseparable and any powerful person could easily be deemed to be a god.

There is little point in speculating too much about such events lost in prehistory, but perhaps these living gods were the men who possessed the secrets of building that they passed on to the pyramid builders before leaving or dying out as a separate race.

The Egyptians believed that matter had always existed; to them it was illogical to think of a god making something out of absolutely nothing. Their view was that the world began when order came out of chaos, and that ever since there has been a battle between the forces of organisation and disorder. This creation of order was brought about by a god who had always been – he was not only there before men, the sky and the Earth, he was in existence before the time of the gods.

This chaotic state was called Nun, and like the Sumerian and biblical descriptions of pre-creation conditions, all was a dark, sunless watery abyss with a power, a creative force within it that commanded order to begin. This latent power which was within the substance of the chaos did not know it existed; it was a probability, a potential that was intertwined within the randomness of disorder.

Amazingly, this description of creation perfectly describes the view held by modern science, particularly 'chaos theory' which has shown intricate designs which evolve and mathematically repeat within completely unstructured events. It appears that the ancient Egyptians were closer to our physics-based world-view than seems possible for a people that had no understanding of the structure of matter.

The details of this earliest time varied a little within the beliefs of each of the great cities; the most influential were (using their later Greek names) Memphis, Hermopolis, Crocodilopolis, Dedera, Esna, Edfu and Heliopolis, the 'city of the sun' which had earlier been known as On. Central to the theology that underpinned these cities was 'a first moment' in history when a small island or hill arose out of the watery chaos, fertile and ready to support life. In Heliopolis and Hermopolis the spirit that had sparked life bringing order was the sun god Re (also known as Ra), whereas in the great city of Memphis he was identified as Ptar, the earthgod. In either case he was considered to have arrived at self-consciousness at the moment that he caused the first island to emerge from the waters. Re/Ptar became the source of the material benefits that the Egyptians enjoyed, and he was the aspiration for all of the arts, the source of essential skills and, importantly, the mystery of building.

The rulers of Egypt, first the kings and later the pharaohs, were gods as well as men who ruled by divine right. Each king was 'the son of god' who at the point of death became at one with his father, to be god in a cosmic Heaven. The story of the god Osiris tells how this cycle of gods and their sons began:

The sky goddess Nut had five children, the eldest of whom was Osiris, who was himself both a man and a god. As became the norm in ancient Egypt, his sister became his consort; her name was Isis. Helped by his right-hand god, Thoth, he ruled the country wisely and the people prospered. However, his brother Set was jealous of Osiris's success and murdered him, severing his body into pieces which he cast into various parts of the Nile. Isis was distraught, especially as Osiris had produced no heir, which meant that the wickedness of Set would reward him with the right to rule. Being a resourceful goddess Isis did not give in; she had the pieces of the body of Osiris located and brought to her so that she could magically have them reassembled and breathe a last brief moment of life into her brother. She then lowered herself onto the divine phallus and the seed of Osiris entered her. With Isis now bearing his child, Osiris merged with the stars where he ruled the kingdom of the dead.

Isis gave birth to a son called Horus who grew up to become a prince of Egypt and later challenged his father's murderer to a duel. In the ensuing battle Horus cut off Set's testicles but lost an eye himself. Eventually the young Horus was deemed to be the victor and he became the first king.

From that time on the king was always considered to be the god Horus and at the moment of his death he became Osiris and his son the new Horus.

The Stability of the Two Lands

Upper and Lower Egypt were united as a single kingdom around 5,200 years ago. We do not know what problems the people experienced before this time, when the gods lived amongst them, but from the start the unification was held to be absolutely central to the well-being of the bipartite state.

The building of the pyramids fulfilled the same need for the Egyptians as the stepped ziggurats had for the Sumerian people in that they were artificial mountains that helped the king and his priests reach up toward the gods. But far more ancient than the pyramid was the pillar, which had the same function of reaching between the world of men and the world of the gods.

Prior to unification, each of the two lands had its principal pillar to connect the king and his priests with the gods. It seems reasonable to assume that when Upper and Lower Egypt became two kingdoms in one, both pillars would have been retained. Each pillar was a spiritual umbilical cord between Heaven and Earth, and the Egyptians needed a new theological framework to express the relationship of their new trinity of two lands and one heaven.

In the ancient city of Annu (later called On in the Bible and Heliopolis by the Greeks) there was a great sacred pillar, itself named Annu – possibly before the city. This, we believe, was the great pillar of Lower Egypt and its counterpart in Upper Egypt at the time of unification was in the city of Nekheb. Later the city of Thebes, known then as 'Waset', had the title 'Iwnu Shema', which meant 'the Southern Pillar'.

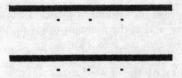

Through analysing later Egyptian beliefs and rituals we believe that these sacred pillars became the physical manifestations of the unification. Symbolising the joining of the lands within one kingdom, the two pillars were considered united by the heavenly crossbeam of the sky god Nut, the three parts forming an architectural doorway. With one pillar in the south and the other in the north, the opening naturally faced east to greet the rising sun. In our opinion this represented stability, and as long as both pillars remained intact the kingdom of the Two Lands would prosper. We found it very pertinent to note that the Egyptian hieroglyph for the Two Lands, called 'taui', was what could be described as two eastward-facing pillars with dots to indicate the direction of the rising sun.

Facing this spiritual doorway from the east, the right-hand pillar was the one in Lower Egypt, corresponding with the Masonic right-hand pillar Jachin, which represents 'to establish'. There is no explanation in the modern ritual as to what this is supposed to mean, but it seemed to us that it stems right back to Lower Egypt; the older of the two lands. According to Egyptian myth it was the place where the world first came into existence from the primordial chaos called Nun and therefore 'Jachin' represents nothing less than the establishment of the world.

For the Egyptians the left-hand pillar marked the connection with Heaven for Upper Egypt and in Masonic ritual it is identified as Boaz, said to mean 'strength or in it is strength'. As we will demonstrate in the next chapter, this association arose when the land of Upper Egypt showed great strength at the time of Egypt's greatest need, at a time when Lower Egypt was temporarily lost to a powerful enemy.

Freemasonry states that the unification of the two pillars represents 'stability' and there is no doubt that describes how the Egyptians felt. As long as both pillars were intact, the kingdom of the Two Lands would prosper. This theme of strength through the unity of two pillars was, we believe, the beginning of a concept that would be adopted in many forms by later cultures including the Jews and, ultimately, Freemasonry.

When studying the history of Egypt we quickly came across an ideal that was absolutely central to their civilisation; it was a concept called Ma'at. In the light of our research you can imagine the amazement and excitement we felt when we found the following definition:

'What characterised Egypt was the need for order.
Egyptian religious beliefs had no great ethical content
but in practical matters there was a general recognition
that justice was a good so fundamental that it was part
of the natural order of things. Pharaoh's adjuration to

the vizier on his appointment made that much clear;
the word used, Ma'at, signified something more compre-
hensive than fairness. Originally the word was a
physical term; it meant level, ordered, and symmetrical
like the foundation plan of a temple. Later it came to
mean righteousness, truth, and justice.[1]

Could there ever be a clearer and more succinct
description of Freemasonry? As Freemasons ourselves, we
don't think so. Freemasonry considers itself to be a
peculiar system of morality based on brotherly love, relief
and truth. The newly made Mason is told that all squares
and levels are sure and certain signs by which to know a
Mason.

Freemasonry is not a religion in the same way that the
concept of Ma'at was not an integral part of some
theological structure or legend. Both are pragmatic real-
isations that the continuance of civilisation and social
progress rests upon the individual's ability to 'do unto
others as you would be done to'. The fact that both use
the design and building of a temple as an example and
observe that human behaviour should be on the level and
upright is surely beyond coincidence. It is rare to find a
moral code in any society that exists outside of a religious
system and it is fair to say that Ma'at and Masonry, stone
for stone, level for level, are a match that could teach the
modern world a great deal.

As we started really to appreciate the strengths and
beauties of Ma'at we felt more and more that Freemasonry, in its current form, was a poor descendant, if
descendant it be. Perhaps people at Grand Lodge identify
with the real values that are indisputably within the Craft,
but we are afraid to say that, in our experience, precious
few work-a-day Freemasons have a clue of the social

[1] P. H. Newby: *Warrior Pharaohs*

splendour with which they are associated. In our modern Western world, decent human values such as pity and charity have become confused with religion, often being described as 'Christian values', which is a great shame. Many Christians are, of course, good and giving people, but we would suggest that this is more to do with their personal spirituality than any theological requirement. Conversely, some of the most horrible, inhuman acts of history have been carried out in the name of Christianity.

Whilst we are dwelling on a modern equivalence of Ma'at, we cannot help but observe that many Socialists and Communists might consider themselves as non-theological seekers of human goodness and equality. If they do, they are wrong. Like a religion their creed demands adherence to a pre-ordained methodology for their 'goodness' to work; Ma'at was pure goodness, freely given. It would seem reasonable to us to say that if Western society ever reaches its broad-based objective of equality and stability, it will finally have rediscovered Ma'at. If modern engineers marvel at the hard-to-emulate skills of the pyramid builders, then what can our social scientists make of a concept like this?

By now we had realised that the link between Masonic values and those of Ma'at was getting hard to deny. Certainly some might claim that Masonry was a fanciful seventeenth-century invention that styled itself on the concept of Ma'at. We felt that that argument does not stand up, as Egyptian hieroglyphics could not be understood until the Rosetta Stone – which translated some hieroglyphics into Greek – was deciphered, a hundred years after the Grand Lodge of England was established. Before then, there was no obvious way that Freemasonry could have known about Ma'at in order to model itself upon it.

In ancient Egypt we had found a civilisation which preached the principles we had learned from the ritual of

Freemasonry, and which also seemed to use a concept of two pillars within its civil structure. There was also a murder and resurrection story linked with the name of Osiris, but it was not connected to the architect of King Solomon's Temple, or even any other temple. We obviously needed to look at the civilisation of the ancient Egyptians in much more detail.

The Egyptians had experienced the limitations of self-seekingness during their formative period and they strove, through the genius of the one all-embracing idea that was Ma'at, to build a new order that would be fit for man and the gods. The future temperament of the Egyptian people has, it seems, been shaped by this spirit of tolerance and friendship. In ancient times Ma'at became a basis for the legal system and soon came to stand for all 'rightness', from the equilibrium of the universe and all heavenly bodies to honesty and fair dealing in daily life. In ancient Egyptian society, thought and nature were understood as two sides of the same reality: whatever was regular or harmonious in either was considered to be a manifestation of Ma'at.[2]

We were aware from our Masonic studies that the appreciation of all that is 'regular' and 'harmonious' is central to all Freemasonry and the right to investigate the hidden mysteries of nature and science is bestowed upon the Fellowcraft, or Second-Degree Freemason.

The story of Set and Osiris we outlined earlier demonstrated to the people of Egypt that the divine rule of legitimate kings could not be broken, even by the powers of disruption and anarchy that Set represented. The concept of Ma'at became the hallmark of a good king and ancient records show that every king and pharaoh was described as 'he that does Ma'at', 'protector of Ma'at' or 'he that lives through Ma'at'. Social order and the balance

[2] Norman Cohen: *Cosmos, Chaos and the World to Come*

of justice cascaded down from the fountainhead of Ma'at, from the living god Horus, the king. Only through the preservation of the divine line of kings could the civilisation of Egypt survive. This presentation of Ma'at and the royal line being inseparable was clearly an excellent mechanism to avoid rebellion and maintain the monarchy.

Not only was the political stability of the country sustained through the embracing of Ma'at, the nation's entire prosperity relied upon it. If the people lived their lives according to Ma'at, the gods would ensure that the Nile brought with it just sufficient flooding to provide the crops to feed the population. Too little or too much flooding would be the fault of the people and the king. Living by Ma'at also ensured victory in war. Enemies of the country were viewed as forces of chaos and would be dealt with because the gods supported the good people of Ma'at.

Eventually Ma'at was perceived as a goddess. She was the daughter of the sun god Re and sailed across the sky with him in a boat, and she is often depicted as standing at the bow ensuring that a true and perfect course is maintained. Ma'at is shown with an ostrich feather in her headdress and an 'ankh' hanging from each arm. The ankh was, and is, the symbol of life. Its form is a crucifix with the top section split down the middle and opened up, to form the shape of an eye or boat in a vertical position.

A further very significant discovery for us was that Ma'at's brother was the moon god Thoth who is often shown at the bow of Re's boat longside Ma'at. Our interest arose after we found references to the fact that Thoth was an important figure in certain early Masonic legends. It was Thoth who taught the Egyptians the art of building and religion and was said to establish what is true. A king that fought evil was said to be 'a good god – an heir to Thoth'.

The Making of a King

As we have shown, Freemasonry has many elements within it that are very Egyptian, from the use of pyramids to the eye of Amen-Ra, but nobody believes that there is any connection. The oral traditions of Freemasonry date the founding of the ritual to be some 4,000 years ago, but nobody believes it to be true. But with the possible ancient Egyptian origin of the pillars and the identical nature of Ma'at we were certainly starting to believe that there was a connection. The starting place for looking for further evidence of similarity of rituals had to be the proceedings of the king and his court.

When the ruler of the two lands died he became Osiris and his son immediately became Horus and the new king. When the king had no son the gods could be relied upon to solve the problem. However, we believe that it was the 'royal Lodge' members who made the decisions, and once the initiation of the new 'master' was complete, the Horus was beyond competition for all time.

One such occasion followed the death of Tuthmosis II in 1504 BC. He had a daughter by his wife, Hatshepsut, but his only son was by a concubine called Isis. This boy succeeded in becoming Tuthmosis III and told the strange story of how the god Amen had chosen him as the new ruler of the two lands. As a young boy he was being prepared for the priesthood and attended the great temple that the master builder Ineni had erected for his grandfather. One day he was present when his father was offering a sacrifice to Amen and the god was brought into the Hall of Cedar Columns, carried within a boat shrine. The god was carried shoulder-high round a circuit of the hall. The boy quite properly prostrated himself on the floor with his eyes closed, but as the shrine reached him, the god forced the procession to stop by increasing his weight so the bearers had to lower the god to the floor. The boy found he had been raised to his feet and at that moment he knew that he had been chosen as the Horus to be, even while his father was still alive.

This story bears a very strong resemblance to the behaviour attributed to Yahweh when he was being carried in the Ark (his boat shrine) by the Israelites. This started us looking at the book of Exodus in a new light and we began to see just how Egyptian the whole story of Moses and his Israelites really is.

In our opinion the coronation ceremony of the new Horus (the incoming king) was also the funeral ceremony for the new Osiris (the outgoing king). These events were conducted in secret and were restricted to the inner sanctum of very senior officials – the Grand Lodge? These obviously included the high priests and the immediate male members of the royal family, but master builders, senior scribes and army generals may also have been included. The funerary liturgy itself was not recorded, but a large amount of the procedure has been pieced together to paint a very illuminating picture.

We found it significant that the accession and the coronation were quite separate events. The accession was normally at first light on the day after the old king's death, but the coronation was celebrated some considerable time later. Despite the extensive records made by the Egyptians, no full account of an Egyptian coronation has ever been found, which suggests that the important parts were entirely a secret ritual transmitted to a tiny group by verbal means alone.

The king-making ritual is known to have been performed in the pyramid of Unas. As in a Masonic Temple, the ceiling of the main chamber represents the sky with stars in place. The commonly accepted view is that the ceremony was celebrated on the last night of the waning moon, beginning at sunset and continuing all night until sunrise,[3] the purpose being a resurrection ritual which

---

[3] J. Spiegel: *Das Auferstehungsritual der Unaspyramide*

141

identified the dead king with Osiris.[4] Resurrection ceremonies were not reserved for the death of the king, indeed they appear to have been quite frequent events conducted in the mortuary temple.[5] It has been suggested that these were rituals to honour royal ancestors, but could it be they were admission ceremonies for new members of the royal inner-sanctum, where they were figuratively resurrected before being admitted to the 'secrets and mysteries' handed down by word of mouth from the time of the gods. It is clear that these secrets would, by definition, require a 'secret society', a privileged group that constituted a society apart. Such a group would have to have had a ceremony of entry; no ancient or even modern élite institution ever fails to have a ceremony of passing from the rank and file into the restricted group.

At the coronation/funeral ritual, the old king was resurrected as the new one, and proved himself a suitable candidate by travelling around the perimeter of the entire country.[6] This was really a symbolic act as the new king was conducted around the temple room to show himself a worthy candidate to those present, which included the god Re and his main assistant. In a Masonic ceremony too, the new member is conducted around the Temple to prove himself a worthy candidate.

After passing all points of the compass he is presented in the south, west and, finally, the east. The first is the junior warden, said to represent the moon (Thoth was god of the moon), the next is the senior warden, representing the sun (Re was god of the sun) and finally the Worshipful Master, who could be said to represent the risen Osiris. Like the Egyptians, Freemasons conduct their ceremonies at night.

The similarities are striking, but what evidence did we have that a secret society existed at all, let alone that the

[4] J. Spiegel: *Das Auferstehungsritual der Unaspyramide*
[5] S. H. Hooke: *The Kingship Rituals of Egypt*
[6] S. H. Hooke: *The Kingship Rituals of Egypt*

principles of the coronation ceremony extended to the initiation of members?

There are many inscriptions indicating a select group whose membership was given knowledge of secret things. An inscription on a false door, now in the Cairo Museum, was written by someone who had been surprised and honoured to be admitted to the inner group of King Teti. It reads as follows:

> 'Today in the presence of the Son of Re: Teti, living forever, high priest of Ptar, more honoured by the king than any servant, as master of secret things of every work which his majesty should be done; pleasing the heart of his lord every day, high priest of Ptah, Sabu. High Priest of Ptar, cup-bearer of the king, master of secret things of the king in his every place ... When his majesty favoured me, his majesty caused that I enter into the privy chamber, that I might set for him the people into every place; where I found the way. Never was done the like to any servant like me, by any sovereign, because his majesty loved me more than any servant of his; because I was honoured in his heart. I was useful in his majesty's presence, I found a way in every secret matter of the court, I was honoured in his majesty's presence.'

This person obviously felt his preferment to this exulted group was very unusual for someone holding his original rank, which indicates that while senior individuals probably had a right to membership, the king and possibly others had the authority to introduce selected people.

Egyptologists have never found an explanation for the expression 'I found the way' in reference to secret matters, but we could interpret this as being instructed in secret knowledge that would thereafter become a way of life. An important point is that the Essenes and Jerusalem Church used the same term for the following of their Law.

Another inscription refers to an unknown builder who was also a member of King Teti's secret holding group:

> *'I did so that his majesty praised me on account of it ...
> [His majesty caused that I enter] into the privy
> chamber and that I become a member of the sovereign's
> court ... His majesty sent me to conduct the works in
> the ka-temple ... and in the quarry of Troja ... I made
> a false door, conducting the work.'*

The nineteenth-century translation 'privy chamber' was selected because it described the modern understanding of a king's personal room, but that does not sit with the term 'sovereign's court' which implies the whole of the palace entourage. Perhaps it could be expressed more meaningfully as: 'His majesty caused that I enter the royal chamber · of restricted access that I might be made a member of the king's élite.'

As we have seen, there was instruction in secret practices for this élite, which must have been bestowed in a ceremony concealed from the view of lesser individuals. This would have represented the highest level of attainment for a man; but for a man who was also a god, the Horus, there was a far more special event – the making of a king. It was an enormously important occasion representing the continued binding of the Two Lands and the prosperity and stability that they enjoyed. However, between the death of the old king and the confirmation of the new one was a point of danger, as it allowed an opportunity for insurrection.

The Egyptologist H. W. Fairman observed:

> *'It is quite evident that at some point in the making of a
> king, in his selection or his crowning, something
> happened that ensured his legitimacy, that automati-
> cally disarmed opposition and claimed and obtained*

loyalty, and that simultaneously made him a god and linked him directly with Egypt's past.'[7]

This view is widely shared, but until now no specific evidence has come to light to identify this key event within the ceremony. In the light of our wider research, a new and startling theory about the special nature of king-making in ancient Egypt occurred to us.

We will start by reviewing what is known of the king-making process:

The coronation took place in two stages. The first stage included anointing and an investiture with a ceremonial collar and apron as well as a presentation of an ankh (symbol of life) and four posies. In the second stage royal insignia were presented and the main ritual began. A crucial part of this was the reaffirmation of the union of the Two Lands and the investiture of the new king by presenting two distinctly different crowns and regalia. At what stage in these proceedings the king became a god is never stated.[8]

We would suggest that the central and crucial process of king-making involved the candidate travelling to the stars to be admitted a member of the society of gods and there to be made the Horus, possibly being spiritually crowned by the dead king – the new Osiris. At some point in the events of the night the old king and the new king journeyed to the constellation of Orion together, one to remain in his celestial home and one to return to rule the land of men.

The new king would have undergone 'death' by means of a potion administered to him by the high priest in the gathering of the inner group of the holders of the royal secrets. This drug would have been a hallucinogenic that slowly induced a catatonic state, leaving the new king as inert as any corpse. As the hours of the night passed the

[7] H. W. Fairman: *The Kingship Rituals of Egypt*
[8] H. W. Fairman: *The Kingship Rituals of Egypt*

potion would have worn off and the newly made Horus would have returned from his sojourn with the gods and past kings of Egypt. The return would have been carefully calculated so that the new king returned to consciousness precisely as the morning star rose above the horizon. From that moment on no mortal would ever think about usurping his power, divinely given in a council of the gods in the heavens above. Once the members of the king's élite, the 'holders of secrets', had decided whom to raise to the sublime and unique degree of Horus, the time for any possible competition had passed.

This logical theory meets all academic criteria for the unknown part of the ceremony that made the new king unassailable. This process would have:

1. Disarmed opposition and ensured total loyalty.

2. Made the new king a god (obviously no man could have conferred this status).

3. Linked him directly with Egypt's past (he had sojourned with all past kings).

Proving the Unprovable

If we had just discovered a new chamber in one of the pyramids and on its walls found a full description of this king-making process, we would have enough proof for most (but no doubt not all) academics to accept our theory as viable. That is not the case, and clearly is not going to happen. The record of events would no more include details of potions administered to the king-to-be than they would give details of the embalming chemistry used on the dead king. As far as the hieroglyphics' failure to record that the candidate for kingship underwent a 'temporary death' and travelled to the stars is concerned, we would say that the main event was the creation of the

Osiris and the creation of the Horus was an implicit event within that. There is some strong circumstantial evidence to support this theory.

Before we go into the reasons why we think this theory is correct, we would like to remind you of the point regarding our two-tier approach to our research. In following this system we have consistently not ignored any proven facts, and have clearly indicated when we have been speculating. In contrast to a number of the other new ideas that we put forward in this book, we cannot provide absolute proof for this process of king-making, but it is a theory that fits the gap in the known Egyptian king-making process, one that is supported by such facts as there are.

The Silent Evidence

Many people have an impression that the Ancient Egyptians built pyramids for the burial of their pharaohs. In fact, the age in which pyramids were built was very short indeed, and it will probably come as a surprise to most readers to learn that Queen Cleopatra was closer in time to the space shuttle technicians than she was to the builders of the Great Pyramid. It is also far from certain that the primary purpose of the pyramids was to provide burial places for dead kings, and the subject of their true meaning is still widely debated. A useful analogy is that St Paul's Cathedral is not the tomb of Sir Christopher Wren, despite the fact that he is buried within it.

The major source of information about the Osiris/ Horus ritual comes from inscriptions called 'the Pyramid Texts', found inside the five pyramids of Saqqara near Cairo, the most important of which was that of King Unas, which dates from the end of the Fifth Dynasty of Kings. Although this is around 4,300 years old it still ranks as a very late pyramid, but the ritual described is considered to be as much as 5,300 years old.

Study of these texts has produced a reconstruction of some of the elements of the ritual, but it is what is missing that is most telling.[9] This reconstruction describes the various chambers ascribing ritual meaning to each; the burial chamber represents the underworld, the antechamber the horizon or upperworld, and the ceiling the night sky. The coffin containing the body of the dead king was brought into the burial chamber where the ritual was performed. The body was placed into the sarcophagus and the members of the élite passed into the antechamber, breaking two red vases as they went. During the ceremony the Ba (the soul) of the dead king left the body and crossed the underworld (the burial chamber) and then, acquiring tangible form in the statue of himself, proceeded to cross the night sky and reached the horizon where it rejoined the Lord of All. The process was then repeated in abbreviated form. For whom? we wondered. The candidate king perhaps?

The most tantalising aspect of this interpretation of the Pyramid Text of Unas is that it contains another ritual running alongside the main ritual. This was a silent ritual, concerned with something like resurrection.[10] It seems to have been observed alongside part of the spoken ritual, starting, as the celebrants passed from the burial chamber into the antechamber, with the breaking of the red vases.

The only tentative explanation for this parallel ritual has been that it was for Upper Egypt, whereas the spoken one was for the more important Lower Egypt. Instead, we wondered if it could have been for the transportation of the temporally dead candidate king, who would have to be resurrected back into human form before the tomb was sealed.

The same ceremonies are known to have been conducted in identical form in other periods and many

[9] J. Spiegel: *Das Auferstehungsritual der Unaspyramide*
[10] J. Spiegel: *Das Auferstehungsritual der Unaspyramide*

experts believe that the ritual is more ancient than the oldest Egyptian history, which is taken to be around 3200 BC.

A prayer from a Sixth Dynasty (2345–2181 BC) pyramid expresses the spirit of the ancient Egyptian theology that was built upon resurrection to the stars and the maintenance of stability on Earth:

> '*Thou standest, ON, protected, equipped as a god, equipped with the aspect of Osiris on the throne of the First of the Westerners. Thou doest what he was wont to do among the spirits, the Imperishable Stars. Thy son stands on thy throne, equipped with thy aspect; he does what thou wast wont to do aforetime at the head of the living by the command of Re, the Great God; he cultivates barley, he cultivates spelt[11], that he may present thee therewith. Ho N, all life and dominion are given to thee, eternity is thine, says Re. Thou thyself speakest when thou hast received the aspect of a god, and thou art great thereby among the gods who are in the estate. Ho N, thy Ba stands among the gods, among the spirits; fear of thee is in their hearts. Ho N, this N. stands on thy throne at the head of the living; terror of thee is in their hearts. Thy name that is on earth lives, thy name that is on earth endures; thou wilt not perish, thou wilt not be destroyed for ever and ever.*'

Consider now a silent prayer for the candidate king about to undergo his brief death to pass through the underworld and meet with the past kings of the Two Lands:

> '*Almighty and eternal Re, Architect and Ruler of the Universe, at whose creative fiat all things first were made, we the frail creatures of thy providence, humbly*

[11] Spelt – an early variety of wheat

> *implore thee to pour down upon this convocation,
> assembled in thy Holy Name, the continued dew of thy
> blessing. More especially we beseech thee to impart Thy
> grace to this thy servant who seeks to partake with us,
> the secrets of the stars. Endue him with such fortitude
> that, in the hour of trial he fail not, but passing safely
> under thy protection, through the dark valley of the
> shadow of death he may finally rise from the tomb of
> transgression to shine as the Stars, for ever and ever.'*

It seems to fit perfectly, doesn't it? Yet this is no
ancient Egyptian ritual; it is the prayer offered up in the
Masonic Third Degree ceremony prior to the candidate
undergoing a figurative death to be resurrected a Master
Mason! We have simply changed the name 'God' to 'Re'
and 'secrets of a Master Mason' to 'secrets of the stars' to
make our point, otherwise it is unchanged.

What then of the suggestion that a narcotic drug was
employed to 'transport' the new king to the stars and back
again? As we have already stated, there would be no
record of this potion as there is no real record of the
coronation ritual at all. It seems reasonable that there is no
record of the massively important moment of king-making
because no one knew what it was; the candidate took the
potion, travelled to the stars and returned the king and
Horus. All his earthly team had to do was present him
with the trappings of office and ask no questions about the
business of the gods, of which the king was now one. The
king himself would no doubt have had strange dreams
under the influence of the drug but was not, of course,
going to reveal anything. By this process the king-making
ceremony put the new Horus beyond all dispute as the
divine choice of the gods as ruler of the Two Lands.

Narcotic drugs have been used in religious ceremonies
in almost every ancient human culture and it would be
surprising if such an advanced culture as that of the early
Egyptians did not possess very sophisticated knowledge

concerning their use. The question is not, could they have used such drugs? It is, why do we think that they would not have used them? The expected method for a man to reach the heavens in death was to traverse the bridge in life, usually with the aid of narcotics.

> *The funerary bridge, a link between the Earth and Heaven which human beings use to communicate with the gods, is a common symbol of ancient religious practices. At some point in the distant past such bridges had been in common use, but following the decline of man it has become more difficult to use such bridges. People can only cross the bridge in spirit either as a dead soul or in a state of ecstasy. Such a crossing would be fraught with difficulty; not all souls would succeed, as demons and monsters could beset those who were not properly prepared. Only the 'good' and the skilled adepts who already knew the road from a ritual death and resurrection could cross the bridge easily.* [12]

These ideas on Shamanism fit what we know of Egyptian beliefs on every level. Demons were warded from the passage of the Osiris by spoken curses, but in fact his course would be quite safe for two reasons. First he lived by Ma'at, and so was a good man; secondly he knew the way from travelling the 'bridge' when he was made Horus. Perhaps the passage of the new king was conducted in silence so as not to alert demons. The new king could then follow the dead king across the heavens, learning the way so that he could in turn lead the next king at his own death.

We later found that Henri Frankfort had detected that the rebirth rites for the dead king were conducted in parallel with the coronation rituals of his heir. [13] This

---

[12] Mircea Eliade: *Shamanism: Archaic Techniques of Ecstasy*
[13] Henri Frankfort: *Kingship and the Gods*

confirmed our view of a double ceremony for the dead and the living kings. Furthermore, a passage from the Pyramid Texts shows that the new Horus was considered to be the morning star, when the new Osiris says:

> '*The reed-floats of the sky are set in place for me, that I may cross by means of them to Re at the horizon. ... I will stand among them, for the moon is my brother, the Morning Star is my offspring ...*'[14]

We believe that the Egyptians adopted much of their theology and technology from the secrets of the city builders of Sumer and that the Sumerians were extremely well versed in the use of drugs for religious purposes.

The next question we had to consider was whether or not such resurrection rituals were exclusively reserved for coronations. The answer seemed to be no, they were not. By the end of the Old Kingdom (circa 2181 BC) some form of royal resurrection ceremony was known to be held annually, and as the Middle Kingdom progressed, the ritual is known to have been applied to well-to-do people, possibly outside the king's central group. These non-royal people would almost certainly not have had the secret knowledge of the royal group.

The Morning Star Shines Again

Now we need to consider a vital element of Egyptian theology. As we said above, the theology of Egypt was very much a development of Sumerian beliefs. Moreover, future Hebrew (and therefore Christian) beliefs were a development of Egyptian theology remerged with later Babylonian versions of the same source material. We had already come across a common identification of the morning star as the symbol of rebirth in the Essene

---

[14] *Pyramid Texts* 1000–1

Community/Jerusalem Church and Freemasonry; we now found the theme again in ancient Egypt. Pyramid Texts 357, 929, 935 and 1707 refer to the dead king's offspring (the Horus) as being the morning star.

It is interesting to note that the Egyptian hieroglyphic for the morning star has the literal meaning 'divine knowledge'. This seems to support our thesis that the candidate for kingship was raised to the status of the new god/king Horus by sharing the secrets of the gods in the land of the dead, where he learned the great secrets before returning to Earth as the morning star broke the horizon just before sunrise.

Hieroglyph for the Morning Star

As we were working on this phase of our research, a new book was published which claimed to throw new light on the purpose of the pyramids by detailing their astrologically inspired design. Robert Bauval and Adrian Gilbert put forward a well argued and researched case that shows how the Giza pyramids are arranged in a deliberate imitation of the stars of Orion's Belt.[15] They also make reference to rituals that were conducted in the stepped ziggurats of ancient Mesopotamia involving the 'Morning Star, seen as the great cosmic goddess Ishtar'. This evidence from a totally different route confirmed what we had found independently by working backwards from the rituals of modern Freemasonry.

In Egypt the new king, the Horus, is the morning star, arising (like the raised Freemason) from a temporary and figurative death. The morning star, usually identified with

[15] Robert Bauval and Adrian Gilbert: *The Orion Mystery*

Venus, was proving itself to be a very important link in our chain.

But, however fascinating were the parallels with the Essenes and Freemasonry which we discovered in Egyptian practices, there remained an obvious question. Was there a route for the ideals of Ma'at, the secrets of the Egyptian Kings and a detailed resurrection ritual to get through to the Essenes? To find out, we needed to look more closely at the Osiris story.

The peculiar fate of Osiris – his brutal murder and dismemberment by his brother Set, followed by his resurrection and exaltation to the stars – is a very early example of the vindication and reward of innocent suffering. Osiris's fate gave hope to the lower orders of society and gave a meaning and purpose to suffering. The cult of Osiris came to be a benign funerary cult, accessible to the ordinary Egyptian. When other gods remained remote in their temples, Osiris could be worshipped anywhere by anybody, alongside the local god.[16]

Change 'the fate' to 'his crucifixion' and this description could be about Jesus the Christ. We now felt positive that we would find the connections we suspected to exist. We did not have to wait long for a powerful hypothesis to emerge. As we were in the midst of analysing the next key period of Egyptian history, the central character of our research, Hiram Abif, emerged out of the mists of time to confront us.

CONCLUSION

We felt at the very least that it was probable the first Egyptian builders had originated in Sumer and that these Sumerian immigrants had brought technology and theology to Egypt. The fledgling Egyptian civilisation was well

---

[16] N Cohen: *Cosmos, Chaos and the World to Come*

established by about 3100 BC and the two kingdoms of Upper and Lower Egypt had already been twinned as two halves of a new single state. This unification of two kingdoms with one divine ruler was to prove important as our investigations developed.

The king's right to rule was based on the story of the murder of Osiris by Set and told of how Isis reconstructed Osiris's body and then had a son, Horus, by him. Horus went on to take the kingdoms of Egypt back from Set in a mighty battle. Each king thereafter was considered to be an incarnation of Horus; literally 'the son of God'. When the king died he merged with Osiris (God the Father) and went to live in the kingdom of the dead and his son became Horus the next living god king.

We had detected that the security of the whole state depended on the two kingdoms working together and this co-operation was symbolised by two pillars, one in the north and one in the south, united by a heavenly crossbeam forming a doorway facing the rising sun. This powerful concept of strength through the unity of two pillars is still a central theme of Masonic ritual and was a theme with which we felt very familiar.

This was not the only link we had found with modern Freemasonry: the concept of Ma'at, meaning righteousness, truth, and justice within a level and ordered symmetrical scheme, summed up the principles we had learnt as Freemasons. This humanistic, ethical code was not a religious commandment, neither was it a legal requirement – it was goodness freely given for its own sake.

We knew that Freemasonry could not have copied this idea from Egyptian history because the concept of Ma'at, long lost to the world, remained so until the decoding of the Rosetta Stone. This stone, which opened the way to translating the hitherto incomprehensible Egyptian hieroglyphics, was not found until nearly a hundred years after the foundation of the Grand Lodge of England.

At this point we had established two circumstantial links with Freemasonry; firstly there was the hint of a resurrection ceremony connected to the Osiris legend; and secondly Ma'at, at first a great truth and later a goddess, was sister to Thoth, the god of the moon and another figure of great significance in Masonic myth.

Whilst investigating the king-making ceremony we had found that although the funerary liturgy itself was not recorded, it involved a resurrection ritual which identified the dead king with Osiris. We also found evidence that suggested that similar ceremonies were much more widely used than just at the making of a king and that they seemed to involve a secret society. The evidence for this secret society we found in translations of inscriptions on artefacts in Cairo Museum — texts which again could not have been translated prior to the discovery of the Rosetta Stone, which happened long after Freemasonry had publicly announced itself.

With the added insight of our Masonic training we had been able to attempt a reconstruction of the Egyptian king-making ceremony which fitted all the known facts.

The most exciting link with the Masonic Third Degree came from references in the Pyramid Texts to the king representing the morning star, which had been such an important part of our own Masonic raising ceremonies. The Egyptian hieroglyphic for the morning or divine star was the same five-pointed star used to represent the five points of fellowship of the Masonic Third Degree. This obviously encouraged us to investigate the Egyptian connection more closely because although we had suspicions, we lacked proof of any practices that were unarguably Masonic.

Chapter Eight

The First Freemason

Much of our energies had been devoted to unravelling the mysteries of Egypt, but while we were starting to focus on particular characters and events which had meaning for us as Freemasons, we were always looking for patterns in history. Sometimes the conventional interpretation of historical events is jarred by facts that don't fit into the accepted pattern. When these historical glitches occur, it is sometimes possible to glimpse a new truth behind the accepted face of history. It was just such a glitch which first directed our attention to the Hyksos period of Egyptian history. Today Egyptologists label this era as the Second Intermediate Period (1782–1570 BC), falling between the Middle Kingdom and the New Kingdom. Here was a major perturbation in the smooth flow of Egyptian history. It was the sort of catastrophe from which few civilisations ever recover, yet we knew that Egypt had not only recovered it but had gone on to reach new heights of achievement, despite the total decline of its traditional monarchy and the domination of the native population for six generations by a group of foreign invaders whom we had first come across by the romantic name of 'The Shepherd Kings'. Why this had happened was a major mystery.

We felt it highly likely that the era of change – from the Egyptian kings to the Hyksos rulers, then back again to the Theban monarchy – would provide further clues, so we concentrated on this period using all possible sources of information, including the Old Testament.

Hiram Abif Discovered

If there was a connection from ancient Egypt to the Jews of the first century AD, it almost certainly would be through Moses, the founder of the Jewish nation who had been an adopted member of the Egyptian royal family. The possibility of finding such a link seemed remote but we kept searching as we reviewed the facts known to us.

Having undergone the Third Degree of Freemasonry, the one that conferred the status of Master Mason on us, we have to say that the references to Hiram Abif and the Old Testament baffled us both. The following words are spoken by the Worshipful Master when first introducing the ancient character to the candidate:

> *'Death has no terror equal to that of the stain of falsehood and dishonour. Of this grand truth, the annals of Freemasonry afford a glorious example in the unshaken fidelity and untimely death of our Grand Master, Hiram Abif, who lost his life just before the completion of King Solomon's Temple, at the construction of which, as you are doubtless aware, he was the principal architect.'*

There is a very clear assumption that the educated candidate should be aware of this character from his existing knowledge, presumably from the Bible. Neither of us had ever heard of such a person and no version of the Bible that we have come across makes any mention of an architect for Solomon's Temple. Because Hiram, King of Tyre provided the labour and the cedar, some have connected the two, but there is no possible link apart from the fact that they share a name. We, like all Freemasons of our acquaintance, accept the Masonic hero despite knowing that he was not recorded as being involved in the creation of Solomon's Temple.

If the name of the master builder had been known to the authors of the Book of Kings, especially in the light of his murder, it seems almost impossible that they would ignore such a key person when telling this story. At first this suggested to us that he must be a much later invention, possibly representing another important character whose role had been played down in history for the sake of a single-strand drama. The only reasonable explanation that we had come across regarding the actual name of the Masonic hero was that Hiram meant 'noble' or 'kingly' in Hebrew, while Abif has been identified as old French for 'lost one', giving a literal description of 'the king that was lost'. By the time we had come to studying ancient Egypt we had stopped trying to find Hiram Abif, because we had no leads at all and thought it an impossible task.

Yet strangely, it was Hiram Abif who emerged from the distant past to find us!

Once we had researched in a far wider manner than we ever set out to, thereby becoming familiar with many details from ancient Egypt, a potential solution to the greatest of all Masonic mysteries slowly unveiled itself. Convinced that there was a secret ceremony central to the king-making of ancient Egypt based on a 'temporary death' and resurrection, we set ourselves the task of trying to understand how the Israelites could have come into possession of these very special mysteries.

Our starting point in connecting the two was easy. The Bible spells out the importance of Egypt in the history of the Jewish people, with such major characters as Abraham, Jacob, Isaac, Joseph and Moses all heavily involved in Egyptian events. The last two of these are presented as very senior members of the royal court, albeit at different times. The later chapters of the Book of Genesis paint a picture of tolerance and co-operation between the Egyptians and the proto-Israelites, yet Exodus depicts a situation of great bitterness between the two peoples. The reasons for this rapid change in relationship became much clearer once we came to understand the period of the so-called Hyksos kings – and the person who was Hiram Abif turned out to be the central figure to the whole story.

The Collapse of the Egyptian State

Working through the development of Egypt we arrived at the low point of that nation's history, late in the Middle Bronze Age, around the end of the third millennium BC. Egypt entered a period of continual decline with weak government and social breakdown. Foreigners from the desert spread across the land, robbery became commonplace and the open, relaxed lifestyle of the people gave way to mistrust and a tendency to rely on themselves for security rather than trust the state. Slowly the spirit and vigour that had made Egypt great sapped away, leaving the country exposed to the wanton gaze of outsiders. Inevitably, invasion followed and the Egyptians became dominated by a people known as the 'Hyksos'. The Hyksos did not suddenly sail up the Nile and demand surrender; the process was far more subtle than that. They infiltrated Egyptian society smoothly and over a great period of time until they were in a strong enough position to force their control on the Two Lands. History provides us for some very specific dates for this loss of national vigour, called today 'the second intermediate period' putting it between the years 1780 and 1560 BC, at the end of much longer section of Egyptian history now called the Middle Kingdom.

We found that 'Hyksos' did not mean 'shepherd kings'; it actually came from the Egyptian term 'hikau-khoswet', meaning simply 'desert princes'. They are believed to have been a mixed group of Asiatic people, mainly

Semites, who appeared out of Syria and Palestine. Their final seizure of power inevitably met with resistance which resulted in the burning of some unco-operative towns and the destruction of temples, culminating in the complete sacking of the Egyptian capital Memphis in about 1720 BC. The Hyksos were no believers in Ma'at and in their search for power they initially dealt cruelly with anyone they felt was an obstacle to their cause; but once established, they were not difficult oppressors, and the Egyptian authorities appear to have largely collaborated with them. By the eighteenth century BC they had extended their rule right into Upper Egypt.

Coming largely from the countries we would now call Israel and Syria, the Hyksos all spoke the same western Semitic language as the people who would later become known as Israelites. The question that immediately came into our mind was: were the Hyksos in fact Jews? The answer had to be no, not in the full sense of the word, because the concept of Judaism did not exist at that time. The scattered nomadic tribes which the Egyptians called the Habiru (Hebrew) were a range of Semitic Asiatics who spoke the same language but were in no way an identifiable race. It is, however, extremely likely that the Hyksos/Habiru peoples did, at a later date, form a substantial part of the tribal co-operative that became the tribes of Israel and eventually the Jewish people. There are several reasons why we believe that there is a direct connection between the Hyksos and the Jews, not least the fact that the first mention in the Bible of the Jewish people coincides precisely with the time when the Egyptians chased the Hyksos out of their land – to Jerusalem!

Recent geological evidence is beginning to show that the desert state of much of the Middle East is a relatively recent occurrence, and that as recently as five or six thousand years ago the terrain around Egypt was a much greener and more fertile area. Records show that there were sudden and dramatic periods of climatic change during the second millennium BC, bringing drought as a seasonal problem across the entire Near East. As believers in the principle of Ma'at, the Egyptians were a generous people and provided the wandering Habiru with water and land on which to graze their sheep when conditions outside the Nile Delta became unbearable. A clear example of this is given in Genesis 12:10:

> *'And there came a famine in the country. And Abram went down into Egypt, to sojourn there; for the famine was very grievous in the land.'*

During the period of decline in Egyptian society, control of these water-hungry Asiatics was poor, and they were allowed to stream in in huge numbers, and were not required to leave when their needs had been met. Without an immigration policy the country became overrun by these nomadic people; furthermore, they were followed by far more sophisticated people, ones who saw an opportunity for gain in the general confusion. These Semitic city dwellers, the Hyksos, were much more warlike than the overconfident Egyptians and possessed highly advanced weapons including horse-drawn chariots which allowed them to take what they wanted without significant resistance from the peace-loving indigenous population.

The Hyksos Kings

It is probable that during the Hyksos period the Habiru tribesmen enjoyed a higher social status and became more assimilated into city life. Prior to this, the only way for one of these desert herdsmen to improve his lot and enjoy the benefits of city life had been to offer himself as a slave to an Egyptian family. This arrangement was not slavery in the sense that most people today might imagine it; it was more like being a servant with a lifetime contract. Wages may not have been good but the quality of life would have been far higher than the vast majority of people could ever aspire to.

Once the Hyksos kings became settled they started to sponsor the building of temples as well as the production of statues, reliefs, scarabs, general works of art and some of the finest literary and technical works of the time. They appear to have had little cultural heritage of their own and quickly adopted Egyptian ways and attitudes. These new rulers started to write their names in Egyptian hiero-glyphics, took the traditional titles of the Egyptian kings and even gave themselves Egyptian personal names. The Hyksos kings at first spread their influence to rule Lower Egypt, the larger and lusher of the two lands, from their newly created city of Avaris where they adopted as their state god a deity which had been especially revered in the area where they had first settled. This god was Set or Seth, who had similarities to their previous Canaanite god Baal. They centred their theology on Set but they also accepted Re as a major god and they honoured him in the throne names that they gave themselves. Later they controlled both the Two Lands from the old capital of Memphis. It is fair to say that there was something of a symbiotic relationship by which the invaders gained culture and theological refinement and the Egyptians new technology such as chariots and other weaponry, includ-ing composite bows and bronze swords to replace their simple and ancient designs. They also gained a further important thing from the Hyksos; cynicism. They had been far too open and easygoing for their own good in the past, with little regard for the proactive defence of their country. The experience of the Hyksos period provided a powerful lesson and a new positive outlook emerged that laid the foundation for the resurgence of the Egyptian spirit in what we call the New Kingdom.

Although they had lost control of the old capital, Memphis, elements of the true Egyptian monarchy continued an existence in the Upper Egyptian city of

Thebes. From records it is clear that the Thebans acknowledged the sovereignty of their Asiatic overlords, with whom they seem to have been on good terms. As in time the Hyksos kings became absorbed into much of Egyptian culture and religious practices, inevitably a politico-theological problem emerged. The invaders started to want spiritual power as well as physical power. For instance, the Hyksos ruler King Khyan (or Khayana) assumed the Egyptian throne-name of 'Se-user-en-re' as well as the titles 'the Good God' and 'the Son of Re', and in addition created for himself the Horus name 'Embracer-of-Regions', a title that suggested worldwide domination. This claim by the Hyksos to be 'the son of god' must have outraged the Egyptian people at every level.

Here, we believe, is a major issue which has not yet been sufficiently examined by modern Egyptologists. We now know that there was a very special point during the king-making process that made the new Horus unchallengable; but the would-be Hyksos kings, for all their stately power and their emulation of Egyptian religion, were excluded from this, the ultimate accolade. How could a foreigner simply change his name from Khyan to Seuserenre and style himself Horus without undergoing the highly secret initiation process known only to the real kings of Egypt and their inner sanctum? The simple answer is that he couldn't. It is completely beyond the bounds of reason to think that the Egyptians would have shared their greatest secrets with these brutish foreigners; but because Khyan desperately wanted this powerful title and had no access to it legitimately, he had little option but to assume the empty title. Superficially relationships between the Egyptians and their new masters were good, but resentment must have been high. Furthermore, despite aping Egyptian styles and customs, the Hyksos remained essentially different. The grafting of the Hyksos onto Egypt was at best superficial. They spoke Egyptian with an amusing accent, wore beards (Egyptians shaved daily unless in mourning), they had a strange dress sense and they transported themselves in wheeled machines they called chariots which were pulled by horses instead of donkeys.

The Loss of the Original Secrets

We continued our research into the Late Middle Kingdom and felt sure that the tensions between the new Hyksos kings and the true royal line must have reached a peak with these false claims to being the Horus. If we had been right about the secret resurrection ceremony of the legitimate kings, there had to be trouble brewing with these presumptuous interlopers pressing to obtain the royal secrets once they had taken everything else. Taking control of daily life was one thing; pushing into the realm of the gods, both heavenly and earthly, must have been intolerable. Once the Hyksos kings were of the third and fourth generation to be born in Egypt and had embraced Egyptian theology, it seems almost certain that they felt entitled to possess the secrets of the Horus, that they considered themselves to *be* the Horus. Perhaps more importantly, they wanted to become Osiris in death and be a star to shine for ever and ever. Having become kings of Egypt, why should they die a Canaanite death, when to die as Horus would give them eternal life?

This was a complex and fascinating epoch and we studied and restudied the events and characters involved. Something about the period in general and about the attitude and actions of the true Egyptian king – Seqenenre Tao II in particular – started to niggle at the back of Chris's mind. This king was restricted to the Upper Egyptian city of Thebes towards the end of the Hyksos rule, and for a whole variety of small reasons Chris had a feeling that the story of Hiram Abif could have started with a power battle between Seqenenre Tao II and the important Hyksos king Apepi I, who took the Egyptian throne name A-user-re ('Great and powerful like Re') and the title 'King of Upper and Lower Egypt – Son of Re'.

For months Chris mulled over the period, looking for more and more evidence that would dispel or confirm some substance to the niggle. Slowly that niggle solidified into a strong hunch. Chris tells how that came about:

'I knew that the Hyksos king Apepi was also known as Apophis. It was a highly significant piece of nomenclature that alerted me to his involvement in a spiritual battle that was nothing less than a re-run of the founding of the nation by Osiris, Isis and the first Horus. I became convinced that Apophis was a man who deliberately set out to get the secrets of the true Egyptian kings for himself – come what may.

'The Hyksos people were warlike and self-centred. They adopted as their chief god Set, the murderer of his brother Osiris; the god who every Egyptian king expected to become. By identifying themselves with Set the Hyksos demonstrated their disdain for the Egyptian people and their allegiance with the forces of evil. The concept of Ma'at must have seemed foolish to Apophis and symptomatic of the "softness" that had allowed his forebears to take the Egyptians' country from them. The opposite of Ma'at was called "Isfet," which stood for negative concepts such as selfishness, falsehood and injustice, and according to Egyptian mythology the leader of these embodiments of "Isfet" was an evil, dragon-like, monstrous serpent god called ... Apophis. I was amazed to find that this power of evil had the same name as the Hyksos king.

'The epithets of this anti-Ma'at monster included "he of evil appearance" and "he of evil character", and for the Egyptians he was the very embodiment of primordial chaos. The serpent that the Hyksos king had named himself after was depicted as being deaf and blind to all things; it could only scream through the darkness and was chased away every day by the rising of the sun. It is little wonder that the greatest fear of every Egyptian was that the wicked serpent Apophis would, one dark night, win his battle with Re and the next day would never come. To defend themselves from this everpresent threat, liturgies were recited daily in the temples of the sun god to give support to this continual battle between the forces of light and darkness.

'I discovered that a vast collection of liturgies has been found describing itself as *The Book of Overthrowing Apophis*. This was a secret book kept in the temple containing hundreds of magical words to ward off the evils of Apophis and provided the novice reader with instructions on how to make wax figures of the serpent which could be trodden into a shapeless mess, destroyed by fire or dismembered with knives. The book required the student to carry out these acts every morning, noon and night and, most especially, at moments when the sun became obscured by clouds.

'Four hundred miles to the south of Avaris, the city of Thebes continued its line of Egyptian kings, although they bowed to the power of the Hyksos and paid to Apophis's tax collectors the dues demanded. Despite being isolated and impoverished, the Thebans struggled to maintain the customs of the Middle Kingdom period that they held dear. They were cut off by the Hyksos (and their puppet rulers of Kush) from the timbers of Syria; the limestone of Tura; the gold of Nubia; the ebony and ivory of the Sudan; and the quarries at modern Aswan and Wadi Hammamat, which forced them to improvise their building techniques. Given the severe limitations they faced they managed to produce excellent buildings, albeit often in mud-brick rather than stone. Nonetheless, the increasing hardships appear to have brought about a resurgence of the spirit and determination that had first made Egypt great, and whilst their quality of life continued to suffer, their learning and culture began to develop. This small city kingdom started to lift itself out of depression and disorder and to stand its ground against the Asiatics in Lower Egypt.

'My hunch was that around the thirty-fourth year of Apophis's rule he instructed the king of Thebes to provide him with the secrets of becoming Osiris so that he could achieve the eternal life which was his due as "rightful" king of the Two Lands. The Theban King Seqenenre Tao II was a tough young man who considered himself to be the Horus and was not interested in parting with his birthright to anyone, let alone a bearded Asiatic named after the "serpent of darkness". His instant rebuff must have quickly built up bad feeling between the two, and King Apophis started to use his power against Seqenenre in every way he could. A particularly significant example of this conflict was an order sent by Apophis over the four hundred miles from Avaris to Thebes complaining to Seqenenre about noise:

> *'Have the hippopotamus pool, which is in the east of the city, done away with. For they do not let sleep come to me by day or by night.'*[1]

'This message was no silly game to simply humiliate Seqenenre. It illustrates a very clear power struggle to establish nothing less than the divine right to rule. Apophis already had all the state power he could need, but what he did not have was the secret of resurrection and the blessing of the gods. His message was deeply political. The Thebans had revived the ritual harpooning of hippopotami in their pool to the east of the city; it was an ancient holy rite intended to guarantee the safety of the Egyptian monarchy. This was clearly bound to irritate Apophis in itself, but it hurt even more because the

[1] W. Keller: *The Bible as History*

hippopotamus was a form of the chief Hyksos god, Set, so a double insult was delivered to the Asiatic king.

'The hippopotamus ritual consisted of five scenes which included a prologue, three acts and an epilogue. The purpose of the play was to commemorate the victory of Horus over his enemies, his coronation as king of the two lands and his ultimate triumph over those who opposed him. The king naturally played himself as Horus and in Act One he casts ten harpoons into a male hippopotamus alternately as Horus, lord of Mesen and Horus the Behdetite representing Lower and Upper Egypt. In Act Three the victim is twice dismembered as a representation of Set.

'The power struggle may have continued for some time, but I believe that at some point Apophis decided to end the impudence of the Theban king and extract the secrets from Seqenenre once and for all. The outcome was to be the killing of Seqenenre closely followed by the expulsion of the Hyksos and a return to the rule of the Egyptian kings.'

By now Chris felt that his original niggle, which had turned into a hunch, was now shaping up into a respectable, if tenuous, hypothesis. He was ready to discuss it in detail with Robert, who quickly agreed that we just might have a candidate in Seqenenre for the origin of Hiram Abif.

The Biblical Evidence

Our next step was to consider an additional important information source which could give us another perspective on the Apophis-Seqenenre struggle. Our insight into the events of the sixteenth century BC had been developed by a new merging of information drawn from written Egyptian history and Masonic ritual; now the Book of Genesis could be added to the mix because, surprisingly, we found it to be rich in information about this period.

The key figures who could, potentially, have any connection with Seqenenre and Apophis are Abraham, Isaac, Jacob, Joseph, and, possibly, Moses. Dating these characters has proved far more difficult for all experts than dating those of the later periods of Jewish history, from David and Solomon onwards, when there are much clearer landmarks in history to cross-refer to. The logical starting point in trying to identify where these famous five figures sit in history was Joseph, the Asiatic or proto-Jew who, the Bible tells us, came to occupy the highest office in Egypt, second only to the king himself.

The story of Joseph, from his being sold into slavery by his brothers to his rise to power in Egypt and his famous coat of many colours (derived from a later, incorrect, translation for a simple long-sleeved coat), is well known and is now generally accepted as being based on a real person. However, the legend was heavily embellished by those later scribes who first committed the oral tradition into a written form. References to camels as beasts of burden and the use of coins are both historically impossible, as neither existed until many hundreds of years after the latest possible dating of Joseph.

According to the Book of Genesis, Abraham first went down into Egypt when he was seventy-five and had his son Isaac when he was a hundred years old, dying seventy-five years later. Isaac had two sons, Jacob and Esau, when he was sixty years of age and Jacob had twelve sons, the second youngest of which was Joseph. It seems safe to assume some exaggeration here, particularly regarding Abraham's age. To work out more realistic time spans, we can start by assuming for a moment that Joseph was at the height of his powers in Egypt between the ages of thirty and sixty. We can then work backwards to a probable time span between his high office and his great-grandfather Abraham's first arrival in Egypt.

Jacob was apparently fond of fathering children by as many women as he could, including both his wives and their maidservants. Joseph was one of the youngest and it is probable that his father was relatively old at the time of his birth, so let us assume that Jacob was sixty. We can accept the biblical age of sixty for Isaac fathering Jacob, but we will have to reduce Abraham's hundred years down to a more tenable seventy years. These ages follow the spirit of the information given in the Bible without accepting the obviously impossible extremes that have crept into the story.

The Book of Genesis tells us that Sarah, the wife of Abraham, was a very beautiful woman and that Abraham feared that the Egyptians would kill him to steal her for themselves, so he passed her off as his sister. The logic is hard to follow, but as they are both later described as old and long past love-making when Isaac is eventually born, it does indicate that both of them were young people when they first went down to Egypt.

At the other end of our scale we get one clue in the story of Joseph that helps us identify an historical date. That clue is the reference to the use of a horse-drawn chariot which clearly places the event in the Hyksos period, because these were vehicles of the Asiatic rulers not the native kings. It is generally accepted that there were Semitic elements among the invaders, and so this would be a period during which Semitic immigrants would be favourably received. Many scholars have commented that the change in dynasty which followed the expulsion of the Hyksos might well correspond to the rise of 'a new king who did not know Joseph' (Exodus 1:8) and that any foreigners left in Egypt would be liable to such treatment as is described in the early chapters of Exodus.[2]

There is little room for doubt that the migration of the

Hebrews to Egypt during a drought in Canaan and the rise of the Hyksos rulers in Egypt parallels the political ascension of Joseph. The pharaoh of Joseph's period welcomed the Hebrews to his kingdom because he was one of the Hyksos and a Semite like themselves. It has been suggested before now that when the Hyksos were overthrown, the new Egyptian monarch regarded the Hebrews as consorts of the Hyksos and therefore proceeded to enslave them.

The experts seem to have been slow coming to the obvious conclusion of this evidence. Verses 8 and 9 in Exodus provide the clearest possible dating for Joseph and the unidentified pharaoh:

> '*In the mean time there arose a new king over Egypt, that knew not Joseph. And he said to his people: Behold, the people of the children of Israel are numerous and stronger than we.*'

We had now come to the firm conclusion that Joseph was contemporary with Apophis, and therefore with Seqenenre Tao.

We had to remind ourselves that we cannot take any of the words of the Old Testament as absolute evidence because of the gulf of time between the events and those who eventually recorded them. Remember the references to camels and coinage; they can be wrong in detail. Nonetheless, the broad shapes are probably a good indicator of what actually happened all that time ago. In simple terms the Bible tells us that Joseph became the most important man in all Egypt save for the pharaoh himself, and therefore we concluded that Joseph was the vizier to the long-reigning Hyksos, King Apophis, the opponent of Seqenenre Tao II.

We worked the chronology backwards from the confrontation between Apophis and Seqenenre, dated by most scholars as circa 1570 BC, and for our general purposes we assumed that the Vizier Joseph was around fifty years old at the time. The following pattern then emerged:

DATE BC EVENT

1570   Joseph Vizier (possibly aged 50)

1620   Joseph born (His father Jacob known to be old, possibly aged about 60)

1680   Jacob born (His father Isaac known to be 60)

1740   Isaac born (His father Abraham said to be very old: say aged 70)

1780   Abraham enters Egypt for the first time (probably aged around 30)

The ages we have given here are as true to the information available in the Bible as it is reasonably possible to be, and working backwards from the conflict between Apophis and Seqenenre we came to place Abraham's entry into Egypt in the precise year that has been identified as the beginning of the Hyksos reign! The dramatic conclusion appears inescapable: Abraham was a Hyksos himself, perhaps even regarded as a prince; remember, the Egyptian term 'Hyksos' simply means 'desert princes' and all the evidence is that Abraham was a high-born man from Ur.

We kept reminding ourselves that the authors of these stories had the distortion of almost a thousand years to deal with and that they, like every other superstitious people, would want to accommodate their prejudices and beliefs into the history that they interpreted and transcribed. The book of Genesis starts with extremely ancient accounts of man's origins but quickly moves from distant legend to relatively recent history for the scribes. Nowhere do the authors openly mention the Asiatic conquest of the Egyptians that is known to have happened in the period somewhere between Abraham and Moses.

Were they ignorant of this period, or perhaps ashamed? We cannot know, but the fact that it is apparently absent from their account of these very significant years in their history struck us as very odd.

The Murder of Hiram Abif

King Seqenenre was fighting a great mental battle with Apophis, the force of ancient darkness who had materialised as a Hyksos king in Lower Egypt, and he needed the full power of the sun god Amen-Re to give him strength to be victorious. Every day he left the royal palace of Malkata to visit the temple of Amen-Re at the hour of high noon, when the sun was at its meridian and a man cast almost no shadow, no stain of darkness, across the ground. With the sun at its zenith the power of Re was at its height and that of the serpent of darkness, Apophis, was at its weakest. This statement – 'whither our Master Hiram Abif had retired to pay his adoration to the Most High, as was his wonton custom, it being the hour of high twelve' – comes from the Masonic Third Degree ritual, which we explained in Chapter One, where it is a previously unexplained comment. Now, in the context of Seqenenre, it made sense to us for the first time.

This is our reconstruction of events. One day, unbeknown to Seqenenre, conspirators sent by Apophis had already tried to extract the secrets of Osiris from the two senior priests, and having failed to get the answers they needed, had killed them. They were terrified of what they now had to do as they were lying in wait for the king himself, each placed at a different exit of the temple. As Seqenenre finished his prayers he headed for the southern doorway where he was met by the first of three men, who demanded to know the secrets of Osiris. He stood fast and refused each. The Masonic Third Degree ceremony explains what happened that day over three and a half thousand years ago in the temple at Thebes. For the sake of emphasising the comparison we have changed the names to the Egyptian ones:

> '*His devotions being ended, he prepared to retire by the south gate, where he was accosted by the first of these ruffians, who, for want of a better weapon, had armed himself with a plumb rule, and in a threatening manner demanded of our Master, Seqenenre, the genuine secrets of Osiris, warning him that death would be the consequence of his refusal; but true to his obligation he replied that those secrets were known to but three in the world and that without the consent of the other two, he neither could, nor would divulge them ... But as for himself, he would rather suffer death than betray the sacred trust reposed in him.*
>
> *This answer not proving satisfactory, the ruffian aimed a violent blow at our Master's forehead, but startled by the firmness of his demeanour, it only glanced down his right temple. Yet with sufficient force to cause him to reel and sink to the ground on his left knee.*
>
> *Recovering himself from this situation, he rushed to the west gate where he stood opposed by the second ruffian, to whom he replied as before, yet with undiminished firmness when the ruffian, who was armed with a level struck a violent blow on the left temple which brought him to the ground on his right knee.*
>
> *Finding all chances of escape in both these quarters cut off, our Master staggered, faint and bleeding, to the east gate where the third ruffian was posted and who, on receiving a similar reply to his insolent demand – for our Master remained true to his obligation even in this most trying moment – struck him a violent blow full in the centre of the forehead with a heavy stone maul, which laid him lifeless at his feet.*'

The secrets of Egyptian king-making died with Seqenenre, the man we call Hiram Abif... 'the king that was lost'.

We were feeling that we had by far the most probable candidate for our lost Masonic Master and we started to look more closely into what is known about this man. We were utterly staggered when we first read the details of Seqenenre's mummy – the incredible facts of Seqenenre's injuries were described in detail:

> *'When, in July 1881, Emil Brugsch discovered the mummy of Pharaoh Ramesses II, in the same cache was another royal corpse, some 300 years older than that of Ramesses, and distinguished by its particularly putrid smell. According to the label this was the body of Seqenenre Tao, one of the native Egyptian rulers forced to live far to the south in Thebes during the Hyksos period, and as was obvious even to the untutored eye, Seqenenre had met a violent end. The middle of his forehead had been smashed in ... Another blow had fractured his right eye socket, his right cheekbone and his nose. A third had been delivered behind his left ear, shattering the mastoid bone and ending in the first vertebra of the neck. Although in life he had clearly been a tall and handsome young man with black, curly hair, the set expression on Seqenenre's face showed that he had died in agony. After death he appears to have fared little better, as his body seems to have been left for some while before mummification; hence the putrid smell and signs of early decomposition.*
>
> *Egyptian records are silent on how Seqenenre met his end, but almost certainly it was at the hands of the Hyksos/Canaanites.* [8]

The impossible had just happened. We had identified Hiram Abif, and what's more, his body still exists.

³ Ian Wilson: *The Exodus Enigma*

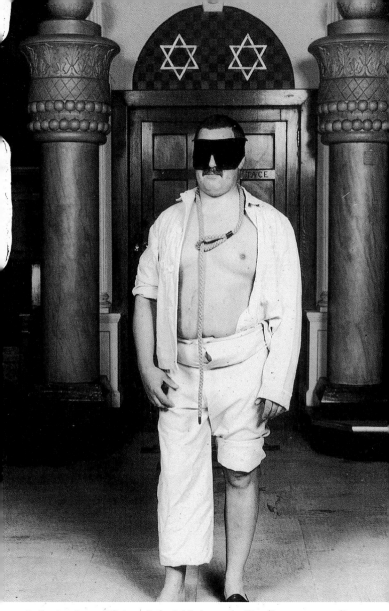

1 A masonic candidate ready for initiation to the First Degree, prepared exactly as a condemned medieval heretic on his way to the gallows.

2 LEFT As the new Master is raised he looks back down at his tomb to see a skull and crossed bones on his death shroud. This symbol of earthly remains was used by the Knights Templar as their marine battle flag.

3 RIGHT A Third Degree candidate being raised by the Worshipful Master from a figurative death – from this moment on he will be a Master Mason.

4 A Knight Templar.

5 ABOVE A Mandaean baptism in the twentieth century – this is probably how John the Baptist looked two thousand years ago when he baptised Jesus.

6 LEFT A cherub found in Jerusalem, similar to the ones that appeared in the Ark and the Covenant – this shows the influence of Egypt on early Jewish theology.

7 and 8 The American maize plants (left), and the Aloe plants (right) carved into the fabric of Rosslyn Chapel decades before Columbus set sail for the New World.

9 The head of King Seqenenre Tao II showing the fatal injuries that are completely consistent with the blows that Hiram Abif received from his attackers, according to Masonic lore.

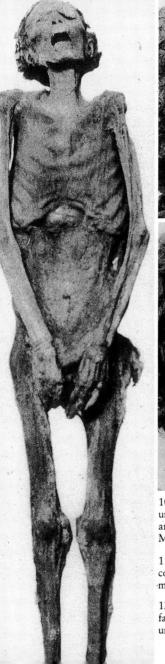

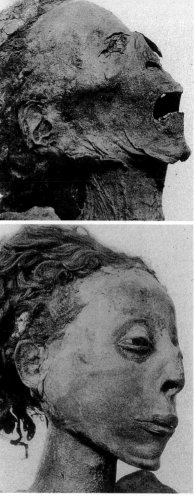

10 LEFT The unwrapped body of an unkown mummy who had been castrated and buried alive – was he the Jubelo of Masonic legend?

11 TOP Detail of the head of 'Jubelo' – the contortion of the features shows that this man must have died in agony.

12 ABOVE A typical mummy showing how facial features were carefully composed – unlike the unfortunate 'Jubelo'.

13 ABOVE LEFT 'Jubelo'. 14 ABOVE RIGHT The head of Ahmose-Inhapi, the widow of Seqenenre Tao, whose skin shows the same unusual ridging as 'Jubelo', suggesting that the same, heavy-handed individual bandaged both. 15 and 16 BELOW The lines on Jubelo's face show how he threw his head back, mouth wide-open after wrapping in a desperate attempt to breathe.

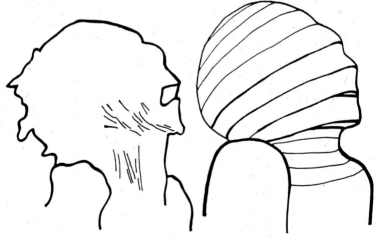

The injuries fit perfectly. A vicious, bone-crushing blow to the length of the right side of his face; he would certainly have reeled and dropped to his knee with such a vicious impact. Being young, tall and powerfully built he found his feet again in the way that strong men do in time of need, but he was met by another assailant who lashed at the left side of his head, again splintering bone. Massively weakened and close to collapse he staggered on, but the last and lethal blow smashed squarely into his forehead, killing him instantly. Another description we found explains the wounds clearly:

> *'The terrible wounds on Seqenenre's skull were caused by at least two people attacking him with a dagger, an axe, a spear and possibly a mace.'*[4]

It took days for our excitement to settle down sufficiently to allow us to think about advancing our investigation. As the elation died down to simmering level, we took stock of what we had got.

The instruments suggested as murder weapons recalled the symbolic Masonic legend in which Hiram was struck with a variety of temple-building implements, including a heavy maul which would produce injuries similar to a mace. The previous description of the early decay of Seqenenre's body shows that the royal embalmers did not receive the body for quite some time after death, which brought to mind the circumstances described in the Masonic Third Degree concerning Hiram Abif's body which went missing after the murder:

> *'... His fears being naturally increased for the safety of his chief artist, he selected fifteen trusty Fellow Crafts, and ordered them to make diligent search after the person of our Master, to ascertain if he were yet alive,*

[4] Peter Clayton: *Chronicle of the Pharaohs*

or had suffered in the attempt to extort from him the secrets of his exalted degree.

A stated day having been appointed for their return to Jerusalem, they formed themselves into three Fellow Craft Lodges and departed from the three entrances of the Temple. Many days were spent in fruitless search; indeed one class returned without having made any discovery of importance. The second class were more fortunate, for on the evening of a certain day, after having suffered the greatest privations and personal fatigues, one of the Brethren who had rested himself in a reclining posture, to assist his rising, caught hold of a shrub that grew near, which to his surprise, came easily out of the ground; on a closer examination, he found that the earth had been recently disturbed; he therefore hailed his companions, and with their united endeavours reopened the grave and there found the body of our Master very indecently interred. They covered it again with all respect and reverence, and to distinguish the spot, stuck a sprig of acacia at the head of the grave, then hastened to Jerusalem to impart the afflicting intelligence to King Solomon.

When the King's first emotions of his grief had subsided, he ordered them to return and raise our Master to such a sepulchre as became his rank and exalted talents; at the same time informing them that by his untimely death the secrets of a Master Mason were lost. He therefore charged them to be particularly careful in observing whatever casual Signs Tokens or Words might occur, whilst paying this last sad tribute of respect to departed merit.'

Take out, for a moment, the placing of Hiram Abif in the time of King Solomon and everything else fits. We were also very interested to discover that King Seqenenre is the only known royal corpse from ancient Egypt to show signs of a violent death.

So now we had the story of a man killed by three blows while protecting the secrets of the Egyptian kings from the Hyksos invaders. But what about a resurrection? Seqenenre had obviously not been resurrected as his body is in the Cairo Museum, so our story was not yet complete. We therefore decided to re-examine our Masonic ritual.

The Killers of Hiram Abif

In Masonic legend the killers of Hiram Abif are named as Jubelo, Jubela and Jubelum, together described as 'the Juwes'. The names themselves sound like symbolic invention; the only meaning we could deduce was that all three names contain 'Jubel', which is Arabic for mountain. This did not seem relevant in any way.

It was the real assassins who interested us, not later symbolism. As we have already shown, the circumstances of Joseph described in the Bible indicates that he was vizier to the Hyksos king Apophis and so it is very likely that he would have been involved in the plot to extract the secrets from Seqenenre.

The Bible also tells us that Joseph's father, Jacob, underwent a symbolic name change later in his life when he became 'Israel' and his twelve sons were identified as the tribes of Israel. This was, of course, the idea of the later authors of Jewish history who were seeking a clearly defined moment in time when their nation formally began. The sons of Jacob/Israel were given historical circumstances which seemed appropriate to the status of the tribes at the time when the writers of Genesis put ink to papyrus. The tribe of Reuben was seen to fall from grace and the tribe of Judah was the new élite, hence we call the descendants of the Israelites 'Jews' not 'Rubes'. Searching for anything approaching a clue in these passages of the Bible, we came across a very odd verse in the King James version of Genesis 49:6 which has no apparent meaning or reference to anything known. It appears at the point where Jacob is dying and reflecting on the actions of his sons, the new heads of the tribes of Israel:

> '*O my soul, come not thou into their secret; unto their assembly, mine honour, be not thou united: for in their anger they slew a man, and in their self will they digged down a wall.*'

Here we had reference to a killing which must have been considered important enough to be included, yet not explained. What secret was sought? Who was slain? The Catholic Church describes this as a certain prophetic reference to the fact that the Jews killed their Christ, but we dismissed that interpretation. Our thesis suggests a more sensible possibility. The fourth to ninth words are unambiguous: 'come not thou into their secret'. In modern English the import of this is, 'You failed to get their secret'! The overall accusation amounts to: 'Not only did you fail to get the secret and to make things worse you lost your temper and murdered him, undermining everything and bringing the whole world down on our heads!'

The two brothers and the future tribes of Israel who are held to account for this unknown murder are Simeon and Levi, the sons of Jacob/Israel by the blind woman Leah whom he despised. These tribes were clearly cursed for what they had done in 'slaying a man' but who was the unnamed victim? Although we thought it unlikely that the killers of Hiram Abif were really called Simeon and Levi and were actually the brothers of Joseph, it did seem very possible that this strange verse contained the folk tradition of the killing of an unnamed man which brought disgrace on two of the tribes of Israel. More to the point, why was the crime important enough to be included in the history of the Jews while the murdered individual goes unidentified?

We were even more convinced that the answer might

lie with Seqenenre Tao. The events leading to his murder, briefly outlined earlier, and its aftermath are so essential to our thesis that we think it important to go through them in greater detail here.

Apophis was outraged. Who did this small-time king of Thebes think he was? Did he not realise that the world had changed for ever and his empire was history, trampled beneath the Hyksos's heel?

The king called in his vizier Joseph, who had ascended to his high rank through his ability to interpret Apophis's dreams, and told him that the time for friendly banter was over; the secrets must be extracted from Seqenenre without delay. The king was getting older and he had every intention of having an Egyptian afterlife.

Joseph was given responsibility for the project, and who better to send than two of his estranged brothers, namely Simeon and Levi? If they were found out and killed it would not matter, as they deserved no better for selling Joseph into slavery all those years ago. If they succeeded, all well and good; Joseph would be a hero himself and his brothers would have paid off an old debt.

The brothers were fully briefed on what to do and the layout of the city. They may have shaved off their distinctive Hyksos beards before they entered Thebes to avoid drawing too much attention to themselves. Once in the city they made contact with a young royal priest of the temple of Amen-Re who was known to be ambitious and easily influenced. The brothers explained that Apophis was tremendously powerful and had decided to destroy Thebes if he could not get the secret from Seqenenre. The young priest (we will call him Jubelo) was told that he alone could avert disaster for the entire population by helping them extract the secrets and making Apophis's attack unnecessary, and besides they could ensure that he would be made high priest to Apophis once the secrets had been secured and the political struggle with Seqenenre was resolved.

Jubelo was extremely frightened of these menacing Asiatics, but he knew what had happened at Memphis when the Hyksos were displeased. Maybe the only thing he could do was betray the trust put in him; in any case he could quite see himself as high priest, even if it was for the evil Apophis. Jubelo explained to Simeon and Levi who the two secret-holding priests were and the optimum time and place to corner them. Perhaps Jubelo even lured them into a trap. Both were caught but refused to provide any details at all, so they were killed to protect the conspirators. Now only one desperate option remained; an attack on the king himself.

Jubelo was terrified by this time but was well past the point of no return, so he led his co-conspirators to the temple of Amen-Re as the sun was just about to reach its highest point. A short time later the King emerged from the doorway where he was told to give up the secrets. He refused and the first blow was struck. Within a matter of minutes King Seqenenre lay dead on the temple floor in a pool of blood. In blind fury and frustration one of the brothers struck the prone corpse twice further. Jubelo was physically sick with fear.

All three knew that they were suddenly alone without a friend in the world. They would be hunted down by the Thebans; Joseph would give them no sympathy; and Apophis would be wild with rage at the permanent loss of the great secrets. Their failure was truly spectacular. The secrets were lost for ever and a fully fledged war to avenge Seqenenre would soon be conducted by Kamose and Ahmose, the sons of the murdered king – a war that would drive the Hyksos out of Egypt for ever. The walls certainly tumbled about their heads!

What then of the treacherous priest? He was caught several days later hiding out in the desert behind Thebes in the place that we now call the Valley of the Kings. He was brought back to the temple and made to explain his part in the treachery, as well as giving details of the whole plan hatched by Apophis and his Asiatic vizier, Joseph. On hearing the full details, Seqenenre's son Kamose was outraged at the wicked act of the Hyksos; but he was also deeply troubled by the fact that he could not be made king himself: the lost secrets would deny him the opportunity to become the Horus. For him and his supporters, this was a disaster beyond compare.

Kamose gathered a council of the surviving senior priests and one of them, destined to become the new high priest, came up with a remarkable analysis of the situation and a blindingly brilliant solution to the dilemma. He observed that Egypt had come into existence thousands of years ago in the age of the gods and that the rise of the two lands had been created through the murder of Osiris by his brother Set. The goddess Isis had not given in and had resurrected the dismembered body of Osiris to cause him to father a boy child, Horus, the son of god. Horus was himself a god who grew to manhood and fought the evil Set in a mighty battle in which the Horus lost an eye and Set lost his testicles. The young god was deemed to have won the battle, but it was nonetheless an indecisive victory with an ongoing tension between good and evil.

The wise priest went on to explain that Egypt had grown strong after this battle but the two lands had slowly aged and gone into decline. The power of the god Set had increased with the arrival of the Hyksos, who worshipped him and the serpent Apophis. There had just been another battle on earth like the battle between the first Horus and Set, but this time Set had won and the current Horus had lost. In this recent battle the king (the Horus) again had had an eye struck out before he died. The answer was to remember the wisdom of Isis and refuse to give up just because a god had been slain. He slowly lifted his hand and pointed a finger at the quaking young priest and shouted, 'There is the manifestation of Set. He will help us defeat the evil one.'

Seqenenre's body was in poor condition through spending many days in its rough interment, but the embalmers managed to prepare him in the usual way. As part of his punishment Jubelo was continually dipped in sour milk and in the desert heat the decaying protein soon caused him to stink, giving him the distinctive hallmark of the 'evil one'. When the time came for Seqenenre's Osiris ceremony, and Kamos's simultaneous Horus ceremony, everything was prepared but there were two coffins, not one. The first anthropoid coffin was splendid and literally fit for a sweet-smelling god/king; the second was plain white without any inscription.

As the moment of the ceremonies drew near the stinking, semi-delirious Jubelo was brought in naked to the embalmers. His hands were held at his sides and with one deft slash of a knife his genitals were struck off and thrown to the floor by Kamose himself, who was about to become the Horus. The whimpering Jubelo was then wrapped in mummification bandages working upwards from the feet. He was allowed to leave his hands touching the wound that was causing him so much agony, as this would demonstrate to every onlooker the point of this evil creature's injury. The bandages finally reached Jubelo's head and the embalmers drew them tightly around his face until he was wholly covered. As soon as the grip was released on him as he was placed in his coffin Jubelo pushed his head backwards to straighten his trachea and forced his mouth wide open in an attempt to breathe through the suffocating bandages. He died within minutes after his coffin lid was sealed down.

Jubelo paid dearly for his betrayal.

The wise new high priest had told Kamose that substituted secrets would have to be created to replace the genuine ones that had been lost with the killing of his father. A new ceremony resurrecting the new king from a figurative death was designed to replace the old method, and new magic words were created to raise him to the status of Horus. The new ceremony told the story of the death of the last king of the first Egypt and with the new king came a reborn nation. The body of Jubelo travelled to the Kingdom of the Dead with Seqenenre so that the battle could continue – Set (in the form of Jubelo) without his testicles and the new Osiris, like the first Horus, without his eye. The priests had cleverly arranged things so that the battle would continue where it was left off at the beginning of time. The war was far from over.

Kamose stuck a very clear finger in the air to Apophis when he chose the throne name 'Wadj-kheper-re', which means 'Flourishing is the Manifestation of Re'. In other words: 'You failed, I'm doing fine with the royal secrets!'

As Kamose was raised from a figurative death, so was his nation. The period we now call the New Kingdom soon started and Egypt became a proud country once again.

The Physical Evidence

The story we have just related is admittedly fictionalised in part to put over the thrust of what we confidently believe happened all those thousands of years ago. Nonetheless, the only parts that we have added to tell this story are the tiny points of detail that glue together the core facts that we have uncovered.

We used biblical evidence to establish an involvement of Joseph and his brothers but the young priest, that we call Jubelo, came to our attention through long poring over ancient Egyptian records. We could hardly believe our good fortune when we came across the remains of a young man who has puzzled Egyptologists for well over a hundred years.

Of all the mummies found in Egypt, two stood out to us as being unusual. Seqenenre's is unique in being the only king to have met a violent end, and another corpse stood out for other radical reasons. Searching for information on all recorded mummies, we were immediately struck by the details of the very strange remains of a young man who in life had been just over five feet eight inches tall. Photographs of the unwrapped mummy were striking because of the appearance of extreme agony on the face as well as the details of the burial, which were unprecedented. The body had not been embalmed, in that there was no incision and all internal organs were in place. Whilst the individual had therefore not been mummified in the usual sense of the word, he had been wrapped in the normal manner. Strangely, no attempt had been made to set the angle of the head or compose the facial features and the initial effect is of a man emitting a long, terrible scream. The arms are not at the side of the body nor crossed on the chest in the usual manner, but stretched downwards with the cupped hands covering, yet not quite touching, the pubic region. Beneath the hands is a space where the genitals should be: this man had been castrated.

His plaited hair is inexplicably covered in a cheese-like material, which struck us as the result one would expect of successive dippings in sour milk with the aim of making him smell evil; the demons of darkness had a highly developed sense of smell and would recognise their own kind. The teeth are in good condition and the ears had been pierced, both of which suggest high birth. The mummy was found in a white-painted cedar coffin which bore no inscription at all, making identification impossible, but experts consider that he must have been a noble or a member of the priesthood. Dating has proved difficult but it is widely felt to be from the Eighteenth Dynasty, which began shortly after the death of Seqenenre Tao. One important clue that has previously been missed lies in the ridges that have formed in the skin of the face. These are highly unusual, but are also present on one other mummy – that of Ahmose-Inhapi, the widow of Seqenenre! These ridges are thought to be due to over-tight bandaging, and this common feature suggests that the same heavy-handed person did the bandaging. Our diagrams illustrate how the angle of these ridges strongly suggest that the young priest was alive when he was wrapped and entombed. This unidentified corpse has not created much interest to Egyptologists, who naturally tend to focus on mummies of the famous, but it has long been suggested that this unembalmed body shows all the signs of having been alive at the time of burial.

The official estimated dating of early New Kingdom was unbelievably close to our target area and we started to wonder if the young man's mummy had been discovered in the Thebes area, thereby having a possible connection to our murdered king. We quickly established that it was found by Emil Brugsch in 1881, not only in Thebes but in the royal cache at Deir el Bahri ... right alongside Seqenenre Tao! This was not the original tomb of either of them, but the likelihood is that they were both moved from the same site at the same time at a later date.

As the possibility of coincidence evaporated, we knew with utter certainty that we had not only found Hiram Abif; we had also discovered the circumstances of the killing and identified one of the murderers, three and a half thousand years after the event. We felt like all detectives feel when they solve a difficult case; we drank rather a lot of champagne that night.

The unfortunate Jubelo, however, never did manage to escape the presence of his victim. The young priest is now in the Cairo Museum, catalogue number 61023 along with Seqenenre Tao, catalogue number 61051.

The Masonic Evidence

Once we sobered up from the celebrations of our solving of the Seqenenre murder, we sat down together and considered our next step. Again we returned to Masonic ritual to search out another clue in our reconstruction of the development of the secrets of the kings. The whole story of Seqenenre and his killers is the story of Egypt undergoing reincarnation and it is the story of Hiram Abif. The two are one and the same. The Bible fills in some blank areas and human remains provide irrefutable forensic evidence, despite a gap of three and a half thousand years. But we found that the Masonic evidence goes still deeper.

Chris turned his attention to the secret words used in the Third Degree ceremony which is the Master Mason raising ceremony. The words are spoken in a whisper to the newly resurrected brother and are never spoken out aloud. They seem complete gibberish. Both words are very similar in structure and sound as though they are composed of a string of very short syllables in the style of the ancient Egyptians. Chris broke them down into syllables and in very short time he sat back and looked wide-eyed at something that made perfect sense. The sounds uttered in open Lodge are:

'*Ma'at-neb-men-aa, Ma'at-ba-aa*'

Those readers who are Freemasons will recognise these words but will be astounded to know that they are pure ancient Egyptian. Their meaning is breathtaking:

'*Great is the established Master of Freemasonry, Great is the spirit of Freemasonry*'

We have translated 'Ma'at' as 'Freemasonry' because there is no other modern single word that comes close to the original complex concept that conveyed a whole bundle of ideas around 'truth, justice, fairness, harmony and moral rectitude as symbolised by the regular purity of the perfectly upright and square foundations of a temple'. Ma'at was, as we saw earlier, an attitude to life that blended the three most important values that mankind possesses, namely the knowledge of science, the beauty of art and the spirituality of theology. That is the craft of Masonry.

The other translations are straightforward on a word-for-word basis.

We have reconstructed these words in hieroglyphics to demonstrate their Egyptian origin although we doubt that they have ever been written down in any language prior to this book.

The question that we had to ask ourselves was how come these few words have survived intact over such a vast period of time. We believe that these utterances have survived the possibility of translation into later languages – Canaanite, Aramaic, French and English – because they have been viewed as the 'magic words', the incantation which made the resurrection of the new candidate something more than symbolic. Their original meaning was probably long lost by the time of Solomon!

Looking back to the very beginning of the New Kingdom, we could sense the power of these words when we imagine Kamose being raised as the first candidate following the murder of his father, the figure we know as Hiram Abif. The import is rather like 'the king is dead, long live the king'. The newly resurrected candidate *is* the spirit of Ma'at (Freemasonry) living on past the deaths of those that have gone before.

This fossilised incantation gave us more powerful evidence to support our thesis. If anyone now wants to question that Seqenenre was Hiram Abif, they have to explain away the fact that the modern Masonic ceremony contains two lines of pure ancient Egyptian at the very core of the ritual.

It has long been established by cultural anthropologists that information is effectively passed on to successive generations by tribal ritual without the exponents necessarily having any idea of what they are transmitting. In fact it is widely agreed that the very best way of transmitting ideas without distortion is via people that do not understand what they are saying. A good example of this can be seen the way in which children's rhymes still survive more perfectly than old stories that have been subsequently written down and embellished by a series of well intentioned 'improvers'. For example, many English children still chant 'Eenie, meenie, minie, mo,' a rhyme based on a counting system that certainly predates the Roman occupation of Britain, and possibly even the Celts! It has survived intact for two or three thousand years and left to its own devices, it might well last as long again.

The fossilised Egyptian incantation concerning Ma'at has come down to Freemasons via two long verbal traditions and a period of 'hibernation' beneath Herod's temple. Reverence for its magical qualities has sustained it long after the meaning of the words had drifted away.

This discovery gave us some really powerful evidence to support our developing thesis, and anyone wanting to question our claim that Seqenenre was Hiram Abif, has now to explain how it is that the modern Masonic ceremony contains two lines of pure ancient Egyptian at the very core of the ritual. We believe that for these sounds to translate into sensible English by coincidence would be to defy odds measured in millions to one, but given that the resulting English words convey a precise and entirely relevant meaning, chance must be ruled out altogether.

We found that other connections with Freemasonry

abound when the structure of the New Kingdom Egyptian priesthood and senior officials are looked at. Descriptions of roles sound immediately Masonic. The First Prophet of Queen Hatshepsut was also known as the 'Overseer of Works' and the First Prophet of Ptah was the 'Master Craftsman' or the 'Master Artificer'. We knew that Masonry could not have copied these descriptions because as we have already pointed out, there was no means to translate Egyptian until long after the Craft was founded.

The more we looked, the more connections emerged. In ancient Egypt a man would serve at the temple associated with the god of his trade. The moon god Thoth was connected to architects and scribes; and it was Thoth that later became an object of interest to early Freemasons. We also found connections with the Essenes, the founders of the Jerusalem Church, in that Egyptian priests would wear only white cloth robes and spent large periods of time cleansing and purifying themselves. They abstained from sexual relations and were circumcised and had taboos on certain foods including shellfish. They used water in an almost baptismal way and used incense to cleanse their clothes. The observances of the Essenes were indeed ancient.

We thought we had extracted as much as we could possibly hope for from this section of our investigation, but then a thought occurred to Robert. Masonic ritual refers to Hiram Abif as the 'Son of the Widow', which has never had any explanation – but suddenly, two connected interpretations emerged. In Egyptian legend the first Horus was uniquely conceived after his father's death and therefore his mother was a widow even before his conception. It seemed logical therefore that all those who thereafter became Horus, i.e. the kings of Egypt, would also describe themselves as 'Son of the Widow', a particularly apt title for Kamose, the son of the widow Ahmose-Inhapi, wife of Seqenenre Tao II.

Seqenenre Tao the Fearless

We could now be certain that the story of Hiram Abif was historical and not symbolic, as most Masons (including ourselves at first) believed. Previously it had seemed to us that a ritualised history had been invented to illuminate important symbolic points, but it was the other way around; the symbolism had been extracted from reality. The event marks a massively important turning point in Egyptian theology, when the secrets of the star cult and magic of king-making were lost for all time. The ancient Egyptians recognised something very special about King Seqenenre, who died at the age of about thirty, because he was given the designation 'the Fearless' in accounts that refer to him. Because of the brutal nature of his injuries some observers have speculated that he died in battle with the Hyksos, although most agree that it is equally likely that he was assassinated. The battle theory ignores records that show there was peace with the Hyksos until the reign of Kamose, and had Seqenenre died a hero in battle Egyptian accounts would not be silent about the means of his death. Seqenenre was obviously regarded as dying a hero for some other, more unusual reason than leading his troops into battle.

We were now certain that this title was bestowed by a grateful people for keeping the greatest secrets of the Two Lands, even in the face of death. Certainly Seqenenre-the-Fearless's death was the start of Egypt regaining its freedom from the invaders, as Thebes prepared for war against the Hyksos in revenge for this wicked murder. Seqenenre's son, King Kamose, eventually inflicted crushing reverses on the 'wretched Asiatic' and the Hyksos were soon routed out of Memphis. The women of the last Hyksos king, Apophis's successor Apepi II, had the terrifying experience of watching the Theban fleet, led by a general by the name of Aahmas, sail up the Pat'etku Canal to the very walls of the Hyksos capital Avaris. The

Hyksos were finally driven completely out of Egypt by Kamose's younger brother and successor, Ahmose, who chased them back to Jerusalem. Unable to escape by sea, no less than two hundred and forty thousand households are said to have made their way across the Sinai and Nagev deserts. Strangely the route they took was known as 'Wat Hor' – the Way of Horus.

In conclusion, the major drama that unfolded in Thebes at the end of the first half of the second millennium BC was a crucial point in Egyptian history; it was an obvious rerun of the battle between good and evil that created the country two thousand years earlier. The Old Kingdom of Egypt had been born, grown, matured, aged and finally died at the hands of the wicked god Set, who had this time brought his followers down upon the people like a plague. Egypt, like Osiris himself, had been dead for a time. After this period of death Amen-Re had fought a battle with the ancient serpent god, the force of darkness, Apophis, who had taken the form of a Hyksos king. Perhaps sensing that Egypt was about to be resurrected, Apophis had tried vainly to secure the secret of Osiris for himself. He failed because of the fearlessness of Seqenenre Tao who died himself rather than betray those great secrets. He was 'the king that was lost' because his body was found too late to allow him to be resurrected personally, and because the secrets of Osiris died with him. From that time onwards the original secrets of how Isis raised Osiris have been replaced by substituted secrets and no king of Egypt ever again joined the stars.

From this time onwards the rulers of Egypt were not kings. They became mere pharaohs which comes from the Egyptian 'Per-aa', a euphemism for king meaning 'great house', rather as the United States of America sometimes refers to its power-base as the White House instead of the president himself. The absolute divine right of the individual was gone for ever. Not only was one king lost, all kings were lost for all time!

Despite the loss of the secrets, the resurrection of Egypt was highly successful and the New Kingdom became the last great period for the Egyptians. The death and resurrection had led to a rebirth that brought new strength and vigour to the whole nation.

The remaining questions that we needed to answer to confirm fully the link between Hiram Abif and Seqenenre Tao were: Why is Seqenenre remembered as a builder, and how did he become associated with King Solomon's Temple? The first part was straightforward: Seqenenre was the greatest protector of Ma'at, the principle of truth and justice that is represented as building the straight and square foundations of a temple. As regards the second part, we would soon go on to establish that the Israelites had direct access to this dramatic story, and it was used in the royal house of David to provide them with a structure of kingly secrets that their new and cultureless monarchy did not have. When the time came to write down the history of this legend, the Jews changed its Egyptian origin and attributed it to the greatest moment in the history of their own nation; the building of King Solomon's Temple. The hero of the Jewish story could not be the king because the story of Solomon was well known. So they created a role that was the next best thing – the builder of the great temple. The secrets of building and the wisdom of the builder were understood by everyone so there could not have been a better 'resurrection' for Seqenenre-the-Fearless.

An Egyptian origin for Hiram Abif solved another problem. Once we realise that our central character Hiram Abif was worshipping not Yahweh but the sun god Re – literally the 'most high', we could understand the significance of noon as the ultimate time of worship. Freemasons today claim always to meet symbolically at noon on the basis that Freemasonry is a worldwide organisation and therefore 'the sun is always at its meridian with respect to Freemasonry'. Masonic reference to God as 'the most high' is therefore a description of Re, the sun god in his ultimate position, the zenith of the heavens at noon. In addition, it is worth noting that the Bible tells us that before the Israelites adopted the name Yahweh, the 'god of our fathers' was referred to as 'el elion', a Canaanite rendering of 'god – the most high'. This strengthens the link between the original Egyptian story and the Israelites who took it with them.

We came across one further piece of circumstantial but highly significant evidence. This concerns King Tuthmosis III who, you will recall from the previous chapter, was made king as a result of the god choosing him in the temple by making his ark too heavy for its bearers. Tuthmosis III was the fourth king after the departure of the Hyksos, and everything about his life tells us that the secrets of the star-based religion and the making of Osiris and Horus had already been lost. The fact that he had to substantiate his claim to the throne by means of the 'ark' story demonstrates that he did not feel that he had a clear and absolute divine right to rule, in contrast to earlier kings. But it is the fact that he was usurped by another is particularly revealing of his lack of divinity.

Tuthmosis II had died without producing a legitimate male heir with his wife and half-sister Hatshepsut and a boy born of a relationship with a concubine had taken the throne, but he cannot have been made the Horus by the secret king-making technique. At first the young Tuthmosis III had no difficulty in establishing his kingship, but things were about to develop in an unprecedented way. Ancient hieroglyphics show how Hatshepsut first came from the background to claim equal status with Tuthmosis, then rapidly overwhelmed him to become the first woman to have the rightful divine progeny of the god Amen-Re. Tuthmosis III was then despatched for military training to ensure that there was no confusion as to who was in control. Like most women who reach the top, she was an immensely powerful person who achieved many great things. Her impressive mortuary temple on the west bank of the Nile remains today as one of the most staggering and beautiful buildings of all time.

Without doubt the noble death of Seqenenre Tao marked the resurrection of the world's greatest civilisation and the point at which the true secrets of the royal line of Egypt were lost for ever. The substituted secrets were created to provide the necessary rite of passage for future pharaohs and their closest advisers, but the absolute right to rule imbued by the original secrets did not pass forward with the new mysteries.

Our success in our quest had continued remarkably smoothly, and Robert posed the question: The answers are coming so thick and fast, could it be that we are starting to see what we want to see? We decided that we should review exactly where we were and the evidence that we had amassed, and having looked dispassionately at each link in the chain of our theory, we were more certain than ever that we were into a new vein of factual history, and what we had uncovered was producing such elegant continuity because it was true.

Our next challenge was to understand how the legend of an Egyptian king killed by proto-Israelites, was transformed into an event in the history of the new nation of the Jews. We now knew that we would have to unravel the circumstances of the greatest legend in the history of the Jewish people – the prophet Moses.

CONCLUSION

Focusing on the Hyksos period of ancient Egypt had produced results beyond all expectation. We now knew who Hiram Abif was, and to add to our joy we had located his body and that of one of his murderers. We had looked at the role of Egypt in the history of the Jews and it became obvious from the Bible that there had been a complete change in attitude towards the Hebrews by the Egyptians. But what was more interesting was what the Bible did *not* say. There is no reference to the period of the Hyksos invasion of Egypt, yet closer investigation allowed us to date the Hyksos period quite accurately from Old Testament information.

Further careful study of the Book of Genesis had allowed us to deduce that Abraham was contemporary with the Hyksos invasion and indeed we suspect he may even have been a Hyksos, which means 'desert prince'. The last influential proto-Jew in Egypt was Joseph and by careful matching of biblical and historical evidence we found that Joseph was vizier to Apophis, the invader king who was involved in a major battle for supremacy with the Theban king, Seqenenre Tao II. Seqenenre was heir to the ancient Egyptian secret rituals of king-making and was by right the true Horus. Apophis had taken an Egyptian throne name but was never privy to the secrets of king-making.

We had found a reference in Genesis 49:6 to the killing of *a man* by the brothers of Joseph whilst trying to force a secret from him, and we had discovered that the mummy of Seqenenre shows most clearly that he had been killed by three blows to the head and then not immediately preserved. This fitted exactly all the facts we knew about the story of Hiram Abif. As we investigated further we found that near Seqenenre a young priest had been buried alive. Using evidence of the pattern of mummy bandages we were able to prove this corpse was dated to exactly the same period as Seqenenre. Using all this evidence and the Masonic story we knew so well, we were able to reconstruct the story of the killing of Seqenenre and how it resulted in the fall of the Hyksos.

Knowing this about the killing of Hiram Abif, we now could finally understand the meaning of two whispered words used in the Masonic Raising Ceremony, which phonetically translated into ancient Egyptian and still made sense in English: 'Great is the established Master of Freemasonry, Great is the spirit of Freemasonry.' Here at last was a firm link with modern Freemasonry. Two meaningless and pointless words which had only survived because Masonic ritual is learned by rote and repetition.

With our link to Seqenenre and the real story of Hiram Abif firmly established, we now faced a gap of nearly 1500 years to the only group who could have buried that information for the Templars to find. We had to trace the development of Judaism up to the flowering of the Essenes, and our Egyptian linkage had to start with Moses.

Chapter Nine

The Birth of Judaism

Moses the Law-giver

Our task was to work forward in time, step by step, to see if we could establish a continuous Masonic-style ceremony linking the Egyptian New Kingdom to the time of Jesus. This was going to be difficult because our only source of information was going to be the Old Testament, but at least we had our Masonic ritual to aid interpretation.

Fortunately the Bible is unequivocal that the Jewish nation started with one man and there is little doubt that an individual by the name of Moses did exist, and that he was connected with some type of exodus of enslaved Asiatics from Egypt. After the expulsion of the Hyksos, Semites of all kinds, including the Habiru, must have been more than a little unpopular and it would explain why the otherwise friendly Egyptians suddenly enslaved many or even all of those who remained in the country during the decade 1560 to 1550 BC. Inscriptions from the sixteenth and fifteenth centuries BC have been found giving details of these Habiru slaves and their forced labour.[1] One tells of how large numbers of these people were forced to work in turquoise mines, which must have been extremely dangerous and unpleasant without ventilation and with naked flames burning up the oxygen. We were interested to find that these mines were just a short

[1] Werner Keller: *The Bible as History*

distance from the mountain of Yahweh, Mount Sinai in the southern mountains of the Sinai Peninsula. Was this coincidence, we wondered, or could the break-out of the Habiru slaves have occurred here rather than in Egypt proper?

We found that records show that although these proto-Jews spoke in the Canaanite language, they worshipped Egyptian deities and set up monuments to the gods Osiris, Ptah and Hathor, which does not tie in with the popular image of the noble, enslaved followers of Yahweh yearning to be led to Jerusalem by 'the god of their fathers'.[2]

The story of Moses is retold to every Jewish and Christian child and therefore tends to stay with the adult as a matter of historical fact, even if most people discount the exotic elements, such as the parting of the Red Sea. Exactly when this event happened is hard to pinpoint but formerly the most commonly held opinion was that Moses led 'his people' out of Egypt during the reign of Ramases II, which would place the event between 1290 and 1224 BC. There is, however, very good evidence recently put together to support a much earlier date, very close to the time of the expulsion of the Hyksos. But before we delve into the issue of dating it is important to consider what we know of the man called Moses and what the Bible tells us about the Israelites and their new god.

We found that the name Moses itself is very revealing. Strangely, the Roman Catholic Douai Bible informs its readers that it is Egyptian for 'saved out of water', whereas it actually means simply 'born of'. The name normally required another name prefixed to it, such as Thothmoses (born of Thoth), Rameses (born of Ra) or Amenmosis (born of Amen). Whilst the 'moses' element is spelt slightly differently when rendered in English, they all mean the same thing and it seems very likely to us that either Moses himself or some later scribe dropped the

[1] *Peake's Commentary on the Bible*

name of an Egyptian god from the front of his name. It is rather like taking the 'Donald' part out of a Scotsman's name, leaving him with Mac, instead of MacDonald.

The Roman Catholic definition is probably wrong, but if there is some historical truth in the idea, it could be that Moses's full name was 'Born of the Nile', in which case he would have been called Hapymoses, which would have been written down as:

The name Moses is unusual as it is one of very few ancient Egyptian words still popular today, in its Hebrew form 'Moshe' and its Arabic form 'Musa'. The Egyptians still call Mount Sinai Jubal Musa – the mountain of Moses.

It is impossible today to know just how much of the story of Moses given in the Old Testament is historical and how much is romantic invention. According to the Book of Exodus, the Pharaoh instructed that all Israelite male children were to be thrown into the Nile. This is almost impossible to believe as an historical event, as such a barbaric decree would have been totally at odds with the concept of Ma'at held so dear by the Egyptians. Any pharaoh giving this command would be giving up his right to an afterlife when his heart was weighed. Further-more, on a practical level it would have been very unpleasant and unhealthy to have thousands of rotting corpses floating about in the population's only source of water.

According to the Old Testament, Moses's mother was determined not to let her infant son die, so she placed him in the bulrushes at the edge of the Nile in a basket daubed with pitch where he was found by the pharaoh's daughter. It has long been noticed that this birth episode is almost identical to that of Sargon I, the king who reigned over Babylon and Sumer many hundreds of years before Moses. A quick comparison demonstrates the obvious similarities:

SARGON	MOSES
My changeling mother conceived me;	... a Levite woman ...
in secret she bore me.	conceived and bore a son ... she hid him for three months, but she could not conceal him any longer.
She set me in a basket of rushes; with	So she got a rush basket for him, made it
bitumen she sealed my lid.	watertight with clay and tar, laid him in it,
She cast me into the river, which rose not over me.	and put it among the reeds by the bank of the Nile.

We concluded that the birth story is almost certainly a fiction created in the sixth century BC echoing, for the birth of the Jewish nation, the ancient theme of creation emerging from the waters. It was also an excellent way of rationalising how a general in the Egyptian army and member of the Egyptian royal family came to be the founding father of the Jewish people. This is something we will come to shortly.

We had no doubt that some aspects of the story were later inventions. One such was the description of Moses's mother as a Levite woman; that was an attempt to put history into an order that suited the story's later authors. Levites became the priestly tribe and so the scribes, using the logic of their own time, reasoned that Moses must have been a priest and therefore a Levite. The Book of Exodus has clear indications of being a patchwork of three

202

oral versions of the traditional history of the coming out of Egypt, with confusion as to whether Moses or Aaron was the main player; even the name of the mountain where Moses met with Yahweh varies between Mount Sinai and Mount Horeb.

We had to keep reminding ourselves that the authors of the early books of the Old Testament were writing down tribal legends from their distant past, the most ancient stories being literally thousands of years old, and even the recent ones such as those of David and Solomon were hundreds of years before their time. The general shape of the supposed events were clear but historical details were completely missing. Different authors filled the gaps in different ways, depending on their political view of the world, and their opinion as to how things should have been. Experts have been able to disentangle these layers of authorship and they have been given such unexciting designations as 'J', 'E', 'D' and 'P'. With modern-day access to far greater historical information than these groups had, we can quickly spot high levels of invention. For example, these authors describe camels as beasts of burden and the use of coins at the time of Isaac and Joseph, when in fact neither occurred until much later. Another significant mistake is the description of Abraham avoiding southern Israel as the land of the Philistines, when we now know that they did not arrive until well after the Israelites had come out of Egypt.

If the Book of Exodus had told us which pharaoh's daughter had found the baby Moses, things would be a lot easier, but clearly the authors had no idea themselves.

We reasoned that there could only be three basic explanations for Moses being at the centre of the Egyptian royal family:

1. He was an Asiatic or Habiru by birth and was taken into the family as a baby or small child as the Old Testament suggests. It is known that the Egyptians did

take in the children of neighbouring countries so that as adults they could influence their people favourably towards the Egyptians. At first this seemed unlikely at a time so close to the Hyksos period when the Habiru were enslaved.

2. He was a high-born Egyptian who as a man found himself on the run for murder and who adopted the Habiru as his outlaw followers.

3. He was a young Semite general in the army of the last Hyksos king and was driven out of Egypt into the wilderness with the rest of the Asiatic hordes when the Theban monarchy regained control. He later returned to lead the Habiru slaves to freedom. This would put the Moses story much earlier than has ever been considered before, but there is no reason why it could not be so – Moses is known to have been a general in the army of an unidentified pharaoh.

This third option has attractions, but we could not at first find sufficient evidence for such an early timing; moreover, to learn the secrets of the Egyptians Moses must have been involved with a true pharaoh, not a Hyksos impostor. We therefore accepted that the truth lay with either the first or the second of these options. In both cases the biblical version of events is accepted as broadly correct. For our purposes we decided not to dwell on the circumstances of exactly how Moses came to lead these proto-Israelites; it is sufficient to accept that an extremely high-ranking member of the Egyptian court became the leader of some of the tribes that would become the nation of the Jews.

Acts 7:22 tells us that:

'Moses was learned in all the wisdom of the Egyptians.'

The Israelites who wrote of Moses all these years later had no reason to invent his closeness with the opponents of their forefathers and they clearly believed that he had been invested with great secrets; indeed *all* of the secrets. By the time that Moses was involved with the Egyptian royal family the New Kingdom would have been established and the 'substituted secrets' would have replaced the 'original' secrets of Osiris. As a senior member of the pharaoh's court, Moses must have been instructed in the principles of resurrection described around the legend of Seqenenre Tao and his fearless sacrifice, which replaced the lost genuine secrets. For the young Moses this ritual was to acquaint him with the secrets of king-making, the highest expression of power, the mere possession of which was a mark of royalty. This must have made a deep impression upon him because he surely carried the story with him, so that it eventually became the new secret rite-of-passage for king-making in the new land of Israel.

Because it was secret and only passed to the smallest possible group of principal Jews, the story of 'the king that was lost' passed on into the royal line of David without much change. The details of the Exodus were a lower level story available to everyone, and truth and fiction merged until little reality remained.

Whatever the route taken, the biblical story of the Exodus clearly demonstrates that the group led by Moses was highly Egyptianised and the worship of Egyptian deities was normal practice. Moses receiving the ten commandments on tablets of stone was absolutely necessary to mark the establishment of a new state. Every king had to be given his 'royal charter' from the gods as proof that he was fit to lead and that there was a basis for law and order in the new society.

These tablets could only have been written in Egyptian hieroglyphics as Moses would not have understood any other script. Because today we rely on the written word on a daily basis it is difficult for us to understand how special writing was considered to be in the second millennium BC. The idea of messages materialising out of marks on stone amazed ordinary people and the scribes who could make 'stone talk' were considered to be holders of great magic. This is easily appreciated when one realises that the Egyptians called hieroglyphics 'the Words of the God', a term that would often be repeated throughout the Bible.

The War God of the Mountains of Sinai

Reading the story of the Exodus carefully and objectively left us horrified. The view that had been formed in our minds during our Christian-focused upbringing was quickly turned on its head. Instead of a noble and great people winning their freedom and finding their 'promised land', we read a disturbing catalogue of primitive demonology, betrayal, mass murder, rape, vandalism and grand theft. It was the most disgraceful statement of origin for a new nation imaginable.

The story of Moses starts with a murder. He sees an Egyptian hitting a Habiru and, after looking around to be sure no one is looking, he kills the Egyptian: the first of tens of thousands of murders this ex-soldier will commit. Unfortunately the crime was witnessed by other Habiru who reported the incident to the Egyptians, so Moses became a wanted man. He went on the run, heading east into the Sinai where he was taken in by the Midianites (also called Kenites) and where he married the king's daughter, Zipporah.

It was here that Moses was introduced to the god of the Midianite tribes, a god of storms and of war whose symbol was a crucifix-like motif worn on their foreheads; it later became known as the 'Yahweh Mark'. This god, who lived in the mountains, provided the inspiration and central theme for the God of the Jews following Moses's conversations with Him on Mount Horeb.

Gods rarely, if ever, spontaneously pop into existence; they develop naturally and undergo metamorphosis as they absorb qualities transposed from other deities. The first recorded meeting with the God of the Jews and Christians seems strangely cold and threatening. When Moses enquired about His credentials and asked for His name he was being very smart; but it did not work. Moses knew from his Egyptian upbringing that gods were not always superior to humans and if a man could extract the name of the god he would have power over him. In Egypt gods usually had many names ranging from a common, widely known one to increasingly restricted names but their fundamental designation was given to no man or other god. If Moses had received the answer to his question regarding the God's principal name, he would have effectively enslaved the god.

Theology and magic have always been totally synonymous concepts until relatively recent times, when we have managed to draw an imaginary line between the two halves of primitive human mysticism. The concept of the god of the Israelites living in his ark is no different to a genie living in his bottle granting wishes to his friends; both indulge in such activities as flying through the air, dividing whole seas, sending out fireballs and generally ignoring the laws of nature. Today we maintain a frail mental separation between the stories of the Arabian Nights and those of the Bible, but there is no doubt they share a common origin. It will be hard for many people to accept, but if we take what the Bible says at face value, then the creator figure, whom the Western world calls simply 'God', started out as a humble genie living on his wits in the mountains of north-east Africa and south-west Asia.

Fearful for his independence, the Midianite god refused Moses's question as to his name and tried to establish his own importance by telling Moses to take off his shoes and keep back because he is on holy ground.

The Book of Exodus tells us that God's reply to the question of His name was:

'*Ehyeh asher ehyeh.*'

This is usually translated as 'I am who I am' but in the parlance of the authors of the work, this carried a stronger import and would be better rendered as 'Mind your own damned business!' The names Yahweh or Jehovah are both modern pronunciations from the Hebrew description of God as YHWH (the Hebrew language has no vowels). This was *not* the god's name; more likely it was a title taken from the given answer meaning 'I am'.

According to the Bible story, Moses eventually returned to Egypt to release the bands of assorted Asiatics whom the Egyptians called Habiru from slavery, supposedly using the powers of his new storm jinn/genie/god to bring misery and death to the unfortunate Egyptians. We are told that 600,000 Israelites left for a forty-year journey through the desert, but it is clear to every intelligent observer that any such exodus could have only involved a fraction of this number. There is no trace of such an event in Egyptian history, and had it been an event on the scale claimed in the Bible there would have been. Had the group been this size they would have represented a quarter of the entire population of Egypt, and given the effect that such a migration would have had on food requirements and labour supply, the Egyptians would certainly have recorded its social impact.

Nonetheless, whatever the number, Moses then took his people into the Sinai back to the Midianite encampment and greeted his father-in-law, Jethro, who congratulated the Israelites and gave wise advice to Moses. The prophet then went back up the sacred mountain for a meeting with the god who still lived there. The storm god who lived in a black cloud told Moses that if any of the Israelites or their animals set foot upon the mountain or even touched it, he would kill them by shooting them through or stoning them. The new god then informed his new followers that they were required to worship him or he would take vengeance not only on the individuals concerned but their children, grandchildren and beyond. He went on to demand that the Israelites give him gifts of gold, silver, brass, fine linen, badgers' skins and shittim wood (acacia) and build an ark completely covered in gold for him to live in. This ark was of classical Egyptian design with two so-called 'cherubim' on top, which are now universally accepted as being a pair of winged sphinxes; that is, winged lions with human heads (see Fig 6).

This new god cannot have made too much of an impression upon the majority of the Israelites as they made a golden calf as soon as Moses had climbed up his mountain to talk to Yahweh. This effigy was most likely a representation of the Egyptian god Apis, which greatly upset the new god. He instructed Moses to command his priests to kill as many of these 'sinners' as possible and, we are told, three thousand Israelites were slain.

And the Walls Came Tumbling Down

As the Israelites moved towards their 'promised land', there was only one obstacle between them and the achievement of their goal; the indigenous population. But Yahweh would lead them to victory over the farmers of Canaan.

The Book of Deuteronomy (Douai version) explains events as God's chosen people started to threaten the city states of Canaan in parts of chapters 2 and 3:

> *'And Sehon came out to meet us with all his people to fight at Jasa. And the Lord our God delivered him to us: and we slew him with his sons and all his people. And we took all his cities at that time, killing the*

209

inhabitants of them, men women and children. We left nothing of them.

Except the cattle which came to the share of them that took them: and the spoils of the cities, which we took.

From Aroer, which is upon the bank of the torrent Arnon, a town that is situate in a valley, as far as Galaad. There was not a village or city that escaped our hands: the Lord our God delivered all unto us ...

... Then we turned and went by way of Basan: and Og the king of Basan came out to meet us with his people to fight in Edrai.

And the Lord said to me: Fear him not: because he is delivered into thy hand, with all his people and his land. And thou shalt do to him as thou hast done to Seehon king of the Amorrhites, that dwelt in Hesebon.

So the Lord our God delivered into our hands Og also the king of Basan, and all his people. And we utterly destroyed them:

Wasting all his cities at one time. There was not a town that escaped us: sixty cities, all the country of Argob, the kingdom of Og in Basan.

All the cities were fenced with very high walls, and with gates and bars: besides innumerable towns that had no walls.

And we utterly destroyed them, as we had done to Sehon the king of Hesebon: destroying every city, men and women and children. But the cattle and the spoils of the cities we took for our prey.'

These passages do not describe battles so much as massacres where every man, woman and child, as well as sheep, ox and ass was put to death by sword.

The Old Testament contains many more passages of this violent type. In addition, Yahweh reminds his people that he is ever-powerful and ready to fiercely punish those that fail to worship him and live by His Word. Deuteronomy 8:19–20 give the following warning:

> '*But if thou forget the Lord thy God, and follow strange gods, and serve and adore them: behold, now I foretell thee that thou shalt utterly perish.*
>
> *As the nations, which the Lord destroyed at thy entrance, so shall you also perish, if you be disobedient to the voice of the Lord your God.*'

Whoever Moses actually was, he became a murderer in Egypt and spent the rest of his life killing huge numbers of people, both strangers and those who had placed their trust in him. We found it difficult to reconcile both this man and his view of God, with the God of modern Jews and Christians. To us this disparity proves the idea of God is not a static entity but a social focus that grows and evolves as He intertwines with other gods, slowly evolving into an idealised figurehead who reflects the morality and needs of the time. It is not so much that God made man in His image; it is more that man continually re-crafts God in *his* image.

The Timing of the Exodus

Some scholars now believe that the gory victories claimed in the Old Testament are exaggerated and that the arrival of the Israelites was more a slow absorption into Canaanite society rather than a bloody replacement of it. However, recent archaeological exploration has uncovered evidence of a large number of destroyed towns and cities indicating a late middle Bronze Age timing for the Exodus. Such a dating would put the Exodus somewhere in the hundred years between the Hyksos expulsion and the mid-fifteenth century BC. This greatly increases the likelihood that Moses was taken into the Egyptian royal family very soon after the Thebans regained control of the country.

We believe it was the training he received in Egypt that gave him the insight and ability to create his own god and establish a new nation in the face of great difficulty. His ruthless methods might have been the only way he could have succeeded. There is much evidence for the strong Egyptian influence on the events of the Exodus, from the design of the Ark of the Covenant to the tablets of hieroglyphics given by Yahweh to Moses, and we think it is entirely logical to assume that the secrets of the Seqenenre resurrection ceremony were taken from Egypt too. Moses clearly treated his people as simple-minded souls and indeed they must have been very unsophisticated compared to their leader who was, as we know, skilled in all of the secrets of the Egyptians.

David and Solomon

The tribes of Israel existed independently for some hundreds of years in a period known as the period of the Judges. These Judges were not primarily judicial or magisterial figures but were localised heroes or more precisely, 'saviours'.

The generally held idea that the twelve tribes of Israel were all involved in the Exodus is certainly wrong; only two or three tribes are now believed to have arrived in this way. At the time of the Judges the tribes of Simeon and Levi had been virtually wiped out and the all-important tribe of Judah was only just becoming recognised as being Israelite at all.

Slowly the nomadic Habiru tribesmen became the Hebrew nation of Israelites and they turned from their wandering ways to become farmers and manufacturers. Those elements of the more advanced Canaanite population which had not been murdered in the invasion merged with the newcomers and taught them the skills they had developed from thousands of years of agriculture.

The oldest book of the Old Testament is the Song of Deborah. This tells us that there was co-operation between some of the tribes when facing a common enemy such as the Philistines. Those tribes that did not provide soldiers for the battle were chided. The role of the Judges was different from kingship, in that each judgeship would have very localised power over one or several tribes and provided little political or economic leadership, with allegiance being voluntary. In short, kings were divinely appointed but judges were not.

All judges, however, were not equal. One of the earliest heroes from the time of the initial invasion was the warrior Jerubbaal who later changed his name to Gideon. (His original name was certainly Canaanite, honouring the god Baal, which probably illustrates that at the time Yahweh was not as entrenched as the later authors of the Old Testament would like us to believe). Gideon was offered the kingship of Israel but declined it stating that Yahweh was king over them all; nonetheless, it is clear that he did hold a special position and has to be viewed as an heir to Moses.

Although Gideon refused the kingship, his authority stemmed directly from Moses and certainly surpassed other judges. He founded a religious centre at Ophrah where he made a cult object known as an 'ephod' which was a type of ark, suggesting that he possessed another god. As a man of influence and power, Gideon kept an extensive harem (possibly including captured Midianite virgins) and reputedly had seventy sons, the principal of these being Abimelech, a name which has suggested to many biblical scholars an increasing royal ideology. It has been taken as evidence that Gideon did accept the kingship but, whether he did or not, his son Abimelech definitely transcended the status of a judge and became king. His temple devoted to Baal-berith has been excavated and found to have been a 'migdal' or fortified temple with walls seventeen feet thick, and on each side of the doorway bases for sacred pillars have been found.[3]

This was a generation after the death of Moses and, importantly, hundreds of years before Solomon's Temple; yet we have two sacred pillars either side of the doorway in a temple belonging to the first king of the Jews. The instruction on the meaning of the pillars and the ceremony that needed to be associated with them could only have come from Moses via Gideon to Abimelech. It seems to us extremely reasonable to assume that the resurrection ceremony based around the story of Seqenenre would have been used by this 'royal family' group, as they could have known of no king-making process other than that which Moses learned in Egypt. The pillars themselves would represent the connection with God and the stability of the new state.

Unfortunately for Abimelech, stability was short-lived. His fledgling monarchy crumbled soon after it was established and he lost his life in a battle with the unco-operative people of the city of Thebez. The period of the judges therefore continued, but the knowledge of the secrets of the royal house and of king-making were kept alive in the line of Gideon's judges.

Throughout this period Jerusalem remained a town that belonged to its ancient founders, the Jebusites; the religious and political centre for the Israelites was the city of Shiloh, some twenty miles to the north. Excavations have shown that Shiloh was destroyed in around 1050 BC, in the war between the Israelites and the Philistines. This event was witnessed by Samuel, who was an important judge, prophet, priest and king-maker.

The war between the Israelites and the Philistines is recorded in the biblical story of Samson, who was a Nazarite (a holy man) of immense strength. He destroyed

[3] *Peake's Commentary on the Bible*

three thousand Philistines by physically pulling down both the left- and right-hand pillars, which we believe is a metaphor for undermining their national stability.

It was Samuel who made the Benjamite, Saul, king in a private anointing ceremony. No explanation is given in the Bible as to how Samuel knew how to do this and there is, of course, no description of the ceremony itself. It appears that the relationship between Samuel and Saul was that of the twin powers of priest and king, the two pillars of a successful society uniting to produce stability. This relationship quickly came under stress when Saul made a sacrifice at Gilgal without the benefit of Samuel's ministrations, and when he failed to follow Samuel's instruction to destroy the harem of the defeated Amalekites, Samuel began to regret his choice.

A new candidate soon emerged, this time from the major tribe of Judah rather than from the smallest tribe of Benjamin. His name was David, and he came from a small town called Bethlehem.

David was, by all accounts, a highly accomplished individual with great skills, first as a courtier then as a soldier and as a statesman. The well-known story of the slaying of Goliath is generally accepted as true, but it was not David who killed the giant Gittite – that was done by another man from Bethlehem called Elhanan,[4] the son of Jaareoregim.[5]

The attributing of the event to David was a later attempt to portray David as a simple shepherd boy unused to war, but the fact was that he was a great soldier and politician throughout his life.

Saul saw the threat from David and tried to have him removed, but eventually it was Saul who lost his life and Samuel created his second king. It is not widely appreciated that when David was on the run from Saul he served

[4] 2 Samuel 21:19
[5] *Peake's Commentary on the Bible*

in the armies of the Philistines against the Israelites; a strange qualification for the founder of the greatest line in Israel's history.

David became king of Israel around 1000 BC and for the first time truly united the tribes into a single people. There was a striking parallel with the role of the kings of Egypt, in that Israel was also two lands, one northern and one southern, united by one ruler. For the first seven years David ruled from Hebron in the southern land of Judah, but his most important role was as the king who took Jerusalem, creating a new capital that sat between the two halves of the united kingdom. Here he built himself a palace, and moved the tent housing the Ark of the Covenant and the altar to the site of a temple that he proposed to build for Yahweh.

David established a well trained army, largely composed of foreign mercenaries, with which he defeated the Philistines who still held cities in the region, eventually gaining control of lands from the Euphrates to the Gulf of Aqaba. Peace appeared to be assured at last when David established a peace treaty with Hiram, King of Tyre, but the unruly behaviour of David and his family soon brought instability.

The events read like something from a Hollywood epic. David fell for Bathsheba and murdered her husband Uriah. David's son, the crown prince Amnon, was killed by his brother Absalom after he had raped his own half-sister Tamar, and Absalom finally tried to take the kingdom from his father by force. After what amounted to civil war, David retained his kingdom and his son Absalom lost his life hanging from the branches of a tree.

All of these distractions prevented David from building the intended temple to house his God, Yahweh. Soon David was on his deathbed and the heir to the throne, Adonijah, was crowned king. However, before the coronation feast was over, another son by Bathsheba called

Solomon was anointed king by Zadok, with David's assistance. Solomon's ceremony was held to be the true one and it was not long before the new king did away with his brother and his supporters in case they should ever consider challenging him again.

Solomon was set on greatness and under his rule Israel reached heights never seen before or since. He married the pharaoh's daughter and was given the strategic city of Gezer on the Egyptian border as a dowry; he created building works across the land; and, most importantly of all, he constructed the house of Yahweh, the holy temple for which he is best remembered. As we have already discussed, the Temple was a relatively minor undertaking but nonetheless, it was lavishly appointed and centrally located. It stood on a hilltop with its porchway facing east towards the rising sun, and because it was sited more or less on the dividing line of the two lands, one in the north, one in the south, the pillars of that porchway stood to represent the harmony and balance of the united kingdom. This was a reconstruction of the Egyptian concept of political stability through unity.

Boaz, the left-hand pillar, stood to the south representing the land of Judah and signifying 'strength'; Jachin stood in the north representing the land of Israel signifying 'establishment' and when united by the lintel of Yahweh the two provided 'stability'. As in ancient Egypt, so long as the two lands were conjoined by the appropriate pillars political stability would endure. This concept was wholly borrowed from the Egyptians, indicating that the structure of the Israelite monarchy and theology still had not lost its ancient origins.

All of this work had to be paid for and as virtually all of the expertise used was foreign – Hiram, king of Tyre provided the skilled workforce and most of the raw materials. This was a great expense for the fledgling kingdom, and Solomon started to run out of money, with many cities being sold to pay off the mounting debts. The population had to endure forced labour, with gangs of ten thousand people being sent for monthly spells in the Lebanon to work for Hiram, king of Tyre. The kingdom was split into twelve regions, with each region responsible for providing taxes to the palace for one month of each year. Tax levels became increasingly high and Solomon's subjects began to lose their enthusiasm for their king's desire for grandeur.

Despite the way the later authors of the Bible preferred to see it, there is abundant evidence that interest in Yahweh was always pretty thin, and other gods were for most of the nation's history held in equal, if not higher, esteem. For many, Yahweh was no more than the Israelite war god, useful in time of battle but a fairly lowly figure when viewed against the full pantheon of the gods. The names given to notable Israelites down the ages shows a strong respect for Baal, and even the most ardent Yahwist would not pretend that the Jews of this period believed in only one god.

So it was with Solomon. Towards the end of his reign Solomon gave himself over to the sole worship of other gods, which caused dissatisfaction with a number of groups, particularly the priests of the Temple at Jerusalem. It was later rationalised that this wickedness of Solomon's was not punished by Yahweh out of respect for his father David. In short, from the time of Moses right through to Solomon, Yahweh does not seem to have impressed his 'chosen people' very much at all. When Solomon – the king famous for his wisdom – died, the country was not only virtually bankrupt, it was Godless.

Solomon's son Rehoboam was brought up to believe in the power of kingship, and although advised to take a conciliatory line with the aggrieved northerners who did not accept him as king, he continued to demand co-operation. The unity of the two lands quickly fell apart and the northern kingdom of Israel had no more to do with Judah, which it saw as the source of its problems.

Let's sum up what we have learned about the Israelites of this period. The aspirations of the new nation to become a major civilisation had been based on a half-structured theology, forced labour and borrowed money. Like all ill-prepared ventures it failed, but it left an imprint in the hearts and minds of future generations who would retrospectively complete that theology and struggle to rebuild the transient glory that had marked out their emergence as a people with a god and a destiny. This was the vision that would never reach its goal, yet it would achieve greatness beyond measure.

Meanwhile, the secrets of the ceremony of initiation through resurrection, and of moral rectitude based on the principles of building a temple, were handed down amongst the royal group. It was no longer an abstract concept taken from the Egyptian story brought to them through Moses, it was real; as real as their temple at Jerusalem that contained the Ark and their God.

Throughout this stage of our research we had found no reference at all to a murdered architect of King Solomon's Temple. Nonetheless, by now we were beginning to see mounting evidence to support our hypothesis regarding the two pillars and the associated resurrection ceremony of Seqenenre Tao that had been taken to Israel by Moses and had become the secret of the Royal House of Israel.

Our next task was to identify when the name of the central character was changed from Seqenenre Tao to Hiram Abif. In order to understand how these guarded secrets could have survived and eventually come to the surface through the actions of the man we call Jesus the Christ, and how the New Testament could be interpreted in the light of our broader findings, we needed to investigate much more closely the next stage of the history of the Jewish Nation.

CONCLUSION

The story of the birth of Moses turned out to have been based on a Sumerian legend and we now felt that it had been adopted as a way of rationalising how a senior Egyptian general and member of the Egyptian royal family came to be the father of the Jewish nation. We were quite sure that Moses had been privy to the substituted secrets of Seqenenre Tao and that he was familiar with the story of the two pillars; he used these secrets to establish a new king-making ritual for his followers. This gave the stateless, cultureless Jews an identity and a secret ritual that was passed onto the line of David.

It was Moses who adopted the Kenite turbulent storm god Yahweh who was identified by the tau symbol, known originally as the 'Yahweh Mark'. Once he had made contact with his new God, Moses went back to Egypt where he was wanted for murder to lead out a group of Habiru. The journey of the Jews into the land of Canaan is depicted in the Bible as one continuous process of slaughter of the indigenous population.

Once the religion of Yahweh was established, the people of Yahweh, the Israelites, were led by a series of judges, starting with Joshua, the leader famous for the battle of Jericho. He was followed by a number of other judges, but both the Bible and archaeological evidence show that the symbol of the two pillars was used by both Abìmelech the son of Gideon[6] and Samson the Nazarite. We felt that this strongly indicated that the Egyptian secrets of Moses were continuing to be used by the leaders of the Israelites.

The Prophet Samuel anointed Saul the first king of the Jews but he was eventually succeeded by David, who was an extremely successful king, in around 1000 BC. David united the kingdoms of Judah and Israel with a new

---

[6] *Peake's Commentary on the Bible*

capital between the two lands at Jerusalem. It was his son Solomon who then built the first Temple in Jerusalem with the two pillars representing the unification of the two kingdoms and forming a gateway that faced eastwards – a pillar in the North representing Israel and a pillar in the South representing Judah. The twin pillars stood in the porchway or entrance to his Temple, showing that the Israelite monarchy still had its Egyptian roots and rituals. Solomon died leaving his country virtually bankrupt, but he left the secrets of the ceremony of initiation through living resurrection, and of moral rectitude, based on the principles of building a temple to be handed down amongst the royal group.

We no longer doubted that we had found the secret role model for the building of the Jewish state. But we had found no reference to a murdered builder of Solomon's Temple and we needed to find out how and when Seqenenre became Hiram Abif.

Chapter Ten

A Thousand Years of Struggle

The Early Jewish Nation

The death of King Solomon occurred almost exactly a thousand years before the final and most famous claimant to the title 'King of the Jews' died at the hands of the Romans.

For the Jews it was a millennium filled with pain, struggle and defeat, but never surrender. It was also characterised by a desperate search for a racial identity and a craving for a theology and social framework that was their own. They had the distant legend of a founding father in Abraham and a law-giver in Moses, but they had little else that amounted to a culture. The early Jewish kings provided a hollow sense of heritage. David, erroneously portrayed as a giant-killer, gave them a role model for their expected victory over their powerful neighbours, and Solomon, humble and ill-starred though his exploits had been, became the focus of national pride. It was not a man, however, who eventually came to epitomise the search for purpose and self esteem, it was a small and unimportant building that Solomon had erected for the god of war, Yahweh.

As we have seen, after the death of Solomon the two lands of the Jews split apart again, with Israel in the north and Judah in the south. They returned to their own respective views of development, which quite soon led to

war against each other. In the northern kingdom assassination of the king became almost a national sport and in
the centuries that followed war, murder and treachery
became the norm. Perhaps the most infamous individual
of this period was Jehu, a general who came to power by
personally murdering Jehoram, King of Israel. He then
murdered Ahaziah of Judah, who was unfortunate enough
to be visiting the north, and had the unfortunate Jezebel
trampled to pieces beneath the hooves of horses so that
only her skull, feet and the palms of her hands were found
for burial. A further one hundred and twelve possible
opponents were killed and all the Baal worshippers in the
land were rounded up and slaughtered. We are told that
God was well pleased with these 'noble' actions, saying in
2 Kings 10:30:

> *'And the LORD said unto Jehu, Because thou hast
> done well in executing that which is right in mine eyes,
> and hast done unto the house of Ahab according to all
> that was in mine heart, thy children of the fourth
> generation shall sit on the throne of Israel.'*

The southern kingdom of Judah continued to be ruled
from Jerusalem and the contrast with Israel in the north
could not have been greater. Judah managed to maintain
genuine stability for almost three and a half centuries after
the split. The Davidic line continued uninterrupted for
over four hundred years in total, which contrasts strongly
with Israel's eight revolutionary dynastic changes in its
first two centuries alone.

The question that we had to ask ourselves was – why
did the two halves of the briefly constituted state fare so
differently?

Geography may have something to do with it. Judah,
the southern kingdom, was off the main east-west route
and the terrain was more difficult for foreign invaders,

giving it a greater sense of national security than the northern kingdom could ever hope to enjoy. We strongly suspected, however, that the main reason for the continuance of the Davidic royal line over such a considerable period was due to the cohesion provided by a 'divine right to rule' conferred by a mystic and secret ceremony. Just as the early Egyptian kings had been viewed as placed in power by the gods, so the descendants of David were considered to be Yahweh's choice and the all-important covenant between the god and his people was the continuity of kingship. We felt that if our suppositions were right, the ruling family and its entourage would have been united by their membership of the secret holding group (the Lodge), and when they 'raised' their chosen candidate to the status of king, insurrection was very unlikely because of the power of this controlling group.

The central importance of the king of Judah was demonstrated in their New Year rituals, which followed Egyptian and Babylonian models. Some of the most important ritual acts were intended to ensure that the king continued to rule, an example of this being a re-enactment by the king of the original battle of the triumph of the forces of light over the forces of darkness and chaos.[1] The king and his priests chanted the 'Enuma elish' – the story that tells how the chaos-dragon Tiamat was overcome to allow the creation to take place. This ritual can be compared to the Egyptian hippopotamus ritual (discussed in Chapter Eight), which reaffirmed the king's ancient and sacred right to rule.

The king's role as 'holder of the covenant' gave him responsibility for the well-being of his people and any catastrophe on a national scale would be attributed to the fact that the king had either overstepped the mark or allowed his subjects to offend Yahweh in some way.

[1] *Peake's Commentary on the Bible*

The Exile in Babylon

The northern kingdom of Israel had struggled from start to finish and it finally collapsed in 721 BC when it was overrun by the Assyrians. Judah lasted over a century and a half longer. On 15 and 16 March 597 BC the great Babylonian king Nebuchadnezzar seized Jerusalem, captured the king and appointed a new puppet king called Zedekiah. The true king, Jehoiachin, was carried into exile with all his court and the intellectuals of the land, the idea being that those that remained would not have the wit to raise a rebellion against their new masters.

The Bible gives us various numbers but it is probable that over three thousand people were taken to Babylon; cuneiform tablets found at Babylon list payments of rations of oil and grain to the captives, naming specifically King Jehoiachin and his five sons as recipients.

The fact that Jehoiachin had not been put to death made many Jews believe that he would be allowed to return, and there is evidence that this may well have been Nebuchadnezzar's original intention. The new puppet king was not as docile as the Babylonians imagined and he was tempted to side with Babylon's enemy, the Egyptians, in order to liberate Judah. At first he followed the advice of his supporters and caused his masters no difficulty. Unfortunately pro-Egyptian pressures in his court forced a rebellion in 589 BC, which immediately prompted Nebuchadnezzar to attack the cities of Judah; in the following January the siege of Jerusalem began. Zedekiah knew that there would be no mercy this time and he held out for two and a half years, but despite an attempt by Egyptian forces to drive off the Babylonians, the city fell in July 586 BC. Jerusalem and its temple were utterly destroyed.

Zedekiah was brought before Nebuchadnezzar at Riblah in Babylonia where he was forced to watch the killing of his sons, and as he stared in horror his eyes were plucked out. With this last terrible sight burned into his memory, the puppet king was carried off to Babylon in chains. According to Jeremiah 52:29 a further eight hundred and thirty-two people were taken in exile at the same time.

For the exiles from Judah, Babylon must have been a marvellous place to behold. It was a cosmopolitan and splendid city that spanned both banks of the Euphrates in the form of a square, said to measure fifteen miles by fifteen miles. The Greek historian Herodotus visited the city in the fifth century BC and described its grand scale, with its gridwork of perfectly straight roads and buildings that were mostly three or even four storeys high. Our first reaction to this description was to assume that this Greek was guilty of exaggeration, but we then discovered that he had also claimed that the city walls were so wide that a chariot with four horses could be driven along them, and recent excavations have shown this to be completely true.

This archaeological support for the standing of Herodotus as a reliable witness caused us to appreciate just how impressive Babylon must have been. We read that inside the gigantic city walls lay expansive parks and amongst its great buildings was the king's palace with its famous 'hanging gardens', which were huge artificial mountain terraces covered in trees and awash with flowers brought from all around the known world. There was also the lofty Ziggurat of Bel, the stepped pyramid with seven tower-like storeys, faced with the colours of the sun, moon and five planets, and upon its summit a temple. This wonderful structure was no doubt the source of inspiration for the story of the Tower of Babel, where mankind was said to have lost the ability to communicate in a single language. Ba-bel was a Sumerian term meaning 'god gate', providing the Babylonian priesthood with a link between the gods and Earth. Amazingly the Tower of Babel still exists, although it is now just a shapeless ruin.

The Processional Way which led to the great Ishtar

Gate must have caused the eyes of the arriving exiles to widen. It was massive in scale and covered with brilliant blue glazed tiles on which were depicted lions, bulls and dragons in raised relief. These animals represented the gods of the city, Marduk the dragon deity being foremost amongst them, along with Adad the god of sky in the form of a bull, and Ishtar herself, the goddess of love and war, symbolised by a lion.

For the deported priests and nobles of Jerusalem, this new existence must have been very strange. They must have felt gratitude that they had not been put to the sword, and sorrow for the loss of their land and Temple. Yet they must have been impressed by what they saw and heard in the greatest city of Mesopotamia, a metropolis that must have made Jerusalem and its Temple look extremely humble. It must have been the kind of culture shock that the immigrant Jews from small European towns felt as they sailed into New York in the early part of the twentieth century.

The whole way of life in Babylonia would have been alien, but they soon found that the theology was surprisingly familiar. Their own Egyptian/Caananite-based legends and those of the Babylonians derived from a common ancient Sumerian source, and the Jews soon found that the gaps in their own tribal stories of the creation and the Flood could now be filled in.

The dignitaries who had been uprooted had been used to running a kingdom and now they had found themselves dispersed around an alien land, usually with only very menial tasks required of them. For men used to running a state they now had little to do but reflect upon the injustice of life, nevertheless the vast majority of them simply accepted that life was cruel and got on with making the best of a bad situation. Indeed a significant number, maybe even the majority, of Jewish families became wholly absorbed into the fabric of life in 'the big city', and stayed on when the captivity ended.

Contrary to popular belief, the Jews of this period were not monotheistic and even if they did hold Yahweh to be the special god of their nation, they would have worshipped Babylonian gods upon their enforced arrival in their new home. Then it was quite normal to show respect to the god or gods of an area one visited as a matter of prudence, because all deities were thought to be territorial in their power. Yahweh's zone of influence lay in Jerusalem and from all of the evidence available it seems that even his strongest supporters never created a shrine to him in the entire period of their captivity.

Whilst most of these Jews got on with life as it came to them, a small number of the deportees were philosophical and fundamentalist priests from Solomon's Temple who can only be described as 'inspired people with a thwarted sense of destiny', and they sought to rationalise the situation as best they could. It is now generally accepted that it was here, during the Babylonian captivity, that most of the first five books of the Bible were written down in a passionate search for purpose and heritage. Using information about the beginning of time from their captors, the Jews were able to reconstruct the way that God had created the world and mankind, as well as gain details about later events such as the Flood.

The writings of these first Jews were a mixture of snippets of accurate·historical fact, chunks of corrupted cultural memories and tribal myths, cemented together by their own original inventions generated wherever awkward gaps appeared in their history. It is obviously very difficult to separate which bits are which, but modern scholars have become remarkably able in identifying probable truths and fictions, as well as breaking down authorship styles and influences. The broad stories have been analysed in depth by teams of experts but, for us, it is the small pieces of oddball information that often provide some of the most powerful clues to origins.

We found the influence of both Sumer and Egypt in

unexpected places. For instance, the figure of Jacob, the father of Joseph, should predate Egyptian influence, yet there are clear signs that those who wrote about him were themselves viewing the world long after the Exodus out of Egypt. In Genesis 28:18 we are told that Jacob erected a pillar to link Earth with Heaven at Bethel, some ten miles north of Jerusalem, and later in Genesis 31:45 he created a second, possibly at Mizpah which was in the mountains of Galeed, east of the River Jordan. This identification of two pillars is strongly reminiscent of the theology that Moses had brought with him from the twin kingdoms of upper and lower Egypt. It is unlikely that either of the towns identified in the Bible existed in Jacob's time and when one looks at the literal meaning of the names of these towns it is clear that they were created to meet the requirements of the story. Bethel means 'God's house', suggesting a point of contact between the heavens and Earth, and Mizpah means 'watchtower', which is a point of protection from invasion.

Most Westerners today think of names as abstract labels and when a baby is expected, parents can buy a book of names from which to pick one they fancy. For most of history though, instead of being merely a pleasant or popular designation, names have conveyed important meanings. It is very significant to note that the late Semitic philologist John Allegro discovered that the name Jacob stems directly from the Sumerian IA-A-GUB, meaning 'pillar' or more literally, 'standing stone'.

When writing down the history of their people the Hebrews gave the key characters titles to communicate specific meanings, which modern readers see simply as personal names. We believe that the authors of Genesis conveyed a great deal in calling this character 'Jacob', and when the script changes his name to 'Israel', this signalled to the contemporary reader that the pillars of the new kingdom were in place and that the nation was ready to be given its own name. This was a necessary precursor to the establishment of true kingship.

The Prophet of the New Jerusalem

One of the strangest and yet most important figures in our reconstruction of the Babylonian exile was the prophet Ezekiel. His brooding, repetitive and often difficult writing style has caused many observers to conclude that this man must have been quite mad. Whether or not he existed and whether he was sane or totally schizophrenic does not really matter because the writings attributed to him, false or otherwise, provided the theology of Qumran, the people who were the Jerusalem Church[2]. Ezekiel was the architect of the imaginary or idealised Temple of Yahweh, and we would argue that it was the most important of them all!

Many twentieth-century experts have concluded that these works were the output of several much later people, circa 230 BC onwards. This would place it close to the dating as the oldest 'Dead Sea Scrolls' found at Qumran, thought to date from around 187 BC to AD 70. If this is the case it would not affect our thesis, serving only to confirm the already massive links between these writings and the Qumran Community, so for convenience we have assumed at this stage that the Book of Ezekiel was indeed written by one man whilst in captivity in Babylon.

The fall of Jerusalem and the destruction of the Temple were of massive significance to Ezekiel, who was a priest at the Temple and, one of the élite taken into exile in 597 BC. The weird visions that he had whilst in captivity are centred around these events. His wife died on the eve of the destruction of the Temple which, for the prophet, was a sign of great portent. However, the disaster in no way surprised Ezekiel, who saw it as Yahweh's

[2] R. Eisenman and M. Wise: *The Dead Sea Scrolls Uncovered*

punishment for Israel's wicked and unworthy history stemming back to its pagan origins and the worshipping of Egyptian idols. The infidelity to Yahweh had continued right up to the time when God allowed Israel's enemies to smite her. Despite all that Yahweh had done for His chosen people, Israel (the two kingdoms) had persisted in behaving in a rebellious, brazen and callous way, unmindful of her holy calling and covenantial bond. The Jews had disobeyed the divine laws and statutes and profaned holy things including the Temple itself – the Temple where His glory dwelt in the Holy of Holies. The destruction of Jerusalem and the Temple represented a death, whilst the expected new City and the rebuilt Temple would be a resurrection, a rebirth with the stain of guilt removed.

Ezekiel saw himself as the architect of the new Temple, one that would fulfil the promise and create a centrepiece for the nation that would be so pure and good, it would be 'the kingdom of Heaven' upon Earth. In his visions obscure allegory and symbolism abound with images of multi-faced men, lions, eagles and such odd items as iron baking plates. He flies though the air back to the Temple and undergoes strange rituals such as shaving off his hair and beard, dividing it into three parts by weighing it. One third of his hair and whiskers is burned, another cut to pieces by a sword and the last third is scattered to the winds. At this time a person's hair represented their dignity, their strength and their power and it seems to us that this imagery must have been representational of the recent fate of the people of Judah and Israel.

A particularly interesting and important vision occurred in November 591 BC when Ezekiel was sitting in his house near the grand canal in the city of Nippur in Mesopotamia (Sumer) with the visiting elders of Judah sitting in front of him. The elders (perhaps including the ex-king himself) had come to hear of any messages from Yahweh when the prophet fell into a trance and saw a man clothed in fire and light who put forth his hand, seized him by the forelock and transported him back to the inner gate of the Temple. Ezekiel saw images of pagan worship to the gods Tammuz, Baal and Adonis before being taken to a door of the court and commanded to dig a hole in the wall through which he saw a remarkable sight.

> '*Through it he sees mural paintings containing pictures of "creeping things" and other mythological scenes, motifs which seem to point to syncretistic practices of **Egyptian** provenance. Seventy elders are engaged in **secret mysteries** with censers in their hands.*'[3]

The bold letters are ours because here we have the elders of Jerusalem (the very people sitting in front of the entranced Ezekiel) accused of possessing 'secret mysteries' of Egyptian origin and conducting private ceremonies in the Temple of Solomon. Ezekiel 8:12 tells that the ceremony was conducted in the dark, as is the modern Masonic Third Degree.

What could the prophet have been referring to?

This part of the vision has never made much sense to Biblical scholars, beyond the general and obvious message that the destruction of the Temple and Jerusalem was believed to be due to a lack of a pure relationship with Yahweh. The Egyptian element has never been explained, especially as it is clear from the vision that it was the elders themselves involved in these secret rites. The verse (Ezekiel 8:8) that introduces this particular vision tells of how the prophet was able to spy on the proceedings, and has some remarkable similarities to Genesis 49:6, which earlier we identified as referring to the failed plot of Joseph's to get the secrets of Seqenenre and the fact that the villains 'digged down a wall'.

[3] *Peake's Commentary on the Bible*

You will recall that the verse in Genesis said:

'O my soul, come not thou into their secret; unto their assembly, mine honour, be not thou united: for in their anger they slew a man, and in their self will they digged down a wall.'

The verse in Ezekiel appears to build directly on the circumstances of the failed attempt to get the secrets of king-making from Seqenenre Tao. It reads:

'Then he said to me, Son of man, dig now in the wall: and when I had digged in the wall, behold a door.'

In Genesis there was a failure to gain the original secrets, but in Ezekiel's vision he found a door and saw what was going on, but this time it was not in a temple at Thebes with the original secrets, but in the Temple at Jerusalem with the substituted secrets. Ezekiel is outraged by the Egyptianesque images on the walls, naming the principal culprit as King Josiah, who in the middle of the previous century had had the Temple repaired and the walls redecorated. The description sounds remarkably similar to the symbolism found on the walls and ceiling of a modern Masonic temple which are based on King Solomon's Temple and, even today, most of the devices are undeniably Egyptian.

The ex-leaders of the kingdom of Judah who huddled in Ezekiel's house in exile in Nippur were there for guidance from the holy man and he gave it. As we read and reread Ezekiel we could not believe how much sense this obscure book now made. Our excitement mounted as it became clear that we had found a major link in our reconstructed chain of events, linking Seqenenre to the Qumran Community. The message that the prophet was putting to the exiled elders concerned their own secret ceremony that had come down to them through the line of

David from Moses. The essence of the prophet's message was something like this:

'*I tell you that we have lost our kingdom through people being unfaithful to Yahweh, worshipping other gods, and you were the greatest transgressors because you have conducted your "secret mysteries" which are from pagan Egypt, based on sun worship and without a role for the God of our fathers. You are the greatest sinners of them all and it is right that Yahweh has punished you.*'

We could imagine the response of these broken men:

'*But those are the secrets given to the Royal House of David by Moses himself!*'
   '*And because of it you no longer have a Royal House, remember Yahweh is the Heavenly King,*' replies Ezekiel.
   '*What should we do prophet? Tell us how to regain what we have lost.*'
   '*You must rebuild the Temple of your hearts first and the Temple of stone will follow. Live according to the law and worship Yahweh alone. You may keep your secrets but you must do away with the Egyptian story and turn the great truths within it to your task of rebuilding the Temple. Know your secrets — but know your God first.*'

We can think of no clearer or more simple explanation for this important vision of Ezekiel's. We believe it was at this point in the history of the Jewish people that the story of Seqenenre became the story of Hiram, the builder of the first Temple that was lost because of the reforming urge of Ezekiel to remove as many traces of Egyptian ritual as he could.

The Book of Ezekiel goes on to tell how he was

commanded in another vision to take two staffs, inscribe them with the names 'Judah' and 'Joseph' and join them into one, symbolically reuniting the two kingdoms. One king will rule over them and Yahweh will save her from apostasy (sliding back into having 'relationships' with other gods), purify her from all uncleanness and bring her into a new covenant relationship. Under the rule of his servant David she will live in obedience and faithfulness and occupy the land of the fathers. The covenant of peace, like all the blessings and benefits of the new age, will be everlasting; but above all Yahweh will dwell in the midst of his people. The presence of his sanctuary in their midst is a pledge that the covenant has been renewed and therefore the nations will see that Yahweh has sanctified his people and has thereby set them apart.

The most famous of Ezekiel's visions was one that occurred early in 573 BC after the prophet had spent nearly a quarter of a century in captivity, by which time his world-view had become particularly refined. In this vision he is transported to a high mountain where he can see a panorama of buildings spread out before him with walls and gates like a city. First he finds himself at the east gate where he meets a man like a figure of bronze with a ten-feet four-inch measuring-reed in his hand; this is his architectural guide. Ezekiel is told to pay close attention for it will be his duty to report everything he sees to the exiles.

First he sees the east gate, also known as the gate of righteousness, in direct line with the main approach to the temple. The main temple area is elevated so as to separate the holy from the profane, and by ascending seven steps they arrive at the threshold and then the passageway of the gate, where there are three guard-rooms facing each other; all of them being a perfect square and of the same dimensions.

The echoes of this vision are very clear in Freemasonry

with the importance of the east gate and the respect for squareness, but of particular significance are the seven steps to the threshold. The candidate in the Third Degree ceremony is required to take seven steps to the Master's pedestal in the east of the Masonic Temple.

Beyond the passageway is a second threshold and the vestibule of the gate that leads to the court. Along the wall of the outer court, to a depth of the length of the gates, runs a large pavement with symmetrically arranged chambers totalling thirty in all. The degrees of holiness are represented by the increasing elevation of the various parts of the Temple. The description of the component parts goes on and identifies the three gates as being in the east, west and south, just as Masonic tradition has it. Eventually Ezekiel is led to the inner court where he sees two rooms at the side of the north and south gates, the former for the priests who control the Temple precincts and the latter for those who have charge of the altar. The court is a perfect square. The vestibule of the Temple is ten steps higher than the inner court, the pillars of which are identified as corresponding with Boaz and Jachin, the pillars of Solomon's Temple. The vision culminates with Yahweh's return, and like the Horus king of ancient Egypt he arises like a star in the east and enters his new house through the 'gate of righteousness'.

Finally the imagination of Ezekiel establishes the rules for the priesthood that would become the landmarks of the Essenes of Qumran.[4] The legitimate priests of the sanctuary are to be the sons of Zadok, the erstwhile chief priest. Known to the people of Qumran as Zadokites, these sons of Zadok would wear white linen garments when they entered the inner court. They could not shave their heads nor allow their hair to grow very long, they could not drink wine before entering the inner court, they

[4] R. Eisenman, M. Wise: *The Dead Sea Scrolls Uncovered*

had to marry a virgin of Israelite birth and they must teach people the difference between clean and unclean. The list of requirements went on and included that they should not have personal possessions nor come into contact with the dead.[5]

The template for the new order had been made and the image of 'the temple to be' became more important than the temple that had been lost.

Zerubbabel's Temple

On 12 October 539 BC a general of the Persian King Cyrus, by the name of Ugbaru, took the city of Babylon without bloodshed. Seventeen days later Cyrus himself rode up to the Ishtar Gate in his chariot, followed by the combined armies of Persia and Medes. The king not only allowed the Jews to return to Jerusalem, he returned to them the treasures that Nebuchadnezzar had taken from the Temple. The Jews regained their city but Judah became a province of the Persian instead of the Babylonian empire.

People who had left Jerusalem as children returned as old men and women. Their memories of the city of their birth must have been dim and the reality of the partly rebuilt community must have come as a shock after a lifetime in Babylonia. It must have been a shock too for the population that had remained in Jerusalem throughout. To see thousands of strangers arriving from the east, demanding not only food and shelter but also expecting to take possession of old family lands and homes, must have been quite difficult to say the least. They brought with them ideas that had been incubated in captivity and these sophisticated relatives soon got down to the business of building a new and powerful covenant with Yahweh.

[5] *Peake's Commentary on the Bible*

The Temple was rebuilt before the end of the sixth century BC by Zerubbabel, the grandson of the last king and the heir to the throne of David. The considerable effect that the captivity had on the Jews is well illustrated by the name of their leader; Zerubbabel means 'seed of Babylon'. As new stones were put one upon the other so new stricter requirements for 'holiness' were being formulated, not only of priests, but now laymen too. We use the term 'men' deliberately here because whilst women were still involved in various aspects of the new religion under the second Temple, they were not allowed to be priests. The book of the law that was enforced by the returning exiles was very precise about what was required of Yahweh's people. Dietary laws were extremely demanding, with long lists of foods that could not be eaten. The list of unclean animals was comprehensive and included: camels, badgers, crabs, lobsters, shellfish, sharks, snakes, bats, swarming insects, rats, lizards, hares, ostriches and, of course, pigs. Animals that were considered acceptable for the dinner table ranged from such understandable choices as sheep, goats, doves and pigeons to what would seem to us to be less tasty morsels, such as crickets, locusts and grasshoppers.

It is important to remember that prior to the return of the exiles, the people of Israel and Judah were not generally monotheists nor fervent followers of Yahweh, the god of Moses. In fact the term 'Jew' (meaning member of the tribe of Judah) was coined in the Babylonian captivity and with it came a new and powerful sense of nationhood that was marked by the construction of Zerubbabel's Temple. The builders of the new Jerusalem saw themselves as a people with something special in their relationship with Yahweh and to protect that specialness they took such steps as banning marriage outside of their own people. In this way the once disparate tribes of the Levant became a race.

The New Threat to Yahweh

The Jews with their new heightened sense of identity had escaped their Babylonian masters, thanks to the intervention of the Persians into whose empire they were now absorbed. The influence of both of these great powers is apparent in the writings of the Old Testament but in the mid-fourth century BC a radically new culture arose that was to have a far more profound effect on the future of Judaism. It not so much influenced as collided with the introverted, spiritual outlook of the Jews. These radical thinkers were the Greeks.

The Greeks had their own pantheon of gods, but unlike the private and inward-looking Jews they were cosmopolitan and eclectic, with a keen interest in the gods of other people. The Jews had built a theology that had originally drawn on beliefs from Sumer, Egypt, Babylon and elsewhere, but now they wanted only consolidation and a focus on their special god – Yahweh. Though the Greeks on the other hand were equally superstitious about the role of other-worldly influences, they were open to new ideas. They had created a clearer separation between the role of the gods and man's right to think creatively, believing that their destiny was dependent upon science, politics, finance and military might.

Whilst in Jerusalem social order was centred around a priesthood and the appeasement of a difficult god, the Greek thinkers were producing a new class of philosophers, scientists and poets. The world found out about this new great power through the military exploits of one of the greatest leaders ever seen; the Macedonian king, Alexander the Great.

Alexander led an army that conquered Egypt, the entire Persian empire and crossed Afghanistan into the Indian sub-continent, yet when he died of fever in Babylon in 323 BC he was still only thirty-three years old. The empire created by this remarkable young king opened up a truly international way of life with knowledge as well as goods being exchanged around the world from the new city of Alexandria, in Egypt, to the Indus valley. The Greek language became the standard for commerce, diplomacy and learning. The Hellenistic way of life and way of thinking became the only way for intellectuals; if a person could not read and write in Greek, they were outside the new international élite.

The crumbling Egyptian society responded to the arrival of the Greeks by declaring the twenty-four-year-old Alexander to be the son of god and pharaoh incarnate. The young warrior who rid Egypt of Persian invaders, but who had himself come from across the Mediterranean Sea, took the throne name Haa-ib-re Setep-en-amen, which meant 'Jubilant is the heart of Re, Chosen of Amen'. Alexander's stay in Egypt was short but his influence was massive, as he restored ancient temples and built the city that still bears his name. The Hellenistic influence in Egypt remained with the line of pharaohs known as Ptolemies who, despite their traditional royal trappings, were Greeks themselves. The most famous of them was Cleopatra, who was reputed to be wise as well as beautiful; certainly she was one of the very few leaders of this dynasty who could even speak Egyptian.

In the city of Alexandria, old Egyptian gods were merged with Greek gods to produce hybrid deities to suit prevailing tastes. The twin pillars of the Two Lands became the Pillars of Hermes and the attributes of the ancient Egyptian moon god Thoth became absorbed into Hermes. Thoth represented wisdom and was, you will recall, the brother of Ma'at. It was said that this god possessed all secret knowledge on 36,535 scrolls that were hidden under the heavenly vault (the sky) which could only be found by the worthy, who would use such knowledge for the benefit of mankind. (It struck us as noteworthy that the number of scrolls is almost exactly the number of days in a century.) Hermes took over the mantle of Thoth as the inventor of writing, architecture, arithmetic, surveying, geometry, astronomy, medicine and surgery.

Both Thoth and Hermes are extremely important in the legends of Freemasonry and the two names are treated in Masonic myth as representing the same person:

> '*In the tomb of Osymandias were deposited twenty thousand volumes ... all of which, on account of their antiquity, or the importance of their subjects, were ascribed to Thoth or Hermes, who, it is well known, united in his character the intelligence of a divinity with the patriotism of a faithful minister.*'[6]

The Ancient Charges of Freemasonry tell us how Hermes/Thoth was involved in the early development of science as this quotation from the Inigo Jones version shows:

> '*YOU ask me how this Science was Invented, My Answer is this: That before the General Deluge, which is commonly Called NOAH'S Flood, there was a Man called LAMECH, as you may read in IV. Chapter of Genesis; who had two Wives, the One called ADA, the other ZILLA; BY ADA, he begat two SONS, JABAL and JUBAL, by ZILLA, he had One SON called TUBALL and a Daughter called Naamab: These four Children found the beginning of all crafts in the World: JABAL found out GEOMETRY, and he Divided Flocks of Sheep, He first built a House of Stone and Timber.*
>
> *HIS Brother JUBAL found the ART of MUSIC He was the Father of all such as Handle the Harp and Organ.*

[6] J. Fellows A.M.: *The Mysteries of Freemasonry*

TUBAL-CAIN was the Instructor of Every Artificer in Brass and Iron, And the Daughter found out the ART of Weaving.

THESE Children knew well that GOD would take Vengeance for SIN either by Fire or Water; Wherefore they Wrote their SCIENCES that they had found in Two Pillars, that they might be found after in Two Pillars, that they might be found after NOAH'S Flood.

ONE of the Pillars was Marble, for that will not Burn with any Fire, And the other stone was Laternes for that will not drown with any Water.

OUR Intent next is to Tell you Truly, how and in What manner these STONES were found whereon these SCIENCES were Written.

THE Great HERMES (Surnamed TRISMAGISTUS, or three times Great) Being both King, Priest and Philosopher, (in EGYPT) he found One of them, and Lived in the Year of the World Two Thousand and Seventy Six, in the Reign of NINUS, and some think him to be Grandson to CUSH, which was Grandson to NOAH, he was the first that began to Learn of Astronomy, To Admire the other Wonders of Nature; He proved, there was but One GOD, Creator of all Things, He Divided the Day into Twelve Hours, He is also thought to be the first who Divided the ZODIAC into Twelve Signs, He was minister to OSYRIS King of EGYPT; And is said to have invented Ordinary Writing, and Hieroglyphics, the first Laws of the Egyptians; And Divers Sciences, and Taught them unto other Men. (Anno Mundi. MDCCCX.).[7]

Here Freemasonry recalls how the Greeks built up their beliefs first from Egyptian legends. The dating

---

[7] *The Inigo Jones Document,* dated 1607

'Anno Mundi' means from the beginning of the world, which is taken by Freemasonry to be the year 4000 BC, the time when the Sumerian civilisation apparently materialised out of nowhere! (Interestingly, the date given in the passage tells us that Thoth/Hermes invented writing and taught the sciences to mankind in 3390 BC; as we now know, this was little more than two hundred years before the consolidation of the first united kingdom of ancient Egypt took place and the earliest known hieroglyphics were produced.)

In the fourth century BC Jewish theology had become mature with detailed legends of its own, and the priesthood did not want any intrusions from the Greeks or anyone else. However, many of their people were quick to forget the more restrictive aspects of their covenant with Yahweh and took to this new cosmopolitan world order with great alacrity. Soon the new race which called themselves Jews spread, establishing their own quarter in just about every Hellenistic city. The Jews had few skills to offer as their young culture had no heritage of building or manufacture, but through cruel circumstances they had learned to live on their wits and extract the best out of any situation. A natural resourcefulness and willingness to keep going in the face of adversity made them particularly suited to becoming traders, buyers and sellers, wheelers and dealers who could make a good honest living by spotting an opportunity for profit that others might miss. Jews quickly became respected members of the new commerce that drove the Greek empire; one commentator described them as 'Greek not only in speech but in spirit'.

The Jews took their belief in Yahweh with them and their sacred books were translated into Koine, the contemporary, city-based version of classical Greek. These writings became known as the Septuagint – the 'Book of the Seventy'. The early scriptures now existed in Hebrew, Aramaic of the Persian Empire and Koine; and from this point on new religious works could be read and even originated in any one of three languages.

Language, however, is a strange thing; it is like a living, creative and special means of communication that works within a community at a given point in time. Translation is an imprecise art and not the scientific replacement of one word with its exact counterpart that many people imagine. The Greek language was developed by a rational, free-thinking, cosmopolitan people who used oratory and philosophy to great effect; by contrast, Hebrew had been developed by an inspired, irrational people with a very different world-view. The Koine-speaking Jews of Alexandria, Ephesus and other cities who translated their scriptures with good intent could not fail but to affect the flavour and import.

The Jewish world outside of Judah was known as the Diaspora, and the faithful minority back in Jerusalem were alarmed at what was happening in the new places beyond their borders. They came to call these Diaspora Jews 'seekers-after-smooth-things', or as we might express it today, 'the easy life'. They wanted the heritage of their Jewish birth but they sought the good things that living the Greek way brought. They interpreted the law as it suited them, and worst of all they 'transgressed' with the invention of the synagogue.

'Synagogue' is not Hebrew at all; it is Greek meaning 'bringing together' and it was originally a place for Jews to meet and organise their community needs in order to uphold the various laws, particularly their food laws. At some point, however, the synagogue turned from a meeting house into a temple, a place at which one could actually worship Yahweh. This was an outrageous idea to those who believed their God could only be worshipped in His house in Jerusalem. The devoted followers of God back in the Holy City were appalled at the growing slackness of the Jews and they began to expect the worst:

Yahweh would punish them horribly unless they got a lot holier.

The religion of Yahweh was by now coming to the attention of occultists who were fascinated by the magical properties they saw in it and who took a very different view of its meaning. The numerological elements seized their attention and even the Hebrew name of God, pronounced Yahweh but written as JHVH, took on special meaning. The Greeks called this name of God the 'Tetragrammaton' and treated the Jewish texts as a source of supposedly ancient, esoteric wisdom. New cults arose in the Hellenistic empire, basing themselves on the scriptures of Yahweh yet not being themselves Jews. These gentiles took what they wanted from Judaism and it was these groups, as we shall see, who were the breeding ground for a later Greek mystery cult called Christianity.

CONCLUSION

The Temple that Solomon had built for Yahweh had incorporated one of the most important symbolic representations of the enduring strength of the revitalised Egyptian monarchy, the symbol of the two pillars and we now knew that this symbol had a direct linkage to the Exodus of Moses via Joshua, Gideon, Abimelech and Samson. It seemed reasonable that if the more public aspects of the ritual of Seqenenre had been handed down to the Israelites by Moses, then the more important king-making initiation ceremonies might also have survived. Once again, there was an historical oddity after the death of Solomon which attracted our attention. Whilst the northern kingdom of Israel was racked by changes in its ruling line, in the southern kingdom of Judah the line of David was uninterrupted for over four hundred years. We came to view this stability as circumstantial evidence of the survival of the Seqenenre resurrection ritual conferring a 'divine right to rule' on the line of David. We had found evidence to support this position in the ritual re-enactment by the king of the original battle of the triumph of the forces of light over the forces of darkness and chaos described in the 'Enuma elish', which reminded us strongly of the Egyptian hippopotamus ritual.

However, it was our detailed study of the Babylonian exile period of Jewish history which finally disclosed the explanation of how Seqenenre's name was dropped. Ezekiel, the architect of the imaginary second Temple of Yahweh, had told the exiled elders of Jerusalem to remove the Egyptian practices of their secret mysteries conducted in the darkness beneath the Temple of Solomon. We knew that to this day the ritual of Seqenenre's resurrection is conducted in darkness, having both experienced it.

We had been struck by the similarities to the earlier verse in Genesis 49:6 which is the only reference in the Bible to the killing of the Theban king. The Book of Ezekiel goes on to tell how the prophet purged the children of Israel of their Egyptian practices and brought them back to the way of Yahweh. So now we knew how Seqenenre Tao had become Hiram Abif, the king who was lost. It was the work of the brooding figure of Ezekiel in an attempt to explain the failure of God to sustain his own Temple from his enemies.

Chapter Eleven

The Boaz and Jachin Pesher

The Dead Sea Scrolls

Our detailed reconstruction of the development of the Jewish people over the last five chapters had finally brought us to the period that directly preceded the events that gave rise to the Christian Church. We had delved deeply into the distant past of the Essenes/Nasoreans, and had learnt a great deal. On the basis of what we had found out, we had the feeling that this was going to be a particularly intriguing section of our quest. So far, we had an emerging hypothesis of kingdoms being built on the power of twin earthly pillars and a heavenly lintel or archway, and we could only hope that a final proof of this paradigm would soon emerge.

Of all the groups that existed in Israel at this time (that is, the period around the birth of Christ), we believe that the most important was the Qumran Community that existed in the Judaean hills. Although it never grew to much more than around two hundred people at any one time, its influence upon the future world was immense.

We already had good cause to believe that the authors of the Dead Sea Scrolls, the Qumran Community, were Essenes, and that they and the Nasoreans and the original Jerusalem Church were all one and the same. Our evidence for such a statement was already strong and it is a view that has received serious consideration by many leading experts, but now our added insight, gained from the Hiram Key, was starting to put it beyond question in our minds.

Our original hypothesis outlined in Chapters Four and Five – that Freemasonry had developed from this group – now seemed entirely possible because of the linkage that we have found between them and the ancient Egyptians, but now we had to look for direct evidence of Masonic attitudes and rites. If we were right that there is a direct connection between Freemasonry and the Qumranians, and that the Qumranians were the first Christians, it follows that Christ must have been, in some sense of the word, a Freemason himself. We were aware that this is a notion that will horrify many modern Christians, particularly Roman Catholics, but we did indeed find the evidence that that is exactly what he was.

It has long been speculated that the Jerusalem Essenes were some kind of proto-Christians, and that Jesus the Christ may have been one of them, but evidence was always very thin on the ground. Things changed radically when some tatty bits of writings were, as we mentioned in Chapter Four, unearthed at the ancient settlement at Qumran. Soon afterwards the whole site was extensively excavated by the Jordan Department of Antiquities, L'Ecole Archéologique Française and the Palestine Archaeological Museum under G. L. Harding and Père R. de Vaux in five campaigns between 1951 and 1956. What they found was the theologian's equivalent to sweating nitroglycerine; the world of Christianity could blow up if the whole thing was not handled with the utmost care. But the lid could not be kept on this explosive issue, no matter how hard the Christian Church tried to do so. Those in charge of the research were not independent scholars, they had a faith to protect and an establishment to maintain. Other scholars involved with the scrolls saw evidence that appeared to change the view of Christ and the New Testament, but they were effectively silenced or discredited.

Accusations of scandal, cover-up and deliberate smothering of the truth have been met by denials and counter accusations of 'over-active imaginations' and 'deliberate sensationalism'. It is a fact that for more than forty years after their discovery, over half of the 800 scrolls discovered had not been published. The academic community was outraged by this unprecedented secrecy of what ought to be public knowledge and after widespread protests, led by the Huntington Library of San Marino, California, the Israeli authorities removed restrictions on public access to the contents of the scrolls in October 1991.

Various versions of biblical texts were found and all of them were over a thousand years older than the oldest surviving Hebrew texts that were produced by Aaron ben Moses ben Asher in AD 1008. Prior to the discovery of the scrolls the Jewish and Christian world did not know for sure how accurate our current Old Testament was, we only knew that during the Christian era even the tiniest deviation has been frowned upon. From the great variety of competing texts, each carefully stored in the caves of Qumran, we now know that there were a large number of different texts and that the one translated into the Greek Septuagint was just one of them – so there is no 'correct' version of the Bible after all.

The whole area of investigation concerning Qumran is a minefield for ordinary Christians, so many have preferred to keep away from the subject. Whilst Judaism and most other religions are based on a broad theme of social and theological thinking, Christianity rests entirely on the idea that on a particular day in history a god/man absolved those members of the human race who were prepared to worship Him of responsibility for their wrong doings by dying (albeit temporarily) under torture. Until recently the only evidence regarding this pivotal event was the three Synoptic Gospels of the New Testament, which were written long after the events they describe by people who were not involved themselves and cannot be properly identified. It is now known that the story of Jesus told in these Gospels is to a large extent a dramatic invention to wrap up his teachings in a 'reader-friendly' format. Analysis of the Gospels of Matthew and Luke have shown that they are an amalgam of two separate Church traditions, based on a combination of the Gospel of Mark and a lost earlier gospel now referred to as 'Q' (derived from the German word 'quelle', meaning 'source'). The birth story of Jesus told in Mark and Luke is now known to be a complete invention by people who had no understanding of the historical and political circumstances of the time. The events as they describe them simply could not have happened. An example of this is the way that King Herod is linked with Roman taxation under Quirinius – when Herod had been dead since 4 BC, at least ten years before Quirinius came on the scene.

Other scholars, such as Morton Smith, have detected the existence of a secret gospel with elements running beneath the four New Testament gospels, which is believed to predate the gospel of Mark.[2] We could not help but wonder that if this secret gospel of Jesus did exist in a written form, it may well be the document at the heart of our mission; the scroll that the Knights Templar found!

This possibility is borne out by the Qumran scrolls which identify that there was a secret tradition that members had to swear never to divulge. These secrets were written down and preserved in readiness for the day when God would visit his people in the last times.[3]

There is little or no reference to Jesus in any recognised third-party documentation, which is very unusual especially when such historians as Josephus, Philo and Pliny the Elder were recording just about everything of note at the time. As we have discussed, it is normally possible to

[1] G. W. Buchanan: *Jesus: The King and His Kingdom*
[2] M. Smith: *The Secret Gospel*
[3] D. S. Russell: *The Method and Message of Jewish Apocalyptic*

understand historical characters through what independent sources and even their enemies say about them, but in this case the early inventors of Christianity did a good job of removing all evidence about a mortal they wanted to portray as a god. They were not thorough enough, however, and through good fortune and modern deductive analysis there is suddenly a lot more information available, and the strange interpretations of the early Roman Church stand to be challenged by the truth.

Christianity is uniquely exposed. There is no sudden influx of information that could fundamentally damage Judaism, Islam, Buddhism or even for that matter the belief systems of the Australian Aborigines or the Amazonian Indians, because they are religions that have grown from a deep spiritual understanding evolved slowly out of their own cultures. Even without Guatama, Buddhism lives; without Mohammed, Islam lives; yet without the resurrection of Jesus, Christianity (as it currently stands) is nothing. It is understandable, therefore, that the Church takes great care in dealing with new information regarding this tiny moment in relatively recent history when they believe the creator of the whole universe decided it was time to become a living Jew. This leaves Christianity exposed to the light of truth.

If the whole basis of Christianity can be shown to be a silly mistake, will the Vatican apologise for the inconvenience it has caused, abolish itself and hand over its wealth and power to the Chief Rabbi? No. Clearly no proof could ever do this, and maybe that is right, because the Church is too large and important to suddenly disappear; but equally it can never be right to hide the truth, because truth must surely be the essence of God. There must be a way for the Church to survive by re-thinking what it knows are mistaken ideas. There is an old Jewish story that makes the point well.

At a gathering of rabbis the wise men were debating a section of Holy Law and one of them found himself at odds with the rest of the group on a point of interpretation. He was coming under great pressure to concede but he knew that he was right and that God would therefore be on his side. So he called upon the Almighty to help him prove his case. 'Please God, if I am right, let the streams of Israel flow uphill,' the rabbi begged. Immediately the waters of the land changed direction. Unfortunately his adversaries were unmoved. 'Please God,' the exasperated rabbi said again, 'if I am right, may the trees bend to the ground.' And they did. But still his fellows were intransigent. 'Dear God,' he called out in rising frustration, 'may you speak aloud and support me.' The clouds promptly parted and a great voice from heaven boomed forth. 'My friends, I have to tell you – you are wrong and he is right. This is what I intended.' The lone elder smiled in triumph but the group remained unimpressed. 'Oh, we pay no attention to heavenly voices,' they said, 'because the correct determination on this point was written down long ago.'

This humorous story says it all. Old scriptures, however inaccurate, take on a life of their own and ultimately religion is not about historical truth at all, it is about faith. But in our modern world blind faith is not enough; not nearly enough – and if religion wants to survive it must not turn away from new information.

To put dogma above truth is no way to honour God.

The Missing Books of Maccabee

Conventional history records the Maccabean revolt as a Jewish cause with right on its side, and the raising of Jonathan Maccabaeus to the high priesthood is viewed as a popular event. Whilst the first part is certainly true, we now know from the scrolls recovered from Qumran that Jonathan was considered by the Hasidim (or strict Jewish establishment) to be an outrageous choice who put politics before Yahweh.

When Jonathan was murdered, his brother Simon became high priest and proceeded to take things even further by declaring his family's hereditary 'right' to the position of high priest, a claim which he had engraved in bronze and set up in the temple. The Roman Catholic Douai Bible tells us how Simon started to see himself as a player on the world stage when he sent an ambassador and offerings to Rome. Simon's illegitimate accession can be found in Psalm 110.

The Qumran Community's views of the Jerusalem priesthood are clear in the following passages from the scrolls:

> *'The priests of Jerusalem, who will heap up wealth and unjust gain from the plunder of the people. (1 QpHab 9:4–5)*
>
> *The city is Jerusalem in which the wicked priest did works of abomination and defiled the Temple of God. (1 QpHab 12:7–9)'*

The names used to describe the rule of the family that took over the high priesthood are confusing; the founder was called Mattathias but the term 'Maccabee' is used for his son Judas and the lineage they produced is collectively called 'the Hasmonaeans' in Rabbinical literature. According to the historian Josephus, this was due to the name of Mattathias's great-grandfather Hashmon. When Simon was murdered he was replaced by his son John Hyrcanus who ruled for thirty years; then his son, Aristobulus, briefly took over and became the first Hasmonaean to call himself king of the Jews as well as high priest. The line continued until roles of king and high priest split again upon the death of Queen Alexandra in 67 BC when her youngest son Aristobulus II became king and her eldest son, Hyrcanus, became high priest.

The Roman Catholic Douai Bible gives a very full story

of this period of political intrigue, murder and wholesale corruption and it portrays the Hasmonaeans as Jewish heroes – yet the King James Bible tells us nothing. The last two books of the Douai Bible are the First and Second Books of Maccabees, scriptures totally absent from the Protestant Old Testament.

Why should this be so? The fact that these two books are missing from the King James Bible actually told us a lot. There must be a very important reason why the Catholic Bible presents the story of the Maccabean Revolt and the Hasmonaean high priesthood as legitimate, and the King James Bible does not recognise any of it as scripture at all. What was wrong with these works, and what could the far-later compilers of the Protestant Bible possibly have known that could cause them to drop these long accepted works, supposedly inspired by God?

The only people who knew that the rise of the Hasmonaean high priests and kings was illegitimate were the Members of the Qumran Community who despised these false high priests and their political panderings to the Romans. Yet the Qumranians were all but destroyed in the war with the Romans in AD 66–70 and the Diaspora Jews/Christians (the seekers-after-smooth-things) were left to tell the story the way they saw it. However, although the Qumranians may have lost the battle, they won the war. By burying the true Jewish story in scroll form, the message eventually got into the hands of the creators of the Protestant Bible – thanks to the early twelfth-century excavations of the Knights Templar.

The Elect of Judah

The Jews who returned from their captivity in Babylon were led back to Jerusalem by Zerubbabel, the man who otherwise might have been their king. He and his inner group, named in the Bible as Jeshua, Nehemiah, Seraiah, Reelaiah, Mordecai, Bilshan, Mispar, Bigvai, Rehum and

Baanah, returned to their city with their secret ceremony of the royal line of David. It was now a little different because following Ezekiel's advice the most overtly Egyptian elements had been exchanged for Hebrew ones – but still it was intact. As they rebuilt the Temple to the design explained by Ezekiel, they were filled with a new confidence; they would build a Temple and a new, unshakeable covenant with Yahweh. Never again would His people err and never again would their God need to punish them so harshly.

The confidence of a new beginning is always special; the 'this time I will make it work' feeling. It is human nature to find strength through hope in a future which always seems as though it will be kinder than the past – but as many experienced people know, it rarely is.

It is most likely that the descendants of Zerubbabel and his inner group known as the Hasidim left Jerusalem sometime between 187 BC and 152 BC. The scroll called the Damascus Document (so called because the Community referred to itself on occasions as Damascus) gives us the best clue to the founding of the Qumran Community:

'For in their disloyalty, when they left him, He hid his face from Israel and from His Temple, and He gave them to the sword. Then when He remembered the covenant of the Patriarchs, He left a remnant to Israel and He did not give them up to annihilation. And in the end-time of anger – 390 years after He gave them into the hand of Nebuchadnezzar, king of Babylon – He visited them and caused to spout from Israel and from Aaron a root of planting to possess His land and to grow fat in the goodness of His earth.

Then they understood their iniquity, and they knew that they were guilty men. But they were like blind men, like men groping their way, for twenty years. And God considered their deeds, that they sought Him with a whole heart, and He raised up for them a teacher of

> *righteousness to guide them in the way of His heart, and He made known to the last generations what He did with the last generation, the congregation of traitors, those who had turned aside from the way.' (CD 1:3–13)*

If we take the reference to the Jews being 'into the hands of Nebuchadnezzar' from the date of his first taking of Jerusalem in 597 BC rather than the city's destruction in 586 BC, the 390 years plus the 20 years of 'groping their way' gives us an early date of 187 BC for the founding of Qumran. This dating should not be taken too literally, but we can be sure that the Community was in place in 152 BC when the Qumranians were in protest at the assumption of the high priesthood by Jonathan, the leader of the Maccabees. Scrolls recovered from the caves of Qumran, particularly the Manual of Discipline and the Commentary on the first two chapters of the Book of Habakkuk, tell us of their particular revulsion at this appointment. Their exile was self imposed and in their desert retreat they saw themselves as the people of the new covenant with Yahweh, the 'elect of Judah', living a harsh, monastic life that would become the model for Christian orders. They describe themselves as 'the men who entered into a New Covenant in the Land of Damascus' (Damascus is now widely considered to be the name that they used for Qumran rather than a reference to the Syrian city).

Excavations have shown that the people of Qumran probably lived in tents and used the caves in the surrounding escarpments as storehouses and dwellings when sheltering from the very occasional winter rains. There were buildings which included a watch-tower, public meeting rooms, a refectory with kitchens and pantries, a scriptorium, a bakery, a pot makers' establishment, various workshops and large cisterns for ceremonial ablutions. Ritual washing was essential to the maintenance of holiness, so large amounts of water were required in this area of very little rainfall.

The members of the Community were divided into three groups: 'Israel', 'Levi' and 'Aaron'. Israel meant the common membership, Levites were lower priests and Aaron designated the most senior and holy priests. Like Freemasonry, any man that could express a firm belief in God was eligible to join the Community – 'the many' as they called themselves. There are a number of distinct similarities in the treatment of new members, starting with an interview with the Council to examine the potential candidate and establish his righteousness after which a ballot was taken. If accepted, the candidate was admitted at a lowly grade for the period of one year, in which time he must not mingle his wealth with 'the many'. The first level of Freemasonry, that of 'entered apprentice', used to be of a year's duration, and in the initiation ceremony the candidate is required to bring in no coins or other metallic objects. In the course of the initiation he is asked to give money, and when he replies that he has none he is told that it was a test to ensure that he had brought no coins or other wealth into the Lodge.

When the new member had been in the Qumran Community for a year he was tested on his learning of the works in the Torah; before proceeding to the status of a Fellow Craft a Masonic brother has to be tested on his learning of ritual. As with Freemasonry in the past, the second stage of membership was as far as the majority got, but for selected individuals there was a third level to which the individual could pass after a further year. This allowed them to 'draw near to the secret council of the Community' – this reminds us of the secrets of Hiram Abif that are revealed to the Freemason that becomes a Master Mason on being raised to their Third Degree. As with Knights Templar practice, once initiates passed their first year they had to pass over all of their wealth;

naturally this is a procedure that Freemasonry cannot adopt without disappearing as an organisation overnight!

The positive virtues taught in the Qumran Community were clearly laid out in the scrolls: truth, righteousness, kindness, justice, honesty and humility along with brotherly love. So similar are the three degrees of the Qumran Community to those of Freemasonry that it transcends mere coincidence. Employing our technique of using Masonic ritual with just the few identifying words changed, it would be easy to believe that this address to a Third Degree initiate was a quotation from the scrolls concerning someone who had just been elevated to the Qumranian third stage, the 'Purity of the Many':

'Your zeal for the institution of the Community of the Many, the progress you have made in the Art and your conformity to the general regulations, have pointed you out as a proper object of our favour and esteem. In the character of a member of the Secret Council you are henceforth authorised to correct the errors and irregularities of Brethren and Fellows and guard them against a breach of fidelity.

To improve the morals and correct the manners of men in society must be your constant care. With this in view, therefore, you are always to recommend to inferiors, obedience and submission; to equals, courtesy and affability; to superiors, kindness and condescension. You are to inculcate universal benevolence, and, by the regularity of your own behaviour, afford the best example for the benefit of others.

The Ancient Landmarks of Israel, which are here entrusted to your care, you are to preserve sacred and inviolable and never suffer an infringement of our rites, or a deviation from the established usage and custom.

Duty, honour, and gratitude now bind you to be faithful to every trust; to support with becoming dignity

*your new character and to enforce by example and
precept the tenets of God's system.*

*Let no motive, therefore, make you swerve from your
duty, violate your vows or betray trust, but be true and
faithful and imitate the example of that celebrated
Artist, Taxo, whom you have once represented.'*

Before we consider the comparative secrets of the two
orders, there are some exclusions from membership which
are strangely similar to each other. A man could not join
the Qumran Community if he were simple or 'smitten in
his flesh, afflicted in the feet or hands, lame or blind or
deaf or dumb, or smitten with a blemish in his flesh
visible to the eyes, or a stumbling old man so that he
cannot hold himself up in the midst of the Congregation'.
Although the rule is no longer rigorously applied,
Freemasonry requires that candidates must be of sound
mind and able bodied; any physical handicap is supposed
to bar admission.

The Community which lived at Qumran for around
two hundred and fifty years is often referred to by modern
observers as an Essene monastery. That they were Essenes
is now fully accepted by most observers, but the term
'monastery' is misleading in that they were not a gathering
of celibate males who spent nearly all of their non-
working time in prayer. We can see from the library of
scrolls that relate to the Community that celibacy was
highly regarded but not essential for membership. Nevertheless, sexual relationships were considered to be deeply
soiling and if a man had even slight contact with a
menstruating woman, a considerable amount of cleansing
was required before he could mix in the Community.
Modern Western minds love labels; we love to be able to
put everything we come across into a pigeon hole – is it an
'A' or is it a 'B'? We have built up so many definitions and
categories that we are slightly fazed if something is
impossible to slot into a box, but the particular point

about the Qumran Community is that it changed dramatically over the quarter of a millennium of its existence, particularly towards its end, under the influence of Jesus and James.

Midrash, Pesher and Parable

Anyone today who studies ancient Judaism is fully aware that the Jewish mind of two thousand years ago and more was quite different to ours today and they have to understand the techniques of 'midrash', 'pesher' and 'parable'. The term 'midrash' corresponds very closely to the English word 'exegesis' and can be defined as 'the investigation and interpretation of the Hebrew scriptures for the purpose of discovering theological truths and instructions to be followed'. This is a closely related concept to a technique of understanding current events called 'pesher', which can be explained as an interpretation or explanation of a verse of Scripture in which a given statement is considered to have meaning regarding an event or a person at the present time or in the future. So 'midrash' was an ongoing process for the priests and prophets of Israel seeking out instruction to improve the spiritual well-being of the people and 'pesher' was a method of making sense of things that were happening around them. They believed that events were not random occurrences but conformed to structured patterns that could be deciphered through the studying of scripture. As a result of these two principles, when they wrote down a story of a recent event, they would be likely to ensure that it followed an ancient pattern. This explains why we find so many references, both in the New Testament and the Qumran scrolls, which are echoes of the Old Testament.

The term 'parable' is well understood by Christians because the New Testament tells us that Jesus the Christ used this form of storytelling to communicate his morality teaching to the unsophisticated people of Judaea. The method can be defined as 'a figurative explanation which may contain either allegory or metaphor or both to transmit a deeper level of meaning than the surface level'. These stories were not only used as simple analogies to help uneducated Jews understand the Law, they were also a technique of explaining complex current events in an allegorical, and therefore, secret way. It is a fact beyond all dispute that Christianity was a Jewish cult and that all of its 'original cast' (Jesus, James, Simon Peter, Andrew, Judas, Thomas, etc.) were people who thought in terms of midrash, pesher and parable. By contrast, what we might call the 'second cast' (Paul, Matthew, Luke, etc.) were quite different and used more Hellenistic thought processes that are closer to the way we think today. The Gospels of the New Testament were almost certainly all written after the destruction of Jerusalem and Qumran and the death of the 'original cast'. These writings were created for a Greek-thinking audience by people who took the teachings that they believed to be those of their Christ, then wove a life story for Christ around them – without the benefit of any actual eye-witness testimony. To separate the fact from the fiction in the New Testament, we have to remove the literalism of Greek thinking and look beneath to study the undercurrent of radical Jewish and proto-Christian thought.

There are fundamental similarities between what the Qumran Community said about itself and what the early Church said about itself. The early Church was known as 'those of the way' or the 'way of God' as a distinct sect (Acts 24:14). The members of the Qumran Community also used this same term to describe themselves. What is more, both groups describe themselves as the poor, the children of light, the elect of God, a community of the New Testament or Covenant. This idea of the Church as a new Temple of God where sacrificial redemption is made once and for all for the entire world comes from the eighth chapter of the Epistle to the Hebrews, which quotes in full the Jeremiah passage which preceded it:

> '... an eternal planting, a holy house of Israel, a most holy conclave for Aaron, witnesses of Truth in judgement, and chosen by divine favour to atone for the earth, to render to the wicked their deserts. This is the tried wall, the precious cornerstone, whose foundation shall not be shaken nor moved from its place.'

We could not help but notice how extraordinarily similar is Peter's description of the Church:

> '... ye also, as living stones, are built up a spiritual house to be a holy priesthood, to offer up spiritual sacrifices, acceptable to God through Jesus Christ. Because it is contained in Scripture, Behold, I lay in Zion a chief corner stone, elect, precious ... But ye are an elect race, a royal priesthood, a holy nation, a people of God's own possession ...'[4]

This close parallel was first noticed in 1956 when it became clear that there was a very special connection between the Qumranians and the Jerusalem Church. What was not commented on was how well these words also fit another organisation – Freemasonry. Whilst all of Freemasonry is concerned with the building of a spiritual temple on the design of Ezekiel's view of Solomon's Temple, the 'address in the north-east corner' immediately comes to mind:

> 'At the erection of all stately or superb edifices, it is customary to lay the first or foundation stone in the north-east corner of the building.
> You, being newly admitted into Freemasonry are

[4] John Allegro: *The Dead Sea Scrolls*

placed in the north-east corner of the Lodge, figuratively to represent that stone and, from the foundation laid this evening, may you hereafter raise a superstructure, perfect in its parts and honourable to the builder.'

The Secrets of Qumran

When Essenes were first forced to leave Jerusalem, we are told that they 'groped around' for twenty years until a man known as the Teacher of Righteousness showed them 'the way' and the Community at Qumran became firmly established. The difficulty with the Qumran scrolls is that they rarely give us names for individuals, so identifying characters by comparison with non-Qumranic sources is impossible. Besides the Teacher of Righteousness, there are major characters who recur in the scrolls, such as 'the wicked priest' and 'the liar', whose identities have provoked much scholarly debate.

Whoever the Teacher of Righteousness was, he must have been a pious, holy man and apparently was a priestly descendant of Zadok, who revealed to his Community that they were living in a time that would be 'the end of days' as predicted by the old prophets. Soon, he told them, God would crush His enemies in a final cosmic battle and usher in the new age of righteousness, and as the Community was the last remnant of true Israel – the people of Yahweh's covenant – it would be they who would fight the battle and would return to Jerusalem to purify the Temple and re-institute proper worship.

The Qumranians had several descriptions for themselves including 'the Community', 'the Many', 'the Congregation of Israel' and 'the Sons of Light'; in addition, the man who would lead them at 'the end of the age', the Davidic Messiah, had such titles as 'Mighty Man', 'Man of Glory' and 'Prince of Light'. It would be this 'Prince of Light' who would overcome the 'Prince of

Darkness' and 'the Congregation of Belial' (Satan). A scroll entitled 'Midrash on the Last Days' tells how the 'Children of Belial' will devise evil plots against the 'Sons of Light' to cause them to stumble and the kings of the nations will rage against the elect of Israel in the last days. God, however, will save His people by the hands of two messianic figures who will arise at the end of time; one from 'the Branch of David' and the other 'the Interpreter of the Law'.[5]

From the scrolls we learned that there were in existence some secret books which contained information about future events and references to certain rituals revealed by God; these were normally transmitted to selected people by word of mouth alone, but they had now been written down in coded form. These secrets were highly restricted and it is claimed that they had been handed down in a long line of secret tradition, to be faithfully preserved until 'the last days'. Father J. T. Milik, who led much of the early work on the Qumran material, identified that certain secret scrolls used cryptic devices. One example was the use of two different alphabets with arbitrarily chosen signs which replaced the normal Hebrew characters; another had the script running left to right instead of the normal right to left.

Everything we found out about the Qumran Community added to our conviction that they were the spiritual descendants of the Egyptian kings and the antecedents of the Templars and Freemasonry. A major piece of evidence came to light thanks to another member of the original Dead Sea Scrolls team and a Nobel Peace Prize nominee. In many of the scrolls Dr Hugh Schonfield discovered a Hebrew code that he called the 'Atbash cipher', which was used to conceal the names of individuals.[6] Staggeringly, before his death in 1988, Schonfield

[5] D. S. Russell: *The Method and Message of Jewish Apocalyptic*
[6] H. Schonfield: *The Essene Odyssey*

found that key words used by both the Knights Templar and Freemasonry are themselves Atbash codes which reveal hidden meaning once deciphered. For instance, the Templars were widely reputed to worship something with the curious name of 'Baphomet', which was never understood until it was written in Hebrew and the Atbash cipher applied to reveal the word 'Sophia' – the Greek for 'wisdom'.

So here was a positive connection with the Templars; and one for Freemasonry followed. Applying the Atbash cipher to the Masonic word 'Tajo' (pronounced 'Tacho'), which was a pseudonym supposedly given to the Grand Master in Spain, produces the name of the man (Asaph) who, according to a number of psalms, assisted at the building of the first temple at Jerusalem.

The subject matter of some of these mysterious works from the Qumran library concern Noah and Enoch, who were said to have been the recipients of divine secrets of Heaven and Earth that had been passed down through certain initiates. There is an ancient belief that the mythical ancestors of the human race were men of superb wisdom, and there are many tales concerning Enoch and Noah as holders of divine secrets. These stories occur in much of the apocalyptic literature and although as ancient as the book of Genesis, they clearly come from some other unidentified source. We believe that this source could be the oral secrets of the resurrection ceremony, as there has long been an unexplained secret tradition attached to the name of Enoch. In Masonic literature there are old rituals associated with the attempt by Sem, Japhet and Ham to resurrect Noah. And we have already mentioned a Masonic side-degree, known as the Ark Mariners, which continues this tradition of the secrets of Noah.

But there is an even more important aspect of secret teachings of the apocalyptic tradition which is connected with both Moses and Ezra (who was known as the second

Moses). It is now believed that there was once a far larger body of writings attributed to Moses than have survived to the present day.[7] One such work that has survived is the *Assumption of Moses*, which is known to be an Essene work.[8] It contains the following instruction given by Moses to Joshua:

> *'Receive thou this writing that thou mayest know how to preserve the books which I shall deliver unto thee: and thou shalt set them in order and anoint them with oil of cedar and put them away in earthen vessels in the place which He made from the beginning of the creation of the world.'*

This reference is talking of secret books which Moses gives to Joshua to be kept hidden.

> *'... until the day of repentance in the visitation wherewith the Lord shall visit thee in consummation of the end of the days.'*

The secret works connected to Moses immediately stood out to us because he was the only man to know the secrets of the Egyptian kings from firsthand experience, and he here gives instructions that at some point prior to the 'end of days' these secrets must be deposited 'in the place which He made from the beginning of the creation of the world'. This described only one place to the Jews; the rock beneath the Holy of Holies in the inner sanctum of the Temple in Jerusalem, because this was the first point of creation. We know that the Qumranians hid the main library of scrolls that they had written down themselves, plus other texts drawn in from around Judaea, in the caves behind the settlement. We also know that

[7] E. Schürer: *The Jewish People at the Time of Jesus Christ*
[8] H. Schonfield: *The Essene Odyssey*

they were devout students of the Law, so they must have followed this instruction from Moses because it is certain that they absolutely believed that the 'end of the age' would happen in their lifetime. It follows that if the Knights Templar excavated towards and underneath the 'Holy of Holies', as we were increasingly confident they had, they must have found these secret scrolls.

We were extremely excited at this point – had we really found an explicit instruction to bury the secrets, handed down from Moses, under Herod's Temple? Such a discovery would instantly turn a compelling theory into an odds-on probability! We immediately decided to investigate further the background to *The Assumption of Moses*. We found that scholarly opinion said that was probably written during the lifetime of Jesus, and that it surveys Jewish history down to the Seleucid era, and then on through the Hasmonaean period to someone who is described as 'an insolent king'. This reference is commonly held to be to Herod the Great. The book goes on to describe a period of persecution, which fits the times of Antiochus Epiphanes; many scholars think this chapter has been misplaced and should stand earlier. Then a mysterious figure, Taxo, appears. He urges his sons to retire with him to a cave, to die there rather than be disloyal to their faith. Their death is to be the trigger for the expected intervention of God in history and the establishment of His kingdom. This kingdom appears to be understood as a Heavenly kingdom, rather than one established on Earth. Many attempts have been made to identify Taxo with a historical character, but none has been really successful so far. Some writers have attempted to identify him as the Teacher of Righteousness.

We now had confirmation of an instruction from Moses to bury the secrets, but we also had a dating which put the origin of the scroll no earlier than the years of Jesus's life, a time when the whole Community was preparing for the great battle before the 'end of the age'. But it was the mention of an unidentified character called 'Taxo' that excited us. We already knew that Taxo and Tacho were forms of the same name, and that the Atbash cipher translates Tacho to Asaph – the man who assisted Solomon at the building of the first Temple at Jerusalem and a name used by Freemasons for the Grand Master.

The name 'Taxo' was no longer a mystery because the discovery of the Atbash cipher used by the Qumranians in their scrolls does confirm earlier suspicions that it refers to the Master of the Community i.e. the Teacher of Righteousness of the last years of their existence.[9] The exhortation in the text 'to die rather than be disloyal to their faith' is also highly reminiscent of the Third Degree of Freemasonry, which is entirely oriented to the idea of 'faithfulness even unto death', summed up by the words of Hiram Abif when he was threatened by the first of his attackers:

> *'I would rather suffer death than betray the sacred trust reposed in me.'*

Our conclusion from this evidence is that the leader of the Qumran Community was considered to be the spiritual descendant of the original builder of the Temple of Solomon, the man that Freemasons now know as Hiram Abif.

The links with the ritual of the Masonic Third Degree now seemed to be fitting into our historical jigsaw pattern but the other main motif of Masonic symbolism still required further explanation. We needed to discover how the story of the two pillars, which is so important in the first two degrees of Freemasonry, could possibly have been transmitted to the Templars.

[9] *Peake's Commentary on the Bible*

The Twin Pillars

Because the Roman Church falsely positioned itself as the inheritor of the teachings of Jesus and because modern Christians erroneously believe that they have some right to the high ground from which to study other groups, they look upon the Essenes/Qumranians as just one group amongst many that existed in the Holy Land at the time of Christ. This is a hopelessly inadequate assessment of the Qumran Community. Its members were the distillation of everything that was important to the Jews as a nation, the guardians of the covenant with their God and the embodiment of all of the aspirations of a people. They were Jewishness in fine focus.

A key point of discussion over the years has been the identity of the individual described as the Teacher of Righteousness, but with the amount of information now available many scholars believe that there must have been not one, but *two* individuals given this title; the first at the founding of the Community and the other at the 'end of the age'.[10] The difficulty is that the Qumran Community was not a static thing but a thriving, rapidly evolving group that had to continually change to meet the pressure brought to bear upon it. Consequently the older scrolls refer to the first Teacher of Righteousness and the later ones are talking about a later spiritual leader, who is identifiable as 'James the Just'. Professors Robert Eisenman and Michael Wise have concluded, as independent observers, that this leader of the Qumranians was James, the brother of Christ and the leader of the Jerusalem Church. It follows that the Jerusalem Church was the Qumran Community.

An early reference to this was made by the second-century historian, Hegesippus, who called James, the brother of Christ 'James the Just', described him as 'a

[10] W. S. LASOR: *The Dead Sea Scrolls and the New Testament*

Nazirite' and said that he interceded in the sanctuary of the Temple for the sake of the people. The same observer described James as 'the Righteous', saying that he drank no wine and ate no animal flesh, he wore the white linen robes of a priest and had knees hard like a camel's from constant prayer.

According to another scroll known as the *Manual of Discipline*, the council of the Community consisted of twelve perfect and holy men who were the 'pillars' of the Community, and we believe that the two principal pillars were highly symbolic, representing the kingly and the priestly aspects of creating and maintaining the 'Kingdom of Heaven'. We bore in mind that this term never did mean anything other-worldly; rather, it pointed to an earthly existence where Yahweh would rule over the Jews in a permanent state of peace and prosperity. These spiritual pillars were, of course, the descendants of the pillars of the united Upper and Lower Egypt that had come down to the Community as the legendary Boaz and Jachin that had adorned the eastern gate of Solomon's Temple. To these pious and cornered Jews, the columns represented both the kingly power of 'mishpat' and the priestly power of 'tsedeq', and when united they supported the great archway of Heaven, the keystone of which was the third great word of Hebrew desire, 'shalom'.

This Qumranian world-view became particularly clear to us reading through vast amounts of information from the scrolls, from the Bible and other contemporary literature, since we have the advantage of our knowledge of Freemasonry and the origins of Hiram Abif. Others have seen all the parts in a fragmented and confused way, but when the broad shape of the late Qumran Community/early Church is properly perceived, all of the confusion and apparent contradictions evaporate. The diagram shown here illustrates this important twin pillar paradigm.

The right-hand pillar is known to Freemasons as

'Jachin', who was the first high priest of the Temple, and therefore it will come as no surprise to learn that this is the priestly pillar which for the Qumranians was the embodiment of holiness embodied in the fundamental concept of 'tsedeq'. This word (sometimes shown spelt 'Zedek') stood for the principle underlying the divinely appointed order usually translated as 'righteousness', although it has been said that a better definition in English would be 'rightness' or 'doing good to others at all times'. In other words, this concept is fundamentally the same as the ancient Egyptian concept of Ma'at. It was clear from our readings that 'tsedeq' was for Canaanites a term associated with the sun god. The Canaanite sun god was seen as the great judge who watched over the world, righted wrongs and shone light onto the dark doings of hidden crimes. When the Jews merged Canaanite beliefs into their concept of Yahweh, 'tsedeq' became one of His features. All the virtues of Yahweh from feeding the people by making the crops grow to destroying Israel's enemies was a part of 'tsedeq'. The word kept its association with the light of the sun and helped become the opposite of darkness and chaos.[11]

Although sun worship is too common in the many theologies that stem from the Sumerian civilisation to

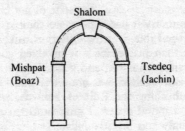

Shalom

Mishpat
(Boaz)

Tsedeq
(Jachin)

[11] Norman Cohen: *Cosmos, Chaos and the World to Come*

make any special point out of it, there *are* interesting similarities between the main Egyptian deity Amen-Re and Yahweh here, in that both of them use their beneficial power of daylight to fight the forces of darkness and chaos.

The left-hand pillar of King Solomon's Temple was called Boaz, who, as any Freemason knows, was the great-grandfather of David, king of Israel. For the Qumranians too, this was the kingly pillar that stood for the house of David and the concept of 'mishpat'. This is often translated as 'judgement', but it stood for more than that; it signified the regular rule of Yahweh as king, and so represented the divinely appointed order itself.

The rule of government and the dispensing of justice were always connected with this pillar: it was at Mizpah (another spelling of mishpat) that Jacob erected his first pillar, and it was here that Saul was acclaimed the first king of Israel.

When these two spiritual pillars are in place with the Teacher of Righteousness (tsedeq) on the left hand of God and the earthly Davidic King (mishpat) on his right hand, the archway of Yahweh's rule will be in place with the keystone of 'shalom' locking everything together at its centre. This Jewish term is perhaps the most famous of all Hebrew words, understood the world over as a form of greeting that means 'peace', the state of not being at war; but needless to say it had a far more complex import for the Jews of the Bible. For the Qumranians shalom meant much more than just peace – it involved good fortune, prosperity, victory in war, and general good fortune and well-being. But 'shalom' was not a free gift – it had to be won by establishing the Rule of Yahweh, which meant establishing a moral order of government, supported by both the kingly and priestly pillars.

The whole essence and mission of the Qumran Community was made comprehensible to its senior members through this symbolism, which they wrote down as per the midrashic instructions of Moses and buried under Herod's Temple, later to be rediscovered by the Knights Templar.

Freemasons have inherited the symbols but have lost the meaning along the way. When the Qumranians knew that the 'end of the age' was drawing near, the need to find the people who were fit to be these pillars became urgent, because God could not destroy the old order until the new framework was in place. Because these positions were 'designate' rather than immediately available, due to the Roman occupation and the false high priesthood in Jerusalem, the candidates were called messiahs; essentially, leaders in waiting.

The more we discovered of the Qumranian 'pillar' paradigm, the more certain we became that their ceremonies had to be the forerunners of Freemasonry today. We became particularly excited when we looked into the remains of Qumran and found that they had erected an imitation Temple entrance with their own copies of the pillars of Boaz and Jachin. The two pillar bases still exist outside the east door of a vestry that leads to what is often referred to as Qumran's 'Holy of Holies'. We could not believe that it was mere coincidence that the only two pillar bases found in the ruins of the whole settlement are either side of the eastern gate to their substitute place of worship. These two pillars must have been the location for the all-important initiation ceremony of senior members and the aspiration for the two messiahs that would come shortly before the 'end of the age'. The Qumranian works we call the Dead Sea Scrolls are full of important information for our investigation and we were particularly thrilled to find a reference to 'the secret of the pillars' in fragment four of a scroll known as the *Brontologion*.

The name 'Qumran' itself is considered to be the modern Arabic word for the location of the Essene monastery and a word that has no meaning. However, we later found that this is not true when we were fortunate enough to come across a copy of a book by the late John Allegro that provides a full translation of the Copper Scroll. Allegro, a Semitic philologist, could see a clear root-meaning to the word 'Qumran'. He describes its origins and states that it would have been called 'Qimrôn' at the time of Jesus and James. The meaning that Allegro detected meant nothing to him and he mentioned it in his book as an interesting aside; but to us it was of explosive interest![12]

The verbal root of 'Qumran' is given as 'vault, arch, doorway or the like'. The Qumranians identified themselves with an 'arched doorway'; or put more precisely, they were the people of the pillars with the arch over it! The doorway was created by the pillars of 'tsedeq' and 'mishpat' with the holy arch of 'shalom'.

Here was unarguably powerful proof of our thesis, connecting the community of Jesus and James with modern Freemasonry. The commonality was going far further than we had ever expected.

Freemasons say that the meaning of the word Jachin is 'to establish'. It was the task of the priestly or 'tsedeq' messiah to establish righteousness in the land of Israel so the Temple could be rebuilt. The left-hand pillar, Boaz, is said by Freemasons to mean 'Strength'. This is the pillar of the kingly or 'mishpat' messiah who would be responsible for the strength of the kingdom in defence from outsiders and in civil law and governmental matters. And Freemasons say that when the two are united, 'stability' is the result. There could be no better single-word translation for the concept of 'shalom'. The bottom line is that modern Freemasons use the two pillars of King Solomon's Temple in exactly the same way that the Qumran Community and Jesus the Christ did. Fragments of a Testament to Levi which is probably older than the version of the Testament of Levi contained in the Bible

[12] John Allegro: *The Treasure of the Copper Scroll*

have been found in the Qumran caves. In this document there are references to the Messiah, which seems to indicate writings came from circles who expected a Levitical (priestly) Messiah rather than a Davidic (kingly) one. The translations of the document we have seen would appear to indicate that the writers expected a priestly leader alongside a civil leader, with the civil subordinate to the priestly.[13]

Many other Qumranian texts, such as the Damascus Document with its references to 'the Messiahs of Aaron (priestly) and Israel (kingly)', confirm these ideas, but the less well known but powerful Testament to Levi makes the point clearly. In Matthew 3:3, John the Baptist is described as 'a voice crying in the wilderness', this is the precise form of words used by the Qumran Community, and it suggested to us that the Gospel writers had a struggle to turn scriptures around to make Jesus come out as the Messiah. It also makes reference to the fact that even as late as the time of the writing of Luke's Gospel it was remembered that people held John the Baptist to be the Messiah. Luke says in 3:15:

> '*And as the people were in expectation, and all men mused in their hearts of John, whether he were the Christ, or not.*'

This verse is probably skimmed over by most Christians who use their scriptures for personal inspiration rather than historical understanding, but it does communicate a key point: the choice of the words 'all men' rather than 'some men' indicates that everybody saw John as the prime candidate for being a messiah. That John and Jesus were joint messiahs has been accepted by many members of the traditional theological community for the last forty

[13] *Peake's Commentary on the Bible*

years.[14] As we discussed earlier, the Mandaeans of southern Iraq are descendants of the Nasoreans and they claim that John the Baptist was the originator of their sect which came into being at the point in time when the Qumranians became a distinct cult instead of being just an introverted, Essene-style community such as those found in Ephesus, Turkey, or on the island of Elephantine in Egypt.

This evidence will frighten many Christians because it seems so alien and threatening to their belief that their Jesus Christ was the one and only Messiah, but this is only a problem to those who cling to the Hellenised, supernatural corruption of the Hebrew term. If the word is given its original correct meaning, it is quite natural to see John as the priestly messiah and Jesus as the 'mishpat' pillar – the kingly messiah.

John lived a hard life in the wilderness, cleansing the spirit of the people by submerging them in the running waters of the River Jordan. That was the preferred technique of the Qumranians who usually had to make do with the static water of their cisterns. He was the personification of Qumranian righteousness, eating only such permissible food as locusts and wild honey and wearing a leather girdle and a coat of camel hair. In John's view the entire Jerusalem establishment was totally corrupt, so as he preached excoriating sermons against it; and he urged his congregation to repent and to accept the Essene/Qumranian rite of purification by baptism. Some observers believe that John was the Teacher of Righteousness, but whilst it may be true we have been unable to find sufficient evidence to support this view.

The story of the baptism of Jesus described in the New Testament is a deliberately enhanced account created by the later gospel writers to keep up the level of magical events to satisfy a Gentile audience, but the reconstructed

---

[14] K. G. Kuhn: *Die Beiden Messias Aarons und Israels*

source material can shed useful light on the relationship between these two important men.[15]

This reveals that the idea that John baptised Jesus was an invention by Mark, and that John only became aware that Jesus existed when his disciples told him about a new wise teacher who had arrived from the north, claiming even that a Roman centurion had shown more belief in the power of God than the average Jew. Jesus must have been a central figure in the Qumran Community and being of the line of David, as well as a very talented student, it is likely that the so-called baptism by John was Jesus's first level of initiation into the Qumran Community. The description of Jesus seeing a dove descend upon him was a standard Hebrew way of expressing the gaining of wisdom.

It is even more interesting to look at what happened to Jesus after his baptism. According to the New Testament he went into the wilderness where he fasted for forty days and nights. It does not say that he left the wilderness after that fasting, indeed the King James Bible tells us that he remained there for three years from AD 27 to 31, and it is important to note that the term 'the Wilderness' is used throughout the Dead Sea Scrolls as the description of the Qumran Community. It was an inability to understand contemporary usage of 'wilderness' that caused Christians to imagine Jesus alone in an actual desert. We can now be clear about its meaning; Jesus was at Qumran passing through the three stages of initiation to reach the highest level of the brotherhood – each of which, you will recall, took precisely one year! Here he learned how to face the temptations of Satan and turn his back on the bribes of the leaders of other nations. At the last stage, after his three years, he was taught the secret technique and words of resurrection handed down from Moses, which raise a candidate from his figurative tomb to live a faithful and

[15] Burton L. Mack: *The Lost Gospel*

righteous life ready for the coming of the kingdom of God.

It is fairly certain that Jesus lived for a year thereafter by the Community's strict sectarian rules, but after John's death in early AD 32 he decided that the fastest and most efficient way to get the people of Israel into shape for the coming 'Kingdom of Heaven' was to bend the rules; a case of the end justifying the means.

From all of the information available to us we have to deduce that Jesus and his younger brother James must have been star pupils and highly qualified Qumranians. As a gifted teacher from the line of David, John the Baptist asked Jesus if he would be 'the one to come', that is, the kingly messiah to form his opposite pillar. Jesus answered the question with a 'pesher' response, 'the blind recover their sight, the lame walk, lepers are cleansed, and the deaf hear, the dead are raised, and the poor are given the good news'. In no way did he mean that he had done all these things; he was referring to the miracles of healing that Isaiah predicted would happen at the time of Israel's restoration. This was a confirmation that Jesus agreed with John that the 'end of the age' was imminent and he was the man to help prepare 'the way'. All physical and mental illnesses were considered to be the result of a sinful life and a driving out of sin would cure the malady.

When it comes to Jesus's expressed view of John in the reconstructed gospel, the message is clear.

> 'You knew that John was a prophet and not to expect royal garments when you saw him. But what you did not know, and what I now tell you, is that John was more than a prophet. He was the one about whom it is written, "look, I am sending my messenger before you". He will prepare your path ahead of you.'[16]

[16] Burton L. Mack: *The Lost Gospel*

This early Christian text incorrectly implies that it is Jesus who has marked out John as the priestly messiah, rather than John spotting Jesus as the kingly messiah. The passage states lucidly that whilst John is the preordained one, people should not expect 'royal garments' because he will not be the king. Many people have been confused by passages in which Jesus describes John as 'the one to come' and John describes Jesus with the same words. Once it is realised that the two of them were pillars in the heavenly gateway, it becomes clear that there is no conflict at all – each needed the other.

The messianic ministry of John the Baptist lasted only six years as he was beheaded early in AD 32. Josephus records in 'Antiquities' that he was killed by Herod Antipas, who feared that John's activities could lead to a revolt because of his 'messianic' nature. It must have come as a major blow to Jesus to hear that his opposite pillar had been murdered. The Qumran Community and all of their followers must have been devastated by the loss of one pillar, ahead of the 'end of the age' and the arrival of the 'kingdom of God'. Despite the rarity of people holy enough to be considered as John's replacement, two candidates appear to have stepped quickly forward to fill this key role. One was to become the leader of the Qumran Community, known as 'James the Just', and the other was his elder brother – the man we call Jesus!

Once we started studying the New Testament and the Dead Sea Scrolls with our now rock solid knowledge of the importance of twin pillars, whole new meanings were clear to see. We wondered how on earth everybody else had missed the obvious; but then, no one had ever connected the rituals of Freemasonry and the ancient Egyptians with this period before. The vein of investigation that we were mining was rich beyond our expectations and we could only hope that our good fortune would hold out as we started to look more closely at the life of the kingly pillar, Jesus the Christ himself.

CONCLUSION

Our review of the Holy Land at the time of Jesus had led us to the conclusion that the Qumran Community was, despite its tiny size, the most important group for our quest. We knew that they were the authors of the Dead Sea Scrolls and we had now come to the firm view that the Qumran Community, Essenes, Nasoreans and the Jerusalem Church were all names for the same group.

When reviewing the Hasmonaean period we came across the fact that the Roman Catholic Bible is at odds with the King James Bible in that the First and Second Books of Maccabees have been removed from the latter. The Catholics portray the Hasmonaeans as Jewish heroes – yet the Protestants clearly do not. This strongly indicated a connection between the anti-Hasmonaean Qumranians and the seventeenth-century English establishment; something that could only have happened through a Templar/Freemasonry route.

We had found many connections between the Qumranians and Freemasonry, from their grading procedures to their banning of coins or other metallic objects during initiation. From the Dead Sea Scrolls we know that they focused on truth, righteousness, kindness, justice, honesty and humility along with brotherly love. This made their position as the spiritual descendants of the Egyptian kings and the antecedents of the Templars and Freemasonry seem certain to us.

From the scrolls we had also learned that there were in existence secret books that contained references to certain rituals revealed by God that were normally transmitted to selected people by word of mouth alone, but had now been written down in coded form. These secrets were highly restricted and it is claimed that they had been handed down in a long line of secret tradition. Additionally we had come across a definite reference to 'the secret of the pillars'.

Our early suspicion that the Knights Templar had excavated the Holy of Holies and found secret writings had been supported by the Qumranian *Assumption of Moses* which instructed the Community to conceal its most precious scrolls in that precise location.

Without doubt the leader of the Qumran Community was considered to be the spiritual descendant of the original builder of the Temple of Solomon, the man that Freemasons now know as Hiram Abif. And we are convinced that James the brother of Christ was 'James the Just' of the Dead Sea Scrolls and the leader of the Jerusalem Church.

The essence of the Qumranian 'pillar' paradigm became clear as 'tsedeq' on the left-hand side of the gateway and 'mishpat' on the right-hand, with Yahweh the keystone of 'shalom' locking everything together at its centre. John the Baptist and Jesus were joint messiahs for a time but after the killing of John the politics of the situation had exploded. We now needed to try and find out exactly what was going on during this key period, most particularly between Jesus and James.

Chapter Twelve

The Man Who Turned Water into Wine

The Race Against Time

We were about to move into the most sensitive area of our investigation of the past and we decided to sit down and carefully review what we were about to do. It seemed certain that our conclusions were going to be controversial, to put it mildly, and we felt that it was more important than ever to substantiate everything we would say. Christians know a Jesus vastly different from the one emerging from our researches and we knew the contrast would be deeply disturbing to many. However, our first responsibility was to the truth, and after some debate we decided to tell whatever we found as clearly as possible. In fact, what we found revealed a character who was immensely powerful and uniquely impressive.

The first thing that surprised us about Jesus was that the entire duration of his ministry was just one year, from the death of John the Baptist to his own crucifixion. It rapidly became clear from all the available evidence that even this short period was filled with bitterness and political infighting, particularly between Jesus and James. Everything points the same way; Jesus, or Yahoshua ben Joseph as he was known to his contemporaries, was a deeply unpopular man in Jerusalem and at Qumran. His agenda was much more radical than his family and most other Qumranians could understand. As we will go on to show, all the evidence suggests that most people backed James, including Mary and Joseph.

While John the Baptist had been alive it was probable that Jesus observed the same strict sectarian rules as John, but with the loss of the priestly Messiah, Jesus's strategy became more radical.[1] He decided it was better to break the law for the good of the nation. Jesus believed that the time of the final battle with the Romans and their supporters was close and he believed that he had the best chance of winning the war for Yahweh.

The Qumranians were happy for Jesus to be the left-hand pillar of Mishpat, making him the kingly Messiah, or king of the Jews in waiting, but they could not accept him as the right-hand pillar as well. The Bible says that Jesus will sit on the right hand of God the Father, which means that he is the left-hand pillar, in that when one faces God looking west through his temple door, God will be facing out towards the east with the Mishpat pillar to his right.

The circumstances strongly suggest to us that James the Just must have told his brother that he was not considered holy enough to become both pillars but Jesus ignored his comments and announced himself to be the two earthly connections in the holy trinity that had God at its apex. As the idea of these three points of power settled in our minds we could not avoid wondering whether this was the source of the Catholic trinity of God the Father, God the Son and God the Holy Ghost.

We had always found the curious concept of a 'Holy Ghost' very difficult to understand as it appears to make no sense at all. None of our Christian friends has been able to explain what is meant by this curious designation. If the early Roman Church had picked up the importance of a godly trinity from the Jerusalem Church, it seems

[1] G. W. Buchanan: *Jesus: the King and His Kingdom*

possible that they may have mistranslated it. Jesus the Christ did claim to be both earthly parts (pillars) of the triangle and we could see how the confusion could have arisen.

As we saw above, Jesus had a military agenda. This may not sit well with traditional images of him, but G. W. Buchanan observed that Jesus was a warrior and concluded that it is not possible for an objective historian to dismiss all the military implications related to the teaching of and about Jesus. It was Jesus's role to lead the war and become the new king.[2]

Of the Dead Sea Scrolls Professor Eisenman has said:

> *'The kind of thing we're talking about in our new view of the Dead Sea Scrolls is a Messianic movement in Palestine that is much more aggressive, much more apocalyptic, much more militant and much more this-worldly orientated – a kind of army of God in camps along the Dead Sea, or out in the wilderness, a group preparing for a final apocalyptic war against all evil on the earth.'*[3]

As a highly intelligent man Jesus knew from the start that time was not on his side; he needed to accelerate the 'end of the age' and protect himself from the powerful enemies who had already cut down one pillar. The first thing he did was to appoint some personal bodyguards to protect him; then he followed a policy of moving around, with only brief stays in any one place. His five principal 'minders' were: James and John, whom he called 'sons of thunder'; two Simons, one called 'the zealot' and the other 'the terrorist' (barjona); and as Judas 'the knife-man' (sicarius). These were no peacemakers – in Luke 22:35–38 we are told that they inform Jesus that they already had

---

[2] G. W. Buchanan: *Jesus: the King and His Kingdom*
[3] Robert Eisenman speaking on the BBC 'Horizon' programme, 22 March 1993

two swords after he had exhorted them to sell their clothes to buy weapons.

> '*And he said unto them, When I sent you without purse, and scrip, and shoes, lacked ye any thing? And they said, Nothing.*
>
> *Then said he unto them, But now, he that hath a purse, let him take it, and likewise his scrip: and he that hath no sword, let him sell his garment, and buy one.*
>
> *For I say unto you, that this that is written must yet be accomplished in me, And he was reckoned among the transgressors: for the things concerning me have an end.*
>
> *And they said, Lord, behold, here are two swords. And he said unto them, It is enough.*'

The two most important requirements for the success of Jesus's plan were more followers and more funding. If he were ever to sit on the throne in Jerusalem, both would have to be in place quickly. The priesthood in Jerusalem was already rich, selling membership of the Jewish religion to Gentiles around the Roman empire, giving them a stone from the Jordan in exchange for large amounts of money, and he needed to unseat these people. His first idea was a stroke of genius, but one that caused panic and outrage in the Qumran Community. He started raising common people to the status of a first-year Qumranian initiate all over the place; worse still, he unilaterally 'resurrected' many of his closest followers to the highest level, giving them the secrets of Moses.

The New Testament indicates that Jesus had an élite that held special secrets. From almost the very start of Jesus's ministry there seems to have been an inner circle of Jesus's closest followers with whom he had shared special secrets. Some observers have detected three additional layers; the premier team; a group made up of less intimate followers that included family and well-disposed acquaintances (to whom the secret had not been revealed); and the outsiders, the indifferent or hostile people of the surrounding world.[4]

There clearly was a secret mystery confined to a select few amongst Jesus's followers, but until now no one has been able to explain what that secret was. We felt sure that we knew the answer, but we had to stay objective and not try and force our solution onto the facts. Fortunately we did not have to, because the Gospels did that for us.

Jesus's first miracle was to turn water into wine at the wedding at Cana. Looking at this story in the context of everything we had found out, we were certain that this was no mere display of conjuring bravado. It was Jesus's first attempt at recruitment outside the Community, at what must have been a substantial gathering. We discovered that the term 'turning water into wine' was common parlance, equivalent to the English expression 'making a silk purse out of a sow's ear'. In this context, it really referred to Jesus using baptism to turn batches of ordinary people into those fit to enter into the 'Kingdom of Heaven', in preparation for the 'end of the age'. In Qumranian terminology the uninstructed were the 'water' and the trained and refined were 'wine'. Taking the phrase literally, as some less informed Christians do, is equivalent to thinking that someone had the power to turn the ears of pigs into real silk purses.

The idea that Jesus went around raising a few selected people from their recent death, in a land where hundreds died daily, is another literalisation of something far more down-to-earth. The method of making a person a member of the inner sanctum at Qumran was, as we now knew, the ceremony that had come down one and a half thousand years to them from Seqenenre's murder in Thebes, that had itself stemmed from the king-making ceremonies of ancient Egypt going back to the fourth millennium BC.

---

[4] Morton Smith: *The Secret Gospel*

We became comfortable with the concept of the initiates being known as the 'living' and everyone else being referred to as the 'dead'. The Qumran Community believed religiously that 'life' could only happen in the Community and according to some Jews, it could only occur in the land of Palestine if it was freed from Roman rule. We found that it was common practice at that time for one Jewish sect to believe that all Jews of other sects were religiously 'dead'.[5]

This preoccupation with a living resurrection we had already come across in our study of the Gnostic Gospels, so the idea of the non-resurrected being referred to as the 'dead' was not such a strange concept.

Our findings to date told us that the Qumranians used simulated resurrection as a means of admittance to the 'third degree' of the sect and it has been indisputably established from the Dead Sea Scrolls that they viewed those outside their order as the 'dead' and it was becoming perfectly clear from the New Testament that Jesus can be seen to have used exactly the same techniques. When he made someone a general member of this splinter cult of the Qumranian sect, he turned 'water into wine' and when he initiated a new candidate into his core group, they were 'raised from the dead'. This two-tier structure was recorded by early Christians, who said that Jesus offered simple teaching to 'the many' but gave a secret teaching to 'the few'. Clement of Alexandria mentions this secret tradition in a letter, as we discussed earlier; Valentinus, a Christian teacher of the mid-second century, also recorded that Jesus shared with his disciples 'certain mysteries which he kept secret from outsiders'. This is confirmed by the New Testament in Mark 4:11:

'And he said unto them, Unto you it is given to know

[5] George Wesley Buchanan: *The King and His Kingdom*

287

the mystery of the kingdom of God: but unto them that
are without, all these things are done in parables.'

The resurrection initiation to bring people in from the
'dead' was called being 'raised' or 'standing up' and it was
reversible for those who contravened the rules of the sect,
which was, quite logically, called being 'buried' or 'falling
down'. A classic example of this process we found in the
New Testament story of Ananias and Sapphira who were
members of the sect at the time of the crisis after the
crucifixion. James ordered that as much money as possible
had to be raised to organise the defence of the sect, and
every member of the inner group was required to sell any
land or property that they owned and to give the proceeds
to central funds. When it was discovered that Ananias and
his wife Sapphira had made their sale but had kept back
some of the money for themselves, they were each, in
turn, brought before Peter, who decided to make an
example of the pair to dissuade others from similar
thoughts. The story is told in Acts 5:1–11:

> *'But a certain man named Ananias, with Sapphira his*
> *wife, sold a possession, and kept back part of the price,*
> *his wife also being privy to it, and brought a certain*
> *part, and laid it at the apostles' feet. But Peter said,*
> *Ananias, why hath Satan filled thine heart to lie to the*
> *Holy Ghost and to keep back part of the price of the*
> *land? Whilst it remained, was it not thine own? and*
> *after it was sold, was it not in thine own power? why*
> *hast thou conceived this thing in thine heart? thou hast*
> *not lied unto men, but unto God.*
>
> *And Ananias hearing these words fell down, and*
> *gave up the ghost: and great fear came on all them that*
> *heard these things. And young men arose, bound him*
> *up, and carried him out and buried him.*
>
> *And it was about the space of three hours after, when*
> *his wife, not knowing what was done, came in. And*

*Peter answered unto her, Tell me whether ye sold the
land for so much? And she said, Yea, for so much. Then
Peter said to her, How is it that ye have agreed together
to tempt the Spirit of the Lord? behold, the feet of them
which have buried thy husband are at the door, and
shall carry thee out.*

*Then fell she down straightway at his feet, and
yielded up the ghost: and the young men came in, and
found her dead, and, carrying her forth, buried her by
her husband. And great fear came upon all the church,
and upon as many as heard these things.'*

For those that read the Bible without understanding of
the terminology of the period it appears that a peevish
God murdered a husband and wife, using supernatural
powers, because they had not supported His chosen group
quite fervently enough. This portrays a god as partial and
vicious as Yahweh in his early days, who is vastly different
from the God of love and forgiveness apparently promoted by Jesus. However, once we know the procedures
of the Qumran Community/Church we can see this for
what it was: a disciplinary hearing that resulted in two
members being thrown out, i.e. sent amongst the 'dead'.
The term 'young men' used in this passage was not an
unnecessary reference to the age of these acolytes; it was
simply a normal Qumranian description for 'novices' –
the opposite of 'elders'. To be cast out amongst the 'dead'
at this crucial time was a terrible punishment to those that
believed the 'kingdom of God' was only days away; they
had lost their ticket to the new order that was about to
arise in Israel.

Sometimes people underwent 'temporary death' by
leaving the inner group and then being readmitted. An
example of this was Lazarus, who lost his nerve when the
going got tough towards the end of Jesus's life. He
explained to his sisters Mary and Martha that he was
afraid and would have to leave the inner group. Four days

later Jesus arrived on the scene and Mary said to Jesus that Lazarus would not have become 'dead' in the first place if Jesus would have been there to talk to him. Jesus then went to find Lazarus and persuaded him to be bold and rejoin the 'living'. The raising of Lazarus has always been considered to be one of the most striking miracles of Jesus recorded in the Gospels but now that we truly understand the terminology of the first-century Jews, we can safely forget the unnecessary necromantic interpretation.

This kind of expression of the 'living' and the 'dead' has been shown, beyond all doubt, to have been the terminology used at the time of Jesus and those that insist upon taking it literally not only deny all the evidence but also do a great disservice to a unique and brilliant teacher. The idea of a rotting corpse being brought back to life would have been a disgusting concept to all Jews of the age, and for modern Christians to think there was ever an age when such things were spoken of in a matter-of-fact way is as foolish as thinking that magic carpets really were once the usual mode of transport in Baghdad. People who are generally pragmatic seem open to believing that the ridiculous could have happened in the remote past in some lost 'golden age'.

The reality is that Jesus was no fluffy softy, dispensing love and kindness wherever he went; by today's standards he was extremely tough as he required his principal followers, his inner group, to cut all ties with their family as he himself had done. An example of this is in Matthew 8:21–22, which has always seemed odd and defied explanation by the church:

> '*And another of his disciples said unto him, Lord, suffer me first to go and bury my father. But Jesus said unto him, Follow me; and let the dead bury the dead.*'

To try and make literal sense of this is rather more

difficult than 'turning water into wine' but it is clear that Jesus meant, 'Let the outside world [the "dead"] take care of itself because we have more urgent business within the Community.' If any reader believes that we are over-emphasising this aspect of Jesus's teachings, they should consider Luke 14:26 where he actually requires his followers to 'hate' their families.

The Bible makes a number of references to a strained relationship between Jesus and his mother and brothers, none clearer than Matthew 12:46–50:

> *'While he yet talked to the people behold, his mother and his brethren stood without, desiring to speak with him. Then one said unto him, behold, thy mother and thy brethren stand without, desiring to speak with thee. But he answered and said unto him that told him, Who is my mother? and who are my brethren?*
>
> *And he stretched forth his hand toward his disciples, and said. Behold my mother and my brethren! For whosoever shall do the will of my Father which is in heaven, the same is my brother, and sister, and mother.'*

This shows that Jesus had no time for the members of his family, but also that they may have been trying to make peace with him after the rift when he had unilaterally taken on the 'priestly' as well as 'kingly' messiah role. It is certain that at some point before the crucifixion, Jesus's brother and competitor for the 'priestly' role, James, had seen the wisdom of the outlandish actions of his brother and became prepared to accept these new teachings.

Jesus was known as Yahoshua ben Joseph, meaning 'saviour the son of Joseph' but in the New Testament there is no report of Jesus mentioning his own father. This is hardly surprising since he had told his disciples to call no man father on earth (Matthew 23:9). The disciples were required to reject their families and live as though they had never existed, so that all of their loyalties could be focused into the group. In the Lord's Prayer, Jesus taught to the apostles that they were instructed to refer to God as our 'Father' as a complete replacement for their genetic parent. It is easy to see from this point how the Gentile, Hellenised Christians who heard this completely misunderstood the Jewish mind and took it literally, believing that Jesus was in some physical way 'the son of God', despite the fact that he also called himself 'the son of man', a common title to apply to a claimant to be the messiah at that time. This description of God as the Father and himself as the eldest or first son can be seen to make perfect sense, because as the man due to become the new Davidic king of the Jews, he would only be an earthly regent for Yahweh, who would always be the supreme ruler in this theocratic state.

The Lord's Prayer is given in the King James Bible as follows:

> *'Our Father which art in heaven, Hallowed be thy name. Thy kingdom come. Thy will be done on earth, as it is in heaven. Give us this day our daily bread. And forgive us our debts, as we forgive our debtors. And lead us not into temptation, but deliver us from evil: For thine is the kingdom, and the power, and the glory, for ever. Amen.'*

This can be translated from the understanding we have gained of the terminology and intentions of Jesus and his splinter group as follows:

> *Yahweh, great is your name. Israel will become your kingdom. The requirements of holy living that you abide by will be instituted in Israel. Sustain us in the time before your kingdom is in place. Forgive us if we*

fall short of your holy requirements, as we forgive those that let us down. And do not make life too harsh for us to test our resolve, but help us to avoid errors in our own holy endeavours.

Israel is yours, and the power to rule us and the splendour, for all time. Let it be so.

It is important to realise that the word 'temptation' had a somewhat different connotation to the way it is used in modern English. It actually meant 'test', in the sense of turning up the pressure to see how much punishment a person can take, rather than the modern sense of resisting pleasures.

From this it is possible to see how odd it is for non-Jews to use this wholly Israelite prayer for their own Gentile purposes. It was only ever intended as a request to a Jewish god to create self-determination in Israel, as Jesus had no interest in anyone outside his little kingdom. Other terms he used, such as 'brothers' and 'neighbours', were also only intended to refer to those in the Community, not the world at large. Our reworded Lord's Prayer is a translation of *meaning*, rather than the mere constituent words, as the Bible does. The fact that the words used by Jesus had an entirely local Jewish political meaning was not discovered by us; it is now widely accepted, even by such mainstream Christian works as *Peake's Commentary on the Bible*. It is now clear that Jesus was only ever talking about his political struggle in freeing the Jews from foreign domination forever.

The New Way to the Kingdom of God

The requirement for the end of the current age and the beginning of the 'kingdom of God' was to have the high priest of 'tsedeq' at the Temple and the Davidic king of 'mishpat' upon the throne so that Yahweh would ensure that 'shalom' was in place for evermore. Yahweh would not assist in these things coming about until a greater state of holiness existed in the land of Israel, and Jesus saw his main task as bringing about an improvement in the common people.

The first thing that Jesus did in his ministry was to go to a large wedding (which could be huge affairs lasting many days) to find converts to his cause. The amazing thing that he did, astounding the strict Qumranians, was to allow in the 'unclean' – such as married men, cripples and, most surprising of all, even women. To Jesus they were all equally able to sin in the sight of God and therefore had as much, if not more, need of salvation than others. This idea of equality was revolutionary for the time and became the hallmark of his teachings.

More than anything else, Jesus needed money and to get it, naturally enough, he had to go to the rich to find it. Unfortunately it was normally precisely this group of people which was considered to be particularly sinful. Following the destruction of the Temple in 586 BC the place of the Lord had been defiled, and pious Jews tried to keep their own homes as undefiled as the altar in the Temple and themselves as undefiled as its priests. This meant keeping Levitical purity laws and Pentateuchal dietary laws very carefully indeed. A member of the Qumran Community would never enter in the house of someone outside (a 'dead' person), because they could be exposed to all types of uncleanness. Jesus offended 'worthy' Jews by entering into the homes of such people as tax collectors, and as a result was being accused of mingling with 'sinners' and 'harlots', 'drunks' and 'prostitutes'. In truth, these people were perfectly respectable and very wealthy, but their devotion to 'the way' was not established, so they were called every unpleasant name imaginable. The term 'harlot', for instance, simply meant that they mingled with Gentiles in their working or social lives, rather than any observation of their sexual promiscuity.

One tax collector became an apostle of Jesus and another, Zaccheus, was actually a chief tax collector before being 'raised' from the 'dead'. He gave half of his wealth to repay for past injustices and the other half to 'the poor', which was the term for the Qumran Community.

The teachings of Jesus appear in something of a list in some of the Gnostic gospels and it is certain that the original gospel 'Q' was not constructed in a story format. Whilst most of the teachings of Jesus were woven into a biography by the New Testament gospel writers, a sizeable number appear in list form in what is called the 'sermon on the mount'. It seems credible that Matthew's ability to weave all of Jesus's teachings into a storyline ran out of steam, so he stuck all kinds of passages together as though they were spoken one after another to a crowd on a mountain top. Had this been delivered verbatim as a single sermon, the poor audience would have been open-mouthed trying to take in such a barrage of information. We therefore believe that most of these sayings and instructions were drafted into this one 'occasion' to avoid interrupting the flow of the overall story.

The actual words of Jesus used on this 'occasion' have focused the minds of Christians right down the ages and they have come out with all kinds of interpretations. However, in the light of what we now know, the meanings have become very straightforward. The beatitudes are particularly simple to interpret:

'Blessed are the poor in spirit: for theirs is the kingdom of heaven.'

This is rendered simply as 'the poor' in Luke, and in both cases it simply means the Qumran Community, for that is how they described their full 'third degree' members.

'Blessed are those who mourn for they shall be comforted.'

In Luke 'those who mourn' is expressed as 'you that weep'. In both cases the reference is to the Qumran Community and other pious Jews who grieved for the Temple of Yahweh in the hands of the unworthy. This saying also appears in a Qumranian psalm.

'Blessed are the meek, for they shall inherit the earth.'

Again the term 'the meek' was commonly used by members of the Qumran Community to describe themselves. The members were required to behave in a meek and humble manner so as to cause the 'kingdom of God' (their inheritance) to arrive. In the light of the evidence from the Dead Sea Scrolls, to pretend that it could mean *any* humble person is to deliberately abuse truth.

'Blessed are those that hunger and thirst after righteousness, for they shall be satisfied.'

The Qumran Community were the people that sought out 'tsedeq' (righteousness) at all times, but until the 'kingdom of God' arrived, they would not be fulfilled.

'Blessed are the merciful, for they shall obtain mercy.'

As in the Lord's Prayer, God will allow the righteous of the Qumran Community their slight errors because they are forgiving of the minor mistakes of their brethren.

'Blessed are the pure in heart, for they shall see God.'

The members of the Qumran Community were taught to keep clean hands and a pure heart because that was the

requirement to enter the Temple of Zion; they would be
the ones to witness the coming of the 'kingdom of God'.

*'Blessed are the peacemakers, for they shall be called
the sons of God.'*

Nothing has been more misquoted than this statement
of belief. The 'peacemakers' here does not mean pacifists
of any kind, it refers to those who were working for
'shalom', the state of peace, prosperity and general well-
being that would arrive when the pillars of 'tsedeq' and
'mishpat' were finally put in place. Once again, the
reference applies solely to the Qumran Community. As
we already know, Jesus taught his followers to cut
themselves off from their families and consider Yahweh as
their father; they became therefore the sons of God.

*'Blessed are those who are persecuted for righteousness's
sake, for theirs is the kingdom of heaven.'*

The Qumran Community had always suffered persecution; John the Baptist, for example, had been taken from
them the previous year.

*'Blessed are you when men revile you and persecute you
and utter all kinds of evil against you falsely on my
account.'*

This is slightly different to the others, as it seems to
apply to Jesus and his splinter group. Luke uses the word
'hate' in place of 'revile', and it is probably a reference to
enmity from the supporters of James within the Qumran
Community. If so, it must have been written just a few
months before the crucifixion, when the rift between the
brothers was at its height.

These 'beatitudes' make pretty unspectacular reading
when seen for what they are; a series of recruitment

slogans which all boil down to 'become one of us and be part of the "kingdom of God" – or be nothing'. They must have worked pretty well. Christians have never, until recently, understood the complex Jewish circumstances that were the backdrop for this inspired recruitment campaign and have used the literal text of Jesus's statements in support of their own belief system. This may often have been a good thing, but it certainly is not what Jesus meant.

For a short period of time, maybe just two or three months, Jesus, with his strange activities, was viewed as having departed from the core of the Qumran Community; but it soon became clear to James that his brother was building a substantial party. Some of the essential tenets of the teachings of Jesus can be gleaned from contemporary works that were excluded from the New Testament. In *logan* 114 of the *Gospel of Thomas* (Jesus's twin brother) Jesus explains his belief that even women are equal to men:

> *'Simon Peter said to them, "Let Mary leave us, for women are not worthy of life." Jesus said, "I myself shall lead her in order to make her male, so that she too may become a living spirit resembling you males. For every woman who will make herself male will enter the Kingdom of Heaven."'*

Needless to say, Simon Peter was not suggesting that all women should be killed when he said that they were not 'worthy of "life"'; this was a reference to the fact she needed to leave the room whilst members of the highest order of the movement (the 'living') discussed secret matters. Jesus must have caused amazement amongst his followers when he replied that he would personally 'raise her from the dead' to be the first woman member of the élite and that every woman had the right to do the same. This passage is certainly from the lips of the radical teacher whom Christians call Jesus the Christ and it is disappointing to see many male priests currently vigorously objecting to women entering the priesthood.

In the *Secret Book of James*, reputed to be written by James the brother of Jesus after the crucifixion, Jesus is quoted as explaining how his followers must understand his teachings:

> '*Pay attention to the Word. Understand knowledge. Love life. And no one will persecute you, nor will any one oppress you, other than yourselves.*'

This man was amazing. We could not believe such wisdom could arise in the midst of such strife. For us these words still provide a marvellous personal lifestyle philosophy.

The Arrest of the Kingly Pillar

Jesus knew that time and stealth were of the essence. He needed to incite a mass revolt against the Romans and the Sadducees in Jerusalem and to arm as many people as he could. This had to be achieved without forewarning the enemy of the strength of the movement, so Jesus and his followers met in secret and preached in out-of-the-way places. Although James still would not accept Jesus's right to be the priestly as well as the kingly messiah, things seemed to be going well. Furthermore, Jesus's network of spies reported that there was no special activity planned against him in Jerusalem.

Jesus needed a show of strength in the capital to demonstrate that he was not afraid to challenge the authorities head on and to establish his right to the throne of Israel. A careful plan was drawn up to show the people of Jerusalem that he was the king who would arise to save them from foreign domination, as foretold by the prophets. His entry into Jerusalem riding on a young ass was a deliberate enactment of the well-known prophecy made in Zachariah 9:9 that predicted that the people of the City would see:

> '... *thy King cometh unto thee: he is just, and having salvation; lowly, and riding upon an ass, and upon a colt the foal of an ass.*'

It is accepted by Bible scholars that the palm-branches had no significance and were probably used by Jesus's supporters to draw attention to the event which otherwise would have gone unnoticed. To ensure that he gained maximum publicity, Jesus proceeded to the Temple and caused a riot by overturning the tables of the traders and money changers who abused the sacred building. A team of Jesus's men must have placed themselves around the area to ensure that the place was safe before the signal was given for the kingly messiah to walk in surrounded by his five 'minders'. He immediately set about kicking down the tables as his followers threw the stallholders to the ground. The people hid in terror as Jesus shouted out his views on their ungodly behaviour; before he beat a swift retreat to Bethany, two miles to the east of the city. The general opinion was, no doubt, that the mission had been a great success, but in fact it was the beginning of the end. From that moment the Roman and Jewish authorities decided to act to end the trouble from this sect at Qumran before it got too big to handle.

James was duly arrested and a wanted poster was issued for Jesus, giving a visual description of the man. All copies and references to this were destroyed a long time ago, because to have a description of a less than perfect god would never do for a growing church. It was, however, reported by Josephus in his *Capture of Jerusalem*. Josephus drew his information directly from the 'forma' produced by Pontius Pilatus's officers. This was the document that carried the description of the wanted man, a copy of which had to be filed in Rome. The New Testament states that a warrant was issued for the arrest of the man that says he is the king of the Jews, and that it was Judas who turned in his master.

Despite Christian censorship a copy of Josephus's description survived in Slavonic texts and came to light in the last century. We cannot be certain that it is genuine but many scholars believe it is, and there is no reason to doubt them. It paints a picture of a man quite different to the image most people imagine:

> '... *a man of simple appearance, mature age, dark skin, small stature, three cubits high, hunchbacked with a long face, long nose, and meeting eyebrows, so that they who see him might be affrighted, with scanty hair with a parting in the middle of his head, after the manner of the Nazarites, and with an undeveloped beard.*'

A height of three cubits would put him at under four feet six inches, which combined with a hunchback and severe facial features would make Jesus the Christ a very easy person to recognise. Whilst this might offend some Christians, we would point out that it ought to be no more important for a god to be of beautiful appearance or tall than it is for him to be born in a palace. That is a modern view, however, and if Jesus had been a small and ugly man the Hellenised world would never have accepted him as a god, so the early Christians would have had to hide the fact. There is additional evidence that Jesus was a man of very small physical stature. The *Acts of John* (which was excluded from the New Testament) says of Jesus:

> '... *I was afraid and cried out, and he, turning about, appeared as a man of small stature, and caught hold on my beard and pulled it and said to me: "John, be not faithless but believing, and not curious."*'

301

In Luke 19:3 we read about a man called Zaccheus who tries to see Jesus through a crowd.

> *'And he sought to see Jesus who he was; and he could not for the crowd, because he was low of stature.'*

This verse can be read in two ways; that the comment on stature be applied to Zaccheus or to Jesus. This ambiguity explains why it has survived the knife of the censor. Was Jesus the small one? No one can ever be sure.

Whatever his height, Jesus was quickly arrested at the Garden of Gethsemane. Everyone who has had any Christian upbringing at all will be familiar with the name of this place that was the setting for one of the most dramatic scenes in the story of Jesus's life, but in studying the position of this small garden it became clear that the choice of location was no accident. In Mark 14:32 the author makes it sound almost like a casual stopping-point on a journey when he says:

> *'And they came to a place which was named Gethsemane: and he saith to his disciples, Sit ye here, while I shall pray.'*

Nevertheless, this was no arbitrary choice – Gethsemane was a deliberate and preordained place to change the course of history. The Garden of Gethsemane is just three hundred and fifty yards away from, and directly in front of, the eastern gate of the Temple – the 'righteous' gateway. As Jesus prayed he may have been high enough to see across the valley the two physical pillars that he represented in the building of the new Jerusalem and the coming 'kingdom of God'. He watched the sun go down over the recently rebuilt Temple, knowing full well that he would be arrested that night. From the passages in the Bible it is clear that Jesus was worried and on edge in the expectation of his arrest, but he was trusting that Yahweh would cause things to go well for him, saying 'Father, all things are possible unto thee'.

Jesus had chosen the timing and the location with great care. The east gate, the gate of 'tsedeq' or righteousness, was the main gate for the highly important celebration of the New Year, which was the Passover at the new moon nearest the spring equinox that fell in late March or early April. It was this gate, so important in Ezekiel's vision, that Jesus, and all of the Qumranians, held so dear. In chapters 14 and 15 of Ezekiel we can read the special importance of the east gate in his vision that he starts by saying happened 'at the beginning of the year':

> '... And the glory of the Lord came into the house by the way of the gate whose prospect is towards the east ...
>
> ... Then he brought me back the way of the gate of the outward sanctuary which looketh towards the east; and it was shut. Then said the Lord unto me; This gate shall be shut, it shall not be opened, and no man shall enter by it; because the Lord, the God of Israel, hath entered by it, therefore it shall be shut. It is for the prince; the prince, he shall sit in it to eat bread before the Lord; he shall enter by the way of the porch of that gate ...
>
> ... Thus sayeth the Lord God; The gate of the inner court that looketh toward the east, shall be shut the six working days; but on the Sabbath it shall be opened, and in the day of the new moon it shall be opened. And the prince shall enter by way of the porch of that gate without, and shall stand by the post of the gate, and the priests shall prepare his burnt offering and his peace offerings, and he shall worship at the threshold of the gate: then he shall go forth ...'

That is exactly what Jesus did. He worshipped as near as he dared to the threshold of the east gate on the night of the new moon at the beginning of the new year. He saw himself as the prince of Israel awaiting to be crowned to undertake the duty given by Ezekiel to 'execute justice and righteousness' (mishpat and tsedeq). Through that night Jesus waited for the morning star to rise, the star that rises in the east that once heralded the arrival of the newly created king of ancient Egypt and in Qumranian belief would be the mark of their new king. This 'star prophecy', found throughout the scrolls and in Numbers 24:17, says 'a Star will rise out of Jacob, a Sceptre to rule the world'; it had a precise meaning for Jesus, but later became confused by the Gentile Christians as a feature of his birth rather than his brief moment of kingship. The author of Revelations, the last book of the New Testament, called Jesus:

> *'The root and branch of David and the bright star of the morning.'*

The 'War Scroll' from Cave 1 at Qumran tells us that they saw the 'star prophecy' in terms of the rising of 'the meek' in some final apocalyptic war. It seems a strong possibility that Jesus thought that in living out the prophesied steps towards the war, he would cause a popular uprising that would be the opening shot of the 'war to end the age'.

The disciples of Jesus knew that he did not expect to survive the confrontation that he was engineering with the Temple and Roman authorities. Further information can be gleaned from the *Gospel of Thomas*. It purports to be the secret sayings of Jesus as written down by Judas Didymos, who is believed to have been the twin brother of Jesus and therefore called Thomas, which meant 'twin'. This gospel was not structured as a narrative; it is a list of the words spoken by Jesus as leader. In saying number 16, Thomas tells us:

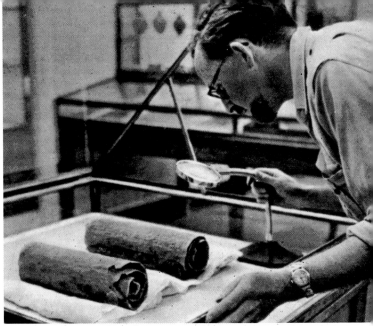

17 The Copper Scroll found in Qumran that identifies the location of all scrolls and treasures buried by the Community shortly before their destruction by the Romans in 70 AD – here being examined by John Allegro prior to opening.

18 A view of the remains of the Essene settlement at Qumran, the name of which has been shown to have the root meaning 'twin pillars with an arched top'.

19 and 20 The face on the Shroud of Turin above betrays an uncanny likeness to Jacques de Molay RIGHT.

Iacob亡 busbul... Sim fr ag... Iacob alfei 54 pher... phi lipp... la fei... Si mon... Iu...

andr eas berz...

per ruG ...riuG

chriG...

lu?...

21 The drawing of 'Heavenly Jerusalem' by Lambert of St Omer who
died circa 1121 AD. Was this a hastily produced copy of one of the
Nasorean scrolls discovered under Herod's Temple by the Knights
Templar, brought to Lambert by Geoffrey de St Omer?

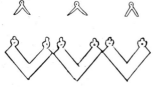

22 The Masonic Square and
Compasses can be seen to have
been built into the design of
Lambert's 'Heavenly Jerusalem'.

23 BELOW The interior of Rosslyn
has many carvings which can be
seen to have been inspired by the
same imagery as found on
Lambert's 'Heavenly Jerusalem'.

24 The so-called Rosslyn Chapel is in fact a reconstruction based on the foundations of Herod's Temple and the imagery of the Nasorean description of the New Jerusalem, built in the fifteenth century to house the Nasorean scrolls. It is covered with Templar, Masonic and Celtic carvings but has no Christian imagery.

25 The authors outside Rosslyn.

26 LEFT The wounded head in Rosslyn. Is this a representation of Seqenenre Tao?

27 BELOW LEFT The tripod with suspended marble block, known as a Lewis, that stands on the floor of every Masonic Craft Lodge. Is this in recognition of the marble block with a ring at its centre that we know gave entrance to the underground vault beneath the sacrificial altar in Herod's Temple, where one of the important Copper Scrolls was concealed?

28 RIGHT The so-called 'Apprentice Pillar' in Rosslyn that is actually the kingly Boaz Pillar.

29 FAR RIGHT The Jachin Pillar in Rosslyn.

30 The skyline of the eastern aspect of Rosslyn shows its many spires, echoing the Heavenly Jerusalem manuscript.

31 The authors in front of the ruin of Rosslyn Castle which was destroyed by General Monk during the English Civil War – like Cromwell, Monk was a Freemason and he spared Rosslyn Chapel from the desecration that every other church in the area suffered.

> *'The disciples said to Jesus, "We know that you will
> depart from us. Who is to be our leader?"*
>
> *Jesus said to them, "Wherever you are, you are to go
> to James the Righteous, for whose sake heaven and
> earth came into being."'*

This clearly indicates that the rift between the brothers
was over and that Jesus had a gloomy view of his own
future. It is easy to see why, three hundred years later,
Constantine would reject the *Gospel of Thomas* from his
'official' Bible as the preferred line of the Roman Church
was that Peter, not James, became the next leader: a claim
that can now be seen as transparently false.

That night Jesus intended to wait for the morning star
to rise as he did not expect to be spotted by the Temple
guards before daybreak, and despite his impending arrest
he conducted a 'third degree' raising ceremony, there on
the hillside, almost in sight of the two great pillars of the
Temple. Who the young initiate was we do not know, but
the initiation may not have been completed before the
arrest occurred. Mark 14:51–52 tells us:

> *'And there followed him a certain young man, having a
> linen cloth cast about his naked body; and the young
> men laid hold on him: And he left the linen cloth, and
> fled from them naked.'*

This incident has hitherto defied explanation, but now
its meaning is clear.

The Trial and Crucifixion

The powers in Jerusalem now had exactly what they
wanted; both pillars of this dangerous messianic movement that was intent upon overthrowing the Sanhedrin
and the Roman Procurator, Pontius Pilatus. The Jewish
priests feared the claim that James made over their right

to the Temple and the Roman was probably little more than uneasy about the politics of the situation. He knew that these Jews had a reputation for causing an amazing amount of trouble when they whipped themselves up into a frenzy, but he had the support of lots of well trained troops behind him. Unfortunately, most of them were two days march away in Caesarea; while that meant that any uprising could be put down within three days, it was quite long enough for him to be hanged from the city walls. Pilatus was no fool. He came up with a plan that satisfied everybody.

The Roman Procurator had James and Jesus, the two who claimed to be pillars of the subversive sect, under arrest and both stood to be executed; but Pilatus knew that he only needed to topple one to undermine the plan, so he offered to let one of them go and he gave the substantial crowd in front of him the choice. Remember that whilst we call the 'kingly messiah' Jesus, that was not his name; it was a description of his role as 'saviour' which in Hebrew was Yahoshua. James's name in Hebrew was certainly J'acov but he too could be referred to as 'saviour' – that is, 'Jesus'. As we had suspected since we realised the true meaning of the name Barabbas, the two people on trial were both called Jesus – Jesus 'the king of the Jews' and Jesus, 'the son of God'. James was called Barabbas – literally, 'the son of God' – here because it was understood that he was the priestly messiah and therefore the one more directly in line to his 'father'.

It is a complete invention of the later Church that there was a custom of releasing a prisoner at the Passover. That simply did not happen and it would have been a very un-Roman and foolish way to run a legal system. The reality is that this was a unique plan of Pilatus's to meet the needs of a delicate situation. Most of the crowd were from Qumran and supporters of James, or as he was described on the day, 'Jesus Barabbas'.

'Jesus – the king of the Jews' did not have enough

voices shouting for him, so he was found guilty, scourged, crowned with thorns and crucified on a 'T' cross with the words 'King of the Jews' above his head. He died unusually quickly, and if he were a hunchback as described in the wanted notice, that could be expected. The process of crucifixion makes breathing very difficult and it is necessary to heave the chest upwards continually, to expel air from the lungs. With a curved or hunched back this would have been very difficult, and suffocation would quickly result.

In researching the whole period of the first century AD, we combed through all kinds of information to build up a picture of what was really going on in Israel. Because we were building a new and unique perspective on the life of Jesus, things that would mean little to others could be major pieces for us in our immense jigsaw puzzle. One of the most important finds imaginable came from obscure passages in a rabbinical text known as *Tosefta Shebuot*, which dates from the early centuries AD. This document records the memories of the surviving Jerusalem Jews and tells the story of events that preceded the calamity of AD 70, and because it comes from a non-Christian tradition, we believe it is authentic and untampered with. In Tosefta Shebuot 1:4 we stumbled across a powerful description that shed a remarkable new light on what happened between Jesus and James at the crucifixion. The passage starts:

> '*Two priests who were brothers were running neck and neck up the ramp, and one of them got within four cubits of the altar before the other.*'

This first sentence is an easily recognisable reference of the race between the two brothers to establish which of them would be the priestly messiah. Jesus was almost there when he died on the cross.

'He took a knife (for the killing of the sacrificial animal) and stuck it into his own heart.'

Interestingly, this next line confirms the Christian idea of Jesus deliberately sacrificing himself before God, an idea that we did not subscribe to until we reconstructed those last hours when Jesus did indeed deliberately lay himself open to arrest. When Jesus died on the cross he was viewed as a 'Paschal lamb' as identified in 1 Peter 1:19.

The last part of the Tosefta Shebuot passage is truly a major find!

'Rabbi Tsedeq came and stood on the steps of the portico of the Temple mount and said,
    "Hear me out, O brothers of ours, House of Israel! Lo, it says, When a corpse is found, and your elders and judges go forth and measure. Now as it is to us – whither and whence shall we measure? To the sanctuary? or to the courtyard?"
    All the people groaned and wept after what he said.'

Here we have sixty-three vitally important words spoken by James, the brother of Jesus, possibly within minutes of Jesus being lifted down from the cross. They ought to be in the Bible, but they are not.

The first part of this Rabbinical Jewish text is a description of the race between Jesus and James to prove themselves the priestly messiah, although both agreed that Jesus was the kingly messiah. This stylised account tells us that Jesus had almost achieved his goal of being both pillars himself when he sacrificed himself. His brother Rabbi Tsedeq (literally 'the Teacher of Righteousness') was obviously deeply upset by this loss and he addresses the members of the Qumran Community present with passion and with anger whilst standing under Solomon's

Portico that overlooked the Courtyard of the Gentiles. James referred to an instruction in Deuteronomy 21:1–9 that deals with assigning guilt for a murder by establishing which city or town is the closest to the corpse. When asking the assembled Jews of the Community whether to measure 'to the sanctuary or the courtyard' he was saying that they, the supposedly worthy Jews, were as guilty as the Sanhedren who made the request for the killing, since they had made a choice for Jesus to die.

We thought it a good idea to find out whether Herod's Temple did have a ramp up to its altar. It did. The altar itself was over fifteen feet high with a fifty-two-foot long ramp rising from the south. This translates to a slope of thirty-six cubits, which means when the leading brother chose to sacrifice himself he was, very symbolically, eleven twelfths of the way to success.

This information means that we can date the 'race' of these brothers to between around AD 20 and 70, because we know that Herod's Temple was destroyed in June of AD 70, very soon after its completion. This makes our interpretation of the brothers being the men we now call Jesus and James seem almost certain, as they were the leaders of the Essene Community at that time.

We were interested to note that at the top of the ramp, in the south-west corner of the altar, there were two drain holes for the sacrificial blood and a large marble block with a ring at its centre. This block could be lifted by its ring to gain access to a cave beneath the altar. In the First Degree ceremony of modern Freemasonry the candidate is addressed by a brother standing in the south-west corner of the Masonic Temple and exhorted to live a moral and upright life. In front of the brother delivering the passage is a marble block with a small ring at its centre, suspended from a pulley in a tripod lifting device. Could there, we wondered, be a connection? (See Fig 27)

We felt that the quotation of James's speech to his

assembled followers was of great importance as it confirms James's role and attitude towards his brother at the time of the crucifixion. Somehow these words were omitted from the New Testament accounts. This is more likely to be deliberate than accidental; as we have noted, there was a definite policy of trying to downgrade James's premier position in the Church after the death of Jesus, in favour of Peter, who came under the influence of Paul.

Proof that this text contains the words spoken by James is given by the story of Pontius Pilatus washing his hands to show that whilst he gave his authority for the crucifixion, he would not accept responsibility for the killing. The technique of washing hands to demonstrate innocence was not a Roman practice, it was a Qumranian/Essene procedure, and therefore it is a later addition rather than a true description of events. It actually comes from the exact passage of Deuteronomy that James was referring to and only applied as a sign of innocence *after* a murder; certainly not before it. Once a body had been found and measurements taken to identify the nearest town, the elders of that town were required to take a heifer that had never drawn a yoke and strike off its head and then to wash their hands over its body whilst reciting the words 'our hands have not shed this blood, neither have our eyes seen it'. The next verse then calls upon the Lord 'not to lay innocent blood unto thy people of Israel's charge, and the blood shall be forgiven them'.

This Old Testament means of claiming innocence of a murder was clearly in the mind of the synoptic gospel writers; Matthew, for instance, puts words in the mouth of Pontius Pilatus in chapter 27, verses 24–25:

> '*When Pilate saw that he could prevail nothing, but that rather a tumult was made, he took water, and washed his hands before the multitude, saying, I am innocent of the blood of this just person: see ye to it.*

Then answered all the people and said, His blood be on us, and on our children.'

If we compare the Deuteronomy passage with Matthew, the parallel is obvious:

'our hands have not shed this blood, neither have our eyes seen it.'
'I am innocent of the blood of this just person: see ye to it.'

The Old Testament claim of innocence relies on a person not having done or seen a murder; here we have Pilatus saying that he is not guilty of doing the deed and it is the Jews who *see it*. Whoever first wrote this version of events was certainly aware of James's words after the crucifixion and built on his reference and accusation of partial guilt to the assembled crowd. James could not have known how his words would soon be twisted by Gentiles to lay a charge of 'theocide' on the whole Jewish nation for all time. The claim that the assembled crowd damned themselves with the words 'His blood be on us, and on our children' is a wicked lie, responsible for two thousand years of anti-Semitism.

The Tosefta Shebuot transcription of James is important as it confirms James's role in the movement and his attitude towards his brother at the time of the crucifixion, and in addition it explains the claimed actions of Pilatus. The omission of James's words from the New Testament was a deliberate downgrading of James's premier position vis à vis 'Jesus'.

Whilst looking further into this rabbinical work we came across a reference in Mishnar Sotah 6:3 that once again brought our eyes out on stalks:

'Forty years before the destruction of the Temple the

*western light went out, the crimson thread remained
crimson, and the lot for the Lord always came up in the
left hand.'*

Forty years was a special number to the Jews of the
time, but it was also just about this period of time before
the destruction of the Temple that Jesus was killed. The
light that went out was the kingly messiah signified by the
royal colour – crimson – and the lot for the Lord coming
up in the left hand refers to the decision of the crowd (the
lot) to vote for James, the 'right-hand pillar' in preference
to Jesus, the 'left-hand pillar'. The crimson thread
remaining crimson tells us that James was the inheritor of
his deceased brother's right to be considered the new head
of the royal line of David, as well as the Teacher of
Righteousness.

There has always been a debate as to whether Jesus
died on the cross or whether he was replaced by someone
else. Muslims have always held that it was not Jesus on
the cross. The Koran says in Sura 4:157:

> *'That they said (in boast), "We killed Christ Jesus the
> son of Mary, the apostle of Allah" – but they killed
> him not, nor crucified him, but so it was made to appear
> to them, and those who differ therein are full of doubts,
> with no (certain) knowledge, but only conjecture to
> follow, for of surety they killed him not.'*

Why is it that some people are convinced that Jesus was
crucified, yet others are equally convinced that he was
not? The answer is remarkably simple. They are both
convinced they are right because they *are* both right. Two
sons of Mary stood trial together and both had recently
claimed to be the saviour or messiah; both, therefore, had
the name 'Jesus'. One died on the cross and one did not.
The one who did not die was James, the lesser of the two

but the one with the higher profile. It is little wonder that some people thought he had cheated the cross.

The Symbols of Jesus and James

The star of David is today fully accepted as the symbol of Judaism but the hexagram is actually two symbols superimposed to create a new, composite meaning, and its origin is not Jewish at all. The top and bottom points of this star are the apex of two pyramids, overlaid one upon the other. The upwards pointing pyramid is an ancient symbol for the power of a king, with its base resting on Earth and its summit reaching to Heaven. The other represents the power of the priest, established in Heaven and reaching down to Earth. In this overlapping form it is the mark of the double messiah; the priestly or 'tsedeq' messiah and the kingly or 'mishpat' messiah. As such, it is the only true sign of Jesus, and it carries the extra meaning as being representative of the bright star of David's line that arose in the morning.

✡

It is called the Star of David, not because David invented it, but because Jesus used it and he positioned himself to be the 'Star of David' that had been prophesied. It is not surprising therefore that this symbol does not appear in any ancient Hebrew books on religious life, and its only use in the distant past of Judaism was as an occasional decorative motif along with other Middle Eastern images, including (ironically) the swastika. It first came into popular use on a large number of Christian churches in the Middle Ages and the earliest examples were, we were amazed to find, on buildings erected by the Knights Templar. Its use in synagogues came very much later. Alfred Grotte, a famous synagogue builder of the early twentieth century, wrote the following concerning the Star of David:

> *'When in the nineteenth century the construction of architecturally significant synagogues was begun, the mostly non-Jewish architects strove to build these houses of worship according to the model of church construction. They believed they had to look around for a symbol which corresponded to the symbol of the churches, and they hit upon the hexagram. In view of the total helplessness (of even learned Jewish Theologians) regarding the material of Jewish symbolism, the megan david was exalted as the visible insignia of Judaism. As its geometrical shape lent itself easily to all structural and ornamental purposes, it has now been for more than three generations an established fact, already hallowed by tradition, that the megan david for the Jews is the same kind of holy symbol that the Cross and the Crescent are for the other monotheistic faiths.'*

We could not help but marvel at the way that history is so often made up of a wonderful series of misunderstandings and cock-ups!

One can see that if the two lateral lines of the Star of David are removed, leaving the upward and downward pointing arrows of priest and king, the result is the Freemasons' square and compasses. The priestly or heavenly pyramid becomes the stonemason's square, an instrument used to measure and ascertain the trueness and uprightness of buildings, and, figuratively, human goodness; the quality that the Egyptians called Ma'at, as we saw earlier. The kingly or earthly pyramid is depicted as the compasses which, according to Freemasonry, marks the centre of the circle from which no Master Mason can materially err; that is, the extent of the power of the king or ruler.

So, if the Star of David is a symbol of the unified messiah-ship of Jesus, it should be the mark of Christianity. Then the question has to be asked, what is the symbol of Judaism? The answer is the cross.

T

This is the mark of the 'tau' and it is this shape of cross upon which Jesus was crucified, rather than the assumed four-armed cross with an extended lower section rising above the cross bar. We saw earlier that the 'tau' was the mark of Yahweh, and that which the Kenites bore on their foreheads long before Moses came across them in the wilderness of the Sinai; it is also the magical symbol that was painted on doors during the Passover.

We were intrigued to discover that the crucifix-style cross used by the Christian Church was an ancient Egyptian hieroglyph and simply flabbergasted that it carried one very precise meaning – 'saviour', which translates to the Hebrew 'Joshua', which in turn translates in Greek to 'Jesus'. In short, the shape of the crucifix is not a symbol of Jesus; it is his name itself!

This takes us back to Freemasonry. The most important symbol of the Royal Arch Degree is the 'Triple Tau', which can be seen on the main banner on the tracing board between the banners of Reuben and Judah. These three interlocking taus represent the power of king, priest and prophet. It is explained by the Order as follows:

> *'The several bearings of the Sceptres denote the Regal,*
> *Prophetical, and Sacerdotal Offices, which all were,*
> *and still ought to be, conferred in a peculiar manner,*
> *accompanied with the possession of particular secrets.'*

The last symbol that we want to review at this stage is the sign of the fish, which has in recent years enjoyed something of a comeback as a mark of Christianity.

Although this is viewed as a Christian symbol it is a very ancient badge of priestliness and was undoubtedly the symbol of the Nasorean party, and when Christians used it to identify their holy places in Jerusalem towards the end of the first century, it was the only mark that existed for them. It may well have been adopted by John the Baptist and, as we have already discussed, the name 'Nasorean' is a form of the word 'Nazrani' which means both 'little fishes' and 'Christians' in modern Arabic, just as it did in Aramaic two thousand years ago.

We knew that James the Just became the first bishop (or, in Hebrew, 'Mebakker'), and that he took to wearing a mitre as a badge of office. This device is now worn by all bishops and there can be no doubt of its origin; it came with Moses from Egypt.

The mitre with its split front and rear sections and its tail is identical to a modern bishop's head-dress and certainly came via the Nasoreans from the ancient Egyptians. This was exactly the hieroglyph that stood for 'Amen', the creator god of Thebes that later became merged with the Lower Egyptian sun god Re as Amen-Re. Once again we saw no room for coincidence. The threads of connections from Egypt to Jerusalem to modern times have combined in our researches to form a virtual rope!

Finally we had to remember how frequently the name of Amen is still vocalised today. It is used daily by Christians at the end of each prayer; could this have originally been to draw the blessing of the god Amen upon the request so that it might become true? As Thebes was the city of Seqenenre Tao we would expect such a prayer ending to pass down to the Israelites via Moses in the resurrection ceremony. The Hebrew language certainly used the word 'amen' to close a prayer with the meaning 'let it be so', and Christians have adopted it from them.

The Rise of the Liar

After the death of Jesus, James the Just retired to Qumran to consider his future, as he was now the sole messiah with responsibility for being both the priestly and kingly pillars. James appears to have been a strong leader and fanatical about living a wholly righteous life. He abstained from absolutely anything and anybody that could contaminate his pureness. So free from sin and 'uncleanness' was he that, unlike all others at Qumran, he was exempt from ritual washing. We are told that 'he never washed', but we think this referred only to the ritual use of water – he did wash in the usual way for reasons of personal hygiene. That James was now important in the early Church is confirmed by Acts 2:17 where Peter sends news of his release from prison to James and the brethren:

> 'But he, beckoning unto them with the hand to hold their peace, declared unto them how the Lord had brought him out of the prison. And he said, Go shew these things unto James, and to the brethren. And he departed, and went into another place.'

The killing of 'the king of the Jews' by a Roman Procurator created a lot of publicity; throughout Israel and beyond, people became interested in the messianic movement. One such person was a Roman citizen by the name of Saul who came from an area that is now southern Turkey. His parents had become Diaspora Jews and he was a young man who was brought up as a Jew but without the culture and attitudes of such pure followers of Yahweh as the Qumran Community. The idea that his job was to persecute Christians is an obvious nonsense as there was no such cult at that time. The Nasoreans, now led by James, were the most Jewish Jews it is possible to imagine and Saul's task was simply to put down any remaining independence movement on behalf of the Romans. The Mandaeans of southern Iraq, as we have discussed, are Nasoreans who were driven out of Judah whose migration can be accurately dated to AD 37; it therefore seems almost certain that the man that persecuted them was Saul (alias Paul) himself.

Saul must have been the scourge of the Jewish freedom movement for the best part of seventeen years as it was the year AD 60 when he was struck blind on the road to Damascus. It is now believed that Saul would not have had the authority to arrest activists in Damascus even if there were any there, which seems very doubtful, and his destination is considered by most scholars to have been Qumran, which was often referred to as 'Damascus'. His blindness and regaining of sight was symbolic of his conversion to one part of the Nasorean cause. The fact that Saul's destination was indeed Qumran is borne out by Acts 22:14 where he is told he will be introduced to the 'Just One', an obvious reference to James.

> '*And he said, The God of our fathers hath chosen thee, that thou shouldest know his will, and see the Just One, and shouldest hear the voice of his mouth.*'

Paul heard the story of the Nasoreans directly from the lips of James, but being a foreign Jew and a Roman citizen he failed to understand the message that he was given and immediately developed a Hellenistic fascination for the story of Jesus's death and his role of a 'sacrificial lamb'. It is certain that Paul was not admitted into the secrets of

Qumran, because he spent only a short time there; as we know, it required three years of training and examination to become a brother. The relationship between the newcomer and James quickly became very strained.

Paul had seventeen years of hunting down potentially rebellious Jews and he was never converted to the cause of John the Baptist, Jesus and James. Instead he invented a new cult to which he gave the Greek name 'Christians', as a translation of the Hebrew word messiah. He called Jesus, a man he never knew, 'Christ', and started to build a following around himself. Because Paul had no understanding of the terminology of the Nasoreans, he was the first person to apply literalism to the allegory in Jesus's teachings and a miracle-working god/man was created out of a Jewish patriot. He claimed that he had the support of Simon Peter, but this was just one of a whole framework of lies. Simon Peter issued a warning against any other authority but the Nasorean leadership:

> *'Wherefore observe the greatest caution, that you believe no teacher, unless he brings from Jerusalem the testimonial of James, the Lord's brother.'*[6]

After reading Robert Eisenman's interpretations of the Qumran texts we had no doubt about the identity of Paul as the 'Spouter of Lies' who battled with James, the 'Teacher of Righteousness'. The use of the word 'spouter' is a typically Qumranic play on words, referring to the baptismal procedures associated with this adversary. The Habakkuk Pesher makes clear that this individual 'pours out on Israel the waters of Lying' and 'leads them astray in a wasteland without a Way'. The word-play on 'Way' relates to 'removing the boundary markers' of the law.[7]

We believe that the 'Liar' and the enemy of James was

---

[6] Hugh Schonfield: *Those Incredible Christians*
[7] Robert Eisenman: *The Habakkuk Pesher*

Paul; the man who lied about his training as a Pharisee, lied about the mission of Christ, taught that the Law of the Jews was not important and admitted the uncircumcised. It is clear from Paul's letters that Apostles from Jerusalem were sent to his chosen territory to disclaim his authority and contradict his teaching. Paul speaks of opponents of unquestionable prestige who were 'reputed to be something' and as 'reputed pillars', and he declares that he is not dependent upon the very chiefest Apostles. He describes them as 'servants of Satan', 'false apostles' and 'spurious brethren'. He is astonished that his Galatian converts are turning to a 'different Gospel' and tells them, 'If anyone is preaching to you a Gospel contrary to that which you received, let him be accursed.' He calls the emissaries of James 'false brethren privily brought in ... to spy out our liberty which we have in Jesus Christ, that they might bring us into bondage'.

Some commentators, such as Hyam Maccoby, have put forward a strong argument that Paul was never a Pharisee rabbi, but was a simple adventurer from an obscure background. Ebonite writings confirm that Paul had no Pharisaic background or training; he was a convert to Judaism, born of Gentile parents in Tarsus.[8] He came to Jerusalem as an adult, and became a henchman of the High Priest. When he was disappointed in his hopes of advancement, he split with the High Priest and founded his own new religion.

Paul acknowledges that there were two opposed versions of the life and mission of Christ: the 'false' teachings of James, the brother of Christ; and his own Hellenistic mystery romance that disregarded the very core beliefs of Judaism. In 1 Corinthians, 9: 20–25 he is not shy of admitting his disregard for the Jerusalem Church, and openly states that he is an unscrupulous liar:

[8] Hyam Maccoby: *The Mythmaker*

> *'I made myself a Jew to the Jews to win the Jews ... To those who have no Law I was free of the Law myself ... I made myself all things to all men ... That is how I run intent on winning; that is how I fight, not beating the air.'*

This open disregard for the Law and a willingness to say and do anything to achieve his own strange ends shows why James and the Qumran Community called Paul 'The Spouter of Lies'. In Romans 10:12 and elsewhere, Paul announces his desire to found a community that would 'make no distinction between Jew and Greek'. This is precisely the kind of ambition which characterised the Herodian family and their supporters. Paul went out of his way to legitimise the forces of occupation that had driven the branch of David out of Jerusalem and had murdered their king/messiah. He reasoned, 'You must obey the governing authorities. Since all government comes from God, the civil authorities were appointed by God.'

Paul's Roman citizenship was clearly well earned.

This hijacker of the cult must have engendered great hatred and fear. His ready access to the circle of Herodian power at Jerusalem is clear in Acts, and marks Paul out as a probable conspirator against James. The danger must have been clear to James, as he took great care to avoid directing the same kind of slanders towards Paul that were aimed at him. Paul continued to steal the 'secrets' of the Qumran Community for his own teachings. In 1 Corinthians 3:9ff Paul uses the 'building' and 'laying the foundations' imagery of the Habakkak Pesher when he describes his community as 'God's building', and he refers to himself as 'the architect' and Jesus Christ as the 'cornerstone'.[9] These are, of course, terms used by Jesus and all

---

[9] Robert Eisenman: *The Habakkuk Pesher*

of the Nasoreans that have been passed down to Freemasonry.

We have already dealt with the anger amongst the Nasoreans at Qumran which was created by Paul's opposition to James the Just as the undisputed messiah, and by Paul's false claim that Peter was leader of the Jerusalem Church. No doubt Paul had tried to take the leadership for himself with his false claims of a training as a Pharisee under Gamaliel (a great doctor of the law), but he had the political instinct to know that he would not make it himself. Just how unpopular Paul was with the people of Jerusalem is evident in chapter 21 of Acts. Here Paul misjudges his authority and enters the Temple, but is dragged out to be lynched by the assembled crowd, who recognise him as the man who taught against the Covenant Community and the Law, when he was at Ephesus. The riot which broke out must have been on a huge scale, as the Bible tells us that 'all of Jerusalem was in uproar' and several hundreds of Roman troops were turned out of the fortress of Antonia, which fortunately for Paul adjoined the Temple courtyard.

Chris visited the amphitheatre at Ephesus where Paul had addressed the massed crowds and where he managed to misjudge the occasion. At that time Ephesus had a cosmopolitan population, including one of the largest Jewish communities outside of Israel. Like the Jews in Alexandria, many were therapeutes, a sect of healers closely connected with the Essenes of Qumran. In the clumsily reconstructed ruins Chris found a large stone inscribed with the mark of the Therapeutai, a staff and serpent, which has become the symbol of medicine across the world. These highly intelligent and well-informed Jews had no time for Paul and his foolishness, and the self-appointed preacher was incarcerated in a small building on a barren hilltop just visible from the amphitheatre. Chris could not help but wonder what a better place the world might have been if they had kept the man there.

Paul escaped the Jerusalem riot with his life but in the year AD 62 it was James's turn to be attacked at the Temple in Jerusalem. The writings of Epiphanius, Bishop of Constantia (AD 315 to 403) tell us that eye witnesses claimed that James took to wearing the breastplate and mitre of a high priest, and claimed, as the first Bishop of Jerusalem, the right to enter the Holy of Holies once a year. It seems probable that James followed in his elder brother's footsteps and forced his way into the Temple unannounced, and was promptly arrested. The New Testament has been assembled to exclude the details of the assassination, but a gospel rejected by the pagan Emperor Constantine, *The Second Apocalypse of James*, does record the event as follows:

> '... *the priests ... found him standing beside the columns of the temple, beside the mighty corner stone. And they decided to throw him down from the height, and they cast him down. And ... they seized him and [struck] him as they dragged him to the ground. They stretched him out, and placed a stone on his abdomen. They all placed their feet on him, saying, "you have erred!" Again they raised him up, since he was still alive, and made him dig a hole. They made him stand in it. After having covered him up to his abdomen, they stoned him.*'

Parts of the Temple were still under construction and the stone that was placed on the abdomen of James would almost certainly have been in a state of preparation for its purpose in the building; as such, it could well have been a rough ashlar, which is the term to describe an approximately shaped block hewn from the quarry. It is interesting to note that in a Masonic Lodge a rough ashlar is placed at the north-east corner of the Lodge.

There is also a story concerning the death of James that

could have Masonic links. Hegesippus, a second-century
Christian authority, wrote:

> '*So they cast down James the Just, and they began to
> stone him since he was not killed by the fall; but he
> kneeled down, saying, "O Lord God, my Father, I
> beseech thee forgive them, for they know not what they
> do." While they were thus stoning him, one of the
> priests of the sons of Rechab, of whom Jeremiah the
> prophet testifies, cried out, "Stop! what do ye? The Just
> is praying for you." But one of them, who was a fuller,
> smote the head of the Just One with his club.*'

The killing blow struck by the fuller's club on the head
of James is not believed to be a historical fact, but it
occurred to us that it may have been a tradition added by
the Qumranians to create an exact pesher of Hiram Abif.
In this way the martyrdom of James, the Teacher of
Righteousness, would have been viewed as a rerun of the
death of the architect of the first Temple of Solomon (and
therefore Seqenenre Tao). A blow to the forehead killed
both Hiram Abif as he stood in the almost-complete first
Temple, and James in the almost-complete final Temple.
The parallels are too strong for this to be coincidence.

The Temple connection continued after death. The
tomb of James is now believed to be in the Kidron Valley
that runs right up to the east gate of the Temple. Hewn
out of the high rock-face, it still stands with its entrance
dramatically marked by a pair of splendid pillars.

Josephus recorded that the inhabitants of Jerusalem
were greatly offended by the killing of James and that they
secretly contacted King Agrippa, urging him to punish
the high priest Ananus for his wicked and unlawful
actions. The Jews apparently got their way and Ananus
was deposed.

The one significant part of our investigation that had
remained a mystery was the source of the Masonic names

of Hiram Abif's murderers; given as Jubelo, Jubela and Jubelum. Apart from the apparently unconnected fact that 'jubal' is Arabic for mountain, we could detect little meaning. However, as we looked closely at the death of James, the Teacher of Righteousness, we came across instructive analysis by Professor Eisenman. Referring to the Habakkuk Pesher found at Qumran, he says:

'The Pesher, which turns on the reference to "wrath" and "feast days" in the underlying texts, discusses how "the Wicked Priest pursued the Righteous Teacher to confound" or "destroy him with his angry wrath at the house of his retreat" (or "at the house where he was discovered"; The usage 'leval'o" does not appear in the underlying text, but it indicates strong action, and as it is used in a seemingly violent context, probably signifies "destroy".' [10]

Eisenman goes on to observe:

'Since the thrust of the allusion to the Lord's "cup of wrath" is one of divine vengeance and retribution for the destruction of the Righteous Teacher (as the pesher itself puts the proposition in the next section referring to the destruction of "the Poor": as he himself criminally conspired to destroy the Poor, so will God condemn him to destruction"/"he shall be paid thee reward which tendered the Poor"), the sense of "teval'enu" here, and as a consequence that of "leval'o"/leval'am" earlier, is certainly that of destruction ...'

Could it be that the three words from the pesher that dealt with the killing of James in the Dead Sea Scrolls, 'leval'o', 'leval'am' and 'teval'enu', were the origin of Jubelo, Jubela and Jubelum?

[10] R. Eisenman: *Habakkuk Pesher Textual Exegesis*

The Treasure of the Jews

It seemed likely to us that the Jewish war of AD 66–70 was caused by the tensions created by the murder of James the Just, and we found that this was borne out by Josephus. Although the original document no longer exists, we know of it because the third-century church father, Origen, made reference to Josephus's observations because they confused him. Origen wrote:

> '*Although not believing in Jesus as the Christ, Josephus, when searching for the true cause of the fall of Jerusalem, ought to have said that the persecution of Jesus was the cause of its ruin, because the people had killed the prophesied Messiah. Yet, as if against his will and not far from the truth, he says that this befell the Jews in revenge for Jacob the Just, who was the brother of Jesus the so-called Christ, because they killed him, although he was a perfectly just man.*'

Many Christians today are somewhat ignorant of the subject that they hold so dear, but when one realises that Jesus's ministry lasted just one year and James's twenty years, it stands to reason that James would have been the more popular figure at the time. The position and influence of Jacob as Jesus's brother is referred to in the ancient records, but is suppressed in Catholic teaching, so that laymen and even many clergy are denied information about it.[11]

The war that broke out in AD 66 started four years of wild ferocity with terrible acts committed by Jews against Romans, Romans against Jews and Jews against Jews. The horrors that occurred were as bad as the world has ever seen, on a par with the worst of the French and Russian revolutions. Josephus, the historian of the Jews, was the

---

[11] Hugh Schonfield: *The Essene Odyssey*

Jewish commander in Galilee – until he changed sides and
hunted down his own former officers with great passion.
At first the Jews did well, defeating the Syrian legion that
marched against Jerusalem, but they could never overcome the might of the Roman army.

The Nasoreans who believed in the power of the sword
to restore the rule of God were called Zealots and it is
certain that they took Jerusalem and the Temple in
November AD 67. Led by John of Gischala, the Zealots
discovered that many of the priests of the Temple and city
leaders wanted to make peace with the Romans. Such
thinking was not tolerated and everyone with such views
was immediately put to death. The Roman forces were
closing all the time and it became obvious to even the
most ardent Zealot that the end could not be far away. In
the spring of AD 68 the decision was made to hide the
Temple treasures, the sacred scrolls, vessels and tithes, so
that they should not fall into Gentile hands. They acted
just in time, because by June the Romans destroyed
Jericho and the settlement at Qumran. Two years later
Jerusalem fell to Titus, and the Zealots were killed or
taken captive, and eventually the last of the Jews who
knew the secrets of the Nasoreans died when the entire
population of Masada committed suicide rather than
surrender to the Romans.

The secrets passed down to the Nasoreans from Moses
were deposited, as the prophet had instructed, in a vault
under the foundations of the Temple as near to the Holy
of Holies as they could get. Other works were secreted in
at least five other locations around the country, including
the caves in the hills surrounding Qumran. One of the
scrolls found in those caves was made of a sheet of copper
eight feet long and one foot wide which had been rolled
from its edges to the centre to form a twin scroll that had
now parted in the middle to form two tubes. The
investigating team were unable to read it at first as it was
completely oxidised, but it was opened by cutting into

strips and reconstructed by a team at Manchester College of Technology in 1955. John Allegro explained the excitement he felt when the content of the copper scroll became clear.

> '*As word after word became plain, and the import of the whole document inescapable, I could hardly believe my eyes. Indeed, I resolutely refused to credit the obvious until more strips had been removed and cleaned. However, after another column or two of the script had been deciphered, I rushed air letters to Harding with the news that the Qumran caves had produced the biggest surprise of all – an inventory of sacred treasure, of gold, silver, and jars of consecrated offerings, as well as sacred vessels of all types ...*'[12]

John Allegro's interpretation of the 'Copper Scroll', indicated that there was at least one other copy, deposited in the Temple itself:

> '*In the Pit (Shîth) adjoining on the north, in a hole opening northwards, and buried at its mouth: a copy of this document, with an explanation and their measurements, and an inventory of each thing, and other things.*'

Could this be the scroll that the Templars found first? If it was, they would have been able to produce a perfect treasure map. In his detailed notes Allegro went on to show that the 'Shîth' (meaning pit or cave) was directly beneath the altar of the Temple; the cave we knew was capped with the marble block with a ring at its centre.

The 'Copper Scroll' lists huge amounts of gold, silver, precious objects and at least twenty-four scrolls within the

[12] John Allegro: *The Dead Sea Scrolls*

Temple. Directions are given to sixty-one different caches; the following are typical of listings:

'In the inner chamber of the twin pillars supporting the arch of the double gate, facing east, in the entrance, buried at three cubits, hidden there is a pitcher, in it, one scroll, under it forty-two talents.

In the cistern which is nineteen cubits in front of the eastern gateway, in it are vessels, and in the hollow that is in it: ten talents.

In the Court of [?] ..., nine cubits under the southern corner: gold and silver vessels for tithe, sprinkling basins, cups, sacrificial bowls, libation vessels, in all six hundred and nine.

In the pit [?] which is in the MLHM, in its north: tithe vessels and garments. Its entrance is under the western corner.

In the underground passages of The Holes, in the passage looking south, buried in plaster at sixteen cubits: 22 talents.

In the mouth of the spring of the Temple: vessels of silver and vessels of gold for the tithe and money, the whole being six hundred talents.' [13]

We knew that the original Knights Templar had found some scrolls by AD 1119; now we understood why they had spent another eight years digging away under the ruins of the Temple. The explanation for the Order's sudden rise to fame and fortune was suddenly a mystery no longer!

* * *

After the Jews lost the war and the Temple was destroyed for the last time, the buried scrolls lay forgotten and the

[13] John Allegro: *The Treasure of the Copper Scroll*

teachings of Jesus and the Nasoreans were replaced by Christianity, which would be better described as 'Paulianity'. But the fact that Christian theology fails to reflect the contents of the surviving teachings of Jesus tends to suggest that the dogma is a much later addition. These doctrines which Paul invented were totally different from the revolutionary egalitarian ideas of Jesus.[14]

Jesus had been a revolutionary and a pioneer of democratic thinking. Thanks to Paul and the non-Jewish hierarchical cult that he developed, Jesus's teachings were buried and forgotten. But we knew that they were due for resurrection.

Now we had pieced together the story of how the scrolls had come to be buried and had developed a sustainable hypothesis about their likely contents. From our trawl through history we now had a continuous thread leading from the murder of Seqenenre Tao via the development of the Jewish nation to the flowering of the concepts of Ma'at within the Qumran Community. We had found the instructions in the *Assumption of Moses* to hide the secret scrolls in the Holy of Holies under the Temple and we had read the accounts of the destruction of the Essenes and the Temple they claimed. This still left a gap of over a thousand years to fill in.

At this point we decided to look again at all the Masonic rituals we knew, from the Royal Arch to the Rites of the 33°. Perhaps in the vast proliferation of Masonic literature and ritual variations we might uncover further clues to help our quest. We had also, at an early stage of our research, looked very closely at the Celtic Church, which had been a very strong influence on the development of Scottish society at the time; we had thought it might well have influenced the Celtic Revival of Robert the Bruce, which had coincided with the fall of the Templars. This work would also need reviewing to see if

---

[14] Rupert Furneaux: *The Other Side of the Story*

we could fill this gaping thousand-year hole in our reconstruction of the story. We decided that our investigation should continue with a closer look at what happened to the remnant of the Jerusalem Church after the Roman destruction of the Temple, to see how – if at all – it linked with the Celtic Church.

CONCLUSION

Reviewing the life of Jesus in the light of information gathered from the Bible, the Dead Sea Scrolls, Freemasonry, the reconstructed secret of the pillars and obscure Jewish texts had proved to be amazingly fruitful. We found that Jesus, or Yahoshua ben Joseph as he was known, had an active ministry of just one year, during which time he was deeply unpopular in both Qumran and Jerusalem because he had announced himself to be both pillars.

We confirmed that Jesus did have an élite that held special secrets and used expressions such as 'turning water into wine' as metaphors for ordinary events. Other descriptions that we now understood included terms such as 'sinners' and 'harlots', 'drunks' and 'prostitutes', which simply meant people who mingled with Romans. Even the Lord's Prayer itself could be translated back into its true meaning.

We had established that the Qumranians used simulated resurrection as a means of admittance to their highest grade, initiates being known as the 'living' and everyone else being referred to as the 'dead'. A good example of how the followers of Jesus used this living resurrection as entry to their inner circle is the story of Ananias and Sapphira, which had shown that membership of this élite was reversible. The tale of Lazarus had further shown that a person could join, leave and join again; the leaving was described as a 'temporary death'.

The role of the pillars was absolutely central to everything that Jesus did, and when he was arrested in the Garden of Gethsemane he was conducting a living resurrection ceremony just three hundred and fifty yards away from the twin pillars of the Temple at Jerusalem. Another direct connection with Freemasonry was found in the 'morning star' imagery: 'the Star will rise out of Jacob, a Sceptre to rule the world'.

Our earlier hypothesis that there were two Jesus Christs was now proven and we now knew that the one that died was Yahoshua ben Joseph – 'the king of the Jews' and his brother James, Yacob ben Joseph, was 'Jesus Barabbas', referred to that day as 'the son of God'. We discovered the long-lost speech given by James after the crucifixion in the Courtyard of the Gentiles, which was twisted by later Christians to create a basis for anti-Semitism that was to last for almost two thousand years.

We now believed that we understood the origin of that curious Christian concept of the Holy Trinity, which describes the Father, the Son and the Holy Spirit as three persons in one Godhead. To us, this three-god format had always proved Christianity to be a non-monotheistic religion. Additionally we could not understand who the Holy Spirit was; either it was Jesus or it was someone else. Christians seem to avoid thinking too much about the Trinity concept because it does not make sense. The origin of the Trinity must be the pillar paradigm. God the Father is the 'shalom' keystone, the son of God is the 'tsedeq' pillar and the king of the Jews is the 'mishpat' pillar. The two pillars are entirely Earthly and when the Heavenly archway or lintel is in place a perfect harmony between God and His subjects is achieved.

The use of the pillars and such descriptions as Jesus Christ – 'the Cornerstone' make powerful connections with Freemasonry, but equally we had found obvious echoes of the Egyptian origin of the secrets of the Jews. The Christian cross symbol turns out to look nothing like the structure on which Jesus died – instead, it is the shape of an ancient Egyptian hieroglyph meaning 'saviour'. The regalia of a bishop, worn by James and still worn today, turns out to be another hieroglyph meaning Amen, the creator god of Thebes.

Even the name Qumran, we found, meant 'an archway over two pillars', confirming that this imagery was central to the Community's world-view.

The beginning of the Christian Church, we found, had nothing to do with Jesus; it was the invention of a foreigner named Saul, or later Paul. We feel certain that he is the character identified in the Dead Sea Scrolls as the 'Spouter of Lies' and it was he who battled with James to hijack the Nasorean cult. And it was Paul and his followers who failed to understand the pillar paradigm, and ended up trying to rationalise Jewish thinking by inventing the peculiar, and highly un-Jewish, idea of the Holy Trinity.

Most importantly, we now knew that the Nasoreans at Qumran believed that the end of the age had arrived, so they hid their most secret scrolls in a vault under the foundations of the Temple as near to the Holy of Holies as they could get. In the war that followed most Jews around Jerusalem were killed or fled, and the buried scrolls lay forgotten until a Templar crowbar broke through to rescue them.

Chapter Thirteen

The Resurrection

The Remnants of the Jerusalem Church

The development of the false creed of the Christ consumed Jesus's Nasorean teachings but we found clear evidence that there were some survivors of the Jewish war of AD 66–70, and that they did communicate the essence of Jesus's message to foreign parts, including the British Isles, via Alexandria in Egypt. A sect called the Ebionim or Ebionites was a direct descendant of James's Church, the name being the same as the Qumranians used for themselves – Ebionim, which as we well knew by now meant 'the poor'. This sect held the teachings of James the Just in high regard and believed that Jesus was a great teacher but a mortal man, not a god. They still considered themselves to be Jews and they believed Jesus to have been the Messiah after his 'coronation' by John. Records also show that they hated Paul, whom they viewed as the enemy of the truth. For a long time after the death of Jesus and James the terms 'Ebionite' and 'Nasorean' were completely interchangeable and these people were condemned, under both names, by the Church of Rome as heretics. However, all descendants of the Jerusalem Church except for the deviant Pauline division believed that Jesus was a man and not a god, so it is really the bejewelled Vatican and its offspring that are the true pagans and 'heretics'.

Robert was brought up in a Welsh-speaking environment, and he has had a lifelong interest in the Celtic Church and the mythology of his forebears. He had been brought up to know that Christianity had first come to Ireland from Alexandria via Spain, possibly as early as AD 200 and that that country's isolation from Romanised Europe permitted the development of a distinctive type of Christianity. In AD 432 Patrick went to Ireland and at some point later in his life he is reputed to have been shipwrecked off the northern coast of Anglesey, where he sought refuge from the storm in a cave on a small island not too far from Robert's current home. Legend says that when the saint eventually came safely ashore on the headland, he built the church of Llanbadrig, to thank God for his safe deliverance. There is a further later church dedicated to Patrick (Sant Padrig in the Welsh language) in the town itself. According to Catholic versions of the story he was supposed to have been travelling from Rome, but this legend has never cut any ice with Celtic scholars because Patrick's surviving writings show him to have been a follower of the 'Arian heresy' in that he did not believe in the Virgin birth or that Jesus was anything other than mortal!

Such ideas were actively persecuted by the Roman Church, but they had no power in the many kingdoms within Ireland, Scotland and northern England until the Synod of Whitby in AD 664. Their tradition of Saint Patrick claims that he introduced mainstream Roman Christianity into the country in the fifth century AD, but the system of bishops with territorial dioceses, modelled on the Roman Empire's administrative system, just did not exist at this time. This version of the legend seems to be a typical attempt by the Roman Church to hijack an existing local saint and change his story to reflect their preferred version of history. The truth is that during the fifth and sixth centuries Irish monasteries became great centres of learning under the auspices of the Celtic

Church, sending out such missionaries as saints Columba, Iltut and Dubricius to the Celtic fringe of Europe.

What was for most of Europe a 'Dark Age' was for Ireland a golden period when it was the greatest place of knowledge in the Christian world. Religious art, such as the *Ardagh Chalice* and the Book of Kells and other illuminated manuscripts, flourished alongside secular, even pagan, artistic achievements, such as the Tara Brooch and the great Irish epic *Tain Bo Cuilange*. The Celtic Church spread from Ireland to Wales, Scotland and northern England, and its hermits and priests built many small churches in the wilder parts of the west of Britain. These were not churches built to serve the needs of the local population for worship, since modern geographical studies show that most of these very early churches were not in centres of population at all.[1] They were, like Qumran, isolated outposts in the wilderness where the holy could refine their righteousness, and consequently the founder of every monastery or convent was considered a saint.

Earlier in our quest we had realised the importance of the connection between the Celts and the theology of the Sumerians, and we referred to the knotted, intertwining designs of the Celts that show a strong relationship to the art of the Middle East. As we said earlier, the origin of these northern Europeans is now beyond doubt as DNA analysis of some modern-day Celts from remote communities, such as that where Robert prefers to live, have shown a match with some north African tribal groups. There is moreover a core to Celtic thinking that has a natural affinity to Judaism, and therefore Jamesian Christianity, which had grown from the land of Sumer and there were strong similarities with Sumerian religion in the Celtic tradition.

On being told the story of Jesus, one Celtic king

[1] E. G. Bowen: *Settlements of the Celtic Saints in Wales*

accepted it right away, saying that 'Christianity had been with them for a thousand years!'[2] The new religion merged with some of the old druidic beliefs and grew to cover Ireland, Scotland, Wales and northern and south-western England. The Celtic Church differed greatly from the Roman type of Christianity that had swept the rest of Europe. It did not believe:

The Virgin Birth

The Divinity of Jesus
That the New Testament Superseded the Old
That Original Sin was inevitable but that it could be atoned by individual will power and good works

It did keep:

The Druidic Tonsure (The front half of the head was shaved)
A Dating of Easter based on the Full Moon and the Jewish Calendar

Eventually, following a fifty-year debate, the Roman Church officially absorbed the Celtic Church at the Synod of Whitby held in AD 664, but the undercurrent of the Nasorean thinking continued to simmer beneath the Catholic surface which, we believe, would later provide a cradle for the reborn teachings of Jesus.

Whilst there were strong grounds for us to believe that Celtic Christianity was connected with the true Church (alias the Nasorean movement), it could not explain the purity and detail contained in the rituals of Freemasonry. It was at this point that we were, for the first time, starting to feel that we might have met a dead end with no obvious next move. The lull lasted no more than a day or two

[2] C. Matthews: *The Elements of the Celtic Tradition*

because Robert managed to get his hands on a very revealing little book whilst visiting another Lodge. Green and inconspicuous, it was no more than four inches by two and a half inches but for us it was worth its weight in gold, several times over.

It was past midnight when Chris was woken by his doorbell ringing, followed by a pounding on his door. His initial irritation soon subsided when the contents of the book on Royal Arch Freemasonry was opened. This edition had been privately printed in London in 1915 and therefore predated the changes that have been made to the ritual of the Holy Royal Arch, due to pressure on Grand Lodge from sources outside of Masonry. Here was the original ritual, recorded before all the recent changes and innovations that have been carried out by men who did not understand the importance of the tradition with which they so readily tampered.

In the pages of this book was nothing less than the complete and unaltered story of the unearthing of the Temple scrolls!

It told us that the candidate for this degree is first tested on the questions of the first three 'Craft' degrees before he is admitted to the Lodge room. The room he enters is very different from the Lodge he has known though the various grades of Craft Masonry, and its officers are not the Worshipful Master and his two Wardens, but the 'Three Principals'. They form what is called a Sanhedrin, the Jewish name for the elder council of the Second Temple, representing the powerful triad of Priest, King and Prophet. They claim to be named after the three principals who are reputed, by the Order, to have held what is called the third, or Grand and Royal Lodge in the second Temple after the return from captivity in Babylon.

Reading on, we discovered that this triad was composed of Haggai the Prophet; Jeshua, son of Josedech the high priest and heir to the traditions of Aaron and the Levites;

and Zerubbabel, King of the line of David. The two previous Lodges were referred to as the First or Holy Lodge, which was opened by Moses, Aholiab and Bezaleel at the foot of Mount Horeb in the wilderness of Sinai; and the second or Sacred Lodge held by Solomon, King of Israel, Hiram, King of Tyre and Hiram Abif in the bosom of Mount Moriah.

As we read the words of the structure of the Royal Arch degree, our jaws were dropping lower and lower. Had we known about this Order at the outset we felt sure that we would have dismissed it instantly as romantic nonsense; but in the light of our work to date we could take it very seriously indeed.

The Master Mason who wants to be 'exalted to the Supreme Order of the Holy Royal Arch' must first prove himself by answering the test questions of the Craft Third Degree before he is given a grip and a password (the meaning of which is 'my people having obtained mercy') to allow him to enter. The candidate wears his Master Mason's apron and is blindfolded with a length of rope tied about his waist. Before the candidate is allowed into the Lodge room (in this degree called the Chapter) the pedestal which features later in the ceremony is covered over. The candidate is questioned about his reasons for wanting to enter the Chapter and is then asked to kneel while a prayer is said, calling on the Almighty and Eternal Father of the universe to bless the proceedings and support the candidate through his exaltation. The First Principal then checks that the Candidate believes in the true and living God Most High before asking the candidate to advance towards the veiled pedestal in a sequence of seven steps which mimic the actions of a Jewish Priest of Yahweh approaching the Holy of Holies in the First Temple. When this is completed, the candidate is told that he has now arrived at the crown of a vaulted chamber into which he must descend. To do this it is necessary to remove a keystone; he is then lowered to his knees whilst Proverbs 2:1–9 and 3:13–20 are read out.

The candidate is then told that he must search in the darkness to see if anything has been secreted there. A scroll of vellum is placed in his hands and he is asked what is on the scroll, but has to reply that deprived of light he cannot tell.

This was incredible. Quite beyond our wildest hopes. A clear description, not only of an excavation into the buried chambers of the Temple, but an absolutely accurate description of the finding of a scroll: not treasure, not an artefact but just as we had predicted – a scroll!

Reading on we found that the candidate is once again 'lowered' into the vault and Haggai 2:1–9 is read. This is a passage about the rebuilding of the Temple and as such, is the very essence of the Qumran Community. The last verse reads:

> *'The glory of this latter house shall be greater than the former, saith the Lord of hosts: and in this place will I give peace (shalom), saith the Lord of hosts.'*

At this stage the candidate is obligated and seals his obligation on the Bible with his lips four times. The blindfold is now removed and the candidate is then asked to read the contents of the scroll that he found in the vaulted chamber. The candidate then reads Genesis 1:1–3, following which the First Principal says:

> *'Such, newly-exalted Companion, are the first words of the Sacred Volume, which contains the treasures of God's revealed will. Let us praise and magnify His Holy Name for that knowledge of Himself which He has vouchsafed to us, and let us walk worthily of that light which has shone around us.'*

The ceremony apparently continues with a ritual telling

of the story of how the scroll came to be found. The candidate leaves the Chapter and is then readmitted, dressed as a Royal Arch Mason; he is joined by two other Companions and the three are referred to as 'the three sojourners', known as the three Master Masons of Babylon: Shadrach, Meshech and Abednego. As they enter they take part in a ceremony known as Passing the Veils, which represents a Priest of the Temple approaching the Holy of Holies of the Temple of Solomon. This ritual completed, they present themselves to the First Principal, describing themselves as three children of the captivity who have heard that he is about to rebuild the Temple at Jerusalem and beg permission to assist in the work. The First Principal questions them about their supposed origins, to which they reply that they are from Babylon and claim to be nobly born, descended from a race of patriarchs and kings who were led into captivity by Nebuzaradan, Captain of the Guard to Nebuchadnezzar until they were released by King Cyrus of Persia. Cyrus defeated the Babylonians and then issued a proclamation:

> *'The Lord God of heaven hath given me all the kingdoms of the earth; and He hath charged me to build Him a house at Jerusalem; which is in Judah. Who is there among you of all His people? his God be with him; and let him go up to Jerusalem, which is in Judah and build a the house of the Lord God of Israel (He which is God) which is in Jerusalem.'*

The sojourners explain that as soon as they had heard this, they had returned to Jerusalem to offer their services. Zerubbabel then congratulates them on their noble birth and acknowledges them as brethren of his tribes before enquiring how they wish to be employed. The three reply that they will be glad to be employed in any way which Zerubbabel is pleased to appoint them. Taking this as a sure indication that they must be qualified for offices of importance Zerubbabel tells them that only lowly tasks are left to be filled and that they will have the job of preparing the foundation of the most holy place, for which purpose they are supplied with the necessary tools. They are also warned that if in removing the ruins they should make any discovery of importance they are to communicate to none but the three Principals sitting in Council. They retire once more from the Chapter.

In the next part of the ceremony the three masons from Babylon again seek admission to the Chapter, bringing with them news of a discovery of importance which they entreat permission to impart to the august Sanhedrin. Once they are admitted the First Principal requests them to relate their story, which is as follows:

'*Early this morning on resuming our labours we discovered a pair of pillars of exquisite beauty and symmetry; proceeding with our work, we discovered six other pairs of equal beauty, which, from their situation, appeared to be the remains of the subterranean gallery leading to the Most Holy Place; on clearing away the fragments and rubbish which obstructed our progress, we came to something which seemed to be solid rock, but accidentally striking it with my crow, it emitted a hollow sound. We then cleared away more of the loose earth and rubbish, when we found that instead of a solid rock there was a series of stones in the form of an arch, and being aware that the architect of the previous structure had designed no part of it in vain, we determined to examine it, for which purpose we removed two of the stones, when we discovered a vault of considerable magnitude, and immediately cast lots who should descend.*

The lot fell on me; when, least any noxious vapours or other causes should render my situation unsafe, my companions fastened this cord or life line round my body, and I was duly lowered into the vault. On arriving at the bottom, I gave a preconcerted signal, and my companions gave me more line, which enabled me to traverse the vault; I then discovered something in the form of a pedestal and felt certain marks or characters thereon, but from the want of light I was unable to ascertain what they were. I also found this scroll, but from the same cause I was unable to read its contents. I therefore gave another preconcerted signal, and was drawn out of the vault bringing the scroll with me. We then discovered from the first sentence that it contained the records of the Most Holy Law, which had been promulgated by our God at the foot of Mount Sinai.

This precious treasure stimulated us to further exertion. We removed another stone, and I again descended into the vaulted chamber. By this time the sun had attained its greatest altitude, and shining in all its splendour, darted its rays immediately into the aperture, which enabled me to distinguish those objects I had before but imperfectly discovered. In the centre of the vault I saw a pedestal of pure virgin marble, with certain mystic characters engraven thereon, and a veil covering the upper face of the altar. Approaching with reverential awe, I lifted the veil, and beheld what I humbly supposed to be the Sacred Word itself. I replaced the Veil on the sacred pedestal, and was again raised out of the vaulted chamber. We then closed the aperture, and hastened hither, to report to your Excellencies the discoveries which we have made.'

The precise moment of discovery must have been at the hour of high twelve, the time when Seqenenre was at his final devotions to Amen-Re and the sun was at its meridian, which it is always said to be for Freemasons. The timing is no doubt symbolic, but what intriguing symbolism.

Zerubbabel then asks the sojourner to tell him what the

word was that he found, and receives this fascinating reply:

> *'That we must beg to be excused from for we have heard with our ears, and our forefathers have declared that in their time and in the old times before them it was lawful for none but the High Priest to pronounce the name of the True and Living God Most High, nor him but once a year, when he alone entered the Holy of Holies and stood before the ark of the covenant to make propitiation for the sins of Israel.'*

Later in the ceremony the candidate is given an explanation of this word which was found on the pedestal. He is told that:

> *'It is a compound word and its combinations form the word Jah-Bul-On. Jah the first part, is the Chaldean [Sumerian] name of God and signifies his essence and majesty incomprehensible; it is also a Hebrew word signifying "I am" and "shall be", thereby expressing the actual, future and eternal existence of the Most High. Bul is an Assyrian word, signifying Lord or Powerful, it is itself a compound word signifying in or on; and Bul signifying Heaven on High, therefore this word means Lord in Heaven or on High. On is an Egyptian word, signifying Father of All, and is also a Hebrew word implying strength or power, and expressive of the omnipotence of the Father of all. All the significations of these words may, therefore, be thus collected: — I am and shall be; Lord in Heaven; Father of all.'*

After hours of digesting the contents of this revealing book we parted shortly before dawn, and Chris spent most of the next morning pondering over what we had found. Our blockage seemed to have been shifted. Did this

Royal Arch story stem from the Templars? We could not think of any other explanation, yet we felt the need to control our enthusiasm.

Chris found the explanation of the word Jah-Bul-On a very interesting construction, but felt that it was not quite accurately explained by the Royal Arch Freemasons. The first part, 'Jah', is the Hebrew word for their god, very probably with a Sumerian connection. It can be seen in this form in the name of the prophet Elijah, which is actually Eli-jah, meaning 'Yahweh is my god' (El being the ancient word for a god). The second part is almost phonetically correct, but would be usually spelled as 'Baal', the great Canaanite god whose name does indeed mean 'Lord on high'. As far as I can ascertain the ancient Egyptian word for father was 'it', not 'on' as claimed here, but 'On' was the original name of Heliopolis, the city of the sun god Re, where he came into existence from the nothingness before he created the first earth there. From this point of view I found it possible to accept that the definition stands. It was also instructive to note that the Greeks identified Baal with their sun god Helios and his city, Heliopolis. However, the final definition of this string of words, given as 'I am and shall be; Lord in Heaven; Father of all', seemed completely nonsensical. My feeling was that 'Jah-Baal-On' was simply the names of the three great gods, of the Jews, the Canaanites and the Egyptians, all of whom were referred to as the 'Most High'. If this was indeed carved upon a stone found at the centre of the Jerusalem Temple, its creators must have deliberately merged the three forms of God into one ultimate deity.

Of course, the idea of a single and same God under many names is not unheard of – it is central to the credo of Freemasonry!

New meanings were becoming clear, but it struck us that Royal Arch Freemasonry by making such a hash of explaining its own ritual indicated strongly that Freemasons did not originate the story, and that it came down to them without its original meaning being clearly explained.

The whole narrative is told as though those conducting the excavation were Jews from Babylon digging in the ruins of the first Temple, but we believe it is actually describing the discoveries of the Knights Templar at the site of the last Temple. It can only refer to the ruins of Herod's Temple because the type of arch described in the ceremony is an arrangement of stones supporting each other in compression to form a curved load-bearing structure which was unknown at the time of Zerubbabel. The curved arch employed wedge-shaped, precisely cut stones requiring little or no mortar, and since it is that type of arch with three keystones which plays such a prominent part in the Royal Arch ceremony, it is absolutely certain that the setting of the story re-enacted in the ritual is Herod's Temple, which was constructed using Roman engineering principles.

We now felt this Masonic legend could well have kept alive the story of how the first Templars, under Hugues de Payen, had found the scrolls which led to the creation of the Order. The most significant part of this story is that in order to gain access to the hidden chamber, the visiting 'highly skilled' masons removed the keystones of an arch and then stood underneath it without in any way shoring up the rest of the arch. They showed great concern about the possibility of being overcome by noxious vapours within the confined space to the extent of fixing a safety rope, but were unworried about the havoc they had caused to the structural integrity of the roof. These were not the actions of stonemasons of any kind, let alone ones supposedly 'highly skilled in architecture', but it makes a lot of sense as a record of the actions of a gang of treasure-hunting knights, searching in underground vaults beneath the ruins of the Herodian Temple.

When we had first looked at the history of the Knights Templar, we had learnt that there is evidence of such Templar excavations and we decided to try and find further details. We had recently discovered that a duplicate of the Qumranian copper scroll had been deposited in the 'Shîth', or cave, directly beneath the altar of the Temple – the cave that was capped with the marble block with a ring at its centre. Had this been the stone that the Templars lifted and descended to the vault below?

The Templars may have been the first people to excavate below the Jerusalem Temple, but they were not the last. We mentioned earlier that in 1894 a group of British Army officers, with a budget of just five hundred pounds, set out to try and map the vaults below the ruins of Herod's Temple. The contingent of Royal Engineers led by Lieutenant Charles Wilson conducted some excellent work under very adverse conditions and they could confirm that the chambers and passageways they found were often vaulted with keystone arches. They also confirmed that they were not the first visitors to the subterranean galleries when they came across Templar artefacts discarded some seven hundred and forty years previously. These consisted of part of a sword, a spur, part of a spear or lance, and a small Templar cross. They are now in the care of Robert Brydon, the Templar Archivist for Scotland. The Royal Arch ritual and the finds made by Wilson's group made us feel ninety-nine per cent sure that our Templar hypothesis was correct; then another stroke of luck added the last one per cent to shift a hypothesis into a certainty.

Some years earlier, when we had first developed the theory that the Knights Templar had found something under the Temple ruins, we had stared backwards to a gulf of over a thousand years wondering what might have been placed there for them to find. Now we had reconstructed a past of several millennia and all we lacked was real proof that it was indeed the nine knights led by Hugues de Payen who found the scrolls. It fell out of a bookshelf onto Chris's lap.

The 'Heavenly Jerusalem' Scroll

Chris was sifting through the many books in his study looking for a small technical reference when an illustration caught his eye. There was something immediately familiar about the picture, something that sent a shiver down his spine. The title was given as 'The Heavenly Jerusalem circa 1200 AD' and it was said to be housed in Gent University Library. The more he looked at the illustration the more he saw. It showed a vision of a rebuilt Jerusalem, only this was no artist's impression; it was a highly symbolic diagram designed to convey meaning to those who knew what they were looking at.

The stylised city shows twelve towers: one principal heavenly tower, two major towers arising from the central pillars, three lesser towers with their own pillars and six background towers. The towers that rise directly from the two main pillars are supporting a curved archway and the central Heavenly tower; both are identified with Jacob, or as we know him – James! This was an exciting find as it confirmed our previous insight that James became both the mishpat and tsedeq pillars after the death of Jesus. As both the kingly and priestly pillars combined, James had adopted the joint messiah role that his brother had originally created.

Important though this confirmation of James's positioning was, it was not that that had first grabbed Chris's attention: the most impactful motifs in the whole drawing were unmistakable – three Masonic squares and compasses!

Chris needed to know more about the origin of this

fantastic manuscript and quickly contacted Dr Martine De Reu, the conservator of manuscripts and rare books at the Universiteitsbibliotheek, who provided a background to the illustration that left little doubt that we were indeed looking at a copy of one of the scrolls buried by James's Church and found by the Templars.

The information provided by Dr De Reu was heart-stoppingly exciting, and it dropped right into the centre of our unfolding story. The full history of the manuscript is no longer known but our research fills in the gaps. We can now dovetail our research with the known history of the Heavenly Jerusalem Scroll:

In around AD 1119 Hugues de Payen and his small band of primitive archaeologists opened up a vault beneath the rubble of Herod's Temple and found the secret scrolls of the Qumran Community, which were in either Greek or Aramaic or a combination of both. Had they been written in French it would not have made any difference, because these knights were completely illiterate; but they were far from stupid. They knew that they had found something of immense significance that was probably very holy, so they decided to get them translated. The nine sat and pondered as to who would be able to understand the strange writings and, more to the point, who could they trust not to interfere in their work or be otherwise indiscreet. The man with the solution was Geoffrey de St Omer, the second in charge to Hugues de Payen. Geoffrey knew an elderly canon by the name of Lambert, who was a retired schoolmaster of the Chapter of Our Virgin in St Omer, who was the wisest and most knowledgeable man imaginable, and who had spent many years compiling an encyclopaedia of human knowledge.

Geoffrey de St Omer set out with a selection of the scrolls on the long journey back to his home town. True to expectation, Lambert did understand much of what he read. The old man must have been overcome with joy to see such fabulous documents in the closing years of his life. He actually died in 1121, sadly without completing his encyclopaedia.[3]

Today, one of the most famous of all of Lambert of St Omer's works is his hasty copy of a drawing that depicts the heavenly Jerusalem. It shows that the two main pillars of the heavenly Jerusalem are both named 'Jacob', and apparently shows the founder to be John the Baptist. There is no mention of Jesus at all in this so-called Christian document. It is no ordinary image and we believe it can have come from only one place; the vaults of Herod's Temple. The symbolism on it is Masonic in the extreme and it confirms that James was both pillars of the Nasoreans!

Lambert's copy was obviously produced in a hurry, as though he had been given a very short period of time to work. One can imagine Lambert asking Geoffrey for the opportunity to copy the scroll in return for translating and explaining its contents, but the Templar was keen to return to the Holy Land. The pen marks show signs of undue speed and there are clearly errors of draughtsmanship creeping in, indicating that the copyist was compelled to work at an uncomfortable speed.

The document dates from over five hundred years before the Masonic square and compasses symbol was first officially used and yet the most dominant feature of the building images are composed of this device. There is no room for mistake in this, because the 'squares' have no possible reason for being placed in the picture. This told us that this symbol of Freemasonry must have been used by the Jerusalem Church. In Lambert's copy he has written the names of twelve pillars of the mystical City in Latin and we can see Jacob (James) on both pillars and Zion (Israel) upon the arch that those pillars support. We believe that this double use of James dates the creation of

---

[3] Private correspondence with the Librarian of Gent University

the original to the nineteen years between the crucifixion of Jesus and the stoning of James.

The illustration shows the three huge squares tucked incongruously into balconies with the accompanying compasses directly above in the apex of each tower. This trio sit beneath the twin pillars of James, indicating their subordinate position. These are named, and although we cannot make out the one on the left-hand, the right-hand one is identified as Andrew and the central one, Peter. Unfortunately for the Catholic Church and their claim to be the direct descendants of Jesus's authority via Peter, this scroll clearly confirms that James was leader of the Jerusalem Church and that Peter was a leading but clearly secondary person.

The line-up of the three towers, each with its square and compasses, is totally in tune with modern Freemasonry in that there are three key figures in a Freemason's Lodge – the Worshipful Master and his two Wardens – who represent the sun (Re), the moon (Thoth) and the master of the Lodge.

There is one last indicator that the scrolls were found by the Templars at the Temple in Jerusalem, and that comes from Masonic ritual itself, when the subject of the lost secrets of Freemasonry is discussed between the Worshipful Master and his two wardens:

> '*Brother Junior Warden, Why leave the east to go to the west?*
>
> *In search of that which was lost, Worshipful Master.*
>
> *Brother Senior Warden, What was that which was lost?*
>
> *The genuine secrets of a Master Mason, Worshipful Master.*
>
> *Brother Junior Warden, How became they lost?*
>
> *By the untimely death of our Grand Master, Hiram Abif, Worshipful Master.*

Brother Senior Warden, How do you hope to find them?
By the centre, Worshipful Master.
Brother Junior Warden, What is a centre?
That point, within a circle, from which every part of its circumference is equidistant.'

These words are meaningless to most Freemasons speaking them time after time, but to us they now revealed everything. At the time of the crusades every cartographer in Christendom produced maps that placed Jerusalem at the centre of the world. The Temple was at the centre of the old city, and at the centre of the Temple itself was the Holy of Holies. The two pillars shown in Lambert's drawing are also at the centre of the new Jerusalem, the exact place where the secrets of Jesus and Moses were found; for the Templars it was unquestionably the most central point on Earth.

We were learning new things rapidly and we had got into the habit of returning to previous source material from time to time to see if our greater understanding would produce new insights. It was on this basis that we reread some of the translations of the Dead Sea Scrolls produced by Robert Eisenman, and found that the concept of a 'Heavenly Jerusalem' or a 'New Jerusalem' was discovered in scrolls recovered from five different caves in Qumran, all based on Ezekiel's visions in which the new city is described in detail with fifteen hundred towers, each a hundred feet tall.

Like all Masonic degrees, the Royal Arch Degree has what is called a 'tracing board' (see illustration on p 355), which is a visual compilation of the subject matter of the Order. It can immediately be seen that it is all about the excavation of the Temple. In the background we see Jerusalem and the ruins of the Temple strewn about, and in the foreground the excavated entrance to the underground vault. Inside a central panel there are seven steps rising to a tessellated pavement on which there are digging tools as well as building tools, a square and compasses and a scroll. Around the edge of this panel are the badges of the twelve tribes of Israel and, at the top, what are claimed to be the four principal banners of Judah (a lion and royal crown), Reuben (a man), Ephraim (an ox) and Dan (an eagle).

With the discovery of the Heavenly Jerusalem Scroll and the story related in the Royal Arch Degree, we were now certain that the Templars did find the secrets of their Order inscribed upon the scrolls buried by Nasoreans and that they did conduct initiation ceremonies based upon a living resurrection, as performed by Jesus.

The Impact of the Nasorean Scrolls

The nine knights who discovered the Nasorean scrolls had found treasure beyond their dreams, but it was a treasure that they could not share with the world at large. The find did have an immediate impact on their home country, France. It took several decades for the Order established by Hugues de Payen and his fellow founders in AD 1118 to become one of the most powerful forces in Christendom. Within fifty years, however, something very extraordinary was happening in France.

In a single century from 1170 no fewer than eighty cathedrals and almost five hundred abbeys were built in France alone, involving more masonry than was ever cut in ancient Egypt![4] These buildings were built to a startling new plan on a scale never seen before. A classic example of these super-buildings is Chartres Cathedral, which soars skyward in a composition of ornate pillars and glass. The masons at this building and others across the country were directed by the Knights Templar, whose mission was stated as seeking to 'rebuild Jerusalem' in a

[4] C. Frayling: *Strange Landscape*

The Tracing Board of the Holy Royal Arch Degree of Freemasonry depicts the excavation of Herod's Temple

glorious new architectural style of pillars, towers and Heaven-seeking spires.

Before, we could find no previous explanation as to why the Templars suddenly took it into their heads to become master builders of a Heavenly Jerusalem in their home country, but now it all suddenly made sense to us. The instructions that the nine knights recovered from the vaults of the Temple at Jerusalem had been left by the Nasoreans just before they failed in their own mission to build Heaven on Earth. James and his followers died without bringing the Kingdom of Heaven which Jesus had promised *his* followers, but they had left a very clear message behind them.

The Nasorean scrolls could not have been found by more responsive people. The Templars took the ancient Ma'at-inspired, speculative Masonic secrets of Jesus and James for their own initiation purposes and proceeded to give the world a new, supreme level of operative masonry. The resurrection was in full swing!

From the discovery of the Heavenly Jerusalem scroll, and others now lost, we now knew that the Templars had became masters of both speculative masonry and operative masonry. We now needed to explore the destruction of the Templars and understand how a remnant of the Order transformed itself into something that became modern Freemasonry.

CONCLUSION

Looking at the Celtic Church we had found that it differed greatly from the Roman variety of Christianity in that it rejected such central tenets as the virgin birth and the divinity of Jesus. Whilst the Celtic Church had been forcibly consumed by the Roman Church in the middle of the seventh century, we believe that much of the old thinking survived as an undercurrent that was to make

Scotland highly receptive to Nasorean thinking when the Templars eventually arrived.

Finding the original ritual of the Royal Arch Degree of Freemasonry was a major breakthrough, as it provided the complete story of the unearthing of the scrolls. One problem that we still had not resolved was why it described the events as happening on the site of Zerubbabel's Temple rather than Herod's. There was no doubt in our minds that it did refer to the discovery made by the Templar knights at the beginning of the twelfth century, because keystones and vaulted arches had not been invented until the Roman period.

The image used on the Royal Arch Degree 'tracing board' had shown us in detail the excavation of the Temple and the layout of the vault beneath the rubble that held the scrolls. In the background we see Jerusalem and the ruins of the Temple.

We would have to continue with our researches and hope that an explanation for this paradox would emerge in time. Despite this small problem, we now understood how this Masonic legend could well have kept alive the story of how the first Templars, under Hugues de Payen, had found the scrolls which led to the creation of the Order.

The identification of the Heavenly Jerusalem as a copy of one of the scrolls taken by Geoffrey de St Omer to Lambert at the Chapter of Our Virgin in St Omer, was another huge breakthrough. The use of the Masonic square and compasses in this picture is blatant, and its identification of James as the two central pillars of the new Jerusalem had confirmed our earlier deductions.

Chapter Fourteen

The Truth Breaks Free

The Prophecy Becomes Truth

In our trawl through post Jewish-war literature we came
across a widespread belief, known as 'Bereshit Rabbati',
that the power of prophecy would return to Israel in AD
1210, and that soon after, the Messiah would appear out
of hiding in the Great See of Rome.[1] Much to our
surprise this is, arguably, what appears to have happened.

In 1244, just thirty-four years after the power of
prophecy was to return to Israel, an infant was born to a
family of minor nobles in eastern France; his name was
Jacques de Molay. The young Knight had a clear sense of
mission and he joined the Knights Templar at the earliest
possible age – twenty-one. He did well and developed a
reputation for organisation underpinned by rigorous
discipline and rose to be Master of the Temple in England
before being made Grand Marshal with responsibility for
military leadership of the Order. When Tibald Gaudin,
the Grand Master of the Templars, died in 1292, Jacques
de Molay was elected to this, the highest office.

By this time the Templars had lost control of the Holy
Land; the Muslim Mamluks had taken Acre the previous
year, thereby more or less bringing the Christian kingdom
of Jerusalem to an end. However, Molay was still an
immensely powerful man controlling a huge number of

[1] Maimonides letter to the Jews at Yemen

estates across Europe as well as a fine army, a substantial battle fleet and an international trading and banking syndicate. From humble beginnings a hundred and seventy-four years earlier, when Hugues de Payen and his small band of knights started digging in the ruins of the Temple, the Order had become arguably the most powerful force in Christendom, rivalling or surpassing the Vatican itself. We strongly suspect that the early Templars did succeed in finding the gold, silver and other treasures buried by the Jews as the Romans swept forward in the war of AD 66–70, as the speed of development of their wealth and influence seems too remarkable to be the simple result of organic growth. It stands to reason that if they did find such treasures, they would have told nobody and history could have no record of it.

As soon as Molay came to power he reimposed the full observance of all rules and maintained absolute discipline throughout the Order. A total illiterate himself, he forbade other knights from wasting their time by reading, preferring to leave such tasks to the clerics.

The Templars reported to the Pope directly but they were a French-speaking Order with most of their connections in that country. At the time France had a particularly self-important and ambitious king in Philip IV, known as 'Philip the Fair', who sought to manipulate the Pope to his own ends, but Boniface VIII was not an easy man to push around. They fell out when the Pope refused to allow Philip to levy taxes against the French Church, and in 1302 Boniface declared that 'the spiritual was greater than the temporal' and that 'to oppose the Pope was to oppose God'. Philip announced to the world that Boniface was unfit to sit upon 'the throne of Peter', accusing the pontiff of every crime imaginable including blasphemy, heresy, murder and even sodomy. His desire to damn the Pope knew no bounds and he tested the extremes of medieval credulity when he levelled the charge that Boniface had had a secret sexual relationship with a demon who lived in the Pope's ring. Not surprisingly the Pope was angered and responded by imposing the highest level of excommunication on Philip personally, rather than on his kingdom. However, the king managed to gain substantial support throughout France and Boniface responded by threatening to proclaim that the country was to be placed in a state of 'interdiction', which whilst less terrible than national excommunication was still an extremely bad state of affairs. For as long as an 'interdiction' was in place, the people of France would not be baptised, attend communion, receive absolution or even be buried with full Christian rites.

Philip knew that such a sanction would bring him down and he sent his henchmen to 'make the Pope an offer he could not refuse'. On 8 September 1303 Guillaume de Nogaret and his team entered the palace at Anagni in Italy and seized the aged Pope, abusing him and threatening him with great damage. Philip's men were unable to escape with the Pope and they knew that to kill him would be fatal for themselves, so they left uttering terrible threats. Boniface never recovered from the ordeal and he died five weeks later, some say at the hands of Philip because of the stress of the attack.

The new Pope, Benedict XI, started out with a friendly tone towards Philip, but as the French king started to increase his demands the relationship quickly soured, to the point that the Pope publicly accused Philip of ordering the attack on Boniface at Anagni. Soon Benedict was dead by poison at the hands of Philip the Fair. The king effectively chose his replacement – one Bernard de Goth, archbishop of Bordeaux. He was a sworn but controllable enemy of the king, but his desire for the throne of Peter was far stronger than his dislike of Philip. Suddenly in 1305 the megalomaniac King of France had control of the Vicar of Christ and, therefore, Western Christendom. Barely solvent, Philip immediately levied a ten per cent tax on the gross revenue of the French clergy. Four years later the puppet Pope effectively transferred the seat of power from the Vatican to Avignon, a situation that endured for the next three-quarters of a century.

With the appointment of a controllable Pope in Clement V, Philip the Fair now had the power he wanted but now he needed money. Guillaume de Nogaret, still the king's henchman, was a very clever fellow and he conducted an act of grand theft on the king's behalf, as cunning as it was wicked. After some extremely careful and skilful planning, the king's troops moved out in small groups right across the country on the morning of 22 July 1306 and arrested every Jew in the country. Shortly afterwards the unfortunate Jews were sent into exile – naturally without their property, which was immediately transferred to the crown.

It is little wonder then, that this greedy king next turned his attention to the Templar Master, Jacques de Molay and all the wealth of the Paris Temple and its estates and business interests across the land. Nonetheless, even Philip could not expect to get away with open piracy towards an order of such high rank. The Knights Templar answered to no man save the Pope, and were outside the laws of every country. The king, however, was a resourceful man when it came to increasing his wealth and power, so he created the necessary circumstances for his plan to succeed without interference.

The belief that the Templars indulged in some unusual rites had been suspected from the beginnings of the Order but as the mightiest and most respected force in Christendom they had been almost immune from serious speculation. Unfortunately the very secrecy of their procedures provided an excellent reason for false charges to seem credible. A plan to destroy the Templars and seize their wealth was carefully put together by Guillaume de Nogaret. He must have had at least one spy planted within the Templar Order, reporting back to him on the nature of the secret rituals of the Templars. Even so, this information alone would not have been sensational enough to bring down the world's most celebrated Order and to allow Philip to seize its wealth. So to compensate for the absence of sufficiently damning evidence, de Nogaret simply arranged for the 'discovery' of new information. False witnesses leaked the stories of foul deeds, and in due course King Philip felt 'obliged' to inform the Pope of the grievous situation.

The king knew that rivalry between the two most important orders of chivalry, the Templars and the Hospitallers, was deep and widespread, and he suggested to Pope Clement that he write to the Grand Master of both, inviting them to a meeting to discuss a plan for the support of the kings of Armenia and Cyprus. It was no secret that the Pope had ideas of merging the Knights of the Temple of Solomon and the Knights of the Hospital of St John of Jerusalem into a single order to be called 'The Knights of Jerusalem' and de Molay almost certainly believed that this was the true agenda. Such a merger was out of the question for him, and he must have felt that given the wealth and power of the Templars he could easily prevent such an unwanted marriage. On the other hand, in all likelihood, the Pope would probably have forced the merger; he had declared his preference for the Hospitallers to take the senior role. Meanwhile, King Philip had failed to convince anyone that his plan to make himself the leader of the joint Order was the best solution.

William de Villaret, the Grand Master of the Hospitallers, was unable to attend a meeting because he was fully occupied with an attack upon the Saracens of Rhodes. De Molay, who was in Limassol, Cyprus, when he received the papal order to travel to France for a meeting with the Pope, collected sixty knights together, packed 150,000 gold florins and set sail for Marseilles. De Molay had every right to expect a magnificent welcome from King Philip the Fair as the Templars had rendered him many great services. They had loaned the king the money he required for the dowry of his daughter, the Princess Isabella, and the Paris Temple had provided a refuge for the king for several days when a public uprising got out of hand. On a personal level, the Grand Master must have felt that the king was a true friend as he had asked de Molay to be the godfather to his son, Robert.

Suspecting that the Pope would raise the subject of a merger with the Hospitallers, de Molay had taken the precaution of having a document drafted that put the case for the continued independence of his Order. Entitled *De Unione Templi et Hospitalis Ordinum ad Clementum Papam Jacobi de Molayo Relentio*, the document was presented to the Pope at Poitiers. As soon as de Molay arrived in Paris he was greeted with honours by the king but the Grand Master soon became deeply worried when he started to hear about some rumours that were spreading about the 'misdeeds' of the Templars.

The secret plan drawn up by de Nogaret was to take the entire Templar force into custody simultaneously. Considering that there were some fifteen thousand Templars in France at that time, the task was a considerable one – but de Nogaret had excellent experience in undertaking mass simultaneous arrests from the previous year, when he had seized the entire Jewish community. The date of arrest for the Templars was set for Friday 13 October 1307. Sealed orders were sent out to the royal seneschals three weeks beforehand with strict instructions that they must not be opened before Thursday 12 October. The orders started with a powerfully written, if somewhat lengthy sentence, designed to overcome any reluctance the seneschals may have had in carrying out the arrest of such famous knights:

'*A bitter thing, a lamentable thing, a thing horrible to think of and terrible to hear, a detestable crime, an execrable evil deed, an abominable work, a detestable disgrace, a thing wholly inhuman, foreign to all humanity, has, thanks to the reports of several persons worthy of faith, reached our ears, not without striking us with great astonishment and causing us to tremble with violent horror, and, as we consider its gravity an immense pain rises in us, all the more cruelly because there is no doubt that the enormity of the crime overflows to the point of being an offence to the divine majesty, a shame for humanity, a pernicious example of evil and a universal scandal.'*

The main charges made from the testimony of an ex-Templar, Squin de Flexian, were:

'All Templars upon admission swore never to leave the Order and to further its interests by any means, right or wrong.

That the leaders of the Order are in secret alliance with the Saracens and they have more of Mohammedan infidelity than Christian faith, every novice being required to spit and trample upon the cross.

The leaders of the Order are heretical, cruel and sacrilegious men who kill or imprison any novice, who upon discovering the iniquity of the Order, tries to leave it. That furthermore they teach women who are pregnant by them how to procure an abortion and secretly murder new-born children.

That they are infected with the errors of the Fratecelli; they despise the Pope and the authority of the church and scorn the sacraments, especially those of penance and confession.

That they are addicted to the most infamous excesses of debauchery. If anyone expresses his repugnance he is punished by perpetual captivity.

That Templar houses are receptacles of every crime and abomination that can be committed.

> *That the Order works to put the Holy Land into the hands of the Saracens.*
>
> *That the Master is installed in secret and few of the younger brethren are present and that he repudiates his Christian faith by doing something contrary to right.*
>
> *That many statues of the Order are unlawful, profane and contrary to Christianity. The members being forbidden, under pain of perpetual confinement to reveal them to anyone.*
>
> *That no vice or crime committed for the honour or benefit of the order is held to be a sin.'*

The arrest of some fifteen thousand Templars including de Molay was completed within the morning of Friday 13th. The principal false witness was de Flexian who had been expelled on the grounds of heresy and other offences. Together with a Florentine called Noffo Dei, he gave evidence against the Order in return for a pardon and release from prison. The Inquisition was given orders to extract confessions and that no torture should be spared in the furtherance of this objective. These skilled torturers were generally expert at inflicting maximum pain without actually killing their subject; only thirty-six Templars died in the Paris area during the early stages of questioning. With the huge influx of prisoners the Inquisition had to make special arrangements as there were insufficient dungeons and instruments of torture to go around. They were highly imaginative men and they quickly came up with lots of inventive ideas for extracting confessions. A good example of this was 'the foot oven', which simply required a platform to strap the subject to, a little oil for his feet and a brazier. This easy-to-make device proved to be highly effective at convincing Templars to tell the Inquisition the 'truth'. One man was carried into court to confess, holding a box in his hands which contained the blackened bones that had dropped out of his feet as they roasted.

Despite the best efforts of the Inquisition the confessions were slow in coming in, but enough were quickly available to horrify the public when they were told that the once pre-eminent Templars admitted that they had denied God, Christ and the Virgin Mary, and that during their initiation they had bestowed the *Osculum Infame*, the 'kiss of shame', which involved kissing the initiator on the mouth, navel, penis and buttocks. With the benefit of current knowledge it is easy to dismiss these trumped up charges as the output of the imagination of the accusers, but some of the confessions which emerged have to be taken much more seriously.

Many countries were very slow in persecuting the Templars, despite orders from the Pope to have all members of the Order arrested and questioned; Portugal, Ireland, Scotland and England were amongst those that were not happy to carry out this instruction. In England King Edward II eventually agreed to meet the papal command but his torturers were not very successful and the Paris Inquisition offered to help them and put men on the job who had more highly developed skills and a relish for their chosen trade. In June of 1311, the English Inquisition came across some very interesting information from a Templar by the name of Stephen de Strapelbrugge, who admitted that he was told in his initiation that Jesus was a man and not a god. Another Templar by the name of John de Stoke stated that Jacques de Molay had instructed that he should know that Jesus was but a man, and that he should believe in 'the great omnipotent God, who was the architect of heaven and earth, and not the crucifixion'. This has surprised a number of experts, because the statement does not fit any theological belief of the time, including that of heretical sects such as the Cathars, who probably did have contact with the Order. Of course, it caused us no surprise whatsoever, as the words are exactly what we would expect of a man who has been initiated into a latter-day Order of Nasoreans on the basis of the messages from the Jerusalem Church of James found in the Temple scrolls. The view expressed by the Grand Master comes from the true teachings of Jesus and predates the 'crucifixion' cult of Paul that had been adopted by the Romans. These views attributed to the Grand Master ring true; they do not reject Jesus – they merely remind people that there is only one God, one supreme being. It seems certain that such thoughts could only have come directly from James's Church where the teachings of Jesus were revered, but where the crucifixion was considered to be a powerful symbol of 'faithfulness unto death' in the mould of Hiram Abif; nothing more. The cross for the Templars was a mark of martyrdom rather than the source of magic that the 'crucifixion' cult of Paul believed it to be.

From all the information that we have gathered in our researches, we strongly feel that while the highest-ranking knights may have had radically atypical views on the divinity of Jesus Christ, the Templars were, throughout their entire existence, a faithful Catholic Order. In the mid-thirteenth century their wealth, possessions, armed might and remoteness from Rome would have allowed them to have established a new type of Christianity if that had been their wish. They were clearly content, holding their special knowledge to themselves and conducting their own secret ceremonies which, like modern Freemasons, they considered to be complementary to their Christian faith. The Knights Templar were betrayed by a Church and a Pope that they had served well.

The Crucifixion

That Jacques de Molay was horribly tortured there is doubt because this powerful warrior broke down and confessed to crimes he did not commit, although he did retract them shortly before being burned at the stake seven years later. The means of persuasion were not recorded by the Inquisition but strangely enough we were to find evidence in a Scottish Templar building which would help us find out what really happened. We believe that we can reconstruct what happened to the Grand Master in those dungeons seven centuries ago, thanks to one remarkable piece of evidence. What happened on Friday 13 October and Saturday 14 October 1307 must have been something like this:

The Grand Inquisitor of France, Guillaume Imbert, had taken a personal interest in the confession to be extracted from the greatest heretic of them all: Jacques de Molay. As a priest torturing a priest Imbert would normally have avoided the spilling of blood – burning, crushing and stretching imaginatively applied were usually highly effective alternatives. In this instance though, Imbert must have been outraged by the evil 'Anti-christ' activities of this once senior man of God. One can imagine him visiting the Paris Temple with the arresting officers and taking immediate control of the Grand Master. He wanders around the splendid building looking for evidence of wrong-doing to confront the accused, and upstairs he finds a large door with a brass plate at its centre and pushing it open he sees nothing but darkness. In the windowless inner Temple he lights one of the large candles that stood at the first pedestal and his eyes slowly scanned the strange sights that could be picked out in the dim flickering light. It was all so terribly pagan, with markedly anti-Christian ornamentation: pyramids with eyes in their centre, a star-studded roof, and the square and compasses. Amazed and unnerved by the ungodly feel of the place he is suddenly certain that the stories are all true and his prisoner must be the most evil heretic ever to walk the earth. Proceeding to the eastern end he pauses in front of two large pillars and a main pedestal and looking down he sees a simple wooden box which he finds contains a white shroud some fourteen feet long, a human skull and two thigh bones. This, he reasons, must be the shroud that he has heard from his spies was used to 'resurrect' the dead. The Grand Inquisitor is horrified that it is clearly true that de Molay has indeed mocked the suffering and holiness of the passion of Jesus Christ by performing resurrection ceremonies with Templar initiates. A novel line of questioning occurred to Imbert right there and then: one particularly suited to the vile impudence of this fallen priest.

That night, in the cells beneath the Paris Temple, with de Molay stripped of his mantle and naked beneath the rough smock of an accused heretic, complete with running noose about his neck, Imbert informs de Molay that he will admit to his crimes in due course, so why not save himself some pain and make a full confession? Much to the relief of the outraged Imbert, the Grand Master refuses. Imbert starts to quote from the Gospels.

'Then Pilate therefore took Jesus, and scourged him.'

De Molay's arms are pinioned high on the wall and the rough smock thrown forward over his head. His naked back is scourged by two assistants using horse whips tipped with twin metal balls. The torturer on the right, being taller and keener than his partner, causes injury to the legs as well as the back but not the upper arms.

'And the soldiers platted a crown of thorns, and put it on his head.'

A crown of intertwined thorns has been prepared and is thrust squarely onto de Molay's head, drawing blood from the scalp and forehead.

'But they cried, saying, Crucify him, crucify him.'

And then the Grand Master is affixed to a roughly assembled cross; square section nails are driven through

369

the wrists. The violence of the nail's impact on the internal structure of de Molay's right hand causes his thumb to swing across the palm so violently that the joint dislocates and his thumb nail embeds itself into the flesh of his palm. The sole of his left foot is pressed against the upright of the cross, known as the 'stipes', and a lengthy nail smashed through exactly in between the second and third metatarsal. As soon as the nail appears at the other side of the foot the torturers place his left foot upon the right so that the same nail can be driven through both feet. Thus de Molay's body is suspended on just three points of searing pain. Blood loss is minimal and he remains fully conscious.

Molay finds the pain indescribable as his body-weight instantly works against him, causing him to sag downwards, producing traumatic tension in the muscles of his arms, shoulders and chest wall. The ribcage is drawn upwards so that his chest is held in a position preventing exhalation, and in order to avoid asphyxiation the Grand Master has no alternative but to push down on the wounds of his nailed feet to raise his body, so that his lungs can blow out and gasp in one more chestful of air. The panic of not breathing is exchanged momentarily for the massive pain of standing upon impaled flesh. The overall effect of this repeated vile dilemma is increased anoxia (shortage of oxygen), leading to agonising cramps and a dramatically raised metabolic rate.

In between questioning Imbert follows his Biblical role model and offers de Molay a rag soaked in vinegar to 'quench' his terrible thirst, again quoting the scriptures.

'And one ran and filled a sponge full of vinegar, and put it on a reed, and gave him to drink, saying, Let alone; let us see whether Elias will come to take him down.'

The hours seem like weeks and de Molay's resistance

begins to fail him. He asks Imbert what he needs to say to be brought down from the cross. Imbert quotes once more.

'But one of the soldiers with a spear pierced his side, and forthwith came there out blood and water.'

Imbert thrusts a knife into Molay's side, not deep enough to cause life-threatening damage but sufficient to complete the deliberate re-enactment of the suffering of the 'son of God'.

Jacques de Molay confesses there and then on the cross, suffering the same vile agony that caused Jesus to lose his faith momentarily some twelve hundred and eighty years earlier. He is lifted down.

The massive trauma to de Molay's body has caused the production of large amounts of lactic acid in his bloodstream, leading to what is called 'metabolic acidosis'; his muscles have become frozen in permanent cramp, blood pressure has plummeted and his heart is pounding. He is lifted down just moments away from the sweet relief of death.

Guillaume Imbert is well pleased with his success and sees one more amusing twist. He has de Molay placed on the very burial shroud that Molay used to mock the Messiah. As the torturers laid him face upwards on the cloth and the excess section is lifted over his head to cover the front of his body, Imbert cannot resist a final quotation from the story of the Passion.

'And when Joseph had taken the body, he wrapped it in a clean linen cloth.'

Patting the shroud around the desperately damaged body, Imbert suggests that the barely conscious man might care to raise himself, if he feels as important as the true Christ!

The Inquisition was under strict orders not to kill the Grand Master of the Templars but had no intention of nursing the confessed heretic back to good health. De Molay had no family in the area to look after him but Geoffrey de Charney, the preceptor of Normandy who was also under interrogation, did. De Charney's family was called in and told to care for both men, who were destined to die together seven years later, when they both publicly retracted their confessions and were slowly roasted over charcoal for their relapse into 'heresy'.

The Physical Evidence

We were able to reconstruct the circumstances of the interrogation of de Molay because one important piece of evidence still survives to this day. The Qumranian/Masonic style shroud that was taken from the Paris temple of the Knights Templar and used to wrap the damaged figure of the Grand Master travelled with de Molay to the home of Geoffrey de Charney, where it was washed, folded up and placed in a drawer. Exactly fifty years later, in 1357, this fourteen-foot-long piece of linen was taken out of store and put on public display at Livey. We cannot be sure as to whether or not it was exhibited because it was its half centenary, but we can be certain as to why it was of public interest.

De Molay's steaming body had been lifted down from his cross and left in a cold, damp underground dungeon where the injured man's morbid fluids – sweat mingled with blood high in lactic acid – had run freely around his body, staining the cloth where contact was firmest. The trauma of the crucifixion caused Jacques de Molay's body to 'paint' the image of his suffering onto his own 'Masonic' shroud.

The de Charney family had removed the shroud and

dressed the wounds and must have spent many months bringing de Molay back to something approaching reasonable health. The shroud itself was put away in the family home without further thought. Geoffrey de Charney's nephew, also called Geoffrey, had been killed by the English in 1356 (the year before the exhibition of the shroud) at the Battle of Poitiers, and it seems likely that knowledge of the true origin of the shroud died with him.

The image on the shroud was remarkably clear. The features of de Molay's body were etched onto the cloth by the lactic acid from the free-flowing blood, reacting with the frankincense used as a whitening agent, which was rich in calcium carbonate. The long nose, the hair beyond shoulder length with a centre parting, the full beard that forked at its base and the fit-looking six-foot frame all perfectly match the known image of the last Grand Master of the Knights Templar (See Figs 19 and 20).

The first people to view the shroud thought that they recognised the image because it fitted their notion of a man that had suffered a similar fate just over one thousand three hundred years earlier; they thought that they were looking at the face of Jesus, and that length of cloth is today called the Shroud of Turin.

The image that the Christian world has learned to love as the face of God is in fact the face of a man tortured and murdered in God's name, not by the Romans but by a money-grabbing French king with the support of the Roman Catholic Church.

Many people have searched for the origins of the Turin Shroud; we believe that we have found the solution because we did *not* look for it. All of the various theories previously put forward previously deny some aspect of the available evidence, but in our quest to find Hiram, the Shroud was just a passing jigsaw piece that helped complete a total picture. In 1988 the Vatican allowed scientific tests to be carried out at three separate carbon-dating establishments; these showed conclusively that the linen of the Shroud could not date any earlier than AD 1260. Given that the Shroud had probably been in use for a few years, that puts it right on target.

Very strangely, the findings of the carbon daters were published on 13 October, the same day of the year that de Molay had been arrested and crucified! There is a one in three hundred and sixty-five chance of this being a coincidence, but we could not help wondering if there was more to it than that. The Vatican has always denied that the Shroud is a holy relic, because the Church knows its origins: could it be that Rome thought it fitting to prove the point on the very anniversary of the Shroud's creation?

The teachings of Jesus effectively 'died' with him, to be replaced by Hellenistic mystery formulae created by Paul, the 'Spouter of Lies', yet the 'resurrected' teachings were released to the world once again by the crucifixion of Jacques de Molay. For the one thousand, two hundred and seventy-four years between the two identical crucifixions, the true teachings of Jesus lay 'dead and buried' under the Temple in Jerusalem. But once released to the world the concepts of equality, social responsibility and the power of human knowledge re-emerged to end the intellectual vacuum of the well-named 'Dark Ages'.

The political power that the Roman Empire had been losing in the first three centuries AD was maintained through the planning of Constantine, who as we showed earlier, had a complex web of superstition woven to wrap up the minds of the masses to keep them in their place. His vision for the common people was to use them to produce goods and wealth in peacetime and provide soldiery in time of war; their reward for their sad, ignorant little lives was the promise of their own personal resurrection and a wonderful afterlife. The Church of Rome positioned blind faith as a virtue and labelled Christian literature referring to knowledge for the individual as 'Gnostic', and this they called evil. 'Gnostic' is simply from the Greek for 'knowledge'. It is no coincidence that the period popularly referred to as the Dark Ages corresponds with time between the rise of the Roman Church and the crucifixion of Jacques de Molay! Thankfully, due to the true teachings of Jesus, the age of darkness that had lasted one and a quarter thousand years started to back away from the shining light of reason.

The Message Breaks Out

Whilst the Grand Master was being crucified, many Templars had slipped the net. A large part of the Templar fleet had been in harbour at the Atlantic sea port of La Rochelle and they must have been tipped off or picked up some rumours, for as the sun rose on the morning of Friday 13 October, the would-be arresting guards could see only water where the fleet had been tied up the night before. The ships of the Order were never seen again, but their battle flag, the skull and crossbones, was.

We now needed to establish what happened to those Templars that managed to escape the clutches of King Philip. From our investigations we found that their presence can be detected in two places soon after the escape: Scotland and America.

We cannot be sure from the surviving evidence, but stories persist of Templar ships going to Scotland and to Portugal. The fleet could have visited both refuges in turn, but it seems more probable to us that they divided as soon as they left port, with one section headed towards Scotland and the remainder sailing to the northern tip of friendly Portugal to stock up with provisions. From there they set out on a voyage that had often been discussed but, due to commitments in the Holy Land, had never been undertaken. They pointed their bows exactly due west and set sail on what is now the forty-second parallel in search of the land marked by the star they knew from the Nasorean scrolls was called Merica, which these

French knights referred to as 'la Merica', a name that later became simply America. They almost certainly landed in the Cape Cod or Rhode Island area of New England in the early weeks of 1308, setting foot on the New World nearly a century and a half before Christopher Columbus was even born.

This is a strong claim, but irrefutable evidence is already in existence to show that the Templars did reach America, settled there and that they carried out journeys to and from Scotland. In the small town of Westford, Massachusetts, there is an image of a knight carved as a series of punched holes into a slab of rock. The now-famous knight can be seen to be wearing a helmet and the habit of a military order and the sword shown in the weathered carving that has been identified as having a pommelled hilt of the style of a European knight of the fourteenth century. But for us the most fascinating feature is the shield which has a clear and simple design upon it; it depicts a single masted medieval vessel sailing west ... towards a star.

At Newport, Rhode Island, there is a second European monument – a puzzling tower constructed in the style of Templar round churches. It has been described as having typically Romanesque architectural details in its pillars and arches. Its dating puts this strange tower right into the century that saw the Templar fleet disappear. It was probably a multipurpose building for the new colonists, serving as a church, a watchtower and a lighthouse. There is no doubt that the building is extremely old, because on a map of 1524 recording the European discovery of this coastline, Italian navigator Giovanni da Verrazano marked the location of the Newport Tower as an existing 'Norman Villa'.

These finds are very powerful indicators of a Templar presence in the New World, but alone they are not conclusive. However, we already knew that Rosslyn Chapel provides the evidence that is beyond debate, as we discussed earlier in this book. Well known as a place where the Templars congregated after the attack by King Philip and the Pope, this elaborate building took some forty years to build and was completed in the early 1480s by Oliver St Clair, which predates Christopher Columbus's arrival in America by several years. Columbus made his first New World landing on the morning of 12 October 1492 on an island in the Bahamas, which Columbus named San Salvador; his first mainland landing was not made until 1 August 1498 when he arrived in South America.

When considering these comparative dates it is extremely instructive to look at the carved decoration of the Chapel because there the apparently impossible is evident. As stated earlier, the archways and ceiling of Rosslyn Chapel have corn cobs (Indian maize) and aloes carved into them as decorative devices; these are two plants that the Scots had no right to know about, let alone illustrate so accurately. Corn was extensively cultivated, in all its present forms, by the Indians of North and South America but it is still believed to have been unknown outside the New World before 1492 at the very earliest. According to official history, seed grains of Indian maize were first brought to Europe and Africa by sixteenth-century explorers and eventually thrived throughout most of the world. These carved plants are very much an integral part of the fabric of the chapel and they must have been started some years before the completion of the building, so we have certain evidence that the men that instructed the masons of Rosslyn Chapel must have visited America at least a quarter of a century before Columbus.

In the light of such solid evidence we can accept the Westford knight and the Newport Tower for what they are – Templar remains in what is today the United States of America.

The Land of the Star Called La'Merika

Before leaving the subject of the first European landings in the New World, we would like to explain why it became our firm conviction that the continent of America took its name, not from the 'also-ran' explorer Amerigo Vespucci, but from the star of the west called Merika, which the Nasoreans believed was the marker of a perfect land across the ocean of the setting sun. Not only did we have the evidence of the true source of the name; we found that the old explanation is easy to disprove.

The standard historical line that is routinely trotted out for the origin of the name of the New World, comes entirely from a silly misunderstanding by an obscure clergyman who never ventured more than a few miles from the monastery of St Deodatus in the Vosges Mountains in the Duchy of Lorraine on the French/ German border. This very enthusiastic priest had a passion for geography and for deeply meaningful names. He gave himself the highly imaginative pseudonym of 'Hylacomylus', from the Greek for 'wood', the Latin for 'lake' and the Greek for 'mill', which was eventually translated back to his native German to create the family name of Waldseemüller. This slightly eccentric man led a small team who had access to a printing press and they gathered what information they could about the world including the inspiring discoveries of the great and mysterious continent across the western ocean. The little group produced and printed a 103-page volume in April 1507 that they called *Cosmographiae Introductio*. It covered the traditional principles of cosmography, including the divisions of the planet, distances between key locations and details of winds and climates, but it was also the source of a mistake that would make an amateur navigator famous for all time. Waldseemüller had found a number of references by various sailors to the general landmass of the great continent to the west, describing it as 'America', and he also found a glowing account of the travels of an Italian explorer by the name of Amerigo Vespucci. He erroneously married the two pieces of unconnected information and wrote:

> *'Now, these parts of the earth (Europe, Africa, Asia) have been more extensively explored and a fourth part has been discovered by Amerigo Vespucci (as will be described in what follows). Insomuch as both Europe and Asia received their names from women, I see no reason why any one should justly object to calling this part Amerige (from the Greek "ge" meaning "land of"), i.e. the land of Amerigo, or America, after Amerigo, its discoverer, a man of great ability.'*

Waldseemüller printed his book and a giant map with the new continent marked as 'America' and it has always been assumed that he was the originator because it was the first printed reference. The words of the monk, given here, have been taken as showing his thinking process on what form of Amerigo Vespucci's name to use, but it is not that at all. Read it carefully and it can be seen that it shows nothing more than that he was musing over why the existing name 'America' is so appropriate. It was a name that in his opinion could have been perhaps better as 'Amerige', but he could quite understand why 'America' was an acceptably meaningful construction. This book was written fifteen years after the 'official' Columbus discovery of the New World and exactly two hundred years after the Templars first landed there. In either case it seems silly to assume that nobody had given this continent a name before this German monk started writing a book called 'Introduction to Cosmography' or that such a non-sailor would have had the audacity to assume that he had the right to christen a new quadrant of the globe.

Waldseemüller got the name right but the explanation wrong. His personal inclination for meaningful names misled him, and the power of the printing press ensured that his error was transmitted widely in a very short space of time. Very shortly after he had written these words, he realised his great mistake and publicly retracted his assertion that Amerigo Vespucci was the discoverer of the New World – but by then it was too late, people had an explanation that seemed to make some sort of sense. It was a classic case of history (to paraphrase Henry Ford) becoming 'bunk'.

Once a convention is accepted it takes intellectual dynamite to shift it. The accidental myth of Vespucci is cultural folklore in the American education system. But those that really want to understand America and the forces that created the modern United States need to follow the evolutionary chain of Nasorean thinking.

CONCLUSION

The downfall of the Knights Templar was the end of a great Order but its demise opened up the way for a whole new world order based upon Jesus's reworking of Ma'at. In reconstructing the crucifixion of Jacques de Molay and tracking the flight of his knights, we felt close to finding the final link with Freemasonry. Why the Templars had provided their secrets to form a new order called Freemasonry was still not clear, but at least we knew where to look for some answers to these gaps in our knowledge.

As we reviewed what we had discovered about the events surrounding the crucifixion of Jacques de Molay, we could not help but see it as the central event in an episode of history that marked out the greatest ever watershed in the course of Western social development. The attack on the Templar Order by a greedy and unimportant French king proved to be the first vital step in the long process of releasing the Christian world from the prevailing principle of intellectual castration, exercised by the Vatican, and allowing it to build a civilisation driven by a desire for knowledge and a recognition of the worth of the individual. This drive from autocracy to democracy in government and aristocracy to meritocracy in social structure, within a framework of theological tolerance, has nowhere been so conspicuously sought, and in part achieved, than in the United States of America.

Chapter Fifteen

The Lost Scrolls Rediscovered

Why, we asked ourselves, does the United States of America exist? It did not have to come into existence and we doubt that without the benefit of hindsight, many modern observers would have given it any chance of being successful in becoming the hub of world culture and the most powerful nation on Earth within less than two centuries. The plan for the United States was not a development of anything obvious that had gone before in Europe; it was something apparently quite new and very radical, but the inspiration for a new country where every individual counts, where the people themselves are responsible for the state and where they personally answer to their God, had to come from somewhere. We felt with growing certainty that it came via Freemasonry and the Templars from the man we know as Jesus, who himself lived in a time of oppression when he sought equality, justice and enlightenment for all his people. His outlook could not and did not go beyond the boundaries of his own nation, but in time the message he gave to the world was heard and acted upon.

We found the following words of especial interest:

'Observe good faith and justice towards all nations; cultivate peace and harmony with all. Religion and morality enjoin this conduct and, can it be that good policy does not equally enjoin it? It will be worthy of a free, enlightened and, at no distant period, a great

> *nation, to give to mankind the magnanimous and too*
> *novel example of a people always guided by an exalted*
> *justice and benevolence.*[1]

They were spoken by George Washington in his farewell address, and the words chosen clearly confirm what is already well known; this first President of the United States was a lifelong Freemason. They also sound strangely reminiscent of the lost teachings of Jesus, talking of the importance of 'freedom', 'enlightenment', 'peace', 'good faith', 'justice' and 'benevolence' as well as aspiring to the building of a 'great nation' and the binding together of religion and morality. These characteristics expressed by Washington may sound to modern ears like the sort of words one would use on such an occasion, but at the time they were spoken they were quite remarkable.

An acceptance of Templar artefacts on the eastern seaboard of the United States does not explain how this outlawed French Order could have possibly influenced the founding principles of that country. To understand the full sequence of events we decided that we first needed to look closely at the other Templar outpost, three thousand miles across the Atlantic Ocean, on the western coast of Scotland.

That many Templars settled in Scotland after the collapse of their Order in mainland Europe is well documented and the evidence is still plain to see today. The church at Kilmartin, near Loch Awe in Argyll, contains many examples of Templar graves and tomb carvings showing Templar figures; furthermore, there are many Masonic graves in the churchyard. On visiting the site in 1990 we had been immediately struck by a maritime monument in the wall of the churchyard to a captain lost at sea during the 1600s. What was so striking was that the monument consists of two pillars framing a

---

[1] W.M. Thayer: *George Washington*

skull and crossbones, the Templar fleet's battle flag and symbol of a master mason, framed by the motif which linked Freemasonry with Seqenenere Tao. This was extremely exciting, but even more exciting was the large number of Templar graves and carvings within the churchyard. As we discussed these finds it seemed to us that if a large enough contingent of Templars had fled to Argyll in the early 1300s, then we would expect more than one site of Templar graves. Over the next few weeks we worked out from Kilmartin exploring all the old churchyards and burial grounds we could find. We soon discovered several more sites with at least one Templar grave, and whilst we were not particularly looking for them, we also found extremely old graves bearing Masonic symbols.

We had long been aware that there was a strong Templar connection with this area of Scotland from the time when Hugues de Payen married Catherine de St Clair. In fact the first Templar preceptory outside the Holy Land was built on St Clair land at a site to the south of Edinburgh now known as Temple. By the beginning of the fourteenth century the Templars had many estates in Scotland and a great deal of affection and respect from the people.

The Scottish Sanctuary

Scotland had always been an important location for the Templar Order but we discovered that the political circumstances in Scotland made it a particularly suitable sanctuary after the attack by King Philip and the Pope.

Following the death of King Alexander III in 1286 the ancient line of Celtic kings had come to an abrupt end because he had no children, nor brothers or sisters. His only direct heir was Margaret, the 'Maid of Norway', but she died *en route* to Scotland, leaving the succession in dispute. The country became weakened by infighting and

King Edward I of England took advantage of the situation by lending support to John de Balliol, who was one of the contenders for the throne, demanding in return for this support that Balliol become a vassal of the English king and do homage for his Scottish kingdom. The people were not fooled and he was an unpopular king, known as 'Toom Tabard' which translates as 'Empty Gown' but meant more accurately, 'glove puppet of Edward I'. The English king had no respect for the man either and treated him as a common vassal, humiliating him publicly on one occasion by insisting that Balliol stand trial for a claimed debt to a London wine importer. Balliol finally turned against Edward in 1296 when he refused the English king's instruction to help fight the French. Edward responded by marching on Berwick and deposing of Balliol, sending him into exile in France and claiming direct rule over Scotland for himself. To ensure that no Celt could make a counterclaim, the Englishman carried off the symbol of Scottish independence; the ancient 'Stone of Destiny', or 'Stone of Scone' as it is also known. This small, roughly hewn, rectangular block upon which the kings of Scotland had long been crowned was never returned and still rests under the English throne in Westminster Abbey.

After stealing the Scots' symbol of independence the English king set about establishing a governor in Scotland to rule it on his behalf, leaving the unhappy Scots heavily oppressed under his dictatorial leadership.

The first resurgence of Scottish nationalism came very quickly, sparked when the nobleman William Wallace killed the Sheriff of Lanark as revenge for the murder of his wife in May 1297. This was an affront to the English king and Wallace would have been severely punished but popular support rose strongly behind him, leading to a fully-fledged battle at Stirling Bridge on 11 September 1297 at which Edward's forces were defeated.

Edward I made peace with the French and then turned

his full attention to the troublesome Wallace, whom he defeated at Linlithgow the following year. Wallace escaped capture and immediately travelled to France, seeking support from Edward's old enemies for his cause. He is reported to have received letters from King Philip the Fair commending his cause to Pope Clement V, and it is certain from the support he gained from the Moray family (whose name has been continually linked with the Templars and Freemasonry) that he made contact with the Templars during this time. He was successful in gaining this support because there was a battle between the Scots and the English at Roslin in 1303 which was won with the support of Templar knights, led by a St Clair. Wallace remained an outlaw hunted by the English Crown for seven years before being betrayed and taken to London and hung, drawn and quartered in 1305. Following his execution and dismemberment, parts of Wallace's body were hung in Newcastle-on-Tyne, Berwick, Stirling and Perth.

Throughout this period of unrest there were two Scots who had a genuine but not indisputable claim upon the throne, one being Robert the Bruce, the eighth Earl of Carrick, and the other John Comyn. Robert was an ambitious man and he first sought advancement by working with Edward I, but his support for the Englishman became weaker as he began to feel that he was not going to get the elevation he wanted. When Robert started to investigate other options for building his personal status in Scotland, his opponent Comyn took advantage of the situation by telling Edward that Robert the Bruce was scheming against him. The king would have disposed of such an irritation without a second thought, but a supporter warned Robert the Bruce of the imminent danger and he had to think pretty quickly. His options were suddenly much reduced and he decided to take a huge gamble. He knew that there was a fledgling Celtic resurgence and that the Scots would not easily accept a king who was an English vassal for ever, so he decided to become the spark that lit the powder keg.

He knew that Comyn was a favourite of the Pope and well liked by Edward I, so he conspired to polarise his position by publicly insulting the Pope and king whilst raising the battle standard for the growing Celtic revival. This he did in one preplanned move when he had Comyn lured to the Franciscan church at Dumfries and attacked him right on the steps of the altar itself. As Comyn lay bleeding Robert refused to allow the monks to aid the dying man, and stood over him until he was sure that his opponent had bled to death. This brutal act committed on sacred ground outraged both Edward and the Pope, but the Scottish patriots took it as a brave deed of open defiance against the English, because Comyn had inherited John de Balliol's claim to the throne and was supported by King Edward I. The Pope responded by announcing on 10 February 1305 that Robert the Bruce was, from that moment, excommunicated. Despite this ultimate punishment from the Pope, thirteen months later Bruce had the total support of the Celtic lords and was crowned King of Scotland by the Countess of Buchan at Scone – without the benefit of the Stone of Destiny.

This then was the situation in Scotland when part of the Templar fleet made the decision to head to Argyll and the Firth of Forth, where they knew Robert the Bruce was engaged in a rebellion against England. The fact that Robert the Bruce was excommunicated combined with the long St Clair family links with Rosslyn was the greatest attraction of Scotland as a sanctuary – it was one of the few places on the planet where the Pope could not get at them. Because of the war with the English the Templars also knew that as skilled warriors, they would be received with open arms.

Just three months before Philip the Fair sprang his trap on the Templars, Edward I of England died, to be succeeded by his weak and ineffectual son Edward II who almost instantly retreated to England, leaving Robert I to tidy up his enemies in Scotland.

History records that the Bruce had nothing but major setbacks in 1306–7 but after that he rallied from an apparently hopeless situation and began systematically winning back his kingdom from the English. The Scots' greatest triumph was the Battle of Bannockburn on 6 November 1314. The battle is recorded as going strongly against Bruce's army until an intervention by a unknown reserve force quickly turned the tide of the whole battle and ensured victory for the Scots. Stories quickly spread that these mysterious warriors had carried the Beausant (the battle flag of the Templars). A Templar intervention indeed seems to be the only possible explanation. So in the same year that Jacques de Maloy and Geoffrey de Charney were roasted alive in Paris, the Battle of Bannockburn was being won by the arrival of a Templar force led by the Grand Master of the Scottish Templars, Sir William St Clair. This victory at Bannockburn declared and put in place the freedom of the Bruce's kingdom in Scotland. The St Clairs' part in this victory was well rewarded as they received a bishopric and additional lands to add to their Rosslyn holdings.[2]

This great victory was the major step in securing a permanent independence for Scotland, and King Robert I spent the remainder of his life fighting the English in Ireland and along the Scottish borders until eventually, in 1328, England formally recognised Scotland as a free nation. A point of Masonic interest concerning the Battle of Bannockburn is that it was fought on the day with the longest daylight in the year – a day still celebrated by all Freemasons as the Feast of St John the Baptist.

It seems that the Templars had found a good haven in Scotland, but it was obviously a symbiotic relationship with the king of Scotland benefiting from the skills of

---

[2] Andrew Sinclair: *The Sword and the Grail*

these professional warriors, probably in terms of strategic planning at first, but eventually in direct combat assistance as well. For a while the Templars were safe with Robert I being excommunicated, but this state of affairs, whilst good for the Templars, was not good for Scotland because a kingdom whose king was excommunicated was viewed as a pagan land, and any Christian ruler was free to mount a Crusade against heathens. Unless good relations were eventually restored between the Scottish king and the Bishop of Rome, Scotland could find itself at great risk of lawless invasion in the future. In 1317 Pope John XXII tried to impose a truce on the Scots and English and was said to have been furious when Robert the Bruce responded by capturing the border town of Berwick in a surprise attack. Papal–Scottish relations deteriorated still further when the English gleefully told tales at the papal court of Scottish war-making and obstinacy and in 1320 the Pope sent two papal legates to serve a further sentence of excommunication against Bruce, James (the Black) Douglas and the Earl of Moray. The defence of these further charges were met with the Declaration of Arbroath which was published by the Scottish Barons on 6 April 1320. It is very Masonic in nature and concerning Robert the Bruce it states:

> '*All were bound to him by right and by the service that he had rendered his people.*' *The nobles said that they fought "not for glory, or riches or honours, but only for liberty, which no true man would yield save with his life".'*

It also gives their definition of kingship:

> '... *the due and lawful consent of all the people, made him our king and prince. To him, we are obliged and resolved to adhere to in all things, both on account of his right and his own merit, as being the person who*

hath restored the people's safety in defence of their liberties. But, after all, if this prince shall leave these principles he hath so nobly pursued, and consent that we or our kingdom be subjected to the king or people of England, we will immediately endeavour to expel him as our enemy, and as a subverter both of his own and our rights, and will make another king who will defend our liberties.'

The senior lords of Scotland were Templars or consorts of the Templars, and it is hardly surprising that their 'Nasorean' style of thought is present in this unusually democratic document that turns the idea of king into more of a president. Certainly one of the signatories to the document was the Lord Henry St Clair of Rosslyn.

Surely, we reasoned, it has to be significant that Nasorean/Templar/Masonic thinking was present at many important points in Western history when the subject of popular leadership and will of the people were the main factors. In England, a hundred years before the Declaration of Arbroath, the Magna Carta was signed by King John under persuasion by a group that included Templars. To this day it is the only document in the English constitution that can be loosely compared to the Bill of Rights of the United States – a document that, as we will show later, was wholly Masonically inspired.

In October 1328, for political reasons which are of no great importance to our story, Pope John XXII released Robert I from the ban of excommunication but the now legitimate Scottish king died at the age of fifty-five on 3 June 1329, just ten days before John XXII published a bull publicly recognising his right to the throne of Scotland. Robert was succeeded by his son David II, who was only five years old, and Lord Randolph, a member of the Moray family and uncle of the Earl of Moray, was appointed as Regent. The death of Robert the Bruce was not the end of his links with the Templars. Before dying he had taken a vow to go to Jerusalem and fight the Saracen and as a mark of respect his embalmed heart was taken by Sir William de St Clair and Sir James Douglas on a last crusade to Jerusalem, but unfortunately they were killed in battle in Andalusia *en route*. Bruce's heart never reached the Holy City and was returned to be buried in Melrose Abbey whilst Sir William was buried at Rosslyn.

As soon as Scotland was once again officially part of Christendom it was imperative that the Templars should disappear from sight by becoming a secret society, as the power of the Vatican was now able to once again prosecute its enemies across the whole of Europe. Fortunately during the transition period a member of the Templar Moray family was Regent, ruling on behalf of the infant King David II, and this gave them the level of control they needed to plan the future of the organisation that had already replaced their doomed Order, so that they could retain the great secrets with which they had become entrusted.

Return to Rosslyn

A new secret Order would ensure the survival of Templar rites and thinking, and the plans for this changeover must have been developed in parallel with the papal negotiations, so that by the time Scotland once again paid homage to the Pope, the Templars of Scotland were invisible to those who did not know where to look – and one of the places worth looking was the St Clair family.

As we discussed in Chapter Five, Rosslyn Chapel, built by the later William St Clair, had already proven itself to be hugely important to our quest because it was the construction of this edifice that provided the interface between the Templars and Freemasonry. The use of American plants in decorative stone carving (the aloe and Indian maize), that should have been totally unknown at the time, had provided us with undeniable evidence that someone connected with the St Clairs had traversed the Atlantic at a remarkably early date.

Our first visit to the chapel built by Earl William St Clair was now some four years in the past and as we had learned an incredible amount in the intervening time, we decided to return to this linchpin of a building. Once again we set out at seven thirty in the morning, arriving shortly after noon in the quiet Scottish village. It was a pleasant early summer day, warm but with a broken cloud cover that caused the sun to throw its beams hither and thither across the green rolling hillsides, lighting the many pinnacles of Rosslyn Chapel in a most dramatic manner.

Entering the chapel was like greeting an old friend. It was familiar and inviting yet interesting and exciting, and hopefully it would have lots of new information to share with us. We certainly had plenty of discoveries to put to the test in Rosslyn.

As we walked into the building we were pleased to find it deserted so that we could enjoy its powerful personality without distraction. Rosslyn Chapel exudes a sense of living spirituality, a feeling of the here and now combined with an infinite past. Both of us have a fondness for church buildings, but every church we know has a lifeless and empty character compared to Rosslyn. It is hard to describe the warm feeling that embraces you in this medieval structure without sounding overly fanciful, but Robert summed it up by observing that it was the only church or chapel where he could happily sleep the night alone.

We strolled through the nave enjoying the place and then turned our attention first of all to the carvings of the maize and the aloe cactus, subconsciously to reassure ourselves that we had not imagined what we had seen on our first visit. There was no need to worry; there has no doubt about what we were looking at. As we studied the cactus lintel a lady vicar approached from the north doorway and, with a warm smile, asked if we had seen the Indian maize. We replied that we had, and she started to discuss the subject.

The Reverend Janet Dyer turned out to have been trained in botany and her husband is a botanist by profession.

'The aloe cactus is remarkable, isn't it?' she said, glancing up at the frieze. 'I suppose it could be something else ... but then, I really don't know what it is, if it is not an aloe.' She swung a little to the left and pointed up towards the Indian maize arch. 'My husband says that maize is accurate, probably a slightly immature plant.'

She continued her helpful commentary by referring to the documented evidence that Prince Henry Sinclair, the first St Clair Jarl (Earl) of the Orkneys had, thanks to Templar money, commissioned a fleet of twelve ships for a voyage to the 'New World'. The fleet under Antonio Zeno landed in Nova Scotia and explored the eastern seaboard of what is now the United States of America prior to 1400. The date is certain because Henry Sinclair was murdered upon his return in that year.

It seemed only logical that lives must have been lost on such an expedition, and the Sinclair family claim that a knight called Sir James Gunn died in the Americas and was buried there. The image of the medieval knight found in Westford, Massachusetts is, they claim, his hastily prepared tombstone. We found evidence to support this in the crypt below the chapel, where a small coat of arms on the wall shows on its left-hand side, above the 'Engrailed Cross' of the Sinclair family, a single-masted, twin sailed ship identical to the one found on the shield of the Westford knight. It too is shown pointing to the west, but instead of furled sails under a western star this vessel is under full sail.

As we looked around the chapel's interior Robert could not take his eye off the Hamilton organ that was housed in the Victorian extension on the west wall. 'May I have a look at the organ please?,' he asked the Reverend Janet.

'Certainly, help yourself.' Her reply was so friendly and relaxed that Robert pushed his luck a little further.

'Would you mind if I played it? I am the organist at Christ Church in my home village.'

Having received permission Robert climbed the spiral staircase to the organ gallery and a couple of minutes later the nave was resounding to the sound of *Cwm Rhondda* as Chris continued filming the many items of interest.

As we started to take in the details of the building our attention was quickly drawn to the freestanding pillars of which there are fourteen in total; twelve identical in form and two special and quite splendid ones at the eastern end of the chapel. The left-hand pillar is known as the Mason's Pillar and is a beautifully proportioned and elegant piece of work. The right-hand pillar is quite different; known as the Apprentice Pillar, it is lavishly decorated with the four, floral swathes spiralling down and around the fluted centre from the corners of the capital to meet the base at its opposite side.

The significance of these symbols was of great importance to the builders of this chapel but the meaning has long been lost. However, our reconstruction of the past allowed us to understand what we were looking at. The so-called 'Mason's Pillar' is actually a rendering of the priestly pillar known to Freemasons as Jachin and to the Nasoreans as Tsedeq, and the 'Apprentice Pillar' is the kingly pillar called Boaz, representing the power of Mishpat.

One thing we had to look for in this conundrum of a building was any reference to Hiram Abif; we would have been surprised if this wholly Templar/Masonic building did not have a figure with a hole in its forehead, the distinctive head injury that we now know came down from Seqenenre Tao. And sure enough, we found it. High up in the corner where the south and west walls meet, and level with the organ, is a head with a severe gash on the right temple and in the opposite side of the west wall is the head of the person who killed him. These heads have been well known for hundreds of years but their true symbolism has been lost, replaced by a harmless but implausible story.

To get a better view we both climbed the spiral staircase to the organ gallery and took in the splendid view of the chapel from what was originally the west wall before the horrendous baptistery was stuck on in 1882. From this vantage point we were very close to the head of Hiram Abif and we could see the head wound with great clarity.

This wound has long been noted, and the generally accepted story is that it is the head of a murdered apprentice and the opposite head is that of his master who killed him. According to this legend a master stonemason went to Rome looking for inspiration for the design of the 'kingly' pillar but while he was away his apprentice quickly designed and made the pillar that stands there today. Because it was so much better than anything the master had done, or could have done, upon his return to Rosslyn he hit his junior with a mallet, striking him dead on the spot.

This story sounds like a corrupted version of the Masonic Hiram Abif legend and it can easily be dismissed as the reason for the presence of the wounded head. We know this because William St Clair himself masterminded the whole construction of the building from its inception to his own death in 1484, just two years before its completion; furthermore, he personally supervised every tiny detail of the work. It is a matter of record that every carving, however small, was first created in wood and submitted for approval, and if so approved it was then carved in stone. William St Clair had brought some of Europe's finest masons to Scotland for this great project, building the village of Roslin to house them, and he paid the master masons the then massive amount of £40 per annum and the lesser masons, a still handsome £10 per annum. The idea that after all this preparation and expense, a mere apprentice would be allowed to produce the centrepiece of the entire building seems unlikely in the extreme.

The current caretakers of Rosslyn Chapel did not know it, but the head high up facing the north-east corner is a representation of Seqenenre Tao, the last true king of Egypt.

Let There Be Light

As we talked about the true significance of the pillars and the wounded head, and the fact that the original reasons for them had become lost, slowly but surely a veil of darkness started to lift from our eyes. Had we been blind? The great light of truth about the building suddenly seemed so blindingly obvious: Rosslyn Chapel was not a chapel at all, it was not even really Christian! For a start there is no altar. To operate as a chapel, a table has been set up in the centre of the building because there is no room in the east where the pillars stand. Behind Boaz and Jachin there are three stone pedestals set against the wall, but these are not altars.

This structure was not built as a place of Christian worship!

We had known that a later William St Clair, who became the first elected Grand Master of the Grand Lodge of Scotland, had been in trouble with the Church for having his children baptised in the building, but the importance of this point had not sunk in before.[3] Upon checking with the official history we found that Rosslyn had to be reconsecrated in 1862; prior to that date there is uncertainty about its consecrated status. In fact one of the

[3] *Year Book of Grand Lodge of Ancient Free and Accepted Masons of Scotland 1995*

objections King James VI raised to this Earl of Rosslyn, as Grand Master of Masons, was that he had had his children baptised at Rosslyn which was not' a Christian place of worship.

The more we looked, the more obvious this fact became. The symbolism is Egyptian, Celtic, Jewish, Templar and Masonic in profusion. A star-studded ceiling, vegetative growths coming from the mouths of the Celtic Green Men, entangled pyramids, images of Moses, towers of the Heavenly Jerusalem, engrailed crosses as well as squares and compasses. The only certain Christian imagery was in later Victorian alterations: the stained glass windows, the revolting baptistery and a statue of the Madonna and child. Some small elements of decoration have been described as Christian by the Episcopal Church, but on close inspection they are not what they seem.

In the area of the north wall there is a small frieze showing the crucifixion. But there are good reasons to believe that this is not the crucifixion of Jesus the Christ; it is the torture of the last Grand Master of the Knights Templar, Jacques de Molay. Firstly, all characters are in medieval garb including hooded members of the Inquisition. The details are correct in that the cross is a Tau or 'T' shape and the nails are being driven through the wrists; two details that medieval artists invariably got wrong, unless of course they knew what had actually happened to de Molay. Another section shows Templars with an executioner next to them and most remarkably, we found a carving here that has figures holding up the Shroud of Turin with the face of de Molay clearly visible. We would have expected that the Templars in Scotland would know of the suffering of their master, but we now also knew that they were aware of the story of his image 'miraculously' appearing on his own ritual shroud.

Further confirmation that this building was not what everybody imagined it to be came when we read that even after its completion it was never used as a chapel because there was a family chapel in the castle, a small distance away. The current caretakers admit that it was odd to spend a large fortune as well as some forty-five years building a chapel and then never use it even once. This seems to stump them as they have put forward no suggestion as to why this was so.

The obvious was starting to descend upon us and we both had a simultaneous attack of goose pimples. Rosslyn was not a simple chapel; it was a post-Templar shrine built to house the scrolls found by Hugues de Payen and his team under the Holy of Holies of the last Temple at Jerusalem! Beneath our feet was the most priceless treasure in Christendom. In comparison to these treasures, the Dead Sea Scrolls are humble also-rans. The Nasoreans/Qumranians were instructed (by the Assumption of Moses) to put their most treasured scrolls under the Holy of Holies in around AD 69, and more mundane material, such as the Community Rule, was deposited around Judaea in places as humble as the caves at Qumran. Following these examples, Rosslyn Chapel was a deliberate replication of the burial-place of the secret scrolls! The unearthing of the Dead Sea Scrolls caused a major sensation; we could not help but wonder how the world would respond to this discovery.

We believe that these scrolls are likely to deal with the story of the Nasorean struggle; the story of Jesus the Christ, the secret ceremony of resurrecting the living and the importance of building the human spirit as though it were a temple. They will tell us about the life of Jesus, and as such must be the lost gospel of 'Q', the gospel that was the source material for Matthew, Mark, Luke and John.

We sat on a pew and stared at the thick stone floor; honoured and numbed with excitement because we suddenly knew with utter certainty that we were just feet away from everything we had been searching for, the reason and purpose for the creation of Freemasonry.

It took ten minutes to compose ourselves sufficiently to continue our fact-finding. We looked at historical information for further clues; they were not long coming. Having decided that the Nasorean scrolls were under Rosslyn it was only minutes later that we knew that they were contained in precisely four trunks! This came to light when we read an account of a fire that occurred in 1447, one year after the foundation stone was laid.

William St Clair held many titles including the Prince of Orkney, and the following account uses that description:

> *'About this time [1447] there was a fire in the square keep [of Rosslyn castle] by occasion of which the occupants were forced to flee the building. The Prince's chaplain seeing this, and remembering all of his master's writings, passed to the head of the dungeon where they all were, and threw out four great trunks where they were. The news of the fire coming to the Prince through the lamentable cries of the ladies and gentlewomen, and the sight thereof coming to his view in the place where he stood upon Colledge Hill, he was sorry for nothing but the loss of his Charters and other writings; but when the chaplain who had saved himself by coming down the bell rope tied to a beam, declared how his Charters and Writts were all saved, he became cheerful and went to recomfort his Princess and the Ladys.'* [4]

What could have been so important in those four trunks that William St Clair could only think of them in the fire and not his own wife and the other ladies? Surely he cannot have been so heartless and insecure as to worry first about simple civil documentation about his lands or

---

[4] Tim Wallace-Murphy: *An Illustrated Guide to Rosslyn Chapel*

titles? In any case, medieval trunks are fairly huge affairs and such papers would not fill a quarter of one of these containers, let alone four. No, those trunks contained the scrolls from Jerusalem that had been brought to Scotland by the Knights Templar and were now entrusted to him as the greatest treasure in the whole world. If those scrolls had been destroyed before he had completed the shrine to house them, he would have been in utter despair.

William St Clair dedicated his life to the construction of the scroll shrine and we are certain that the four trunks are still there, beneath three feet of solid rock.

The more we looked and the more we read of Rosslyn's history, the more confirmation we got. Apparently it is generally considered that the building was erected very quickly but the foundations took a curiously long time. From the commencement of work to the completion of the foundations took four years, a ridiculous length of time as the 'chapel' is a relatively small single room with a very tiny crypt at a lower level in the east. This has puzzled historians, but we now knew exactly why it took so long.

The mission of William St Clair was to recreate the underground vaults of Herod's Temple exactly as Hugues de Payen and the other eight knights had found them over three hundred years earlier. We suspected that the underground system was far larger than everything above ground and that the scrolls had found a final resting place in a reconstruction of their original home. It was at this point that our one major inconsistency resolved itself: we now knew why the Royal Arch Degree described the location of the excavation as Zerubbabel's Temple instead of Herod's Temple.

Those who first created the Royal Arch Degree – either ageing, disenfranchised Templars or their descendants in Scotland – relied on stories handed down in the verbal traditions of Hugues de Payen, which told that the setting of the excavation was Zerubbabel's Temple. It is now known the crusaders believed that the Muslim Dome on the Rock, which dates from the seventh century, was Herod's Temple, and the ruins beneath it those of Zerubbabel's.

From the outside, Rosslyn is a representation in stone of the Heavenly Jerusalem as depicted in Lambert's copy, with towers and a huge central curved, arched roof. Inside the Rosslyn shrine, the layout is a reconstruction of the ruin of Herod's Temple, decorated with Nasorean and Templar symbolism. In the north-east corner we found a section of the wall carved with the towers of the Heavenly Jerusalem complete with the Masonic compasses, styled exactly as they are shown on Lambert's scroll. Upon a more detailed examination of the bases that had once carried statuettes, we realised that this image of the Heavenly Jerusalem appeared many times.

As we looked directly upwards from the organ loft, we could see that the arched roof had a running series of keystones down its length, just like the one the Royal Arch Degree describes as found in the ruins of Herod's Temple! Over three feet thick of solid rock, those keystones were locking together a huge weight. Carved into the under-surface of the roof above us was a starry firmament as found in the pyramids and Masonic lodges, and tucked in between was the sun, the moon, a cornucopia, a dove and four heavenly figures.

Thinking about the Royal Arch Degree we realised that if our idea that the Rosslyn building was a reconstruction of the ruined Temple of Herod, we should expect the design of the building to conform to the description given in the ritual. We remembered the relevant words spoken in that degree.

'Early this morning on resuming our labours we discovered a pair of pillars of exquisite beauty and symmetry; proceeding with our work, we discovered six other pairs of equal beauty, which, from their situation,

401

appeared to be the remains of the subterranean gallery leading to the Most Holy Place.'

Fourteen pillars in total; exactly as we saw before us in Rosslyn! William St Clair had followed his script with care. We consulted the ritual of Royal Arch to see if there were more requirements that should predict the layout of this shrine. There is a reference to the so-called 'lights' of the Order which definitely refer to a planned formation:

'These lights are placed in the form of an equilateral triangle, each of the lesser bisecting the line formed by two dividing the great triangle into three lesser triangles on the extremities, which, by their union, form a forth triangle in the centre, and all of them equal and equilateral, emblematic of the four points or divisions of Masonry. This symbolical arrangement corresponds to the mysterious Triple Tau ...'

We recalled that it was the mark of the Tau that the Kenites wore upon their foreheads when Moses first met them and the shape of the cross upon which both Jesus and de Molay had suffered. In Rosslyn, we observed that the fourteen pillars had been arranged so that the eastern eight of them, including Boaz and Jachin, were laid out in the form of a Triple Tau. The formation and the proportions were exactly as the Royal Arch Degree depicts this device today.

There can be no coincidence here – all of the pillars of Rosslyn are laid out to a precise plan according to ancient wisdom and as given in the Royal Arch ritual!

Another point that has puzzled historians was the fact that the 'chapel' was never finished and was 'clearly intended as the first section of a much larger and grander building – a major cathedral'. There is no known reason why the St Clair family should have suddenly stopped building and forget the forty-five-year-old project if it had been their intention to build a collegiate church. Yet the west wall is huge, totally incompatible with the rest of the structure and very obviously incomplete. It has decoration on what is now its exterior side that has been taken to indicate that it was intended as an internal wall for some non-existent larger building. To all intents and purposes it looks like a ruin of a much larger structure, except it is known that there never was one.

But we know that there was. Thinking about it, it would have been strange to complete a small chapel if the intention was to build a great medieval church; and a cathedral in the middle of nowhere at that. The west wall is incomplete and the obvious normal conclusion is that it was never finished – but there is another reason why single walls remain; they are the remains of a ruined cathedral, or more precisely in this case *a ruined temple*. We could not forget that Hugues de Payen and his team found the scrolls whilst investigating ruins, and the Royal Arch ritual reminds us of the fact:

> '... *on clearing away the fragments and rubbish which obstructed our progress, we came to some thing which seemed to be solid rock, but accidentally striking it with my crow, it emitted a hollow sound. We then cleared away more of the loose earth and rubbish ...*'

The Rosslyn shrine was completed exactly to plan; there never was any intention of building further because that huge west wall is a carefully executed reconstruction of the ruin of Herod's Temple that the Knights Templar first entered in their exploration in Jerusalem in AD 1118. We then recalled the next part of the ritual which says:

> '... *when we found that instead of a solid rock there was a series of stones in the form of an arch, and being aware that the architect of the previous structure had designed no part of it in vain ...*'

Just as 'the architect of the previous had designed no part in vain', neither had William St Clair. Every facet of this fascinating structure was there to tell a story. Today the original western entrance has lost its intended dramatic effect of the reconstructed Herodian ruin because the Victorians stuck an ill-conceived baptistery right onto it. The sooner this invasive 'carbuncle' is sliced off this wonderful shrine the better!

The Lost Secret of Mark Masonry Rediscovered

The more we looked, the more we realised that there was nothing accidental about this building. Every detail was carefully considered and important to the great story frozen into the Rosslyn shrine. The fact that all carvings were first made in wood and taken for approval to overseers and finally to Lord St Clair himself reminded us of the ritual used by the Masonic degree known as 'Mark Masonry'.[5]

The ceremony revolves around events that supposedly occurred during the building of King Solomon's Temple and the candidate performs the role of a Fellowcraft Freemason (the rank of a Second-Degree Craft Mason) and tours the Lodge room as the last of three workmen who put forward their work for the approval of the Junior, Senior and Master overseers who are placed respectively at the south, west and east gates.

The three pedestals are visited in turn and at each the first two workmen (the deacons of the Lodge) have their work tested against the plan and approval is given. When the candidate presents his work it is a small keystone and does not meet with approval. The Junior and Senior Overseers state that it is a curiously wrought stone that does not meet with the plan, but because of its fine workmanship they will allow the workman to pass on to

[5] Robert Brydon: *Rosslyn – A History of the Guilds, the Masons and the Rosy Cross*

the next gate. Finally the Entered Apprentice arrives at the pedestal of the Master Overseer, who flies into a rage because the candidate has had the audacity to present a stone to him that is not required for the building, and he orders the stone to be cast into the waste of the quarry.

The workmen are then called to go and receive their wages in the middle chamber of King Solomon's Temple and the Candidate joins the queue and puts his hand through a small hole, known as the 'wicket', to take his payment. He is immediately grabbed by the hand and denounced as an impostor, and an axe is brought down as though about to sever his hand at the wrist. Thankfully, he is spared.

It is then detected that all work has stopped for the lack of a keystone to complete the arch. The overseers state that they recall such a stone being brought to them and a search is made for the lost keystone that will lock the arch together. It is found by the candidate who is then made a Mark Mason and is provided with a mark (a small symbol) that becomes his personal trade mark.

Rosslyn shrine has hundreds of such masons' marks carved into it.

Chris was made a Mark Mason, and at the time none of his initiation had made very much sense either to him or those initiating him, but now the mystery was clearing rapidly. It is possible for us to understand how the murdered apprentice legend developed at Rosslyn as a composite of the Hiram Abif story and the Mark Mason story. William St Clair had an obvious problem with security; the masons building his scroll shrine had to know the layout of the underground vault network and they knew that this strange building was to house something of great value.

William St Clair was a brilliant and talented man and we believe that he devised the First Degree of Craft Masonry and the Mark Mason Degree to give his operative masons a code of conduct and an involvement in the secret, without telling them the great secret of living resurrection which was reserved for speculative Masons. It is a matter of record that he had two grades of stonemason on site; the £10-a-year standard masons (or apprentices) and the £40-a-year 'mark masons' who were honoured by the possession of a personal mark in the continental fashion. Both classes of craftsmen must have been aware that they were rebuilding King Solomon's Temple for some strange reason (although it was actually Herod's Temple).

When Sir William St Clair first planned the building of his scroll shrine, he needed to be certain that he had the loyalty and fidelity of his stonemasons, so that they would keep his 'lawful secrets as securely as their own'. In order to do this he would have to bind them to secrecy, and we believe that the Entrant's Degree of Freemasonry, known today as that of 'Entered Apprentice' was developed by Sir William at the outset of building, using selected elements of the Templar initiation ceremony so that he could ensure that any necessary secrets he had to pass on to these people were within a system of obligation. To maintain differentials he had to provide the £40-per-year senior craftsmen with an extra secret so that they had something more than their lesser masons.

We believe that both grades were told the secret of the kingly or Boaz pillar, and were called, as they are today, Entered Apprentices, and the higher ranks were told the importance of the keystone of the arch because they were Mark Masons. Neither rank was ever allowed to know the secret of the priestly pillar or the significance of twin pillars and the keystone combined:

(MISHPAT OR KINGLY OR BOAZ)	+	(TSEDEQ OR PRIESTLY OR JACHIN)	= STABILITY

or more simply ... STRENGTH + ESTABLISHMENT = STABILITY

The great formula that secured stability in ancient Egypt had to be preserved and reserved for the philosophers; the speculative masons. Men like William St Clair himself.

The masons who worked in stone knew secrets, to an appropriate level; but none was ever raised, by living resurrection, to the rank of a speculative Master mason.

We now could be certain, without any shadow of doubt, that the starting place for Freemasonry was the construction of Rosslyn Chapel in the mid-fifteenth century; later historical developments confirm this view because the St Clair family of Rosslyn became the hereditary Grand Masters of the Crafts and Guilds and Orders of Scotland, and later held the post of the Master of Masons of Scotland until the late 1700s.

As we well know, many modern Freemasons believe that their organisation is descended from the semi-literate working-class ritual practices of the medieval guilds of stonemasons. It is an origin theory that is riddled with problems, yet it did seem to explain the well-documented references to the early operative lodges of Scotland. The true reason is more the reverse; it was speculative masons (Templars) who adopted operative masons (stone workers) and introduced them to lower level secrets concerning Solomon's Temple.

We believe that these Mark Masons and their Entered Apprentice understudies were thrilled to be part of the secret of Rosslyn and they had no ideas of the fabulous 'treasure' that would be housed there. They did not question the absence of normal church imagery because they knew it was secret and special. The only biblical imagery that we could conclusively identify was a carving of Moses sporting a fine pair of horns. Whilst from our studies of Exodus we think that this death-dealing fanatic may have deserved them, we cannot think why the Templars would have thought this way. For a short time we thought we had found just one definite New Testament figure in a tiny statuette of St Peter, but we soon worked out that it was not the disciple at all.

It is said throughout Masonic ritual that the workmen went into the middle chamber of King Solomon's Temple to receive their wages but from the greater knowledge that our historians of today have discovered, we know that the original Temple did not have a middle chamber; however, the Rosslyn shrine did. The crypt of the supposed chapel is in the south-east, with steps down to it immediately to the right of the kingly pillar. These steep steps are hugely worn with deeply arched risers making it quite difficult to descend and ascend. The official guidebook says of these steps:

> *'These well worn steps indicate that many pilgrims visited this chapel in the ninety or one hundred years between its completion and the Reformation. The exact reasons for this pilgrimage are, as yet, unclear, but it is possible that Templar knights had deposited some holy relic of ancient veneration here.'*[6]

But what was this ancient relic?

Halfway down is a door with hinges that reminded us of the hinges on the door in Lambert's copy drawing of the Heavenly Jerusalem. Once inside this lower chamber, the first thing that struck us was how small it was. There was nothing in it except a few tiny wall decorations, an even smaller room to the north and a fireplace with a chimney that was built into the main southern wall of the building. The heavily worn steps told us that this room was used a great deal, and the presence of a fireplace told

[6] Tim Wallace-Murphy: *An Illustrated Guide to Rosslyn Chapel*

us that it was designed to be used for reasonably extended periods. Unless a person was down there for some hours a fireplace would have been unnecessary for the hardy knights of the mid-fifteenth century.

It was next to this fireplace that we found the small figure that we first took to be St Peter, because he was carrying a key. We found this odd because, more than any other imagery this is the most Catholic and the least Nasorean/Templar we could think of, being the basis of that Church's false claim to the teachings of Jesus. Then we realised that the figure had only one large key in his hand, whereas St Peter normally sports several and the handle of the key was a perfect square – 'a true and certain sign to recognise a Freemason'. Suddenly we knew that this was marking the entrance to the scroll vaults; this little rock carving was holding nothing less than *The Hiram Key*.

We believe that this was the middle chamber of this Templar shrine, because up until the completion of the project the west wall of the crypt was open, giving access to the labyrinth beyond. The Nasorean scrolls themselves were probably kept behind a locked door within the vaults so that the St Clairs and their fellow 'resurrected' Masons could refer to them before they were finally sealed away until the end of time. The room, which is now referred to as the crypt, was the middle room of the reconstructed Temple, because it linked the main upper room with the underground vaulted room that took the holy scrolls. It was here that the masons received their wages, and no doubt it was here that they were initiated and sworn to secrecy as Mark Master Masons or Entrant Apprentices.

Before the vaults were sealed off at the completion of the building, several of the latter-day Templars were granted the right to be buried alongside the holy scrolls. It is a matter of historical record that there are knights buried here who are not in coffins, but their full suits of armour. This was normally a privilege reserved for kings alone. Sir Walter Scott immortalised this practice in his poem, *The Lay of the Last Minstrel*:

> *'Seemed all on fire that chapel proud,*
> *Where Roslin's chiefs uncoffined lie:*
> *Each baron, for a sable shroud,*
> *Sheathed in his iron panoply ...*
> *There are twenty of Roslin's barons bold*
> *Lie burid within that proud chapelle.'*

As we scanned the main hall we reflected on how unfortunate it was that all of the principal statues that once stood on the many wall plinths have disappeared. They are said to have been removed by local people when the Parliamentary troops were closing in during the English Civil War and are believed to be buried in the vicinity. We would dearly love to know who they depicted: David and Solomon maybe, and perhaps even Hugues de Payen and Jacques de Molay?

We then found a small carving that could possibly add more weight to our earlier interpretation of the first Templar seal which depicted two knights on one horse. Chris had earlier put forward the tentative suggestion that this motive was intended to represent the two levels of membership of the early Order; those that were raised or resurrected into the secrets at the front of the horse and those that were not a party to the full secrets on the back. Here in Rosslyn we found a small sculpture that was a three-dimensional representation of this seal, except that the knight on the front is elbowing the rear knight off the mount. Could this depict how, after the fall of the Order, those of secondary rank were ejected to maintain maximum security for those who were party to the main secrets? It is still a minor bit of speculation, but it is an answer that could fit the facts well.

The Lord Protector Who Protected Rosslyn

Perhaps the most remarkable evidence to support our view of Rosslyn is that it is still there at all. During the English Civil War, Cromwell and his Parliamentary forces roamed Ireland, Wales and Scotland as well as England, bringing damage to Royalist and Catholic property wherever they could. Cromwell himself visited Rosslyn and whilst he destroyed every Papist church he came across, he did not so much as scratch this building. The official line, as told to us by the Reverend Dyer, is that he was a Freemason of high standing and aware that Rosslyn was a Masonic shrine, and for once we fully agree with present caretakers. The circumstantial evidence that we already had strongly pointed to the Lord Protector being a senior Freemason, and his deliberate sparing of Rosslyn seems to bear this out.

The St Clairs (or Sinclairs as it later became spelled) were naturally on the Royalist side and Rosslyn castle was utterly destroyed by General Monk in 1650 yet again the shrine at Rosslyn went untouched; had it been viewed as a Catholic chapel it would have been felled in an instant!

We left the Rosslyn shrine with great reluctance because it had told us so much in such a short space of time, and we drove the very short distance to the place down the road that is called simply – Temple. This was the Templar headquarters in Scotland, although the picturesque ruin that stands there now is a far more recent structure, built from stones reclaimed from the original Preceptory. In the graveyard we found numerous Masonic graves, most sporting the symbolism of the Royal Arch Degree, and many the ancient twin pillar and lintel motif.

These graves are extremely old and they have not been restored or protected in any way, so it was difficult to make out their precise dates. One, perhaps a more recent one, could be seen to be dated 1621 and like many others it carried the pick and shovel of Royal Arch (commemorating the digging up of the scrolls) as well as the skull and cross bones, the Templar symbol of resurrection that became their battle flag. Such a date means that the remains below it are of a man that was a Royal Arch Freemason at least a hundred years before the official foundation of Freemasonry in London in 1717.

It is, of course, the Royal Arch ritual that tells of the Templar discovery of the scrolls in the ruins of Herod's Temple, and we therefore believe that it must date from long before Rosslyn and Mark Freemasonry as well as the Craft Second Degree which we now believe is a development of the Mark Degree – and not the other way around, as is generally believed. The men who were Royal Arch Masons at the end of the fifteenth century may well have been Templar descendants.

As we headed back to England from Rosslyn that day, we reflected on the huge number of revelations that we had uncovered and the vital information that had come to light which filled in sections of our quest. Reading through the guidebook we were excited to find that William St Clair had had many titles including 'the Knight of the Cockle and Golden Fleece'. This immediately caught our eye, as Freemasonry describes itself as 'more ancient than the Golden Fleece or Roman Eagle'. Put simply, this told members in the early years of the Order of Freemasonry that the ritual was no invention of the St Clairs; indeed it not only predated them, it even predated the great Roman Empire. Reading more about the official view of Rosslyn we also found a couple of intriguing comments that hinted at the truths that we had just uncovered. The first read:

> '*The vaults themselves may yet be far more than a simple tomb, other important artefacts may be contained therein. The one recorded action of the Lords Sinclair that apparently contradicts their well earned reputation*

> *for chivalry and loyalty may also be explained if the vaults are opened, for it is just possible that some clue as to the whereabouts of certain treasures of great historical interest may also be discovered.'*

How true. The author did not know what great secret Rosslyn holds and yet the building has always been known to be much more than meets the eye. Other comments seemed to be premonitions of our decoding:

> *'We must acknowledge this when we attempt to understand the motivation of both the builder of this unique and magnificent chapel and of the gifted artists and craftsmen who executed its design. The fruits of this open-minded approach will inevitably lead us to hypotheses which will direct us in further study to locate evidence that, at present at least, may be hidden or has been overlooked for any one of a variety of reasons...'[7]*

We trust that when we formally request the opening and investigation of the vaults beneath the Rosslyn shrine we will be met by such reasoned and mature thinking. Not to search the vaults could deprive the world still longer of a great and ancient wisdom that will tell us about Jesus and his contemporaries and lead us into the third millennia AD with a certain knowledge of what truly happened at the beginning of the Christian age.

We found a Latin inscription carved onto the Rosslyn shrine and we thought it a very appropriate comment in a single motto. Humorous though it is, we can only assume that it came from the Nasorean scrolls:

*WINE IS STRONG, A KING IS STRONGER,
WOMEN ARE EVEN STRONGER*

[7] Tim Wallace-Murphy: *An Illustrated Guide to Rosslyn Chapel*

413

BUT TRUTH CONQUERS ALL

Beneath Solomon's Seal

One evening, over a week after our visit to Rosslyn, when we were discussing the great detail of symbolism that William St Clair had built into his Scroll Shrine to match the descriptions provided in the Royal Arch Degree we looked up the definition of the Triple Tau. We had been excited when we saw that the principal pillars in the east of the building formed a perfect Triple Tau because we knew that it was the badge of Royal Arch Freemasonry as well as being an ancient mark that predated Moses. We had not, however, thought about its precise definition as given in the original ritual of that degree.

Chris read the words aloud:

'The Triple Tau, signifying, among other occult things, *Templum Hierosolyma*, "the Temple of Jerusalem". It also means *Clavis ad Thesaurum* – "A key to a treasure" – and *Theca ubi res pretiosa deponitur* – "A place where a precious thing is concealed", or *Res ipsa pretiosa* – "The precious thing itself".'

It suddenly became crystal clear why William St Clair had to arrange the pillars in this way. The central arrangement of the shrine was a symbolic way of saying that the structure did represent the Temple at Jerusalem, and that it is the place where a precious treasure is concealed!

This was a wonderful find. On the same page of explanation Chris could not help but notice the meaning given for the Seal of Solomon (the Star of David) within the Royal Arch Degree. Once again he read aloud:

'The Companion's Jewel of the Royal Arch is a double triangle, sometimes called the Seal of Solomon, within a circle of gold; at the bottom is a scroll bearing the words, *Nil nisi clavis deest* – "Nothing is wanting but the

Key", and on the circle appears the legend, *Si tatlia jungere possis sit tibi scire posse* – "If thou canst comprehend these things, thou knowest enough".'

Robert let out a low whistle. These references sounded as though they had been created as clues for the individuals who would, one day, unlock the mystery of Rosslyn. The words were meaningless in any other context, yet now they carried a very precise import.

The one problem was that neither of us could recollect seeing a Seal of Solomon anywhere in Rosslyn and we set about studying our photographs, video and the ground plan to see if there was anything we had missed. There was.

Chris drew a line through the bottom pillars of the Triple Tau, and taking out a pair of compasses, set them to the width of the building on the plan and described an arc out from each wall. The two arcs intersected exactly between the most westerly pillars to form an equilateral triangle. He then drew another line across the width of the building between the second two pillars from the west entrance and described two further arcs in an easterly direction; they intersected right in the centre of the central pillar of the Triple Tau, forming a perfect Seal of Solomon. Even the two pillars inside the symbol were placed at the precise crossing point of the lines of the star.

At the very centre of this invisible Seal of Solomon, in the arched roof there is a large suspended boss in the form of a decorated arrowhead that points straight down to a keystone in the floor below. It is, we believe, this stone that must be raised to enter the reconstructed vaults of Herod's Temple and recover the Nasorean Scrolls.

The configuration of Rosslyn is no coincidence. Had any one of the aisles been a few inches wider or the pillars just slightly in a different position, none of this geometry would have worked. From that moment we knew with a complete certainty that these symbols had been the starting point of the whole design, to mark out the treasure held beneath in the great stone vaults. The explanation of the symbols was almost certainly added to the Royal Arch Degree, by William St Clair, after the design was complete, to provide the clue for some future generation to discover '*the key*'.

The words in the ritual say 'If thou canst comprehend these things, thou knowest enough'; we did now comprehend and we did indeed know enough to be certain that we had found the meaning of Freemasonry.

Excavating the Nasorean Scrolls

We cannot conceive of more powerful proof of our whole hypothesis than the discovery that Rosslyn is the Scroll Shrine. The question to be asked is: are the scrolls still there? The answer is almost certainly, yes they are. There is no evidence, historical or physical, of any tampering with the foundations of the building, despite the wars and battles that have raged on the turf around it.

Ultrasound groundscans have already established that there are cavities under the floor of Rosslyn and we intend to use our new evidence as powerfully as we can to gain the authority to excavate below the building and recover the scrolls, and then have scholars investigate the wisdom contained therein; wisdom so special that it has already changed the world whilst still buried!

As we thought about that downward-pointing arrow, we reflected on the words of the first Templars as given in the Royal Arch Degree:

'... we determined to examine it, for which purpose we removed two of the stones, when we discovered a vault of considerable magnitude, and immediately cast lots who should descend.

The lot fell on me; when, lest any noxious vapours or other causes should render my situation unsafe, my companions fastened this cord or life line round my

Plan of Rosslyn

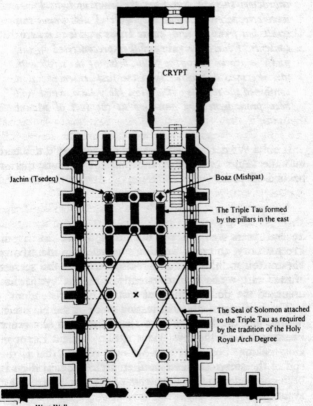

CRYPT

Jachin (Tsedeq)

Boaz (Mishpat)

The Triple Tau formed
by the pillars in the east

The Seal of Solomon attached
to the Triple Tau as required
by the tradition of the Holy
Royal Arch Degree

West Wall

body, and I was duly lowered into the vault. On arriving at the bottom, I gave a preconcerted signal, and my companions gave me more line, which enabled me to traverse the vault; I then discovered something in the form of a pedestal and felt certain marks or characters thereon, but from the want of light I was unable to ascertain what they were. I also found this scroll, but from the same cause I was unable to read its contents. I therefore gave another preconcerted signal, and was drawn out of the vault, bringing the scroll with me. We then discovered from the first sentence that it contained the records of the Most Holy Law, which had been promulgated by our God at the foot of Mount Sinai.'

If only! We determined that one day we would descend into the vaults of Rosslyn and find the treasure that is beyond all price.

* * *

Several years ago we set out to find the origins of Freemasonry, and now we have succeeded. In identifying Hiram Abif we have not only rediscovered the lost secrets of the Craft; we have, inadvertently, turned a key that has unlocked the door to the true history of Christendom.

The locating of the final resting place of the Nasorean Scrolls was the last link in a chain that connects every Freemason with the mysterious rites of ancient Egyptian king-making. For most non-Masonic readers that is the end of the story – at least until an archaeological dig has been completed and the contents of the scrolls are at last available to the world.

* * *

But for those with a special interest in how Freemasonry

developed and how it impacted upon the world in the sixteenth, seventeenth and eighteenth centuries we have continued our story in Appendix 1.

Postscript

Having started out on some entirely private research we had got into the habit of keeping everything close to our chests, sharing our discoveries only with one Masonic past master and one Church of England clergyman. They passed comment at various stages and managed to convince us that we were making a lot of sense. We found this immensely valuable, because we were too close to our subject to know whether or not we were conveying the excitement and import of the discoveries we were making at an ever-increasing rate.

Shortly before making the presentation to our publisher, Century, we decided that it was important to tell the people currently concerned with Rosslyn about the content of our book, so one sunny afternoon we met with the curator, Judy Fisken, and Bob Brydon, a Masonic and Templar historian connected with the Chapel who proved to be a mine of information. The discussion took five hours, but at the end they both felt that we had found something quite remarkable that would have major implications for the future of Rosslyn. Judy duly arranged to meet with Niven Sinclair, a London-based businessman, President of the Friends of Rosslyn. Two weeks later we met Niven for lunch and once again explained our findings. Over recent years Niven has devoted a large part of his time and substantial amounts of money to the upkeep and promotion of Rosslyn Chapel, and solving the mysteries of the building has become a driving passion for him. This fascinating and energetic Scot was just the man we needed on our side.

A further meeting was then arranged to present our discoveries to the group called 'the Friends of Rosslyn'. About thirty people arrived and once again we ran through our story, keeping to the essential parts that affected their building. The audience included historians, Scottish Grand Lodge members, two clergymen, the most senior Knights Templar in Scotland and Baron St Clair Bonde who is a direct descendant of William St Clair (and who has since proved to be a great ally). No one found any reason to challenge our view, and indeed several people came forward to tell us that they had important information that would support what we had just said.

However, the night before this presentation, we made one further significant discovery about the secrets concealed in Rosslyn. As Chris was preparing the overhead slides something rather interesting happened. We had previously decided that Rosslyn was a spiritual interpretation of Herod's Temple and to see if there was any significant similarity between the two Chris overlaid the acetate drawing of the foundations of the ruined Herodian Temple on top of the plan of the chapel.

They were not similar. They were the same!

Rosslyn is not a free interpretation of the ruins in Jerusalem; as far as the foundation plan is concerned, it is a very carefully executed copy. The unfinished sections of the great western wall are there, the main walls and the pillar arrangements fit like a glove and the pillars of Boaz and Jachin stand precisely at the eastern end of what would be the inner Temple. The spot that we identified as being at the centre of the Seal of Solomon turned out to correspond exactly with the centre point of the medieval world: the middle of the Holy of Holies; the spot where the Ark of the Covenant was placed in the Temple at Jerusalem.

The parallels continued outside the building. The land

at the eastern end of Rosslyn falls away just feet in front of the twin pillars, in an identical manner to the site of the original Temple. This discovery prompted us to look more closely at the landscape surrounding Rosslyn and we found that the area appeared to have been selected because it reflected the topology of Jerusalem. To the east lies Scotland's own Kidron Valley and in the south runs the Valley of Hinnon.

William St Clair was indeed a genius.

From this new understanding of the surrounding landscape and from further clues found in the building of Rosslyn, we believe that we have finally cracked the encoded message left by the Earl half carved into stone and half interlaced into Masonic ritual. We now know exactly where the copper scroll, the treasure map of the Essenes and the Templars, is hidden.

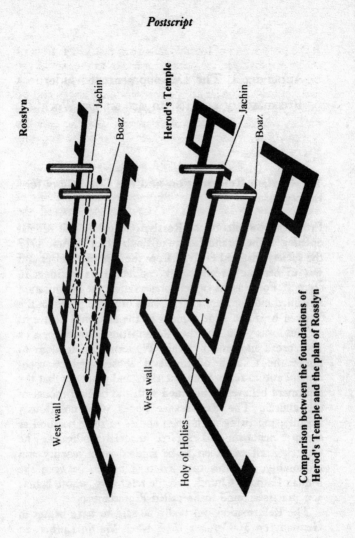

Comparison between the foundations of Herod's Temple and the plan of Rosslyn

Rosslyn

Jachin

Boaz.

West wall

Herod's Temple

Jachin

Boaz.

West wall

Holy of Holies

Appendix 1: The Development of Modern Freemasonry and its Impact on the World

The English Reformation and the Conditions for Emergence

From the completion of Rosslyn Chapel to the official opening of the Grand Lodge of England on 24 June 1717 the society that had evolved from the Templar Order and was to become Freemasonry conducted its business in secrecy. For reasons of self preservation the organisation remained hidden from general view until the power of the Vatican began to slide rapidly in the sixteenth century.

This was due to the Reformation, which was a widespread movement within Western Christendom to purge the Church of medieval abuses, reduce papal control and to restore the doctrines and practices that the reformers believed conformed with the biblical model of the church. The Renaissance popes were notoriously worldly, practising such open abuses of their position as simony, nepotism and carefree financial profligacy. The Church itself was seen to be riddled with venality and immorality, and this that led to a breach between the Roman Catholic Church and the reformers, whose beliefs and practices came to be called Protestantism.

The Reformation can really be said to have begun in Germany on 31 October 1517, when Martin Luther, an Augustinian university professor at Wittenberg, issued ninety-five theses, inviting debate over the legitimacy of the sale of indulgences. The papacy immediately saw this as a political threat to a profitable international dictator-ship and proceeded to label the free-thinker as a heretic. Luther's three famous treatises of 1520, *An Open Letter to the Christian Nobility of the German Nation Concerning the Reform of the Christian Estate*; *The Babylonian Captivity of the Church*, and *On the Freedom of a Christian*, won him widespread popular support. Luther believed that salva-tion was a free gift to all people through the forgiveness of sins by God's grace alone and that it was not therefore necessary to have a pope at all. Not surprisingly, such Jesus-like thinking was not welcomed by the papacy and he was excommunicated in 1521. But Luther was a very clever man and in April of that year he stood before Holy Roman Emperor Charles V and the German princes at the Diet at Worms and refused to recant unless proven wrong by the Bible or by clear reason.

Although England had its own religious reform move-ment based on the ideas of Martin Luther, the English Reformation occurred, not to stem papal excesses, but apparently as a direct result of King Henry VIII's personal trouble with his marriage to his first wife, Catherine of Aragon. The breakaway from papal power was masterminded by Thomas Cromwell, chief minister to the King, who passed the Act in Restraint of Appeals through Parliament in 1533, followed the next year by the Act of Supremacy which fully defined the royal control of the Church. Thomas Cranmer, the Archbishop of Canter-bury, authorised the translation of the Bible into English, and was largely responsible for the Book of Common Prayer.

The Roman Catholic Church was replaced by the Church of England, though there was a brief reversal during the reign of the daughter of Henry VIII by Catherine of Aragon: Queen Mary I ruled from 1553 to 1558, who had been ditched by Henry because she had not borne him a male heir. Once in power Mary proceeded to restore Catholicism, re-establishing the traditional services and the authority of the Pope, and earning the epithet Bloody Mary for the executions of Protestants. In 1554 she married King Philip II of Spain, son of Holy Roman Emperor Charles V; the event sparked several rebellions, which were harshly put down, and afterwards 300 Protestants were burned at the stake for their beliefs. Under her successor, Queen Elizabeth I, England grew into a strong and Protestant nation.

The King Who Built the Lodge System

Freemasonry today consists of almost a hundred thousand individual cells called Lodges, each of which has a Worshipful Master and a full set of officers who are allowed to conduct ceremonies of initiation and advancement. It is possible to trace the development that led to this from the St Clair family's building of Rosslyn Chapel through to the modern day.

It appears that after the building of Rosslyn the concept of 'operative' Lodges (those made up of skilled stonemasons) continued to flourish in close association with the more senior 'speculative' Lodges (made up of aristocrats who had been admitted through living resurrection). As we saw, once the building of the Rosslyn shrine was complete, it was not possible simply to dissolve the secret organisations with which these proud stonemasons had been provided. They had their own rites and a part in an Order that linked them with their Lords and the mysterious ancient past of King Solomon and beyond.

For the next hundred years these operative masons grew in Scotland as a remote extension of the speculative masons, but eventually the St Clairs dropped into apparent obscurity and the origin of the system was lost to living memory. Slowly but surely circumstances arose wherein the ceremonies were repeated with pride, but no understanding of their origins.

King James VI of Scotland (also later James I of England) was the only child of Mary Queen of Scots and the first king to rule both England and Scotland. He was also the first king known to be a Freemason, being initiated into the Lodge of Scoon and Perth in 1601 at the age of thirty-five.[1] Born on 19 June 1566, James was only fifteen months old when he succeeded his Catholic mother to the Scottish throne, but did not begin his personal rule of Scotland until 1583. He received an excellent education from his principal tutor, George Buchanan who undoubtedly had a strong influence on the young king. Buchanan himself had been educated at the universities of Saint Andrews in Scotland and in Paris and was a man of great intellect. He had lived in Europe for thirty years where he developed a reputation for being one of the leading humanists of the age and has since been considered to be one of the greatest Latin scholars and poets of the late Renaissance.

The young king had a good brain and under the intellectual guidance of Buchanan, James successfully asserted his position as head of Church and State in Scotland, outwitting the nobles who conspired against him. Being eager to succeed the childless Elizabeth I to the English throne, he merely made a mild protest when his mother was executed for treason against Elizabeth in 1587.

At the age of thirty-seven, two years after becoming a Freemason, James became the first Stuart king of England, and he devoted himself largely to English affairs thereafter. Although raised as a Presbyterian, he immediately antagonised the rising Puritan movement by rejecting a petition for reform of the Church of England at the Hampton Court Conference in 1604. Roman Catholic hostility to a Protestant monarch was widespread and in

[1] *Year Book of the Grand Lodge of Antient Free and Accepted Masons of Scotland,* 1995

1605 a Catholic plot led by Guy Fawkes failed in an attempt to blow up both king and Parliament. Despite this assassination plot, there was suspicion in England that James was secretly rather pro-Catholic because he had concluded peace with Spain in 1604. James was a speculative mason and also wrote books about kingship, theology, witchcraft, and even tobacco; significantly he also commissioned a new 'Authorised' version of the Bible which is called after him – the King James Bible (it is the version that omits the two anti-Nasorean Books of Maccabees). The introduction that still appears in the front of this Protestant Bible reveals no Catholic sympathies; one section reads:

> '... *So that if, on the one side, we shall be traduced by Popish Persons at home or abroad, who therefore will malign us because we are poor instruments to make God's holy Truth to be yet more and more known unto the people, whom they desire still to keep in ignorance and darkness ...* [2]

This passage betrays a new kind of outlook where 'knowledge' and 'the people' are seen as things that should be allowed to come together, in contrast to the secretive and political selfishness of the Catholic Church at that time.

Modern Freemasonry is non-sectarian and it boasts that it always has been so; but we think there was a period of anti-Catholicism that shows itself in this introduction to the King James Bible. The circumstances of the early seventeenth century provided the perfect conditions for the secret society of masons to emerge into the public arena. With the king a speculative mason himself and the power of the Pope blocked for all time in Scotland, the

[2] Introduction to the *King James Bible*

need for utter secrecy was suddenly gone. King James was a thinker and a reformer and he must have felt that the structure of the growing Masonic movement needed to be more formalised, so fifteen years after he had taken active control of his Scottish kingdom, two years before being accepted as a Freemason and five years before becoming the English monarch, he ordered that the existing Masonic structure be given leadership and organisation. He made a leading Mason by the name of William Schaw his General Warden of the Craft and instructed him to improve the entire structure of Masonry. Schaw started this major project on 28 December 1598 when he issued *'The statutes and ordinances to be observed by all the master maissouns within this realme,'* signing himself as *'the General Warden of the said craft'*.

Schaw did not give much thought to the fact these gatherings had originally been introduced by the St Clair family, who had held what was known as a Court of Crafts nearly two hundred years earlier under the reign of Robert the Bruce. By Schaw's time it appears that the St Clairs had lost much of their influence, because they had sought to gain financially through their control of operative stonemasonry. Towards the end of the year 1600 a new document was drawn up by the masters, deacons and freemen of the masons of Scotland and issued with the consent of William Schaw, who is described in the document as the King's Master of Works. This became known as the First St Clair Charter. It states:

'From age to age it has been observed amongst us, it is stated that the lairds of Rosslyn have ever been the patrons and protectors of us and our privileges, but within the past few years by negligence and slothfulness the office had passed out of use. This had deprived the lairds of their just rights, and the craft of their patrons, protectors, and overseers, leading to many corruptions,

in the craft and to potential employers abandoning many great enterprises.'[3]

This was signed by Officers of the Lodges of Dunfermline, St Andrews, Edinburgh, Haddington and Aitchisons's Haven. Despite this dip in the fortunes of the St Clair family, the Scottish masons stood by tradition and turned down Schaw's offer of a Royal Warrant for the Order if King James was accepted as Grand Master. Although the St Clairs had no veto over James appointing himself Grand Master, they had the support of the Lodges against him.

The ritual of the Schaw Lodges was regularised, but it was still fully based on the 'Old Constitutions' and the Mason words and means of recognition were still those of an older verbal tradition, which Schaw indeed refers to on many occasions. He called the gatherings of speculative masons 'Lodges' and two years after his work had begun, the previously secret Lodges of Scotland starting listing the names of their members and keeping minutes of their meetings. They still did not broadcast their existence but we can easily identify them today. The geographical location of the first registered Lodges show how the rituals cemented at Rosslyn by William St Clair became a major movement during the reign of James VI.

It was the regulation of both operative and speculative masonry by William Schaw (James VI's General Warden of the Craft), that formalised the ritual into what we now know as the three degrees of Craft Freemasonry. He did this by re-establishing the separate operative masons as junior subsidiaries of the speculative masons, thereby creating 'incorporations' for the stonemasons, each of which would be attached to a 'Lodge' of speculative masons. An absolute requirement of membership of a speculative Lodge was that a candidate had to be a

---

[3] *The First Schaw Statute, Library of Grand Lodge of Scotland*

Freeman of the borough in which the Lodge was situated, and soon a speculative mason was distinguished from an operative mason by the title 'Freemason'. Every incorporation was required to be attached to a Lodge, but every Lodge of speculative masons did not have to have an incorporation.

From this point onwards, Freemasonry had a Lodge structure which would soon spread to England, and eventually the entire Western world.

The Architects of the Second Degree

We believe that the current content of the three degrees of Craft Freemasonry was largely present in just two degrees prior to Schaw's reorganisation that inserted an extra level of speculative masonry, in between Entered Apprentice and Master Mason (which was originally known as the Master's Part). This new degree was introduced and designated the Fellow Craft, derived we think from the fact that these masons were not workers in stone but workers in the 'fellow craft' of speculative masonry. We are now sure that this degree was a development of the Mark Mason degree (and not the other way around, as most Masons believe).

When James VI of Scotland became James I of England in 1603, one of his first acts was to confer a knighthood on Francis Bacon, who was one of his favourite thinkers as well as a fellow Freemason. Six years later Bacon was appointed the king's Solicitor-General. The elevations continued as James went on to give Bacon the position of Attorney-General, Lord Keeper of the Great Seal, and eventually Lord Chancellor in 1618, at which point he took the title Baron Verulam.

Brother Bacon was one of history's finest philosophers, and he sought to purge the human mind of what he called 'idols' or 'tendencies to error'. He planned a large work, the *Instauratio Magna* ('Great Restoration') laying out his ideas for the restoration of humankind's mastery over nature, which was to contain six parts:

1. a classification of sciences.

2. a new inductive logic.

3. a gathering of empirical and experimental facts.

4. examples to show the efficacy of his new approach.

5. generalisations derivable from natural history.

6. a new philosophy that would be a complete science of nature.

In the end he only managed to complete two parts: *The Advancement of Learning* in 1605 (later expanded as *On the Dignity and Growth of Sciences* in 1623) and *The New Organon* in 1620, which was an attack on Aristotle's *Organon*. This last work he personally presented to his patron, James VI. The culmination of Bacon's work was an inductive philosophy of nature, which proposed to find the 'forms' or natural laws of bodily action, and he devised so-called tables of induction (of presence, absence and degrees) designed to discover such forms with the goal of mastery over nature.

Although Bacon could never be called a great scientist, he is highly regarded as a man that gave an impetus to the development of modern inductive science. His works were held in high esteem by diverse seventeenth-century thinkers and scientists including Robert Boyle, Robert Hooke, Sir Isaac Newton and Thomas Hobbes. A century later the great French philosophers Voltaire and Diderot described this English thinker as nothing less than, 'the father of modern science'.

It is highly likely that Brother Bacon was the driving

force behind the styling of the new second degree introduced by his close colleague William Schaw. No one in the king's group of Freemasons had more passion for the advancement of science and the opening up of thinking about nature. Bacon, however, let his Masonic knowledge mingle with his public aspirations when he published his book *The New Atlantis* which openly spoke of his plan for a rebuilding of King Solomon's Temple in spiritual terms. This pure Ezekiel-esque vision, he said, was to be 'a palace of invention' and 'a great temple of science'; it was visualised less as a building than as a new state where the pursuit of knowledge in all its branches was to be organised on principles of the highest efficiency.

In this work the intellectual seed germ of the constitution of the United States of America was firmly planted.

The New Heresy

The Second or 'Fellowcraft' Degree of Freemasonry gives very little extra knowledge to the candidate but it does introduce the idea of 'hidden mysteries of nature and science' and makes a clear reference to what is called the 'Galilean Heresy'. Whilst we are certain that the central subject of this degree is as ancient as any in Freemasonry, it nonetheless is evidently of much more recent construction, due largely to Francis Bacon. The parts that were taken for this new ceremony were concerned with nature and man's right to investigate and understand it.

The whole idea of understanding the mysteries of nature seemed to us to recall the botanical encyclopedia encapsulated in the decoration of the Rosslyn shrine. As we showed earlier, its finely worked carvings record details of hundreds of plants, including the 'impossible' American varieties.

Liberal thinking elsewhere had already led to the invention of a new form of heresy by the Vatican who, quite rightly, saw great danger in this idea of 'uncontrolled thought'. The Roman Catholic Church was persecuting those who investigated science and came up with conclusions which conflicted with the Cardinals' dogmatic view of their scriptures. Most significant of these 'wicked' people was Galileo, who used new techniques to confirm the view that the sun and not the Earth was at the centre of the universe. Although this concept had been first described by the Egyptian Eratosthenes in the third century BC, it was known as Copernicanism after the more recent proponent of the idea (Nicholaus Copernicus 1473–1543) and despite all protests the Holy Office at Rome issued an edict against Copernicanism early in 1616. The heresy referred to by Galileo and outlawed by papal bull, is quoted in the answer to a paradoxical question that forms part of the ritual of passing from the First to the Second Degree of Freemasonry. The questions and answers go as follows:

> *Q. Where were you made a Mason?*
> *A. In the body of a Lodge, just, perfect and regular.*
> *Q. And when?*
> *A. When the sun was at its meridian.*
> *Q. As in this country Freemasons' Lodges are usually held and candidates initiated at night, how do you reconcile that which at first sight appears a paradox?*
> *A. The sun being a fixed body and the earth continually revolving about the same on its own axis, and Freemasonry being a universal science, diffused throughout the whole of the inhabited globe, it necessarily follows that the sun must always be at its meridian with respect to Freemasonry.*

This reference is unlikely to have been inserted before 1610, the date when Galileo publicly announced his conviction that Copernicus was indeed correct in thinking that the earth revolved around the sun. Francis Bacon, we believe, immediately set about incorporating this new truth of nature into his recently created Second Degree.

It is important to remember that the Fellow Craft Degree was not an invention; it was made from sections taken from Mark Masonry and possibly the original two degrees (the Entrant's Degree and the Master's rank), with some new elements added where they seemed to fit. This has given rise to a major contradiction within this ritual: the candidate is told that a secret sign is made by holding the hands in a certain way above the head, as used by Joshua:

'When Joshua fought the battles of the Lord in the Valley of Joshoshaphat it is in this posture that he stood and fervently prayed the Lord to stay the Sun in its course and extend the light of day until he had completed the overthrow of His enemies'.

There is an obvious contradiction in being told first that the Earth goes around the Sun, then that God stopped the sun going around the Earth to help Joshua. We believe that story was left in because it was too old and too important to remove or change, despite the contradiction with newer material.

This explanation of the Fellow Craft sign apparently applies to Joshua 10:12, but this verse actually refers to the valley of Ajalon, not Joshoshaphat. Joshua, you will recall, was the leader of the Israelites after Moses but it was not until the time of David that the valley of Joshoshaphat became Israelite territory (as we have already mentioned, Joshoshaphat is another name for the Kidron Valley which runs to the south and east of Jerusalem). We discussed earlier how the Old Testament legend of Joshua depicts him as a marauding, murderous Habiru with no obvious relevance to the tenets of Freemasonry. The passage in the Old Testament to which the quotation is attributed is one of the many appalling catalogues of the mass slaughter of innocent men, women and children for no reason other than the rapacity of such marauders as Joshua, and the apparent insanity of Yahweh. The passage boasts how, on God's orders, five kings and all of their subjects and animals were slaughtered by the advancing Habiru and how, from one end of the land to the other:

> 'he left none remaining but utterly destroyed all that breathed, as the Lord God of Israel commanded.'

Since this Joshua was about as un-Masonic as a person can get and predates King Solomon's Temple, we cannot imagine why anyone would assume that this piece of Masonic ritual should refer to him, unless they were ignorant of any other explanation.

There was, however, another far more special biblical figure known by the name of Joshua, or Yahoshua, who is vitally important to Freemasonry and who did fight the greatest 'battle of the Lord' in the valley of Joshoshaphat. That man of course, was Jesus, who stood with his supporters in the Garden of Gethsemane (which is in the valley of Joshoshaphat) where he finally confronted and sought the overthrow of his enemies. Because he was aware of the ancient story of Seqenenre Tao/Hiram Abif he is likely to have called upon God to metaphorically stay the sun at its meridian, which was a way of asking that the forces of darkness be held at their weakest and the forces of goodness be at their height for the duration of the coming conflict. Unfortunately he lost that battle, but thanks to the Templars, he eventually won the war.

This knowledge makes perfect sense out of an otherwise peculiar explanation of the Fellow Craft, or Second Degree sign. In Chapter Twelve we showed how James's speech at the crucifixion and his subsequent leadership of the Church meant that he was deeply impressed by his brother's actions and it is unreasonable to think that an episode as important as the prayers in the Garden of Gethsemane would not have been written down in the scrolls that the Templars discovered. James and the other Qumranians would have viewed what Jesus had done in the Valley of Joshoshaphat as a pesher of Joshua 10:12, and this interpretation of the Second Degree sign makes sense of a ritual that was previously unfathomable.

The Old Charges

It is clear that changes to the content of the old ritual were kept to a minimum and that the 'Old Charges' from the verbal tradition were first written down to ensure that deviation would not occur. William Schaw is known to have sought to protect the 'ancient landmarks of the Order' and the written evidence is available today to tell us what Masonry was about prior to the improvements ordered by James VI and carried out by Schaw, Bacon and others. There are a number of these documents in existence; one such is the 'Inigo Jones Manuscript' of 1607, but there is some doubt about its authorship; it has been attributed to the famous architect and Freemason. However, it is suggested by some experts that it could have been written as much as fifty years later, possibly by a member of the Inigo Jones Lodge.

A more reliable document is the 'Wood Manuscript', written in 1610 (the same year as Galileo first declared his views on the structure of the solar system) on vellum in the form of eight strips folded to give sixteen leaves with thirty-two pages. It starts by identifying the sciences with which masonry has always been associated, which are given as: *Grammar, Rethorick, Logicke, Arithmetick, Geometrye, Musick and Astronomie*. These are ancient classical subjects lost in the Christian world during the Dark Ages. They had been recognised again from the tenth century onward, through contact with Arab scholars in Spain,

Sicily, and North Africa, and Greek thinkers in Constantinople. Amongst other things, the lost works of Aristotle had been rediscovered; in addition, Arabic scientific and mathematical works were translated for Western use. By the beginning of the seventeenth century they were again the natural subjects of all educated people, and were in no way peculiar to Freemasonry.

The Wood manuscript goes on to say that geometry is the greatest of the sciences and has been since the beginning of time. It traces the history of the Order from two pillars that were found after Noah's Flood, one made of a marble that would not burn with fire, the other made of a substance known in Masonic legend as Laterus, which would not dissolve, sink or drown in any water. One of these pillars was found and upon it were inscribed the secrets of the sciences from which the Sumerians developed a moral code that passed to the Egyptians through the Sumerian Abraham and his wife Sarah. The script goes on to describe Euclid teaching geometry to the Egyptians, from whom the Israelites took it to Jerusalem, which resulted in the building of King Solomon's Temple.

Some of these seventeenth-century manuscripts do not refer to Hiram Abif, which has led some to believe that the character was an invention of this relatively recent period. However, the name Hiram Abif was only one designation for this central figure; he is also referred to as Aymon, Aymen, Amnon, A Man or Amen and sometimes Bennaim. It is said that Amen is said to be the Hebrew word for 'the trusted one' or 'the faithful one', which fits the role of Hiram Abif perfectly. But we also know that Amon or Amen is the name of the ancient creator god of Thebes, the city of Seqenenre Tao. Could there be an ancient linkage here? We think so.

The name 'A Man' particularly interested us because it brought to mind the description of the writers of the Book of Genesis in 49:6 which we referred to in Chapter Eight;

that, you will recall, we thought could be a description of the killing of Seqenenre:

> 'O my soul, come not thou into their secret; unto their assembly, mine honour, be not thou united: for in their anger they slew a man, and in their self will they digged down a wall.'

Could it be that the apparently unnamed victim was actually named because they were referring to 'A Man' – the early Masonic name for Hiram Abif and the name of the creator god of Thebes? And is it coincidence that Christians call on 'Amen' at the end of their prayers in an appeal for their wishes to be made true?

The other name, Bennaim, has caused Masonic researchers some difficulty. It has been noted that the ending 'im' in Hebrew creates a plural (as in pesherim), whilst the first part is said to mean 'builder'. We would go further and suggest that it is based on the ancient Egyptian term for a sacred pillar, which was topped by a small pyramid called a 'benben' stone. This word could therefore be said to be a very ancient description, meaning 'builder of the sacred pillars'. That would indeed make a whole lot of sense as a literal description of Hiram Abif, and a metaphoric one of Jesus.

It seems to us that by the time Freemasonry was being formalised by King James's team from the speculative/operative marriage of the Rosslyn Templars, its origins had become confused and in parts lost. These seventeenth-century Freemasons had a direct line back to almost the beginnings of human history, but all the stages through which the motifs had now passed were obscuring much of the story. However, whilst they were unclear about where their Order had come from, they did understand the import of the wisdom that it contained and were invigorated by the ground-swell of learning that arose in the seventeenth century. Freemasons were ready to take advantage.

In the Second Degree ceremony the candidate is asked, '*What are the peculiar objects of research in this degree?*' The answer he is required to give is: '*The hidden mysteries of nature and science.*' On completion of the making of the new Fellow Craft he is told: '*You are now expected to make the liberal arts and sciences your future study.*' This was an invitation that the great Freemasons of the mid-seventeenth century could not refuse. Having analysed the seventeenth-century developments in Freemasonry, our final task was to understand how Freemasonry went on to make its mark on the modern world.

In 1625 the Freemason King James VI died and his second son Charles succeeded to the throne (James's elder son, Prince Henry, had died in 1612). We felt sure that the new king would have followed in the footsteps of his father by becoming a Freemason. It is significant that a number of graves, rich in Freemasonic symbolism, are built into the north wall of Holyrood Abbey in Edinburgh which he refurbished for his own Scottish coronation in 1633. However, Charles made an inauspicious start in the eyes of the Protestant majority of his people when he married Henrietta Maria the Catholic princess daughter of King Henry IV of France. Like James, Charles was a firm believer in the divine right of kings, which he displayed with arrogance, causing conflict with Parliament and leading ultimately to civil war. The young king was strongly influenced by his close friend George Villiers, the 1st Duke of Buckingham, whom he appointed to be his chief minister despite widespread disapproval.

Charles remained at permanent loggerheads with his Parliaments, dissolving three of them in just four years because of their refusal to comply with his arbitrary demands. When the third of these Parliaments met in 1628, it presented the 'Petition of Right', a statement demanding that the king make certain reforms in exchange for funds. Charles was forced to accept the petition, but after making this concession, he responded by dismissing Parliament once again and had several Parliamentary leaders imprisoned. Charles lacked his father's flair for political management and his ongoing confrontation with Parliament led to a period where he reigned for eleven years without any Parliament at all. During this time he introduced extraordinary financial measures to meet governmental expenses which compounded his deep unpopularity. The whole kingdom started to become unstable under Charles's autocratic rule and, whilst at any other time such social upheaval could only be a bad thing, the peculiar circumstances of the time paradoxically made it a period of opportunity. New kinds of thinking abounded and the break-down of the continuity of the old, established order of things put all possibilities into the melting pot.

It may sound odd at first hearing, but we increasingly started to feel that there are pertinent parallels between this period in seventeenth-century England and the circumstances found in Israel at the time of Jesus and the Nasorean movement. These similarities were to make the teachings found in Freemasonry particularly relevant to all of the main groups concerned in the English Civil War. The first of these parallels concerns a conflict in the process of connecting with God. As with the Jews sixteen hundred years earlier, virtually everyone in the country thought that God was at the centre of all matters, but there was a growing diversity of opinion on the best way to relate to him. In Jesus's time there were the Sanhedrin, who constituted the appointed authority of the Temple which was the only official route to Yahweh, and there were the Sadducees, who recognised the rule of the Roman Emperor. Even the supposedly righteous Pharisees were accused by Jesus of losing sight of the very basis of their faith and Jesus openly opposed their power. In our view, Jesus was nothing less than a republican himself; attempting to establish the rule of the 'righteous' people, with himself as legislative leader upholding the laws of God. He was an anti-bureaucrat who wanted to remove the self-important self-seekers who claimed control of the route to God. He was undoubtedly anti-establishment, and we think it is not unreasonable to describe him as a Puritan of his time: a man who strove for simplicity, religious rigour and freedom – and was not afraid to fight for it. In the sixteenth and seventeenth centuries the Catholic Church was run by comfortable conservatives that had lost sight of Godliness beneath their own inflated egos, and their insistence that only the Pope had the right to interface with God had worn very thin with those that had the wit and the opportunity to think for themselves.

Some of the criticisms of the Pharisees found in the reconstructed original gospel known as 'Q' sound very much like the kind of accusations that the seventeenth-century Puritans were levelling at the Roman Catholic Church. Some of the words attributed to Jesus in QS 34 (of the reconstructed gospel 'Q') struck us as being very pertinent to these later times:

> *'Shame on you Pharisees! for you clean the outside of the cup and the dish, but inside you are full of greed and incontinence. Foolish Pharisees! Clean the inside and the outside will also be clean.*
>
> *Shame on you Pharisees! for you love the front seats in the assemblies and greetings in the market place. Shame on you! for you are like graves, outwardly beautiful, but full of pollution inside ...*
>
> *Shame on you lawyers! for you have taken the key of knowledge away from the people. You yourselves do not enter the kingdom of God, and you prevent those who would enter from going in.'*

How easy it would be to transpose the words 'Phari-sees' or 'lawyers' for the word 'Cardinals' to create a passage that would sound remarkably Puritan!

Our second connection between the two periods con-cerns the ending of papal power in England and the combining of sacerdotal and secular authority in the single figure of the king. For the first time since the establish-ment of the Church, the ambition of Jesus to unite both priestly and kingly pillars in one was achieved. Whilst working on this appendix we decided to look through material we had collected about the English Civil War. We came across a seventeenth-century illustration that confirmed everything we had detected about a link with the Jerusalem Church. Earlier on in our research we had had frequent celebrations as we came across some artefact or gem of information that locked in another section of the growing picture. By this stage, however, we were starting to accept that remarkable pieces of evidence would keep cropping up because our core thesis was correct and we were mining a continuous and endless vein of historical truth. What we found at this point was a seventeenth-century engraving that showed in graphic detail the kingly and priestly pillars of 'mishpat' and 'tsedeq' – exactly as we had perceived them from reading ancient Jewish texts. It was not just similar to the way we had come to envisage this core imagery; it was identical, or almost identical.

The single real difference was the figure that was the keystone: in this version, King Charles I had assumed the role of both pillars by identifying himself as the keystone that locked them together. Here the left-hand pillar is 'tsedeq' in the form of 'THE CHURCH', surmounted by the figure of 'truth'; the right-hand pillar is 'mishpat' in the form of 'THE STATE', surmounted by 'justice'. Interestingly enough, Charles's son King Charles II was to build this design into the entrance to Holyrood House when he rebuilt it after the Civil War in 1677.

In using this symbolism, King Charles I was following
fully in the footsteps of Jesus, but the king lacked both the
Jewish leader's utter brilliance and his republican clarity.
Jesus had believed that when social order was run in tune
with the laws given by Yahweh, there would be no need
for an active high-priestly role because God would act
directly through his earthly king to maintain a state of
'shalom'; in contrast, the English king simply saw a joint
role for himself, with God only a distant figure. Freemasonry was passing on an ancient message that had already
lost some of its original and all-important meaning!

In England, those who sought new social order would
do battle before they found a unique solution to their
differences – a solution that came from the Craft and one
that would ensure the continuity of the monarchy in the

United Kingdom when nations around them would put their rulers to the sword.

The Rise of the Republicans

Three years after Charles I came to the throne, a young commoner with republican ideas entered Parliament as member for Huntingdon. His name was Oliver Cromwell and his family was originally from Wales with the name Williams. They had risen from obscurity through the favour of Henry VIII's minister, Thomas Cromwell, who was the uncle of Oliver's great-great-grandfather, and they adopted the name of their patron in recognition of his help. The newly named Cromwell family soon became prominent in the Cambridgeshire town of Huntingdon, where Oliver was born on 25 April 1599. The now well-to-do Cromwells had their son educated in the town by a leading Puritan called Thomas Beard; a man who was outspoken concerning his wish to 'purify' the Church of England of its remaining Roman Catholic elements. Cromwell later attended the predominantly Puritan Sidney Sussex College and Cambridge University as well as studying law in London. In August 1620 he married Elizabeth Bourchier and returned to Huntingdon to manage his father's estate and became member of Parliament for Huntingdon some eight years later.

Over the following decade Cromwell developed a full-blown Puritan outlook and his personal fortunes dipped before rising again when he inherited some property in Ely from his wife's uncle. In 1640 Cromwell returned to Parliament just as the relationship between King Charles I and the Puritans reached crisis stage and conflict became inevitable. Two years later, on 22 August 1642, civil war broke out between the Puritan-dominated Parliament and the supporters of the king. Cromwell's astute military mind was quick to understand that religious passion could produce the fighting spirit which won battles and he rapidly raised a regiment of headstrong cavalrymen to fight on the Parliamentarian side. In the first two years of war, after both sides had raised armies, the Royalists (or Cavaliers as they were known) became increasing successful. After a bloody but indecisive battle at Edgehill in Warwickshire in October 1642, the Royalists looked as though they would advance on London, but were successfully driven back. At the end of the first year of war the Royalists held most parts of England except London and the eastern side of the country. Cromwell's ability as a fine commander was recognised and by 1644 the single-minded soldier was a lieutenant general under Edward Montagu, Earl of Manchester. His promotion was well deserved; he led the Parliamentary forces, known as Roundheads, to victory in the crucial Battle of Marston Moor, earning for himself and his regiment the name 'Ironsides'.

This victory proved to be something of a turning point for the Parliamentarians, and the Royalists were again defeated by Sir Thomas Fairfax's New Model Army at Naseby in Leicestershire. Battle after battle went the way of the Roundheads until the Royalist capital, Oxford, fell on 24 June 1646, and Charles, who had surrendered himself to the Scots, was turned over to Parliament and became a prisoner. The Staffordshire town of Lichfield held out for a few weeks, but the first and most important part of the civil war was over.

Many observers believe that Oliver Cromwell was a Freemason himself, and whilst no definitive record still exists to prove this contention, it does seem extremely likely. Certainly his superior and close friend Sir Thomas Fairfax was a member of the Craft and the Fairfaxs' family seat in Ilkley, Yorkshire still has a Masonic temple off the library which is entered down a spiral stairway leading onto a black and white paved room with two free-standing pillars. The building today is a corporate headquarters for a large firm of electrical contractors, but a few miles away in the village of Guisley there is still a Lodge named 'Fairfax'.

One of the best sources of information about Freemasonry during this period was the diary of Elias Ashmole, a formidable tome running to six volumes of diary and a further volume of index. The librarian at Robert's University Library was surprised when he took out all seven volumes over one summer with a view to reading the whole diary! We had discussed how to find out about the period and had come to the view that as it was the period of the great diarists, reading them would be a way to find out about the times. We did not know what we were looking for, so it was necessary to read everything to see what was there. This was not a wasted exercise because we found references to some very odd meetings which helped throw light onto the events which led to the formation of the Royal Society and the Restoration.

Elias Ashmole was the King's Controller of Ordnance at Oxford at the time of the surrender and he is also one of the most important figures in the official history of Freemasonry. Four months after he saw his side lose the war, Ashmole travelled to Warrington to be initiated into the Craft. His diary entry for 16 October 1646 reads:

> '*4H.30' P.M. I was made a free Mason at Warrington in Lancashire, with Coll: Henry Mainwaring of Karincham in Cheshire.*
>
> *The names of those that were then of the Lodge, Mr: Rich Penket Warden, Mr: James Collier, Mr: Rich: Sankey, Henry Littler, John Ellam, Rich: Ellam & Hugh Brewer.*'

Travelling from Oxford to Warrington in those days must have been a long and arduous journey, yet the very next day after his initiation Ashmole set out again, this time to the Parliamentary stronghold of London.

This was a strange thing to do because tension was still

high and all ex-Royalist officers were banned from coming within twenty miles of the City of London. As he had so recently served as the king's Controller of Ordnance, Ashmole could not hope to go unrecognised, so he must have had good reason to go there and must also have had some guarantee of protection. A note dated 14 May 1650 in the papers of the Public Record Office, State Papers Domestic, Interregnum A. confirms the unusual nature of the visit and that it was not a temporary arrangement:

> *'He (Ashmole) doth make his abode in London notwithstanding the Act of Parliament to the Contrary.'*

There is good reason to suppose that this Royalist Freemason was able to live openly in London for many years and that he consorted with high-ranking Parliamentarians. There can be little doubt that this was due to the fact that he was a Freemason, and therefore a member of the only non-religious, non-political organisation that provided a fraternal structure in which Cavalier could meet Roundhead and Catholic could meet Puritan without fear and without malice. Once again Ashmole's diary provided us with valuable information. The entry for 17 June 1652 reads:

> *'IIH.A.M: Doctor Wilkins & Mr: Wren came to visit me at Blackfriers. this was the first tyme I saw the Doctor.'*

The Mr Wren referred to is the great architect Sir Christopher Wren, who built many fine churches including St Paul's Cathedral after the City of London was largely destroyed in the Great Fire of 1666. Wren may have been a Freemason but there is no evidence to support the idea and some that suggests that he was not. Doctor Wilkins, on the other hand, was most definitely a member of the Craft. At the time of this meeting John Wilkins was Warden of Wadham College Oxford (Wren was a fellow of the same college at that time) but he later became Bishop of Chester and a founder member of the Royal Society. Wilkins was a Parliamentarian supporter and a Puritan of considerable seniority, being the husband of Oliver Cromwell's sister Robina and a past chaplain to Cromwell himself.

By the time that Ashmole met Wilkins he had been in London for six years and much had happened. The king had renewed the war with the help of the Scots but had been defeated and taken prisoner at Preston and a Freemason king finally lost to a Freemason Parliamentarian. On 20 January 1649 Charles I was put on trial in Westminster Hall in London. The king refused to recognise the legality of the court and did not enter a plea in response to the charges of being a tyrant, murderer, and an enemy of the nation, and a week later he was sentenced to death and publicly beheaded on 30 January. With the monarchy gone and England under his control, Cromwell's first task was the subjection of Ireland and Scotland. The massacres following his capture of Drogheda and Wexford were terrible and excessive, the result of his burning hatred for both the Irish and for Roman Catholics. The name of Oliver Cromwell still evokes fear and anger in Ireland, three hundred and fifty years after the event.

Scotland was a focus of Cromwell's wrath, where he destroyed Royalist castles and Catholic churches wherever he found the opportunity. As we saw earlier, the Masonic shrine at Rosslyn was known for what it was to both Cromwell and General George Monk and therefore survived the war intact.

Despite Cromwell's talent for violence, his main success was in maintaining relative peace and stability and, paradoxically, his provision of a framework that allowed a measure of religious toleration. Whilst he had no love of

Catholics, he allowed Jews, who had been excluded from England since 1290, to return in 1655 – an action born out of his knowledge of Masonic ritual. Cromwell's vigorous foreign policy and the achievements of his army and navy gave England a prestige abroad that it had not enjoyed for over half a century.

With the beheading of Charles the throne of England was abandoned and the country became the world's first parliamentary republic in a period known as the Commonwealth. The following year the dead king's son Charles landed in Scotland to continue the war; in 1651 he was crowned king of that country and promptly invaded England. The new Parliamentarian regime was too well established and organised to be upset by this bold but under-planned attack and Charles was soundly defeated at Worcester; he was lucky to be able to slip away to France.

Throughout this tumultuous time, the ex-Controller of Ordnance for the old king was living untroubled in Cromwell's London and consorting with some of the most intelligent and influential men from both sides. Ashmole obviously had permission from the highest level to pursue a mission that transcended mere politics and, whilst what he was building was wholly derived from Freemasonry, it was developing into something very new and very important.

Ashmole became the friend and acquaintance of astrologers, mathematicians, physicians and other individuals who were advancing their knowledge into the hidden mysteries of nature and science, as Francis Bacon's redefined Second Degree of Freemasonry required them to. The word was out; there was an 'invisible college', a society of scientists that could not be identified as a group, but whose presence was very evident.

Cromwell died a natural death on 3 September 1658, and was interred in Westminster Abbey. His son, Richard, whom he had named as his successor, was weak and failed to retain his power. The country quickly drifted toward anarchy but the slide was halted by the commander of the army in Scotland, General George Monk, who marched into London with his troops in May 1660. He recalled the Long Parliament and had them restore the monarchy by placing Charles II on the throne. The new king did not take long to seek revenge on the man who had caused him so much pain. He had Cromwell's body disinterred and his rotting corpse hanged as a traitor before his head was put on a pole mounted above Westminster Hall.

The Royal Society Emerges

The change back to a monarchy from a republic may well have been welcomed by Ashmole on a personal level, but it also brought benefit to the 'invisible college'. In 1662 King Charles II granted a royal warrant to it, thereby creating the Royal Society; the world's first assembly of scientists and engineers dedicated to understanding the wonders created by the 'Great Architect of the Universe'. The freedoms built into the fabric of Freemasonry had first created a fledgling republic and when that failed, they gave birth to the organisation that would push the boundaries of human knowledge forward to create an age of enlightenment and lay the foundations for the industrialised society of the nineteenth and twentieth centuries.

The brief spell that England spent as a republic was not wasted; monarchs from then onwards forgot the primitive notion of the divine right to rule and held office through the affection of the people and the authority of the House of Commons, which spoke for the democratic will of the nation. In years to come that democratic right spread to poor people and eventually women – the vision of the man called Jesus took a long time coming.

At this point of our research we had no doubt that

Freemasonry carries the seed of the mind of the Nasoreans and most particularly Jesus, and equally we can be sure that the Royal Society germinated from the hothouse of thinking that was released by Bacon's definition of the Second Degree of Freemasonry well before people such as Ashmole and Wilkins pieced it all back together after the traumas of the Civil War. John Wallis, the eminent seventeenth-century mathematician writing about his recollections of the beginnings of the Royal Society, said:

> '*I take its first ground and foundation to have been in London, about the year 1645, if not sooner, when Dr Wilkins (then chaplain to the Prince Elector Palatine, in London) and others, met weekly at a certain day and hour, under a certain penalty, and a weekly contribution for the charge of experiments, with certain rules agreed amongst us. When (to avoid diversion to other discourses, and for some other reasons) we barred all discourses of divinity, of state-affairs, and of news, other than what concerned our business of Philosophy.*'

This description of the earliest meetings of the new thinkers is unquestionably Masonic. The weekly meeting at a known hour, the known penalty and the utter abstinence from all topics of politics and religion are still the hallmarks of a Freemason's Lodge.

This indiscretion of Wallis's was corrected by the Masonic hierarchy of the early Royal Society who commissioned Spratt to write the official history of the Royal Society which made no mention of the Masonic rules which Wallis had incautiously revealed.

One of the most influential scientists to be involved with Ashmole was Robert Hooke, who was appointed the Royal Society's first curator of experiments. His prolific experiments, demonstrations and discourses over the next fifteen years were a strong factor in the Society's survival during its early period. Hooke was one of three city surveyors after the Great Fire of London and he was an early proponent of the microscope for biological investigations, coining the modern biological usage of the word 'cell'.

The great men of the age all sought to join the Royal Society, and perhaps the greatest of them all was Sir Isaac Newton who achieved many things including a remarkably detailed analysis of the gravitational structure of the universe. In 1672 Newton was elected a Fellow of the Royal Society and later that same year he published his first scientific paper on his new theory of light and colour in the Philosophical Transactions of the Society. A quarter of a century after the Royal Society had been awarded its royal warrant, Newton published the *Philosophiae Naturalis Principia Mathematica* (The Mathematical Principles of Natural Philosophy), or *Principia* as it is universally known. This remarkable work is, by common consent, the greatest scientific book ever written.

Whilst virtually all of the early members of the Royal Society were Masons, as time moved on Freemasonry appears to have taken something of a back seat to its new offspring because the gatherings of the intelligentsia no longer needed the secrecy and the protection of the Craft to overcome religious and political obstacles.

The new Society took up a great deal of the time and energy of Elias Ashmole, Robert Moray (recorded as being the first man initiated into Freemasonry on English soil in 1641), John Wilkins, Robert Hooke and Christopher Wren, who was made President in 1681. It is very clear from these well-documented facts that Freemasons had established the Royal Society and that the focus on the reconstructed Second Degree had served its purpose and moved the world forward into a new scientific age. During Sir Isaac Newton's presidency some years later, a well-known senior French Freemason by the name of Chevalier Ramsey was made a member of the Royal Society, despite a lack of any scientific credentials. With most of the foremost intellects of Freemasonry devoting their time and energy to the new Society it seems that the Craft in London was suffering from a certain amount of neglect.

Freemasonry Finds Its Feet

By the year 1717 Freemasonry in the London area was at a very low ebb. There were only four Lodges meeting regularly:

> The Goose and Gridiron, in St Paul's Churchyard.
> The Crown, in Parker Lane near Drury Lane.
> The Appletree Tavern, in Charles Street, Covent Garden.
> The Rummer and Grapes Tavern, in Channel Row, Westminster.

There can be no doubt that the Craft in London was suffering from a crisis of loss of traditional identity. Why did it still need to exist? Freemasonry was suddenly a victim of its own success; it had overcome the long-standing threat from the Church and it had kick-started democracy and a climate of ongoing scientific enquiry. Around the rest of the country, however, Masonic Lodges were starting to become regular and were increasingly popular. A Grand Lodge, formed at some unknown time before 1705, had been meeting regularly in York and this first Grand Lodge, which was continually supported by members of the nobility, claimed the title 'Grand Lodge of All England'. Something had to be done in London and so the four Lodges listed above met at the Appletree Tavern in February 1717 and voted the most senior Mason present into the Chair of the meeting. This senior Mason does not seem to be named anywhere in the literature, but the gathering certainly resolved to call a full meeting of all four Lodges at the Goose and Gridiron to

be held on 24 June for the purpose of electing a Grand
Master to govern the entire Order. Accordingly on St
John the Baptist's Day the same year the assembly and
feast was held, and Mr Anthony Sayer was elected first
Grand Master for the ensuing year. It is interesting to
note that at this time they choose a Grand Master from
amongst themselves 'until such a time as they should have
the honour of a Noble Brother at their head'. This could
well be a reference to the fact that Scottish Freemasonry
claimed a Noble Brother as Grand Master from the time
of the First St Clair Charter in 1601.[4] The new English
Grand Lodge drew up a number of regulations.

*'That the privilege of assembling as Masons which had
hitherto been unlimited should be vested in certain
Lodges or assemblies of Masons convened in certain
places; and that every Lodge hereafter convened, except
the four old Lodges at this time existing, should be
legally authorised to act by a warrant from the Grand
Master for the time being, granted to certain individuals by petition, with consent and approbation of the
Grand Lodge in communication; and that without such
warrant no Lodge should be hereafter deemed regular or
constitutional.*

*That every privilege which they collectively enjoyed
by virtue of their immemorial rights, they should still
continue to enjoy; and that no law, rule, or regulation
to be hereafter made or passed in Grand Lodge, should
derive then of such privilege, or encroach on any
landmark which was at that time established as the
standard of Masonic government.*

*The necessity of fixing the original constitutions as
the standard by which all future laws in the Society are
to be regulated, was so clearly understood by the whole*

---

[4] *Year Book of the Grand Lodge of Antient Free and Accepted Masons of Scotland,
1995*

> *fraternity at this time that it was established as an*
> *unerring rule, at every installation, public and private,*
> *to make the Grand Master, and the Masters and*
> *Wardens of every Lodge, engage to support their*
> *constitutions; to which also every Mason was bound by*
> *the strongest ties at initation.'*[5]

By forming a Grand Lodge under the control of an elected Grand Master, the four Lodges had effectively set up a control system for Masonry which ensured that only they were exempt from its dictates but all other Masons had to conform to its edicts. They could declare a Lodge to be regular or have it struck off the list of regular Lodges. Their right to do this was challenged by other Masons, particularly those in York, who did not accept London's self-appointed mission to ensure that no new heretics emerged who did not agree with the regular and approved heresy of the Order. In trying to formalise itself as a regular institution, English Freemasonry was already starting to lose its way. Nonetheless, the new structure did pull everything together after a long period of infighting, and the higher echelons of the Craft were slowly taken over by the royal family who sought to maintain their influence in the most republican organisation in the world. This linking of Freemasonry and the royal family has, in our opinion, been the main reason for the survival of the British monarchy.

We have constructed a listing of English past Grand Masters and the gravitation towards the aristocracy and the royal family is clear to see (Appendix 3). When this list is compared with the record of Scottish past Grand Masters (Appendix 4) it is clear that from its earliest records Scottish Freemasonry has been closely associated with the Lords of the Realm as well as with the humblest of working stonemasons; a tradition still proudly held in

[5] Preston: *Illustrations of Freemasonry*

Scotland to this day. The Craft soon spread throughout the world.

It was the fundamental influence of Freemasonry on the American and French Revolutions, combined with the tendency of Scottish Freemasons to support the Jacobite cause, that was finally responsible for the Hanoverian kings of England adopting the Craft as their own. In 1782, four years after the Declaration of Independence in the United States, the Duke of Clarence, brother to George II became Grand Master. In the year of the French Revolution, 1789, the Prince of Wales and his two brothers were initiated into the Craft, and within a year the Prince of Wales was Grand Master and received loyal addresses from Masons throughout the world including George Washington, at the time master of Alexandria Lodge, No. 22 on the roll of the Grand Lodge of New York, and also from many French Lodges. By this means the Hanoverian kings used the Masonic system to offer a democratic reason for keeping the loyalty of their Masonic subjects. Masonry in England was now well on the way to becoming the social and dining club that it is today and was starting to lose sight of its original heritage. Its true secrets were indeed becoming lost.

The Spread of Freemasonry

Soon after the Formation of the London Grand Lodge, the second Grand Master, George Payne, collected many manuscripts on the subject of Masonry, including copies of the Ancient Charges. In 1720 it was resolved to publish the Book of Constitutions and at this time it is claimed that a number of valuable old manuscripts 'were burnt too hastily by some scrupulous brethren' rather than have them fall into the hands of an opposing element within the Order known as 'the moderns'. It is claimed that the original of the Inigo Jones copy of the Ancient Charges was lost at this point. In the same year it was agreed in future the new Grand Master should be named before the annual meeting and that every Grand Master when installed should have the sole power of appointing his deputy and wardens. In 1724 the then Grand Master, the Duke of Richmond, set up the first Committee of Charity to provide a general fund for the relief of distressed masons; this had previously been suggested by his predecessor, the Duke of Buccleuch. This seems to be the first recorded instance of a Masonic organisation for charity, which is so important to modern Freemasonry.

In January 1723, after only nine months in office, the Duke of Montague resigned as Grand Master in favour of the Duke of Wharton, who was so keen to become Grand Master that he had even tried to get himself elected at an irregular meeting of Masons. By now the regular succession of lords of the realm had been established and was to continue. The sorts of common men who had been early Grand Masters never again held that office, or indeed the position of Deputy Grand Master: nobles of lesser noble rank took that role, carrying out the Grand Masters' administrative work.

The growing organisation was in need of secondary centres of administration and in 1727 the Office of Provincial Grand Master was instituted as a means of assisting the ruling of the greatly increased and geographically extended Craft. On 10 May 1727 Hugh Warburton was installed as the first Provincial Grand Master, his province being North Wales, and on 24 June 1727 Sir Edward Mansell Bart. was installed as Provincial Grand Master for South Wales. Also in 1727, the first recorded warrant for an overseas Lodge was issued by the London Grand Lodge to Gibraltar, closely followed by permission to hold a Lodge in St Bernard's Street, Madrid.

Freemasonry was spreading like wildfire and by 1728 the London Grand Lodge started to establish itself in the future British Empire, as a deputation was granted to George Pomfret to establish a Lodge in Bengal. The scope of the Provincial control of the Craft was increased with the appointment of Provincial Grand Masters for Lower Saxony, New Jersey in America and Bengal. In 1730 the first prince of the royal blood was initiated; Francis, Duke of Lorraine, Grand Duke of Tuscany, later to become Emperor of Germany, was initiated by the Earl of Chesterfield at a special Lodge convened at the Hague; the Duke received the first two degrees of Masonry, and was later raised to the Third Degree at the house of Sir Robert Walpole at a Lodge again chaired by the Earl of Chesterfield. In the same year the range of foreign Masonry was further extended by the granting of deputations to form Lodges in Russia, Spain, Paris and Flanders.

By now the Order was fast becoming a stylish dining club for the nobility and in 1730 they held their first country meeting of the jurisdiction of London at Hampstead on 24 June, for which purpose cards of invitation were sent to several of the nobility. By 1733 there were fifty-three Lodges represented at the Annual communication of Grand Lodge, so the range of power and influence of the London Grand Lodge was growing. At this 1733 meeting several new regulations were confirmed concerning the operations of the Charity Committee, including the right to hear its own complaints before any were brought before Grand Lodge. At the same meeting a collection was taken to be distributed amongst distressed Masons and to encourage them in the founding of a new colony in Georgia. During the year deputations were granted to open Lodges in Hamburg and in Holland. In 1738 James Anderson (the then Grand Secretary) published a revised *Book of Constitutions*. It is this work on the history of the Craft which has caused some authors to attribute to him the creation of Craft Masonry. At about this time regulations were introduced to the effect that if a Lodge ceased to meet for more than twelve months, then it would be erased from the list and lose its seniority. It was also fixed at this time that all future Grand Masters would be elected from the Grand Stewards' Lodge, to encourage gentlemen to serve the office, while resolutions were passed concerning what were described as illegal conventions of Masons. This removed the democratic right of the brethren to elect whom they saw fit to rule them. The territory of the Grand Lodge of York was encroached upon by the warranting of Lodges in Lancashire, Durham and Northumberland, which reportedly caused all friendly intercourse to cease between the two Grand Lodges.

By this time warrants had been issued to hold Lodges in Aubigny in France, Lisbon, Savannah in Georgia, in South America, Gambay, West Africa. Provincial Grand Masters had been appointed to New England, South Carolina and Cape Coast Castle in Africa. During the year 1737 Dr Dasaguliers (Part Grand Master 1719) initiated Frederick, Prince of Wales, at a Lodge convened for the purpose at Kew later in the same year, passing him to the Second Degree and then raising him to the sublime degree of a Master Mason. At the communication of Grand Lodge sixty Lodges were represented and Provincial Grand Masters were appointed for Montserrat, Geneva, the Coast of Africa, New York and the Islands of America.

In 1738 two further Provinces came into being: the Caribbean Islands, and the Province of Yorkshire, West Riding, which was considered yet another encroachment on the rights of the Grand Lodge of York. This widened the original breach between the two Grand Lodges and resulted in a total breakdown of relations. On 15 August 1738 the Scottish Grand Lodge scored a major victory in the quest for seniority amongst the Grand Lodges by initiating Frederick the Great of Prussia at a Lodge held in Brunswick for the purpose. Frederick went on to set up a Grand Lodge in Berlin under the Scottish Constitution.

The Development of Masonry in America

We had now reached the recorded history of the Craft and in a way our quest was complete, but we still had an outstanding curiosity about the long-term fate of the land of the star of Merica. To complete our picture we decided to look briefly at the development of the United States of America.

It is no secret that Masonry was a major moving force behind the American Revolution and the founding of the Republic of the United States of America. The anti-British tax demonstration known as the 'Boston Tea Party' was organised in 1773 by the members of the St Andrew's Lodge, which had amongst its members such famous individuals as Samuel Adams and Paul Revere. The Lodge, which met at the Green Dragon Tavern in Boston, did not itself organise the 'Tea Party' but its members founded a club called the Causus Pro Bono Publico, of which Joseph Warren, the Master of the Lodge – later to become Grand Master of Massachusetts – was a major force. Henry Purkett is reported to have said that he was present at the 'Tea Party' as a spectator, and in disobedience to the Master of St Andrew's Lodge, who was actively present.

The men who created the United States of America were either Freemasons themselves or had close contact with Freemasons. They used the thinking that had developed in Britain during the previous century as the building blocks of their own constitution. They did not know it, but by their devotion to Masonic principles of justice, truth and equality for their new country, they were undertaking an attempt to build a land that would be driven by a rediscovered Ma'at; a modern state that was the genuine heir to the greatness of ancient Egypt. In some ways the architects of the United States did succeed; but in all too many ways they have, so far, failed. It took a terrible civil war to end the enslavement of the southern black population and even today in many states the word 'equality' is still an aspiration of reasonable people and an irrelevance to the unreasonable. Like Freemasonry itself, the United States is an imperfect ideal that deserves to win, but has the failing of being made up of mere mortals.

Of the men who signed the Declaration of Independence on 4 July 1778, the following were Masons: William Hooper, Benjamin Franklin, Matthew Thornton, William Whipple, John Hancock, Phillip Livingston and Thomas Nelson. It was said at the time that with just four men out of the room the assembly that remained was more than enough to hold a Masonic Lodge in the Third Degree! It could also have allowed in most of the army leaders. Leading Freemasons here included such men as Greene, Marion, Sullivan, Rufus, Putnam, Edwards, Jackson, Gist, Baron Steuben. Baron de Kalb, the Marquis de Lafayette and George Washington himself.

When Washington was sworn into office as the first President of the Republic on 30 April 1789 it was by the Grand Master of New York and he took his oath on the Masonic Bible, which was normally used as the Volume of the Sacred Law of St John's Lodge, No. 1 on the roll of the Grand Lodge of New York. He had been a Freemason all his adult life, being initiated into the Fredericksburg Masonic Lodge five months before his twenty-first birthday on Friday 4 November 1752. As his mother Lodge met on the first Friday of the month, he was passed to the Second Degree on 3 March 1753 and raised to the 'sublime degree' of a Master Mason on 4 August 1753 in the same Lodge. At the time of his initiation he had just completed surveying the Virginian estates of Lord Fairfax, whose forebear had introduced Oliver Cromwell to Freemasonry. The Fairfax family were very active Freemasons in the Grand Lodge of York and his elder brother Lawrence, with whom George was living at the time, had been educated in England and was married to Lord Fairfax's niece. The Lodge that Washington attended probably followed an *ad hoc* 'York Rite' Lodge rather than a 'Scottish Rite', but six years after his inititation, in 1758, Fredericksburg Lodge received a Charter from Scottish Grand Lodge which formalised its position.[6] When Washington was made First President of the United States of America he had been a member of the Craft for almost thirty-six years and was at the time a member of Alexandria Lodge, No. 22.

Searching through old manuscripts we came across a contemporary record of George Washington's speech after being presented with an inscribed *Book of Constitutions* by the Freemasons of Boston on 27 December 1792. From the date of the presentation we assume this must have been to celebrate his forty years in the Craft. We show it here in the form we found it, complete with the use of a letter 's' that looks like a modern 'f'. It reads:

> *'FLATTERING as it may be to the human mind, and truly honourable as it is, to receive from our fellow-citizens teftimonnies of approbation for exertions to promote the public welfare; it is not lefs pleafing to know, that the milder virtues of the heart are highly refpected by a Society whofe liberal principles are founded in the immutable laws of truth and justice.*
>
> *To enlarge the fphere of focial happinefs is worthy – the benevolent defign – of a Mafonic Inftution; and it is moft fervently to be wifhed, that the conduct of every member of the fraternity, as well as thofe publications that difcover the principles which actuate them, may tend to convince mankind, that the grand object of Mafonry is to promote the happinefs of the human race.*
>
> *While I beg your acceptance of my thanks for "the Book of Conftitutions" which you have fent me, and for the honour you have done me in the Dedication, permit me to affure you, that I feel all thofe emotions of*

[6] *Year Book of Grand Lodge of Antient Free and Accepted Masons of Scotland, 1995*

*gratitude which your affectionate Addreſs and cordial
wiſhes are calculated to inſpire; and I ſincerely pray
that the Great Architect of the Universe may bleſs you
here, and receive you hereafter in his immortal temple.'*

It was also in 1792 that Washington laid the foundation
stone of the White House – on 13 October, the anniversary of de Maloy's crucifixion! That year the dollar was
adopted as the unit of currency for the United States of
America. The symbol for the dollar is an 'S' with a double
vertical strike-through, although, in print, it more usually
appears today with a single vertical line: $. The 'S' was
borrowed from an old Spanish coin but the two vertical
lines were the Nasorean pillars of 'Mishpat' and 'Tsedeq',
better known to the Masonic founders of the United
States as 'Boaz' and 'Jachin', the pillars of the porchway
to King Solomon's Temple.

Today the dollar bill bears the image of a pyramid with
an eye set within it, which is the most ancient of all images

in daily use because it has come down to us from before the time of Seqenenre Tao, escaping the purge of Egyptian motifs of the king-making ceremony caused by the prophet Ezekiel during the Babylonian captivity of the Jews. It represents God (in the form of Amen-Re) having an ever-present eye, casting His gaze over His people to judge every action they make in life, so that they will receive their just deserts in death. The whole basis of Ma'at was a measurement of the goodness done in life as seen by God. On the obverse of the one dollar bill is Brother George Washington and on the now-defunct two dollar bill there was the image of another famous Freemason – Brother Benjamin Franklin.

On 18 September 1793 George Washington laid the cornerstone of the Capitol building in Washington, and he along with fellows were all dressed in their full Masonic regalia.

The United States of America is still a very young country. To match the longevity of ancient Egypt it will have to maintain its powerful status until at least AD 4500, and to match that country's first great peak it still has some four hundred years to go. But we suspect that the Masonic experiment that found its home in the cosmopolitan land across the ocean to the west will find a far greater conclusion, because it is only another stepping stone on a journey set in motion in southern Iraq at least six thousand years ago.

Appendix 2

Pre-1710 Masonic Lodges in Scotland with the Date of the First Recorded Mention[1]

1599	9 Jan.	Aitchison's Haven
1599	31 July	Edinburgh
1599	27 Nov.	St Andrews
1599	28 Dec.	Kilwinning
1599	28 Dec.	Stirling
1599	28 Dec.	Haddington
1600		Dunfermline
1613	31 Dec.	Glasgow
1627		Dundee
1654	2 Mar.	Linlithgow
1658	24 Dec.	Scone
1670		Perth
1670		Aberdeen
1674	28 Dec.	Melrose
1677	20 Dec.	Cannongate Kilwinning
1678	27 Dec.	Inverness
1687	20 May	Dumfries
1688	29 May	Leith and Cannongate
1691		Kirkcudbright
1695	25 Mar.	Hamilton
1695	Apr.	Dunblane
1701	2 June	Kelso
1702	22 Dec.	Haughfoot
1703		Banff

[1] Stephenson: *Origins of Freemasonry*

1704 27 Dec.   **Kilmolymock**
1707   **Edinburgh Journeymen**

Appendix 3

Early Grand Masters of English Freemasonry

1717	Mr Anthony Sayer
1718	Mr George Payne
1719	Dr Desagliers
1720	Mr Anthony Sayer
1721	John, Duke of Montague
1722	The Duke of Wharton
1723	The Duke of Buccleuch
1724	The Duke of Richmond
1725	Lord Paisley, Earl of Abercorn
1726	Earl of Inchiquin
1727	Lord Colerane
1728	Lord Kingston
1729	The Duke of Norfolk
1730	Lord Lovel, Earl of Leicester
1731	Lord Teynham
1732	Lord Montagu
1733	The Earl of Strathmore
1734	The Earl of Crawford
1735	Lord Weymouth
1736	The Earl of London
1737	The Earl of Darnley
1738	The Marquis of Carnarvon
1739	Lord Raymond
1740	The Earl of Kintore
1741	The Earl of Moreton
1742–43	Lord Ward
1744	The Earl of Strathmore

1745–46	Lord Cranstoun
1747–51	Lord Byron
1752–53	Lord Carysfoot
1754–56	The Marquis of Carnarvon
1757–66	Lord Aberdour
1762–63	Lord Ferrers
1764–66	Lord Blaney
1767–71	The Duke of Beaufort
1772–76	Lord Petre
1777–81	The Duke of Manchester
1782–89	The Duke of Cumberland (brother of the king)
1790–95	The Prince of Wales

Appendix 4

Early Grand Masters of Scottish Freemasonry

1736	William St Clair of Roslin
1737	George, 3rd Earl of Cromartie
1738	John, 3rd Earl of Kintore
1739	James, 14th Earl of Morton
1740	Thomas, 8th Earl of Strathmore
1741	Alexander, 5th Earl of Leven and Melville
1742	William, 4th Earl of Kilmarnock
1743	James, 5th Earl of Wemyss
1744	James, 8th Earl of Moray
1745	Henry David, 10th Earl of Buchan
1746	William Nisbet of Dirleton
1747	The Hon. Francis Charteris Amisfield
1748	Hugh Seton of Touch
1749	Thomas Lord Eskine, Earl of Mar
1750	Alexander, 10th Earl of Eglinton
1751	James, Lord Boyd
1752	George Drummond, Lord Provost of Edinburgh
1753	Charles Hamilton Gordon
1754	James, Master of Forbes
1755–57	Sholto Charles, Lord Aberdour
1757–59	Alexander, 6th Earl of Galloway
1759–61	David, 6th Earl of Leven and Melville
1761–63	Charles, 5th Earl of Elgin and 9th of Kincardine
1763–65	Thomas, 6th Earl of Kellie

1765–67	James Stewart, Lord Provost of Edinburgh
1767–69	George, 8th Earl of Dalhousie
1769–71	Lieutenant-General James Adolphus Oughton
1771–73	Patrick, 6th Earl of Dumfries
1773–74	John, 3rd Duke of Atholl
1774–76	David Dalrymple
1776–78	Sir William Forbes of Pitsilgo
1778–80	John, 4th Duke of Atholl
1780–82	Alexander, 6th Earl of Balcarres
1782–84	David, 11th Earl of Buchan
1784–86	George, Lord Haddo
1786–88	Francis, Lord Elcho
1788–90	Francis, Lord Napier
1790–92	George, 16th Earl of Moreton
1792–94	George, Marquis of Huntly
1794–96	William, Earl of Ancram
1796–98	Francis, Lord Doune
1798–1800	Sir James Stirling, Bart, Lord Provost of Edinburgh

Appendix 5

Chronology

BC

28000	First evidence of religious practices
12000	Grindstones used for flour production
9000	Animal husbandry developed in Mesopotamia
8000	Fully domesticated wheat, barley and pulses cultivated in Fertile Crescent
6000	Painted kiln-fired pottery in Sumer
5500	Irrigation systems built in Sumer
4500	First ploughs used in Sumer
4500	First use of sails in Sumer
4100	Probable date of Noah's Flood
4000	Sumer known to have a complete social structure – the first known civilisation
3400	First walled cities in Egypt
3250	Earliest known writing in use in Sumer
3200	Secret Egyptian king-making ceremony known to exist
3150	Emergence of the unified Egyptian state with capital at Memphis
3000	First Egyptian hieroglyphics
2686	Egyptian Old Kingdom starts
2600	First true pyramids constructed in Egypt
2530	Great Pyramid of Khufu at Giza
2500	Emergence of city-states in northern Mesopotamia

2300	City-states of southern Mesopotamia united by Sargon of Akkade
2150	Collapse of Egyptian Old Kingdom
2040	Egyptian Middle Kingdom established
1786	Hyksos kings begin rule over Egypt
1780	Abraham travelled from Ur to make his first visit to Egypt
1740	Isaac born to Abraham
1720	Hyksos sack Memphis
1680	Jacob born; later to be renamed Israel
1620	Joseph born
1570	Joseph is vizier to Hyksos king Apophis
1574	Seqenenre Tao becomes king of Egypt but confined to Thebes by the Hyksos
1573	Seqenenre Tao murdered at the temple. His young son Ahmose takes throne
1570	Egyptian New Kingdom begins under Kamose, the second son of Seqenenre
1567	The Hyksos are driven out of Egypt
1450–1500	Most probable period for the Exodus under Moses
1020	Saul becomes first king of Israel
1002	David king of Israel
972	Solomon becomes king of Israel and builds his Temple for Yahweh
922	Solomon dies leaving religious and financial chaos across Israel
721	Northern kingdom of Israel collapses
597	First Babylonian captivity
586	Final destruction of Solomon's Temple
573	Ezekiel's visions whilst in captivity
539	Start of the building of Zerubbabel's Temple
187	Earliest date for the Qumran Community
166	The Maccabean Revolt in Israel
152	Jonathan Maccabee becomes high priest

152	Qumran Community known to exist
153	Jonathan Maccabee killed
6	Probable date of the birth of Jesus
AD	*******
27	Jesus spends three years at Qumran (in the wilderness)
31	Jesus leaves Qumran and is held to be king of the Jews
32	John the Baptist killed; Jesus assumes priestly as well as kingly messiahships
33	Crucifixion of Jesus
37	The Mandaeans are driven out to Mesopotamia by Saul
60	Saul becomes Paul and invents Christianity
62	Killing of James the Just at the Temple
64	Jewish Revolt begins at Masada
70	Destruction of Qumran, Jerusalem and Herod's Temple by the Romans
190	Clement becomes Bishop of Alexandria
200	Celtic Christianity reaches Ireland from Alexandria via Spain
325	Council of Nicaea established by Emperor Constantine
337	Constantine dies
432	Patrick travels to Ireland to establish the Celtic Church at Slane and Tara
563	Columba sets sail from Derry to set up an abbey on Iona
596	St Augustine arrives in England to convert the population to Catholicism
664	Synod of Whitby caves in to the Roman Catholic Church

THE DARK AGES BEGIN

1008	Oldest surviving texts of the Hebrew Bible
1118	The Order of the Poor Knights of Christ and the Temple of Solomon founded
1120	Templars find hidden Scrolls

THE DARK AGES END

1215	Magna Carta signed by King John
1244	Birth of Jacques de Maloy
1292	Jacques de Maloy elected last Grand Master of the Templars
1305	Robert the Bruce excommunicated
1306	Robert the Bruce crowned King of Scotland
1306	The arrest of all Jews in France
1307	Friday 13 October: the destruction of the Templars by Phillip the Fair
1307	Jacques de Maloy crucified and Shroud of Turin created
1308	Arrival of Templar fleet in America
1314	19 March: Jacques de Maloy burnt at the stake in Paris
1314	Battle of Bannockburn – won by the intervention of a Templar battle force
1328	England recognises Scotland as an independent nation
1329	13 June: Pope accepts Robert I and his successors as Kings of Scotland
1330	William St Clair dies taking the heart of Robert I to Jerusalem
1357	First Known Exposition of the Shroud of Turin
1440–1490	Building of the Chapel of Roslyn. Introduction of the First Degree and Mark Masonry by William St Clair, First Grand

	Master and Founder of Freemasonry
1534	The English split with the Roman Catholic Church
1583	James Stuart becomes James VI of Scotland
1598	First Schaw Statutes set up the Lodge System
1599	Second Schaw Statutes published
1599	First documented minutes of a Masonic Lodge
1601	First St Clair Charter affirms St Clairs as Grand Masters of Masons
1601	James VI joins Lodge of Scoon and Perth, No. 3 on the present roll of the Grand Lodge of Scotland, at the age of 35
1603	James VI of Scotland becomes James I of England
1604	Fellow Craft Degree of Freemasonry introduced by Francis Bacon
1605	Guy Fawkes plot to blow up king and parliament
1607	Inigo Jones Manuscript
1610	Galileo publicly confirms the structure of the solar system
1625	Charles I comes to the throne
1628	The Second St Clair Charter confirms the Earl of Rosslyn as Grand Master Mason
1633	Charles I refurbishes Holyrood Abbey for his Scottish Coronation and incorporates Masonic tombstones in its north wall, including one for the Earl of Sutherland
1641	Sir Robert Moray initiated into Freemasonry at Newcastle by a warrant from Lodge of Edinburgh St Mary's Chapel
1643	The English Civil War starts
1646	The end of the main phase of the English Civil War at Oxford
1646	Elias Ashmole initiated in Warrington in an

	ad hoc Lodge
1649	Execution of Charles I
1649	The establishment of the Commonwealth under Oliver Cromwell
1650	Rosslyn Castle destroyed but the Chapel preserved by Cromwell and Monk
1652	First meeting between Wilkins, Ashmole and Wren
1660	Charles II restores the monarchy
1662	Formation of the Royal Society of the Advancement of Science by Freemasons
1672	Isaac Newton elected a Fellow of the Royal Society
1677	Charles II builds the Holy Royal Arch Symbol of the Crown, originally used by his father Charles I in his campaign against Parliament, into the entrance to Holyrood House
1714	First recorded minutes of the Grand Lodge of York
1717	Formation of English Grand Lodge
1721	First Noble Grand Master, John, Duke of Montague, elected to English Grand Lodge
1725	Formation of Irish Grand Lodge
1726	Earliest documented record of a Masonic Third Degree ceremony in Scotland
1737	Formation of Scottish Grand Lodge: William St Clair elected first Grand Master
1738	First Papal Bull against Freemasonry issued
1747	First Charter to a travelling military lodge issued by the Grand Lodge of Scotland
1752	George Washington made a Freemason in the town of Fredericksburg at Lodge Fredericksburg
1758	Lodge Fredericksburg receives a formal charter from the Scottish Grand Lodge

1773	The Boston Tea Party
1778	William St Clair, first Elected Master of the Grand Lodge of Scotland, dies
1778	American Declaration of Independence
1789	George Washington becomes the first President of the USA
1790	Hanoverian Prince of Wales becomes Grand Master of England
1792	George Washington presented with *Book of Constitutions* at Boston
1799	Rosetta Stone found, enabling Egyptian hieroglyphics to be read
1945	Discovery of the Nag Hammadi cache of Gnostic gospels
1947	Discovery the Dead Sea Scrolls at Qumram
1951	Excavation of Qumran starts
1955	The Copper Scroll opened and deciphered as an inventory of hidden treasures
1988	Carbon dating of the Turin Shroud establishes its earliest possible origin to be 1260
1991	First public access to full collection of the Dead Sea Scrolls

Appendix 6

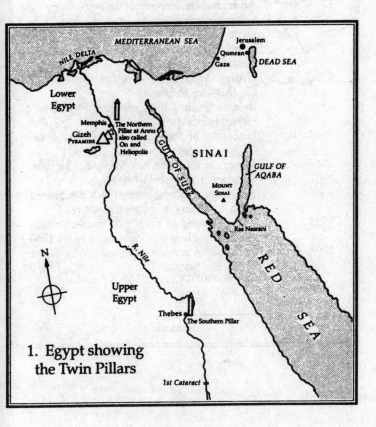

1. **Egypt showing the Twin Pillars**

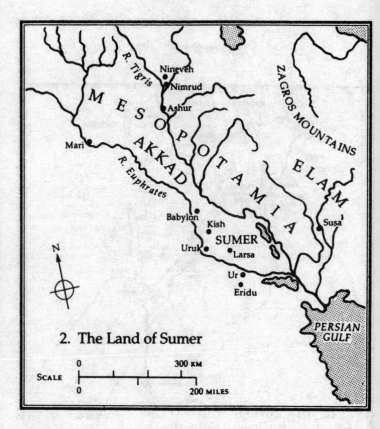

2. The Land of Sumer

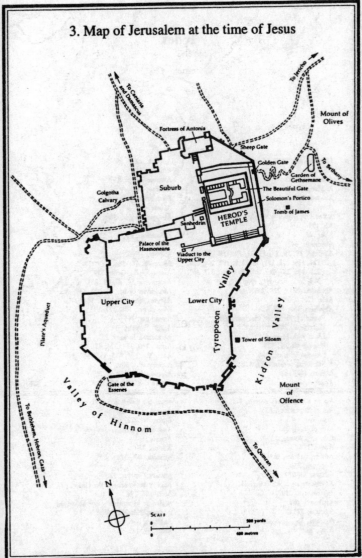

3. Map of Jerusalem at the time of Jesus

Index

Index

Index

The Hiram Key

Index

Index

Index

The Hiram Key

Index

Index

495